Backstage Passes &
Backstabbing Bastards

Backstage Passes & Backstabbing Bastards

Memoirs of a Rock 'n' Roll Survivor

Al Kooper

Backbeat
Books

An Imprint of Hal Leonard Corporation

New York

Backbeat Books
An Imprint of Hal Leonard Corporation
19 West 21st Street, New York, NY 10010

Published by Backbeat Books in 2008

Previously published in 1998 by Billboard Books/Watson-Guptill Publications

Printed in the United States of America

Book design by Robin Lee Malik, Buddy Boy Design

The Library of Congress has cataloged the Billboard Books/Watson-Guptill Publications edition as follows:

Kooper, Al
    Backstage passes and backstabbing bastards / by Al Kooper.
    p.   cm.
    Includes index.
    ISBN 0-8230-8257-1
    1. Kooper, Al. 2. Rock musicians—United States—Biography.
    I. Title
    ML420.K8A3 1998
    782.42166'092—dc21
    [B]   98-22172

Backbeat ISBN: 978-0-87930-922-0

www.backbeatbooks.com

Contents

Contents

This book is respectfully dedicated to my parents, Samuel (1909-1998) and Natalie; my son, Brian; and my dog, Daisy. Any of them, at any given moment, could put a gigantic smile on my face....

(Photos: Al Kooper Collection.)

"Is it the lies?
Is it the style. . . ?
It's a mercenary territory
I wish you knew the story
I've been out here so long dreaming up songs,
I'm temporarily qualmless and sinking
But I did my time in that rodeo
It's been so long and I got nuthin' to show
Well, I'm just so plain loco,
Fool that I am
I'd do it all over again. . . ."

Introduckshun

(Photo: Dorene Lauer.)

I know what you're thinking. It's gotta be one of two things:

1. Who wants to read a book now by or about Alice Cooper?
2. I know who Al Kooper is, but I read this book twenty years ago and it was a lot cheaper to buy then.

Let's clear the air.

This is *not* a book by or about Vincent Furnier (né Alice Cooper.) It is a book by and about Al Kooper. If you don't know who Al Kooper is, that's fine. But don't let that stop you from perusing these eye-opening accounts of encounters with Bob Dylan, Jimi Hendrix, Gene Pitney, The Royal Teens, Bill Graham, Quincy Jones, Blood, Sweat & Tears, Mike Bloomfield, The Rolling Stones, Lynyrd Skynyrd, George Harrison, Miles Davis, The Tubes, Nils Lofgren, Stevie Ray Vaughan, and all the other wonderful people I've been fortunate enough to cross paths with over the last forty years.

Yes, the first edition of this book came out twenty years ago, albeit in truncated

Introduckshun

form. Published in 1977, the original book concerned itself with the years 1958-1968. That was a fascinating time in American music and general sociology, and that is why I spat out an autobiography at so tender an age. So much happened to me in those ten years, that it lent itself to a fast-paced, adventurous, rather humorous tale of a boy caught up in a wave he could not and would not stop surfing.

As time went by, the book slipped out of print and many other new milestones whizzed by me, until, as I approached my fortieth year in the music business, it became apparent that this book had to live again. But this time, instead of ten measly years, why not let the reader in on forty (1958-1998) wild, metamorphic years that even I can't believe I'm still alive to recount?

Ben Edmonds worked closely with me on that first book. This version omits his side-bars from that first printing; however, I owe a great debt to him for asking me all the right questions, thereby unlocking the little tidbits of information I had previously forgotten. A lot of his editing is sprinkled in the sections that deal with 1958-1968. From 1968 to 1998 I was strictly on my own.

In 1995, the cult following for the original out-of-print book placed a $100 bounty on its cover for a rare paperback or hard-cover copy. Time has shown that the hard-covered ones all came undone with pages trailing behind them in the wind. This time, we're publishing in trade paperback only, which means it's a paperback, but larger in size than the ones you see in the drugstore or at the airport. No hardcovers. It's only rock 'n' roll. . . .

The rather lovely Beverly Keel encouraged me to take the first steps. David Lane ran interference for me so I could sit typing in Nashville for months, uninterrupted. Beverly, Jeff Tamarkin, Kathy Alpert, and Jaan Uhelszki were indispensable in their support and tireless editing. Kathy Alpert kept all the distractions at bay in Boston so that I could finish on deadline. Our band, The Rekooperators—Jimmy Vivino, Anton Fig, and Mike Merritt—still keep the joy and spontaneity in the music for me. And, finally, my dog Daisy was always full of sage advice and had the good sense not to chew up this book.

One of the horrible offshoots of rock 'n' roll history books is revisionism. That is, someone who is a lazy researcher publishes an untruth in a book that is used by other researchers. The untruth becomes used so many times that it becomes "the truth." The difference with this book is that I was present when these events took place and they are not up for conjecture. In the course of the last two weeks, I have read in recently released "factual" books how I dated Linda McCartney before Paul (not true), formed The Blues Project (not true), and many other so-called facts that never happened in my life. I urge the writer who does research to try and speak with someone who was in the room when something happened, as opposed to taking the word of

Introduckshun

some hack on assignment. Otherwise, we are doomed to see things in the future like *The National Enquirer Book of Rock*. That would be unfortunate. So strike out against the forces of revisionism and read this book. It's the truth. It's factual. Getting the "real" story out to you is satisfactual. . . .

It's time to get comfortable and begin reading. Because herein are tales told on people, myths debunked, hilarious moments caught in mid-air, and things you couldn't possibly imagine happening if you were born after 1965. Rare photographs (which include many a fashion faux pas) have been added to document events and make them even more enjoyable. I'm sure this will interest you if you love rock 'n' roll. And twenty years from now, God willing, you can pass it on to someone born after 1995 with a subtle, knowing grin on your face.

Al Kooper
April 1998

Preamble:
Roots

Prior to the invention of California, the uncontested center of the music industry universe was a five-block stretch of Broadway in New York City. Three buildings in particular—1619, 1650, and 1697—summed it all up. Like three octogenarians in a rock 'n' roll rest home, they each assume very distinct personalities once they start telling their tales about the faces they've seen and the times they've shared.

1619 Broadway (at West 48th Street) is more commonly known as the Brill Building. Having been constructed in 1931, it is the youngest of the three, and yet it's the most notorious. It was the first of the lot, however, to gamble on show-biz by painting ASCAP and BMI on its opaque glass doors instead of MD or DDS. The inherent Jewish/Italian balance was not disturbed by this changeover; the fate of those entering the building was merely transposed from healing to stealing.

Throughout the years, revisionist tomes have insisted that the music business rose and fell at the Brill Building. This simply is *not* true. The Tin Pan Alley era

4

Preamble

(1930-1955) flourished at the Brill Building, but in the mid-fifties the action moved over to 1650 Broadway, which unlike the Brill Building was an edifice without a name, just a number. All the glory and the music that came to be known as "the Brill Building Sound," in fact, came from 1650 Broadway. So, what was the Brill Building's story? Here goes:

The Brill Building stood against a fairly standard New York backdrop of camera stores and record shops that had been going out of business since they opened. One of the most lucrative ventures in this particular neighborhood was painting "Going Out Of Business" signs. To the right of the entranceway you couldn't miss a gnarled specimen of humanity astride a fire hydrant (his only visible means of support). This was the notorious Broadway Larry, the unofficial doorman of the Brill Building and one of the most outrageous characters in all of New York City. He'd been standing out in front with his shopping bag and unshaven face for as long as anybody could remember, assailing random passersby with an X-rated stream of abuse. When long hair first came into vogue, aspiring hippies were subject to an extra helping of his verbal shit-rain. But the guy's charm was that he so obviously considered *anybody* deserving of his hostility. Some of his best victims were immaculately-dressed corporation executives, who'd turn twelve shades of purple when dropped in their tracks by a loud "Hey asshole!" from the lips of my man. A great guy, Broadway Larry; a credit to his race.

The Brill Building was where Elvis Presley's publishing interests were looked after, and where the entire Southern rockabilly scene came to pick up its weekly allowance checks. It was the base of operations for the Goodman family, who handled the Arc publishing empire, which encompassed the songs of Jimmy Reed, Muddy Waters, Willie Dixon, Chuck Berry, Howlin' Wolf, and nearly every other Chicago blues singer of note. Arc's fortunes, unlike those of so many of the other fifties' musical giants, remained unaffected by the renaissance of the sixties. Every white blues-based band, from The Beatles and Rolling Stones on down, still recorded Arc songs in order to achieve their cultural authenticity.

Bobby Darin, Don Kirshner, Perry Como, and Frank Sinatra were once just faces in the 1619 hallway crowd. Jerry Leiber and Mike Stoller, the Hardy Boys of rock 'n' roll songwriting and refugees from California, set up shop there and ground out "Young Blood," "Black Denim Trousers and Motorcycle Boots," "Hound Dog," and a good piece of the foundation upon which rock was built. Their sixties' record company Red Bird operated out of the Brill Building.

When Bob Dylan, The Beatles, and others changed the attitude of the music business in 1964, the new messiahs were already ensconced and successful in 1650 Broadway, not wishing to be associated with any bygone era. Nashville went big business, pulling its interests southward. Little by little, 1619's charisma faded. By the mid-seventies, the Brill Building was only a third occupied. Still, its legend could not be stopped. An older, wiser, Broadway-beaten Paul Simon still has an office there. The superintendent of the building at the time, Mike Mihok, informed me that the film business was now the building's major source of tenant revenue. *Sic transit gloria mundi.*

Though 1650 boasted a Broadway address, its entrance was actually on West 51st Street, between Broadway and Seventh Avenue. The building was erected in 1922, when musicians were relegated to using the side door. In contrast to the relative seediness of the Brill Building neighborhood, 1650 was on the perimeter of the theater-hotel district.

In 1945, the building changed hands, and the new owners had the foresight to renovate for the coming musical onslaught. The new music business wasn't buying the shirt-and-tie, opaque-glass-door ambience of the Brill Building. Believe me, it was necessary for 1650, like so many of its tenants, to maintain a facade of youth. The rents were cheaper than at 1619, and the restrictions were virtually none, rendering it possible for almost anyone to obtain office space if they had a speed-rap capable of clubbing the rental agent into submission. Many did.

Soon 1650 hosted a wide-ranging clientele of hustlers and would-be music moguls who didn't have the credentials the Brill Building required and therefore had to establish an alternative order. 1650 was not a place in which to rest on your laurels; it was a place to earn them. This kind of tension created by people hungry for success gave the building an electricity that immediately distinguished it from the Brill, and transcended anything that had ever come before it.

Aldon Music, the hottest song-publishing concern of the early sixties and perhaps of all time, dominated 1650's action. Ironically, as I mentioned before, much of what today is called "the Brill Building Sound" actually originated at 1650 right in Aldon's offices! The product of Al Nevins, a performer (The Three Suns) and writer ("Twilight Time"), and Don Kirshner, whose television rock programming established him as a mainstay of the seventies, seemed to have the top of the charts padlocked until The Beatles finally intervened. In 1962, Carole King, Gerry Goffin, Barry Mann, Cynthia Weil, Neil Sedaka, Howie Greenfield, Helen Miller, and numerous others competed for space at Aldon's piano to compose the hits that would monopolize the airwaves. Even The Beatles recorded Aldon songs when they first started out. The standards of today had their origins in 1650 behind Aldon's doors: "Will You Still Love Me Tomorrow," "On Broadway," "You've Lost That Lovin' Feelin'," "Chains," "It Hurts To Be in Love," and "We Gotta Get Outta This Place" are just a fraction of the titles that come to mind.

Preamble

Though the late George Goldner seldom receives credit, he made records while in residence at 1650 that had as much to do with defining the New York R&B sound as did Ahmet Ertegun over at Atlantic Records. George's indie labels included Gee, End, and Gone Records. "I Only Have Eyes for You" by The Flamingos, "Why Do Fools Fall in Love" by Frankie Lymon and The Teenagers, "Maybe" by The Chantels, and "Tears On My Pillow" by Little Anthony and The Imperials are just a few of George's claims to fame. Alan Freed, the Akron, Ohio disc-jockey who made the phrase "rock 'n' roll" a household word, and is the father of the radio art form as we know it, maintained an office here, run by his manager, Jack Hooke. For the sake of history, it is interesting to note that Alan Freed's son, Lance, at the time of this writing, has been running Almo Music—the publishing wing of A & M Records—for the past thirty years. George Goldner's daughter, Linda, was married to contemporary super-producer Richard Perry and produced several records herself. Until he contracted California fever, Neil Diamond occupied a cubicle at 1650. Leo Rogers, who managed The Royal Teens, and Aaron Schroeder, who today administers the Barry White publishing catalogue, had office space there. It also housed Ray Rand's cooking little venture, Adelphi Recording Studios. The latter three gentlemen all played an important part in my early education, and we'll return to them soon.

Above the entrance to the building is a sign bearing the inscription: "1650 Broadway, the best known address in the entertainment field." An exaggeration, perhaps, but ironically not by all that much. I wish it just said, "The place where rock 'n' roll exploded." So remember—it wasn't the Brill Building; it was 1650 Broadway. Tell a friend.

1697 Broadway could have been the place where the adjective "funky" was coined. Built in 1907 (my father wasn't built until 1909) and originally called the Hammerstein Building (my father was originally called Kuperschmidt), this was the smallest and craziest of the three. It penetrated the theater district even further than 1650, and sat in a weird neighborhood hybrid of Cadillac and Chevrolet showrooms, office buildings, and respectable hotels. On the east side of Broadway, somebody had picked up the tab for extensive renovation in the form of modern high rises, and formerly ugly residences had been transformed into cute little office buildings. But if you walked one block west to Eighth Avenue you'd find yourself in the middle of Dylan's "desolation row," an area infested with whore houses, sleazy bars, and porno-supermarkets totally beyond renovation or redemption (although they're giving it the old college try in the late nineties).

The ground floor of 1697 was given over to the CBS-TV soundstage from which *The Ed Sullivan Show* beamed its way into millions of American homes every

Preamble

Sunday night (which is about as far from funky as you can get; it is now the TV home of David Letterman). Up the stairs and around the corner, however, lurked the spectre of rhythm and blues, a festering sore on the face of "white American culture." This building was predominantly rented to African-Americans, to the extent that the few white people who took office space there almost felt obligated to have at least one R&B hit (i.e., The Tokens, Jewish as the driven snow, who produced a sizable R&B hit in "He's So Fine" by The Chiffons, and later, as publishers, ended up winning a suit against George Harrison for borrowing more than a few bars from their song for his "My Sweet Lord"). Upstairs were countless dance studios, recording facilities (most notably Broadway Recording, now defunct), and rehearsal studios where you'd have to fight for listening space in the stairwells (I did!) when Ray Charles cracked the whip over his big band or James Brown ran his supersweat revue through its paces.

Okay. Now you have a picture of the jungle. Let's drop young Tarzan in and see what happens.

1958-1964:

BASICS:

MOVING TO QUEENS,

THE ROYAL TEENS,

GENE PITNEY, COLLEGE,

"THIS DIAMOND RING,"

AND THE GREAT BLACKOUT

I popped out into the world in Brooklyn, New York, on February 5, 1944 (12:15 p.m. if you're doing a chart). When I was four, my parents got in the Conestoga wagons with all their belongings and followed the brave pioneers to the "other" borough, Queens. Unlike Brooklyn, this was comparatively underdeveloped, new real estate and at bargain prices. Our initial Queens abode was upstairs in a two-family, attached home with my father's brother and his family downstairs. As the corner lots got snapped up over the next five years, my parents got serious and took their life savings in order to buy a one-family home two miles further up Union Turnpike on 214th Street (number 80-07 in case the tour bus doesn't stop there). After a premature birth claimed my potential sister, it became apparent that three people didn't need that big ol' house and we moved another mile up Union Turnpike to an apartment in a six-floor elevator building surrounded by two other six-floor elevator buildings.

The area south of Union Turnpike was primarily low-income, World War II veterans' housing in the area between Union Turnpike and Jamaica Avenue. The area above it was middle-class affluent from Union Turnpike to 73rd Avenue. It was right in the middle of these two factions that I really grew up from the ages of twelve to twenty-one, and where my mother resided until March 1998.

Early on, when I was six years old, my parents took me to a friend's home that had a piano. I had never had access to one before and sat down fascinated by it. In an hour, I was playing the number one song at the time, "The Tennessee Waltz," albeit on the black keys. (You know, Irving Berlin only played on the black keys. I should never have integrated my playing!) My parents were impressed with this apparent gift from God, but alas, they could not afford a piano. A ritual began that day: If they were visiting someone who had a piano, I would tag along and sit and play for the entire length of their visit; if there was no piano, I opted to remain at home or was dragged along kicking and screaming.

When I reached the age of twelve, my folks finally sprang for a spinet. Within a year, I had fallen under the spell of Elvis, and turned my back on the keyboard in favor of the guitar. It's a good thing my mother was not aware of the post-partum defense!

I started a kid band called The Aristo-Cats with some local lads in late '57. We played temple and church dances for forty dollars split four ways. I played guitar and piano. Our parents took turns driving us to gigs. It was at this time I met Harvey Goldstein (soon to be Brooks) who was in a rival band, The Valentines.

I stumbled into the professional music biz picture in 1957 at the tender age of thirteen. I'd gone to summer camp with this guy named Danny Schactman, a guitar player with a group that actually had a record out. The record was the original "Baby Talk," which didn't become a hit until Jan & Dean picked it up a couple of years later. Danny was two years older than I was. As a fledgling guitar "virtuoso," I was fascinated by his comparative stardom and generosity with his guitar knowledge. We cultivated a friendship that lasted well beyond summer camp.

Shortly before I was due to be inducted into the eighth grade, I spent a week at Danny's house in Brooklyn. One day, we journeyed to Leo Rogers' (his manager's) office at 1650 Broadway. Leo Rogers was a man in his middle fifties who discovered and managed some of the more dubious one-hit wonders of that time. Leo subscribed to a comparatively underhanded style of doing business, and there were always students and stooges at his feet hoping to pick up the finer points of his locally legendary style. There was also an abundance of kids in my situation, dying for a chance to do *anything* for the experience it offered. We knew we were being taken advantage of, but our financial interests at such a formative age were strictly secondary. I was auditioned as a guitar player.

The Aristo-Cats, 1958. (Left to right) Vampire Al, Joe Heyman (now a gynecologist), Bob Tannenbaum, Eric Krackow (now a Scientologist). (Photo: Lou Krackow.)

ဢ

"Okay, kid," Leo said wearily, "show us your stuff."

I wailed out reasonable facsimiles of Link Wray's "Rumble" and "Rawhide" on my Sears Roebuck forty-dollar black and silver electric guitar. To my surprise, it made everyone smile. (Later, I found out why they were smiling.) I was offered a job for that very night, backing a group called The Casuals. Since I was staying at Danny's that week, I accepted. My parents would never have to know that their under-age darling was consorting with hardened musicians long after he should have been home safely in the Schactman family guestroom. A group of us piled into a car and headed for the scene of the crime, a high school gym somewhere on Long Island.

Even though my prior experience consisted mainly of playing along to the radio and Chuck Berry records, the gig was easy. In those days, the average set ran about twenty minutes. You'd play your hit, and whatever else was popular at the time (i.e., whatever songs the band happened to know).

I had a cursory knowledge of the chords to the hits of the moment, so someone would just call out the key and we'd be off. Before the show you'd get an iridescent jacket and a bow tie (which never fit, not that it mattered; I usually looked like David Byrne with the Big Suit on) and the rest was pretty automatic. At the end of the evening, you might pick up fifteen dollars for your efforts. It seemed like heaven.

From then on, whenever I had money in my pocket I'd become the phantom of 1650 Broadway. Hanging out at Rogers' office promised an education more useful than anything junior high was offering, and when you don't know nothin', you got plenty to learn. If I was lucky enough to be hanging around at the right time, I might even get a shot at earning my subway fare back home for the week. Which is how I came to join The Royal Teens.

The Royal Teens (managed by Leo Rogers) had scored one national smash with a cute little novelty item called "Short Shorts." One day I happened to be in the office when the call went out for a guitar player. The only problem was that I wasn't staying at Danny Schactman's house that weekend, and so my parents had to be brought into the negotiations. I was fourteen years old at the time. Protective animals by nature, my folks demanded an audience with Rogers. Leo explained to them that the job was in Monticello, a four-and-a-half-hour drive from the city, and that he'd assure my safety by personally driving me home. Thus assuaged, my parents sanctioned the ceremonial donning of the iridescent jacket and bow tie, a move destined to fill them with remorse for many years to come.

By the time we finished up in Monticello it was one in the morning, which already put the promised hour of my safe return well out of reach. We piled into Leo's car, and I fell sound asleep. I awoke at 4:00 a.m. to find myself surrounded by five snoring faces, and the car pulled off the road in a cornfield. I shook Leo awake (he was the only one old enough to drive) and without a word he turned the key in the ignition and headed toward home as if he were on automatic pilot. *God knows what he really was on!* When I woke up again it was 5:30 a.m. and I was being dropped off in the heart of Manhattan, miles from my doorstep. Nothing to do now but phone the folks and brace myself.

"Hi," I said as casually as you can when you know you've already been tried and convicted. "We just got back into town and I guess I'll be getting on the subway."

"Subway? Do you realize what time it is? Where's Leo Rogers?"

"Oh, he's gone home. . . ."

For the next two minutes there was nothing but the sound of two mature adults going completely berserk on the other end of the line. When they regained partial control of their faculties, I was ordered to get my barely-teen-age-ass into a Queens-bound taxicab. Their treat.

This is a scene that I've never been able to forget: Sitting in the back of that taxi-cab in the Big Suit, with my Sears guitar and cheezy little 25-watt Ampeg Rocket amp in the seat beside me, watching the first sunrise I'd ever seen against the Manhattan skyline. Then pulling up in front of our house in Queens one step ahead of the milk truck. Passing my father on the front walk, he on his way to work, me just returning from mine. And that *look on his face* as he hurried past me, as if an inner voice was telling him, "Your son has been lobotomized by Martians carrying electric guitars. He'll never be the same again." It would have made a perfect portrait.

Thus ended any pretense I might have had about leading a normal existence.

It also ended my officially *endorsed* career as a musician. Leo Rogers was shit-listed, and from then on I was forced to operate undercover. The capper to the incident was that I didn't even get paid for that gig! It turned out to be my "audition" for The Royal Teens.

I continued my clandestine romance with rock 'n' roll as a member of The Royal Teens. Whenever a job would pop up, I'd have to invent a reason to be staying overnight at a friend's house. I'd be playing in Boston, and my parents would be convinced that I was only around the corner. With an intricate network of liars covering my tracks, the deceptions usually worked. Still, my parents must have thought it odd that their son was so preoccupied with staying overnight at other guys' houses.

In those days there were no Elton John albums to take home and share with your parents. Rock 'n' roll was the line of demarcation, and the life-style attached to it had to be led surreptitiously. I embraced it all: black leather jacket (mine was actually brown—one of many such concessions), rolled-up sleeves, greasy hair, and engineer boots. I would've had sideburns if I could've grown them. A "soul patch" had to suffice: a line of hair grown under the bottom lip à la Ray Charles or Dizzy Gillespie. *That* I could grow.

Naturally my parents weren't buying any of this, so I was forced to keep a stash of contraband clothing in a friend's garage. I'd wake up in the morning and get dressed, bid my parents good-bye, and head directly for that garage, where I'd real-ly get dressed for school. On more than one occasion, my mother would "happen" to be driving by the bus stop, spot me dressed illegally and bust me. I think she made a point of driving that route every morning. But her plan wasn't enough to stop me; I smuggled my clothes into school and changed every morning in the bathroom. Super-Punk!

I worked hard at an aura of toughness, but if actually faced with a fight, the facade wouldn't have lasted longer than the first punch. Luckily, being a musician had its advantages. The bad guys knew us and they left us alone, to paraphrase one of Brian Wilson's songs and that's pretty much the way it was. If I didn't push the tough-guy pose too far, I'd never get called on it. This explains how I managed to pass through the New York City public school system in one piece.

The one time I couldn't avoid a fight, neither my mouth nor my guitar could've saved me. I was on my way home from a gig in one of New York's innumerable lousy neighborhoods and had all the arrogance beaten out of me by three black youths in a deserted subway station. I'd recently begun an infatuation with black music, and the beating was as much psychic as physical. "Hey," I kept wanting to scream, "if you knew how much I liked Jimmy Reed, would you do this to me?"

"Who the fuck is Jimmy Reed, whiteboy?!" would probably have been the reply.

To become an accepted member of The Royal Teens' inner circle, one had to suffer an initiation as the butt of many practical jokes. State of the art was the put-on. Like we'd be driving home from a show, and one of the guys would turn and say, "Hey, let's be honest, fellas." That was the tipoff to the routine; the only one who wasn't in on it was the intended mark. "How many times a week do you jerk off?" Like they're in the habit of unlocking their most private secrets just to kill some time on the drive back from a gig. Each guy would pick a number and do his own confessional. "Now come on, you gotta be really honest, that's the whole point of this," doing a straight-face setup on the poor schmuck. So you'd blurt out your awful truth, and they'd take it every bit as seriously as they'd taken their fabrications. Then they'd let you sit for a couple of hours, feeling good about the bond of intimacy you'd created, until one of them would turn and casually say, "You know that thing we did back there about jerking off? Well, we all made up our answers." You couldn't do anything except sit there red-faced, in a puddle, thinking "Oh shit," over and over again all the rest of the way home.

Another favorite on the mental cruelty hit parade was a game called "Who's The Star This Week?" One of the guys would pop the question in the dressing room, well within earshot of the newest member, who'd go for the bait immediately. "Well, every week," we'd explain, "one of us gets to be the star and can tell everyone else in the band what to do. That means Leo, too. Like last week, Al was the star, and he had Leo shine his shoes right before we went on stage. Leo can't ever be the star, 'cuz he's the manager and that means he's always the star. That's why we set up the star system.

Of course it was always the new chump's turn to be the star, and you could see him swell up with imagined authority. When Leo ambled into the room, the kid would unknowingly deliver the punch line. "Hey, Leo," he commanded. "Bend over and kiss my ass before I go on tonight!" Leo would stand up there in total disbelief, suddenly developing a suntan that Coppertone couldn't have matched. When all the blood reached his brain, the top of his skull would blow off. "What the fuck izza matter wichoo," he'd scream. The kid would usually opt for the nearest exit with his tenor sax between his legs.

When faced with an interview or the presence of somebody we didn't like, we had a bit where we'd jabber in mock Chinese. When a normal person (in those days we called them squares) was confronted with a number of potentially dangerous look-ing adolescents ranting in tongues, his first impulse was to be someplace else. Which was precisely the point. It was like a square alert, a defense against a world none of us felt much a part of when we put on those iridescent jackets. But squares were such easy targets that we only used these tactics in self-defense.

There were times when cheap laughs were the only remuneration we could expect. I was lucky to average ten dollars a night. So when The Royal Teens' comet showed signs of cooling off, I took my ass elsewhere: to 1697 Broadway and the offices of Jim Gribble.

Though he never seemed to be a manager in any active sense of the word, Jim Gribble manipulated the fortunes of some of the legendary local doo-wop heroes, among them, The Passions ("Just To Be with You") and The Mystics ("Hush-a-Bye"). He was an imposing figure—a hefty 6 feet 4 inches, 250 pounds, and a slow, deliberate talker in the John Wayne tradition. In contrast to the authoritarian Leo Rogers attitude, he was incredibly patient and seemed to take genuine interest in his musicians, though it was perfectly understood that his patience would be suit-ably rewarded if they happened to make it big. Jim Gribble was never as success-ful as Leo Rogers, most likely because he lacked that razor-sharp killer instinct, but his office certainly offered more possibilities. At the ripe old age of sixteen, I was writing songs and hustling my ass into whatever sessions I could, and Gribble's office provided a much more receptive atmosphere in which to peddle my flesh. Gribble, you see, was always very kind-hearted about your exploitation. He'd throw a token ten bucks your way for piano accompaniment at one of his several daily auditions, or sometimes just when you looked like you needed it.

The point of connection at Gribble's was a kid about my age named Stan Vincent, who did whatever needed to be done, from emptying ashtrays to arranging to some-times even producing a session. Though he didn't always get credit for his studio

You have to wonder what sort of a young man takes a full-grown guitar into a twenty-five-cent photo booth with no inhibitions. New York City, 1960.
(Photo: A. Photo Booth)

tasks, I zeroed in on his position as exactly what I was looking for myself. Having youth and musical aspirations in common, it was natural that we became friends. And by hanging out with him, I was assured a bit of work here and there. It's even conceivable that in the course of our relationship we taught each other a thing or two. Stan later went on to write and produce "O-o-h Child" by The Five Stairsteps, one of my favorite singles.

I'd get out of school at noon and go directly to Gribble's office. (The official schoolday didn't end at noon, but *mine* did.) There'd be people crowding the waiting room and spilling out into the hall, each one with a hustle they hoped was better than the one that hadn't worked for them the week before. Guys with guitars. Guys with songs. Guys with pretty faces and no talent. Guys with nothing going for them but their mouths. You were in competition for everything, from your seat in the outer office to your gig at the afternoon's demo session, and the point of the game was to make yourself as conspicuously available as possible. The oldest profession in the world.

It didn't matter that you ran the risk of making the same nothing for playing at a session that you could just as easily make by sitting at home watching the Knicks game; what we were all grasping at was the opportunity for *involvement*. My philosophy was that you couldn't afford the luxury of trying to be in the right place at the right time. You had to be *every* place at *every* time, and hope that you might wind up anyplace at all. As I look back, I see myself at sixteen as someone who had ten percent talent and ninety percent ambition. At age 54, I see myself with the equation completely reversed!

Jim Gribble died shortly thereafter, a fate most of his groups shared with him at the time. I went to his funeral; it was ill-attended and depressing. Jim Gribble was a good man, one of the few who made sure that his door was always open to unsolicited talent.

In my junior year of high school, a talented pianist friend of mine recommended his private piano teacher to me. On Saturdays, my dad would drive me out to Long Island for two-hour classes with a Mr. Gerald Knieter. Let me tell you the reason I remember his name. The first hour of my lesson was an advanced piano lesson. The second half was music theory. After three classes, he suggested to my father that we drop the piano lesson entirely and proceed with two hours of theory class. "Your son will never be a great keyboard player," he opined to my Dad, "so let's not waste each other's time pursuing that avenue." My respect was so high for this man, that I took his opinion as gospel, and my ability to play keyboards was stunted at that early age. Subliminally he kept me from formative growth at a time I really needed it. The theory helped tremendously, but I didn't grow up to be a theorist, did I?

After Gribble's passing, I drifted back to 1650 Broadway. In the building was a music publishing company that Dick Clark had owned, called Sea Lark. (C-lark, get it?) He owned a few hit copyrights, among them "Sixteen Candles" and "At the Hop." When the payola scandal hit, Clark had to quickly divest himself of his music publishing holdings or go down in a conflict of interests. The company was purchased by a moderately successful songwriter named Aaron Schroeder ("Good Luck Charm," "Stuck on You"), who kept the company alive in its infancy by channeling his own writing into it. He was looking for songs and writers at the same time I happened to be in need of a publisher, so right away it seemed like a mutually agreeable arrangement. He bought a few of my songs for his catalogue, and his door was always open to me.

I came armed with a full repertoire of terrible songs. I guess Schroeder was really desperate to fill his catalogue, because the shuffling of papers was about the only action these songs ever saw. Most of them now qualify as blackmail items (for both of us).

One Saturday morning, with nothing better to do, I hopped a subway into the city to see if I could scrounge up a session. People seldom came in on weekends, but I stopped by 1650 to check the offices anyway. Schroeder happened to be in, and welcomed my company. He had a kid coming in to audition for Musicor Records, his fledgling label—a friend of a friend from Rockville(!), Connecticut. He wanted my opinion, something I've never been known to be at a loss for, and invited me to stick around.

While I thumbed through the latest *Billboard* magazine in the waiting room, this guy walks in wearing a salt and pepper jacket, heavily greased-down DA ("Duck's Ass") hairdo, and white bucks. Three dressing schools tied together; very strange. The creature was quickly ushered in, sat down at the piano, and proceeded to mesmerize us for two uninterrupted hours with his incredible songs and bizarre voice. He was an original, and the impact on me was like hearing soul music for the first time. But one of the mightiest music business ordinances encourages the "poker-face," so Schroeder and I did our utmost to refrain from hailing him as the unique talent we knew he was. After the kid split, Schroeder nonchalantly asked me what I thought.

"What could anyone think?" I said, knowing that we both knew the answer perfectly well. "Sign that guy!"

"Should we change his name?" Schroeder asked.

"Don't make no difference what you call him," I answered. "Gene Pitney is gonna be a big star!"

My analysis was proven correct, with no small thanks to the energies of Aaron. He cleared out all the legal deadwood around Pitney, then signed him to a contract so thorough it might've included bathroom privileges. Gene even moved into Schroeder's apartment; his campaign was carefully and intelligently planned.

The first step was to cut demos of all Gene's material, some of which I played on (and a few of which eventually found their way into circulation disguised as real records). When Schroeder discovered that nearly every record company enthusiastically seconded his high estimation of Pitney's worth, he resolved to use him to establish his own boutique record label, Musicor Records.

Though Pitney didn't take off until "Town Without Pity," his name was beginning to ring a few bells, thanks to Schroeder's boundless hustle. He placed choice Pitney material with classy customers: "He's A Rebel" with The Crystals, "Hello Mary Lou" with Ricky Nelson, "Today's Teardrops" with Roy Orbison, and "Rubber Ball" with Bobby Vee. Before Pitney's own records could claim the power to make teenage hearts flutter, the rest of the industry could see it coming. And when the powers-that-be accept an inevitability, it takes an act of God to prevent it (witness Bruce Springsteen!).

Soon Phil Spector was producing sides with Gene. Then it was Burt Bacharach (whom Schroeder also spotted early on). Aaron had an eye for good combinations, a knack you can acquire only by a thorough understanding of the artist you're dealing with and the marketplace in which his work will be peddled.

Pitney's influence on me was more pervasive than I realized. We became friends and spent a healthy amount of time in each other's company. Unconsciously, I assimilated aspects of his style. I started to sing like him. I started to play the piano like him. I started to write songs that only he could have inspired. At that time, I was still a lump of clay in search of a benevolent pair of hands, and his proved to be as strong and artistic as were needed. To this day, I still possess a few Gene Pitney habits that've never been broken, subtle colorings that still show up on my canvases. As a point of information, "Just One Smile," the Randy Newman song on the first Blood, Sweat & Tears album, originated on an old Pitney LP. Newman, you see, was at that time also contracted to Schroeder as a songwriter.

I, meanwhile, had committed a drastic error in judgment by enrolling as a music major at the University of Bridgeport. I did it partially to appease my parents, who had yet to be convinced that my fixation with the music business was anything but a collision course with an unsavory fate or (at best) a slowly passing fancy. I viewed college as an opportunity to fill in the details of my not-yet-voluminous technical musical knowledge. If I was gonna be a bum, I was gonna be a bum who could read, write, and compose music.

I should've guessed that higher education was not to play a part in my future when I discovered I couldn't major in either of the instruments I played. I had the feel, but not the fingers required of a piano major; and the concept of a guitar major had not yet occurred to the faculty, so this rock 'n' roll animal wound up majoring in bass fiddle.

Things were *not* as they are today in academia. There were *no* courses in popular music, and rock 'n' roll was looked down upon and was therefore unavailable in any college curriculum. A music major was meant to be spat out as a music teacher or a musical virtuoso. I had no desire to spend my young life teaching. I had already tasted rock blood and I wanted more. Once I became embroiled in the classes there, I realized these people could not help me.

To keep in touch with the outside world (and to make sure I had enough money to buy magazines and records) I would write "ghost" arrangements in my spare time. (This means that I wrote arrangements for overbooked arrangers for no credit and quick cash.) I could usually earn an extra two or three hundred dollars by driving into New York City to pick up the songs on a Monday and returning the finished arrangements on Friday night. Far as I could tell, I learned more from this side trip than from any course I was taking at the time, and the comparative enormity of the task made it a cinch for me to breeze through my college homework.

One assignment for music theory class included a simple four-part Bach chorale, with one missing part that the student was to fill in. It took me about eight seconds; it was so trivial compared to the ghost arranging I was doing. When the homework was handed back the next day, mine was covered with red marks. After suffering through hours of uninspired classes and being taught page after page of extraneous information I knew I would never use, this was the ultimate insult. When class was dismissed, I approached the professor's desk and asked him why he'd decorated my homework so colorfully. Then I sat down at the classroom piano and played my version of Bach for him.

"It's not the way Bach would have written it," my teacher criticized.

"Sir, I'm no expert in reincarnation," I said, "but, taking an educated guess, I would say that if you picked your head up from those papers and actually looked at me while I'm speaking to you, you would immediately notice I am *not* Bach—just a student trying to enrich his knowledge in an effort to bolster his own *creativity*."

The teacher looked up at me for the first time in the conversation. "*Mr.* Kooper," he said, "you must first learn the rules before you can break them."

This astonished me.

"Well, sir," I replied, "now that I have divined your teaching philosophy, I think it's safe to say that you will never see this face in your classroom again." And he never did. I didn't need Bach. I needed Burt Bacharach. . . .

I tried to back out of the whole college thing gracefully at the six-month mark. But my parents, in a last-ditch attempt to salvage their investment, dragged a commitment out of me to see the whole year through. I made the compromise and stayed, but nothing was said about actually *studying or attending classes*. So I didn't.

I maintained a residence in the dormitory at Bridgeport and wrote free-lance arrangements for people in New York, while my classmates fought the typical sixties' paranoia that if they didn't make it in college, they were doomed to sweep bus station floors and drive taxis for the rest of eternity. I also put together an eccentric little student jazz combo called the Experimental Jazz Quartet (EJQ, don'cha know) to keep my performing chops in order.

Eventually I got so bored that I even performed manual labor at the local pizzeria, where I had the opportunity to stock the jukebox with my own material. I went so far as to have some of my own demos pressed onto singles, and thus became the "Artist of the Week" on the pizzeria Seeburg: Al Kooper, the Jukebox King of Bridgeport. That and a goatee were my only tangible college accomplishments. If you wanted to teach music to a bunch of human cookie dough cutouts who wanted to teach music to a bunch of human cookie dough cutouts, then studying music in college in 1961 was just what the doctor ordered. All the universities in the world couldn't tell you as much about music as one tour with Dick Clark's Caravan of Stars package! Years later, schools popped up that taught *exactly* what I needed to know at that time (I teach at one now!) but, unfortunately, the chronology just didn't work out in *my* behalf.

It was nobody's loss when I finally packed it in and went home. I made yet another deal with my folks: If by the end of a couple of years in the music business I hadn't achieved anything significant, I'd return to college. I didn't have the slightest intention of honoring my end of that bargain, of course, but it temporarily gave me the kind of freedom I needed to get on with my "career."

My first brush with gainful employment in the real world was as a stockboy in the record department of one of New York's immense department store nightmares. My memory of this tenure is hazy, but I seem to recall that carting Christmas inventory up from the basement for one hellish week cured me of any notions I might've had about the value of honest labor. I still blanch at the sight of anybody's *Christmas Favorites* album.

My next foray into the business world was an out-and-out Kooper scam, the work of a desperate, clever lad. I'd mastered the basics of a few instruments, and while I wasn't exactly the picture of grace on any of them, through the magical process of overdubbing (recording in tandem from one mono machine to another) I could turn out a record all by myself. This was a cheap way to make demos of the songs I wrote; they were acceptable as long as you didn't actually *listen* to them.

Backed by an extensive catalogue of limited skills, I convinced Ray Rand, the owner of Adelphi Studios at 1650, to donate space in his stockroom for my use as an office. The scheme was that I would solicit publishers to hire me for the purpose of producing their song demos. For a package price of ninety dollars a song, I'd give them a vocalist and a full rhythm section playing an arrangement, with all the studio time provided for. This was quite a bargain, as long as nobody got wise to the fact that this one scrawny kid was playing everything, and poorly at that.

So, in January of 1963, with a hundred business cards and printed statements to prove that I was serious, Ko-op Productions came into being. Also included in my arrangement with Ray Rand was responsibility for sweeping the studio floor at day's end. This task earned me the title "apprentice engineer."

At first, I did a lot of sweeping. When the boss went home, however, the engineers would loosen up and occasionally impart a few tricks of their trade. In this way, I picked up an introduction to the art of engineering, and promptly used that knowledge to make demos of *my* current songs, exhausting countless hours of studio time that somehow never showed up in the log books. There were no multitrack machines at Adelphi in those days—I bounced the genesis of each song back and forth between two mono machines, sometimes eight times (!), retarding the sound quality and mix with each regeneration. I had no choice at the time.

Finally the Ko-op bait landed someone—an old-line publisher in the building who sent down music sheets to three songs he needed immediate demos of. A paying customer! I slaved for three days, and though the outcome was every bit as crude as you might imagine, I felt like Phil Spector when the demos were sent to the publisher for his approval. When he heard them, however, he let out a shriek that is reported to have stopped traffic as far away as Newark. And the next day he was in the studio himself, re-cutting the songs with authentic musicians. My cover was blown, and I was back to soliciting the halls of 1650.

While I was "patrolling the halls" one day, a publisher named Hal Webman suggested that I might work well with a pair of lyricists he had under contract. Bob Brass and Irwin Levine had already enjoyed a couple of hits—"A Thing of the Past" by The Shirelles and "Little Lonely One" by The Jarmels—but they needed a bona fide musician to work with. Bona fide? I'm sure that if they asked the publisher from the Ko-op debacle an estimate of my musical worth, he'd have given them a whole other set of adjectives. However, I was always one for challenges and took on the task of catching up to their level of professionalism. Ko-op was abandoned and Hal Webman's company, We Three Music, assumed the responsibility of paying me the princely sum of the twenty-five dollars a week that Adelphi Studios previously had.

The alliance between the three of us was an easy one to forge. Brass and Levine were about three years my senior, had gone to high school together in Union, New Jersey, and had also embraced the let's-dispense-with-college philosophy to take a stab at the music biz. With two hits under their belts, they were confident, fairly talented, and Jewishly fearless. My background was reasonably similar, and while my comparative youthful inexperience made me their scapegoat too often for my liking, it was a workable situation that taught me a lot.

Our environment consisted of a little corner in Hal Webman's office where there happened to be a piano, and we wrote "follow-up" songs for a living. In other words, if Bobby Vee had a hit out called "Please Don't Ask About Barbara," we'd compose a ditty called "Don't Mention Martha" for him in the same key and tempo with roughly the same chord changes. We repeated this process for every hit record that was out. Unfortunately, the hit artists never recorded our follow-ups but, with credit to Hal Webman, they did get the opportunity to *hear* them. Meanwhile, there were enough has-beens and carbon copy performers to insure fairly steady action on our songs.

First Keely Smith recorded one (she sang it on *The Ed Sullivan Show*; my folks loved that), then (the original) Johnny Thunder (remember "Here We Go Loop-de-

Loop"?) included one on the *Loop de Loop* album. None of these were hits, but they kept our names out there and removed the Christmas inventory from my back.

The job was so mechanical that every now and then we'd have to resort to some bizarre caper to preserve our collective sanity. I remember there was a power struggle going on in the office between Webman and his partner, Larry Spier, Jr. I'm not sure that we even knew the details of the conflict, but Hal Webman was the one who signed our paychecks, and so that automatically tipped the scales in his favor.

One night the three of us stayed late to work after the office staff had departed, and a bottle of Scotch was discovered in an unguarded desk drawer. Between the three of us it was emptied in no time at all. It must have been a particularly tough day for me because I had already been diagnosed as a probable ulcer victim, but didn't think twice about downing the Dewar's. All of a sudden we were seized by the inspiration to break down Junior's door.

"Okay," Irwin said, "if we can actually break his door down, I'll take a shit on his desk."

Really drunk.

It became imperative to break the door down, because Brass and I desperately wanted to see Irwin do the dump.

Had to have it.

So we did the thing like in the movies. The three of us grouped at the far corner of the room and barreled into the door. The only thing that happened, of course, was that we hurt ourselves. This wasn't the movies, obviously. (In the movies guys don't promise to shit on desks, either.) Then we decided we'd *kick* the door down. First we tried kicking around the handle, three rounds of ten kicks apiece. Again nothing happened. Coming to the conclusion that our heads must have been as thick as the door, we tapped all over it until we ascertained that the middle was the weakest section. It was here that we concentrated our ten-kicks system until the first crack appeared. We collapsed in a drunken pile on the floor, hysterical 'cause we knew it was only a matter of time. We smashed at that fuckin' door with a vengeance; it looked like some crazy animal had attacked it. When we had a big enough hole in the door, I reached in and opened it.

"Okay Irwin, time to do your stuff."

Opting to give his performance in private, Irwin temporarily banished Brass and me from the room. All this time we were convulsed, exercising a level of humor thought to have been left behind in kindergarten. Irwin emerged five minutes later wearing a self-satisfied grin, and, while fastening his belt, announced, "Boys, come in here—I got a TEXAS TWISTER to show y'all!" The sight of that smoldering pile of excrement sitting on Junior's desk was like fitting the last piece in some scatological jigsaw puzzle. It crippled us.

When the laughter finally subsided, paranoia set in. "Hey," it suddenly occurred to Irwin, "we could get in trouble for this."

We immediately decided that it couldn't have been us that had done this perverted thing. In a burst of drunken logic, we took magazines, office supplies, and plants and began scattering them all over the room. "We'll make 'em think that robbers were here." Yeah, right! Ten minutes into our campaign to make it look as though the office had been burglarized, Brass tapped Irwin on the shoulder. "You know, schmuck," he said in an uncharacteristic moment of clear light, "robbers don't shit on desks." Good point. On that note, we decided it would be intelligent to evacuate the premises *pronto*. We killed a few minutes in another office to cover ourselves with an alibi ("But, officer, we couldn't possibly have been at the scene of the crap. We were two floors down talking to Bob Yorey at the time."). As we were leaving the building, we passed the doddering old janitor shuffling out of the elevator talking to himself. "*Jesus*," he muttered, shaking his head in disbelief, "*they done broke down the door, splinters an' evuhthang!*"

A police car was pulling up as we made our getaway, but the Scotch had numbed our paranoia, and even the appearance of the law couldn't dampen our spirits. "Can you imagine the cops when they find that turd on the desk! Can you imagine the janitor finding it!" So we went and treated ourselves to a Chinese dinner at the appropriately named Ho Ho Restaurant.

Over another Scotch aperitif we realized that it would be expedient to call Hal Webman and give him our side of the story first. Okay, we'd draw straws. We took three toothpicks and made one short. Of course, always the scapegoat, I strawed the shortest pick. I stumbled to the pay phone and dialed Hal Webman's home number.

"Hal, we got drunk, we kicked in Junior's door, and threw a bunch of things around; we'll pay for all the damage. I think the police are there now, 'cause after we did it the janitor saw it."

"Okay," he said, "I'll take care of it."

Grinning, I hung up the phone and returned to the table. That wasn't too difficult. The two of them were in hysterics.

"Al, what did he say when you told him Irwin shit on the desk?"

"I forgot to tell him."

"Call him back," they screamed.

"Do I have. . . ."

"Call him back," they screamed even louder.

I sheepishly made my way back to the phone booth. Busy. Of course it's busy. I tried it again. This time, unfortunately, he answered.

"Hal," I began hesitantly, then hit full stride. "I forgot to mention that Irwin shit on Larry's desk."

Long pause, followed by a disbelieving "He *what*. . . ? Oh my God, I'll see you tomorrow." Click.

Early the next morning, Hal called us at home and said that if we'd apologize to Junior as soon as we came in, it would square everything; he had already made arrangements on our behalf to pay for the door. I arrived at the office first and said, "Larry, I'm really sorry, you know. We were just drunk and it got out of hand." He said okay. He evidently never got to see Irwin's organic buttwork.

Irwin came in next and did the same. Everything was going fine until Brass's entrance. He took one look at the splintered door and broke into a horse-laugh which transformed Irwin and me into instant hyenas. We almost lost our jobs thanks to Brass's ill-timed outburst. But at least we knew shit from Shinola. There had been no Shinola on Junior's desk.

After awhile, we convinced ourselves that we'd outgrown Webman's firm. When Hal's contract ran out, we began freelancing our material. This made things a little more difficult, because instead of a regular salary, we had to sell a song or three every week to survive. This is where I really came of age in the music business. Our asses were on the line, and that is the surest way I know to bring any discussion of ethics to a swift conclusion. When desperation overtook us, we'd resort to preselling a song we'd written by getting it recorded ourselves. This involved browbeating some weak-willed producer into recording our masterpiece—the function normally reserved for the publisher. What we were doing was actually lessening the publisher's workload by about seventy-five percent, and it was infinitely easier to convince him to purchase an already-recorded song than some turkey he'd have to go out and hustle himself.

We'd often have appointments with three different publishers a day. Not having a championship track record to fall back on, we had to rely on sharp wits and a heavy dose of professional sweet talk to open doors. We'd go in and sing our current crop, me like the spinster piano teacher leading her charges through another recital, working our show around to the song that was presold. If they went for it— and you can hardly go wrong by appealing to the laziness in men—we might unload the thing for an on-the-spot advance of three hundred dollars and keep ourselves in burgers for another week. The three hundred was strictly "front-money"; it was understood we'd receive royalties if the song took off.

Our hero at this time was a little African-American gentleman who went by the name of "Run" Joe Taylor. Joe was a writer who worked solo. He would start at the top floor of a building and hit every publisher's office in the building. The problem usually was that he only had one song at a time to sell. But it usually was a good one. If he sold it on the eleventh floor, he had no compunction about selling it on every other floor on the way down. Sometimes he'd sell the same song six times in one building. This was fine unless one of the six publishers got the song recorded. Then his nickname came into quick use: *"Run, Joe!!!"*

During our freelance period, we manufactured a bright little R&B item that none of us figured to be worth all that much. Nonetheless we managed to sell it for three hundred dollars to my old friend Aaron Schroeder, who, by now, had developed a very smooth and profitable publishing concern and was interested in signing us to an exclusive writers' contract. We'd written this particular song with The Drifters in mind. They were hot, riding a chain of hits telegraphed out to them via the Aldon pipeline (among them "Up on the Roof" and "On Broadway"). The Drifters turned the song down, but a West Coast producer named Snuff Garrett, then successfully masterminding Bobby Vee's recordings, picked up on it. By the time Garrett's production was finished, we had quit freelancing and were signed to Schroeder for two bills a week apiece, quite a chunk by our depressed standards. Garrett had cut a white version of our tune with Jerry Lewis's thoroughly inoffensive white son Gary and sent us a copy the day it was released.

We were revolted. They'd removed the soul from our R&B song and made a teenage milkshake out of it. Never mind that who-were-we-to-be talking-about-soul in the first place; this was disgusting. We dismissed "This Diamond Ring" by Gary Lewis and the Playboys on one hearing, and hoped Schroeder would get us covers that might have some chance of selling a few copies.

To our surprise, after a hype-ridden sendoff on *The Ed Sullivan Show* (once again; several of our songs were showcased by Sullivan acts, as you recall), all you could hear on the radio was our turkey milkshake. Suddenly we were on the charts: 82, 65, 30, 20, 12, 8, 7, 3, 2, 2, and then, after knocking Aldon's "You've Lost That Lovin' Feeling" out of the top slot, our song became the number one song in the country! America had finally seen fit to recognize our "talent." We conveniently forgot our previous animosity toward the record and concentrated on basking in as much of the glory as we could squeeze out of it. The day the record hit number one, we just stared at the charts and laughed and laughed.

We had the biggest song in the country, yet, we were still broke. Recompense for a hit record can be delayed a year or more in arriving. Let's also not forget about the inevitable three-way-split. It's just another music biz irony that you can be at the top of the charts and still be bumming chump change from all your pals. The only course of action is to milk your newfound reputation for dear life; hustle in a bigger ball park.

We drew advances against our forthcoming royalties (not suggested as a great idea) and affected the trappings of success. Occasional barbershop shaves for that freshly manicured look; dinner at Jack Dempsey's (a nearby restaurant that was a hangout for music-biz successes) to *feel* important. And as our milkshake Frankenstein came plummeting down the charts, another Brass-Kooper-Levine special began a hesitant climb up. This one was called "I Must Be Seeing Things," and was courtesy of my old friend Gene Pitney.

Once again, being signed to Schroeder gave us the inside track. Schroeder managed and produced Pitney, owned the record company, and could keep his house perfectly in order by recording songs he already published. But when other artists were not "appreciating" our songs, it was always Pitney who'd take one of our teen traumas and tack it onto an album or make it the flip side of a single, just so's we could eat. When "I Must Be Seeing Things" hit the charts, it felt good to be doing something to repay Gene's kindness for recording various gems of ours like "(We Are) The Last Two People on Earth," "Don't Take Candy from a Stranger," and "Hawaii."

With two solid chart records, you'd think that all would've been peachy keen in the wonderful world of Brass-Kooper-Levine. But alien forces were afoot, and the tide of public taste was pulling out on us. The Beatles were giving Aldon the bum's rush, and an unholy alliance between Bob Dylan and marijuana was fucking with my head in a fierce way. Grass was showing me the same pure visions that it freely dispensed to everyone else at that time, and I found that I could no longer Clearasil-ically compose music. I suddenly saw the inherent dishonesty in what I'd been doing, and prayed to a stack of jazz albums for forgiveness. That's the way pot made you think, at least at first. It wasn't until years later that I discovered that the crooks and con men had been smoking it for decades before I had stumbled upon it.

A split was inevitable. The first to go was Brass, who renounced the vagaries of the music business in favor of a comparatively honest blue-collar job at the Fulton Fish Market, and from then on it was just Kooper-Levine. Our percentages took an instant leap from thirty-three percent to fifty percent, and that helped dry our tears. I had recently married my childhood sweetheart, Judy Kerner, and needed every extra penny I could reel in as the twenty-one-year-old newly proclaimed breadwinner.

One afternoon Irwin and I took some organic mescaline and decided to go to the movies. (Now there's a good family man!) We were in midtown Manhattan, and we chose the first-run *The Loved One*, a film I had already seen earlier in the week but was eager to see again, especially stoned and with Irwin. We arrived at the theater about ten minutes after taking the mescaline, so we weren't high yet. About three-quarters through the show we were *really* loaded and all of a sudden the movie got slower and slower and finally just stopped altogether. I looked at Irwin and said, "I'm so high I can't even see the movie anymore." He concurrred and we realized that the movie had actually prematurely *stopped*. An usher announced that the power would be restored in a moment. Just then another usher of Jamaican persuasion rushed in screaming, "Come see! De lights is out all over de whole damn city!" Irwin and I laughed hysterically as everybody rushed out to the street to check it out. The staff had to coax us out of our seats for *a few minutes* before *we'd* go outside. We were immediately transported into the middle of a powerless New York in the throes of the Great Blackout (October 9, 1965) with rush hour at its peak. Heavy stuff.

Irwin and I were quickly separated in a scene not unlike the climax of *Day of the Locust*. On my own, I got into a heavy Ray Bradbury trip, walking east to west for countless blocks, looking at all the weird situations: People prevented from commuting home crashed out by the hundreds in hotel lobbies. Coffee shops jammed with people eating by candlelight. Then, at the height of my high I got pushed onto this downtown bus. The bus was stopping at every block and people were forcing their way in the back doors and it was really panicsville. When the bus was as jammed as it could be, the driver passed by the lines at all the stops along his route. When he'd have to stop to let someone off, the bus was violently attacked by frustrated would-be passengers who rocked it back and forth in an attempt to get inside. By this time, the mescaline coupled with the violence caused me to be silently crying and people were looking at me like *I* was crazy!

The bus headed downtown, and I was soon in relatively familiar territory. I ran into some folks I knew, and we retired back to the relative safety of their apartment. On the way there, we noticed junkies breaking into stores and cops trying to deal with them without using Gestapo tactics (New York cops were usually the sanest at that time). Anyhow, my friends fed me and cooled me out. I called home to the suburbs, chilled out my wife, and told her I'd return when the power did.

My friends and I then set out on a tour of Greenwich Village, visiting friends, observing various psychodramas, and killing the whole night until we returned to their apartment to crash. By this time, I was down from the mescaline and exhausted physically and mentally. I lay my head down on the pillow and shut my weary eyes, when all of a sudden the TV went on, the radio went on, the light over the bed went on, and the garbage disposal went on. Frankly, it was the most horrendous sound ever heard as every appliance in New York swung back into action at the same time. I looked at my watch and noted that it was almost twelve hours to the second since the blackout began. Weird science, eh?

Around this same time, one of the producers we had bombarded with our material took a shine to me and I was invited to attend a session he was producing the next day. The producer was Tom Wilson; the artist he was producing was a guy named Bob Dylan.

1965:

THE YEAR OF LIVING FAMOUSLY:

BOB DYLAN AND LIFE AS A SESSION MUSICIAN

In 1965, being invited to a Bob Dylan session was like getting backstage passes to the fourth day of creation. And make no mistake about it, a formal invitation was prerequisite. There was no just-happened-to-be-in-the-neighborhood of Columbia Studios when Bob Dylan was recording. Sessions for Dylan albums at that time might as well have been strategy meetings for the direction the new alternative culture would take, and it wasn't very often that one of the foot soldiers got the opportunity of watching the five-star general in action.

I'd been aware of Dylan since the beginning; you could feel his presence in the air. I bought his first two albums because I always made a point of checking out the various musical trends going on around me. Although I had played his records, nothing happened. I was coming off of a four-year intensive jazz-listening binge, and this was comparatively too primitive and antimusical to digest in one or two listens. I confess that I just couldn't hear it at first.

At that time I was playing occasional gigs with a neighborhood friend, the not-yet-famous Paul Simon and his bandleader dad Lou, a society bass player who'd book all kinds of big band jobs. Paul would sing and play rhythm and I would play lead guitar. We'd sit on the bandstand with our guitars, strumming along with the standards, albeit with our volume turned all the way off. Every forty-five minutes, Paul would jump up and sing two twist songs and I would take the prerequisite guitar soli. For playing eight songs in four hours we would receive fifty dollars each.

One night we played a prom at C. W. Post College with that square band. (You've got to remember that the kids were square in those days, too. They still went for big bands rather than rock 'n' roll on those "important" occasions.) While setting up, Paul said, "Man, have you heard 'Baby Let Me Follow You Down' by Bob Dylan?"

"Yeah."

"Isn't it fantastic?"

"Well, I couldn't dig it, couldn't get next to his voice."

"Fuck his voice; listen to the way he plays guitar. Listen to this," he said and began to spew it out note for note on the *electric* guitar, which made a *big* difference to me.

"Yeah," I admitted, "I'll have to go back and re-listen."

And so I did, actually enjoying the records this time around. I also quickly discovered that if I played a Bob Dylan album too loud, it would bring my mother storming into the room in exactly twelve seconds. "Who is that? That's terrible. It sounds like a fingernail on a blackboard. Turn that crap off." His singing definitely struck a discordant note in parents; they were extremely intimidated by the sound of his voice. This helped it all make sense to me (and to millions of others my age, I'm sure, as well).

Little by little, the Dylan influences crept into my Tin Pan Alley work. "Paper doll princesses" and the like began to show up in our songs, and I made a concerted attempt to convert Irwin Levine. I must say he was into it fiscally before he understood it intellectually. His cash register brain immediately saw that it would be advantageous to at least take a stab at understanding this weirdness that had infected so many people around him. I began fooling around composing songs on my own—blatant Dylan ripoffs. I was writing bubble-gum songs by day, working in bar bands by night, and trying to squeeze every possible alternative into the time between. I wrote a song called "Thirty-Eight People," a topical little situation comedy based on a true incident, about a girl named Kitty Genovese, who'd been murdered at a Long Island Railroad station while thirty-eight people looked on from neighboring apartments and did nothing to help her. (Stop me if you've heard this one before.) It was not a funny song.

1965

There was a folk club in Forest Hills called the Cafe Interlude, and I wandered in there one open-mike night. I wasn't into the scene deeply enough to be anything but a weekend folkie. For instance, I had a Goya gut-string guitar; I didn't know that you were supposed to play a steel-stringed guitar. I was a rock 'n' roll guitar player; what did I know from beards and bongos? When I arrived at the club and had to sign in to play, all of the above suddenly occurred to me. "Shit," I thought to myself, "Al Kooper would never do this. It's almost embarrassing. I'll be—uh—Al Casey." So I took the stage that evening and performed "Thirty-Eight People" as Al Casey. What I wasn't aware of was that the incident the song describes had taken place *right outside the club's window*, and several of those thirty-eight people I was singing about were very probably in the audience, making for a tension that I didn't quite pick up on until the song was over.

"Hey, man," said an agitated voice from the back of the room, "that bitch was killed right outside this club. Did you know that?"

Stop. "Well, I . . . err . . . thank you very much, ladies and gentlemen. See you next week." Exit Al Casey.

My first appearance hadn't been what you could call a smash, but I stuck with it. The Cafe Interlude became my new hangout, and I quickly assimilated the exotic life-style it represented to me. Within two weeks the Goya went the way of all Goyas, and I had the right guitar (Gibson J-200), knew all the right names (Woody Guthrie, Ramblin' Jack Elliott, etc.), and even knew a few of the right songs ("Tom Joad," "There But For Fortune," etc.). The people who frequented the club were rigid Pete Seeger types; local communists still hung over from the Beat days and maintaining an unabashed contempt for the dishonesty they inherently saw in rock 'n' roll. I wasn't necessarily falling for *that* part of the sales pitch, but I adapted my profile to their attitude as best I could, helped along considerably by their guidance in the finer points of dope smoking. My mom wanted to know what all those rolling papers were doing in my pants pockets. My new "friends" had sketchy knowledge of my other life, but most likely thought it was just a day gig to keep Al Casey fed. I would've been boiled in oil if they knew I had anything to do with Gary Lewis & The Playboys.

Through sheer persistence I was eventually offered a weekend gig, three nights opening for somebody named Henry Gibson. I had my folkie set all worked out: a few traditionals, tunes by some contemporary folk writers, Dylan's Dylan songs, plus *my* Dylan songs, one of which, "Talking Radio Blues," was an ironically self-righteous putdown of commercial radio, a toothless chomp on the hand that was feeding me. Nonetheless, the weekend was ill-attended; I guess the weather was bad or something. Henry who???

About that time, Mike Wallace was putting together a CBS radio documentary on the thirty-eight people incident. He came to the club to tape some interviews and somebody told him about my spiny topical song, which he then recorded for use as part of the presentation. Figuring this exposure to be an ideal selling point, I started pestering Tom Wilson, Dylan's producer at Columbia Records, with the idea of getting a single of it out as soon as possible. It took five or six visits before I talked my way past his secretary, but when I finally did get to play it for him, he liked it to the extent that we went in and cut the song. He didn't, however, like it to the extent that a record was ever released. It's a good thing in hindsight. It would have been quite the embarrassing item today.

Still, through this experience, Wilson and I became tight. I let him in on the Al Kooper side of me, the Tin Pan Alley songs, some of which he later cut during his tenure at MGM. Our relationship progressed to the level where I could walk past the secretary and straight into his office, which I made a point of doing as often as possible when he wasn't around. I'd sift through his records and cop all the acetates of as-yet-unreleased Dylan material, take them home overnight, and commit them to memory before slipping them back into Tom's pile the next day. These "exclusives" would immediately be incorporated into my Al Casey act and gave it the *only* bit of charisma it ever had.

Tom had just cut "Subterranean Homesick Blues," Dylan's first electric single, and played it for me prior to its release. Of course, on that day, my folkie apprenticeship came to an end. I saw that it was now possible to be both Bob Dylan and rock 'n' roll Kooper at the same time, and kissed off Al Casey forever.

Wilson felt comfortable enough to invite me to watch an electric Dylan session, because he knew I was a big Bob fan. He had no conception of my limitless ambition, however. There was no way in hell I was going to visit a Bob Dylan session and just sit there pretending to be some reporter from *Sing Out!* magazine! I was committed to *play on it.* I stayed up all night preceding the session, naively running down all seven of my guitar licks over and over again. Despite my noodling at the piano, I was primarily a guitar player at the time and having gotten a fair amount of session work under my belt, I had developed quite an inflated opinion of my dexterity on said instrument.

The session was called for two o'clock the next afternoon at Columbia Studios, which were at 799 Seventh Avenue, between West 52nd and West 53rd Streets. Taking no chances, I arrived an hour early and well enough ahead of the crowd to establish my cover. I walked into the studio with my guitar case, unpacked, tuned up, plugged in, and sat there trying my hardest to look like I belonged. The other musicians booked on the session (all people I knew from other sessions around town) slowly filtered in and gave no indication that anything was amiss. For all they knew, I could have received the same call they'd gotten. Tom Wilson hadn't arrived as yet, and he was the only one who could really blow the whistle on my little charade. I was prepared to tell him I had misunderstood him and thought he had asked me to *play* on the session. All bases covered. *What balls!*

Suddenly Dylan exploded through the doorway with this bizarre-looking guy carrying a Fender Telecaster guitar without a case. It was weird, because it was storming outside and the guitar was all wet from the rain. But the guy just shuffled over into the corner, wiped it off with a rag, plugged in, and commenced to play some of the most incredible guitar I'd ever heard. And he was just *warming up*! That's all the Seven Lick Kid had to hear; I was in over my head. I embarrassedly unplugged, packed up, went into the control room, and sat there pretending to be a reporter from *Sing Out!* magazine.

Tom Wilson then made his entrance—too late, thank God, to catch my little act of bravado. All was lost, but I wanted to know the identity of the dragonslayer, so I asked Tom who the guitar player was. "Oh, some friend of Dylan's from Chicago, named Mike Bloomfield. I never heard him but Bloomfield says he can play the tunes, and Dylan says he's the best." That's how I was introduced to the man who can *still* make me pack up my guitar whenever his music is played.

The band quickly got down to business. They weren't too far into this long song Dylan had written before it was decided that the organ player's part would be better suited to piano. The sight of an empty seat in the studio stirred my juices once again; it didn't matter that I knew next to nothing about playing the organ. Ninety percent ambition, remember? In a flash I was all over Tom Wilson, telling him that I had a great organ part for the song and please (oh God please) could I have a shot at it. "Hey," he said, "you don't even play the organ."

"Yeah, I do, and I got a good part to play in this song," I shot back, all the while racing my mind in overdrive to think of anything I could play at all. Already adept at wading through my bullshit, Tom said, "I don't want to embarrass you, Al, I mean . . . ," and he was then distracted by some other studio obligation. Claiming victory by virtue of not having received a direct "no," I walked into the studio and sat down at the organ.

Me and the organ: It's difficult to power up a Hammond organ. It takes three separate moves, I later learned. *If the organist (Paul Griffin) hadn't left the damn thing turned on, my career as an organ player would have ended right then and there.* I figured out as best I could how to bluff my way through the song while the rest of the band rehearsed one little section. Then Wilson returned and said, "Man, what are *you* doin' out there???" All I could do was laugh nervously. On the

Highway 61 Interactive CD-ROM, you can actually hear this moment taking place. Wilson was a gentleman, however. He let it go.

Imagine this: There is no music to read. The song is over five minutes long, the band is so loud that I can't even *hear* the organ, and I'm not familiar with the instrument to begin with. But the tape is rolling, and that is Bob-fucking-Dylan over there singing, so this had better be me sitting here playing *something*. The best I could manage was to play hesitantly by sight, feeling my way through the changes like a little kid fumbling in the dark for the light switch. After six minutes they'd gotten the first complete take of the day and everyone adjourned to the control room to hear it played back.

Thirty seconds into the second verse of the playback, Dylan motioned toward Tom Wilson. "Turn the organ up," he ordered. "Hey, man," Tom said, "that cat's not an organ player." *Thanks, Tom.* But Dylan wasn't buying it: "Hey, now don't tell me who's an organ player and who's not. Just turn the organ up." *He actually liked what he heard!*

If you listen to it today, you can hear how I waited until the chord was played by the rest of the band, before committing myself to play in the verses. I'm always an eighth note behind everyone else, making sure of the chord before touching the keys. Can you imagine if they had to have stopped the take because of *me*? At the conclusion of the playback, the entire booth applauded the soon-to-be-classic "Like A Rolling Stone," and Dylan acknowledged the tribute by turning his back and wandering into the studio for a go at another tune. I sat, still dazed, behind my new instrument and filled in a chord every now and again. No other songs were gotten that day. Later, as everyone was filing out, Dylan asked for my phone number—which was like Claudia Schiffer asking for the key to your hotel room—and invited me back to play the next day. Elated, I walked out into the street realizing that I had actually lived out my fantasy of the night before, *although not quite exactly as I had planned it.*

I was twenty-one at the time of this incident, married, and residing uncomfortably in the suburb of Forest Hills, Queens. My hair was relatively short, and I wore a shirt and tie because I liked the way it looked. You have to admit—the freakier a man looks, the more dashing he becomes in a suit and tie. Imagine Frank Zappa in black tie versus Bill Clinton—who would you wanna chat with? I was very confused about what was wrong or right, a condition compounded, I believe, by a great deal of pot-smoking done at the time. Though I wasn't aware of it, my life was changing in ways I wouldn't begin to comprehend until much later (like now).

I returned to the studio the next day with a little more confidence. My moment as a daring organ commando was behind me, and that release of pressure allowed

Listening to the playback of the keeper take of "Like A Rolling Stone." (Left to right) Roy Halee (engineer), Tom Wilson (producer), Pete Duryea (assistant engineer, standing), Albert Grossman, Artie Mogul, Dylan, Vinnie Fusco (partially obscured) Sandy Speiser (foreground), Al (pondering his future). (Photo: Al Kooper Collection.)

☙

me to get down to figuring out what the hell I was doing sitting behind an organ in the first place. The other keyboard player was Paul Griffin, who, with a strong Baptist church background, was probably the best damned studio keyboard player in all of New York City and certainly the funkiest. I leaned in his direction heavily that day, borrowing a bass line here, a rhythm part there, and generally picked up a lot of basics and the beginning of a style that can only be traced directly to Paul's playing.

We cut two tracks that day: "Tombstone Blues" and "Queen Jane Approximately." I was adequate. And delirious. That was the last date on Dylan's recording schedule for awhile, and thus ended my contact with him—unless he planned to use that phone number I'd given him.

Eventually the time rolled around for one of the grandest East Coast traditions, the

Newport Folk Festival, and my wife and I made our annual trek north. Despite my pop songwriting and Broadway habits, I had always maintained a healthy affection for this event. Whatever your musical proclivity—even if there was no proclivity at all—Newport was one of the nicest social gatherings you could possibly attend. Most of the musicians from downtown made the pilgrimage annually, and it was like a Greenwich Village block party moved to the seaside. There was a lot of new electric folk music being played on the barbarian AM radio airwaves that summer, and some of it found its way past the guardians of the Newport tradition.

Afternoons were given to slow-paced workshop sessions, which one (*this* one, that is) would browse like a bookstore, doing more socializing than serious perusing. On one such late afternoon stroll, I was accosted by Albert Grossman, Dylan's manager. "Bob's looking for you. Here's some passes; meet us backstage tonight." And then he was gone. Backstage! Wow! We quickly sold the remainder of our tickets and got prepared for our preferred ringside accommodations.

When my wife and I arrived backstage that evening, Dylan came running over wearing this top-hat (?) and grabbed me in a bear hug. "Al Kooper," he said. "How are you? We've been calling you for days. [I had been in Newport.] Good to see you," etc., etc., etc.

What Dylan and Grossman had in mind was to put the electric sound of the recording sessions on stage at Newport. "Like A Rolling Stone" was blasting out of every transistor radio smuggled onto the festival grounds, and Dylan wanted to make the penetration blatant. This included my incompetent organ playing, which had suddenly become a publicly recognized trademark of the "new Dylan sound." The irony, oh, the irony. . . .

The group Mike Bloomfield played with, The Paul Butterfield Blues Band, was debuting at the festival that year. So not only was Bloomfield available for duty, but Dylan also got the use of drummer Sam Lay and bassist Jerome Arnold. A friend of Bloomfield's, Barry Goldberg, was "recruited" to play piano. (He begged for the chance!) The night before the scheduled performance, we rehearsed until dawn in one of those huge Newport mansions overlooking the ocean.

Our portion of the show opened with "Maggie's Farm" and concluded with "Like a Rolling Stone." In the middle of "Maggie's Farm," somebody fucked up and Sam Lay turned the beat around (played the snare on beats 1 and 3 instead of 2 and 4), which thoroughly confused everyone onstage until the song mercifully stumbled to its conclusion. But "Like A Rolling Stone" was played perfectly and we really got it across. Dylan came off and appeared to be satisfied, and people were yelling for an encore.

If you've read any accounts of that infamous evening, chances are they centered on how Dylan was booed into submission and then returned for a tearful acoustic rendering of "It's All Over Now, Baby Blue." A romantic picture, perhaps, but that's just not the way it was. At the close of the set, Peter Yarrow (of Paul and Mary fame and the emcee for the evening) grabbed Dylan as he was coming offstage. These two were both managed by Grossman and were close friends. The crowd was going bonkers for an encore, as we had only played fifteen minutes! I was standing *right there*.

"Hey," Peter said, "you just can't leave them like that, Bobby. They want another one."

"But that's all we know," replied Dylan, motioning toward the band.

"Well, go back out there with this," said Yarrow, handing his acoustic guitar to Bob.

And Dylan did. That's all there was to it. I was right there. Most other acts played a forty-five-minute set. Many young kids (like myself) came to the three-day event especially to see Dylan's set. He was the King of Newport. Can you imagine them sitting through the Georgia Sea Island Singers, Son House, or Mance Lipscomb for forty-five minutes each, and then staring in disbelief as Dylan left the stage after fifteen minutes??? Damn right, they booed. But not at Bob—rather, at whoever was seemingly responsible for yanking him offstage after fifteen minutes. We had just run out of rehearsed material and that's why we stopped. But these were representatives of our college-age generation. They belonged to frats and sororities, swilled beer like nobody's business, and had begun smoking the dreaded marijuana. They had journeyed many miles to p-a-r-t-y with their hero, but he just wanted to drop off his present at the front door and leave.

Bob, seizing the moment, returned to the stage with Peter's acoustic guitar and sang "It's All Over Now, Baby Blue" to these people; banishing the acoustic-folk movement with one song right at the crossroads of its origin. If ever there was a galvanizing moment in musical history, this was it. The more coherent members of the audience were the ones with tears in their eyes—not Bob. They realized that things might never be the same again, and it was a rude awakening standing there amidst the crowd at Newport. But the media misconstrued (or manipulated) the whole point. They attributed the booing to Dylan's electric appearance. Hell, Butterfield played electric the day before, and The Chambers Brothers played electric earlier in the show. Bob wasn't trailblazing a plugged-in performance on that stage. But when he said to everyone, *"You must leave now, take what you need you think will last . . . ,"* [1] he was pretty much telling them to hang on to his albums; that this was not the end—but rather, a genesis.

---

[1] "It's All Over Now, Baby Blue," © 1965 Warner Bros. Inc; © renewed 1993 Special Rider Music (SESAC). Used by permission. All rights reserved.

Energized by the Newport reaction, we went back to New York and straight into the studio to finish work on *Highway 61 Revisited*, as that album was to be called. Then, once again, when those sessions were completed, I returned to my little cubicle lovenest in Forest Hills to lead the comparatively mundane life I had lived before I got my organ caught in the tail of that comet.

Prior to my recent Dylan association, I had been playing in bars with my good friend Harvey Goldstein, a bass player. We were partners. If one of us got hired for a gig, he would strenuously rally to get said employer to hire the other one of us, if it was at all possible. Of course, Harvey almost got me killed once. He occasionally played with this singer named Bobby Marico. I would play with them when Harv could get me on the gig. One night we had an engagement in upstate New York at a lovely place called the Luau Nyack. We were supposed to start at 9:00 p.m. and play until 2:00 a.m. Five sets, forty-five minutes on and fifteen minutes off = $400. We got real lost on the way up there and had to call the club to get directions from wherever we were. We arrived at 8:45 p.m., set up quickly, and started playing at 9:15. Bobby, who fronted the band, told the owner we'd play late to make up for the fifteen minutes we had lost by arriving late. There were only ten people in the audience when we started playing in the first place. At the end of the night, the clubowner deducted half our pay for being late. Bobby Marico went ballistic. He screamed at the guy and walked into the guy's office yelling at him. We followed like sheep to watch his back. The guy opened his desk drawer and pulled out a gun.

"Does this change the argument at all?" he inquired, smiling and pointing the gun at Bobby. Harvey and I were incredulous. Bobby was not.

"Hey, before you pull that fuckin' trigger you should know my father is good friends with Angelo D'Ambrosio [not his real name]."

Amazingly this stopped the guy.

"Hey kid, you don't throw names like that around here, y'unnerstan'?"

Bobby didn't back down. I was trying to remember if I told anyone I was going to Nyack that night and wondering if I would just be missing for all time or if miraculously they'd find my body in the woods around the club.

"I'm not throwin' any fucking names around, pal. My father knows Angelo D'Ambrosio and I think you should put that gun away and give us our money!!" God, that Bobby had *balls*!

Amazingly, the guy put the gun down and gave him *all* the money.

"Awright, you little punks, take the fucking money and don't ever come around here again."

Yeah. Like we were gonna come back the next night just for a coupla drinks. In the car, I asked Bobby if his dad really knew that guy. Bobby said he did and that mentioning Angelo D'Ambrosio's name had saved him two other times from compromising situations. I wasn't Italian-looking enough to remember Angelo's real name for the future, fortunately.

Harvey and Bobby Marico got a gig for the whole summer of '64 at the World's Fair. Harvey talked Bobby into hiring me as well. This was a great payday and a three-month steady gig, not far from our homes. I owed Harvey. I talked Dylan into trying Harvey out on one of the *Highway 61* sessions because I could tell Bob liked having people closer to his age around.

Harvey met with Bob's approval and stayed on. Things went so splendidly that Dylan decided to assemble the studio band to accompany him on his upcoming concert tour. Bloomfield was another story. Harvey and I had lunch with him one afternoon.

"You guys going on the road with Dylan?" he asked us.

"Yeah, sure, aren't you?"

"I can't," he said. "You guys will be big stars, be on TV and in the movies, have your picture on the cover of *Time*, but I can't do it. I want to stay with Butterfield."

"Why?"

"All I want to do is play the blues, man. Ah *loves* tuh play de blues," he grinned.

So that was it for Bloomfield. Bobby Gregg, the drummer on the album, also opted to stay home; something about having enough session work to keep him busy. As it turned out, Mary Martin, a Canadian-born secretary who worked at Albert Grossman's office, took Dylan out to a club in New Jersey to see a journeyman band called the Hawks, who hailed from her native Canada and had formerly backed up Ronnie Hawkins. Bob apparently liked what he saw that night, because suddenly guitarist Robbie Robertson and drummer Levon Helm were in the picture in addition to Harvey and me. This gave us a young, rockin' quartet behind Bob (though it did effectively break up the Hawks at that time). We rehearsed exhaustively every day over a two-week period, and the pieces fell together nicely.

After rehearsals, I fell into the habit of tagging along at night with Dylan and his left-hand man, Bob Neuwirth, in their regal odysseys around the Village. Hanging out at the Kettle Of Fish, eating at the Limelight (not the recent disco, but a now-defunct, low-key eatery on Seventh Avenue in the West Village), going to an endless succession of clubs, parties, and recording sessions. With a completely flexible song-writing and session schedule, I had plenty of time to devote to hanging out and soaking it all up. Plus here was a guy who, for no charge, was rerouting my entire train of thought. It was like taking a blackboard with all my former values written on it, erasing everything, and starting all over again.

Dylan would hold court at a back table at the Kettle Of Fish, a seedy little bar on MacDougal Street in the Village that was distinguished only by its musical clientele. Once the place was fairly full, they'd lock the doors and Dylan would take over. Word that Dylan was inside circulated on the street, and people would jam up outside the front window hoping to catch a glimpse of the action.

Dylan, as always, was buying the drinks. Neuwirth would carry the money, pay the bills, and make all the *necessary* apologies. It was never very long before the room was on a collective drunk (except for yours truly, whose raging ulcer precluded anything stronger than soda). The cast of characters usually included Dylan, Neuwirth, Eric Andersen, Debby Green, Phil Ochs, David Blue, Dave and Teri Van Ronk, Ramblin' Jack Elliott, Clarence Hood (who owned the Gaslight, the club next door), myself, and Paul Rothchild (a staff producer at Elektra).

If Dylan got drunk enough, he'd select a target from among the assembled singer/songwriters, and then pick that person apart like a cat toying with a wounded mouse. Making fun of a person's lyrics, attire, or lack of humor was the gist of his verbal barrage. Dylan was so accomplished at this nasty little game, that if he desired, he could push his victim to the brink of fisticuffs. It was all relative to how much alcohol was being consumed by the party of the first part, the party of the second part, or the party in general. When temperatures would threaten to shatter the room's emotional thermometer, it would be good ol' Bob Neuwirth's job to step in and negotiate a temporary truce over yet another bottle of Remy. These nights would usually end with everyone carrying everyone else home and Neuwirth paying a tab that was well into the hundreds.

Dylan maintained a fierce rivalry with his "children" (as *Life* magazine called them), although underlying his antagonism was a comprehensive awareness of their latest albums and career moves. Maybe he wanted to keep everyone on their toes, or perhaps he was just trying to stay awake.

After rehearsing for two weeks, we were ready to take this new electric Dylan on the road. Grossman had booked a couple of impressive dress rehearsals: the Forest Hills, New York, Tennis Stadium for one night; and the Hollywood Bowl a week later. The day of the Forest Hills gig, we spent the entire afternoon doing a sound-check and getting acquainted with the big room. It had rained earlier in the day, God's little preview of what the night held in store.

This concert took place a brief six weeks after the Newport show, which had been ballooned by the media into a major boo-fest to suit the purposes of the countless articles being written about Dylan "selling out" to crass rock 'n' roll. America was ready for hand-to-hand confrontation with its reckless idol, and Forest Hills would

Forest Hills concert—afternoon soundcheck. New York City, 1965. (Left) Bob (with senses reeling); (right) Al (with Beatle boots, kneeling). (Photo: Al Kooper Collection.)

prove to be the battleground. We had no way of knowing this in advance, however.

The concert started off smoothly enough, with Dylan sailing through a well-paced acoustic set to the delight of the overflow crowd. At intermission, Dylan cleared the backstage area and called the band into a huddle.

"I don't know what it will be like out there. It's going to be some kind of a carnival, and I want you all to know that up front. So just go out there and keep playing no matter how weird it gets." Yeah, well . . . sure.

While we had this little band meeting, the concert promoter had decided to have the electric half of the show introduced by the self-proclaimed "Fifth Beatle," Murray the K. Murray represented the antithesis of what Dylan was all about and could have even been a character in one of Dylan's current songs. When Murray was introduced, the crowd was in total disbelief. I still don't know how Albert Grossman let this detail get past him. When Murray hit the stage, a wave of booing swept over him, the likes of which he had probably never endured before. He was like the proverbial turd in the punchbowl.

Our instruments were pushed into place and we walked out on stage. Suddenly an ill-timed wind whipped through the stadium, dropping the temperature at least ten degrees in as many seconds. The crowd stirred at the sound of the tentative drum rolls and guitar tunings; an ominous rumble from the other side of the darkness.

The lights went up and we were into "Tombstone Blues" full force, but the audience got quiet. Too quiet. The wind churned around the stadium and blew Dylan's hair this way and that, as if reprimanding him for this electric sacrilege. The conclusion of the song was greeted with the boos all these kids had read so much about and probably felt obliged to deliver. Of course, the barrage was peppered with "Dylan, you scumbag! . . . Get off the fucking stage!" and other subtle pleasantries characteristic of our generation.

Bob didn't flinch. He just bulled his way straight through the hour-plus set. It seemed that even the hero worshippers were unusually aggressive on this particular evening. They'd try to claw their way onto the stage to make contact with Dylan, and the police were sparing no tactic to keep them back. One kid was chased behind me by a cop and as he flew by, he hooked his leg on my stool, taking me with him as he went down. I was on my ass and not the least bit pleased about the situation.

Three-quarters of the way through, Dylan stood at the piano to play "Ballad Of A Thin Man," a song from the as-yet-unreleased *Highway 61* album. It had a quiet intro, and the kids persisted in yelling and booing all the way through it. Dylan shouted out to us to "keep playing the intro over and over again until they shut up!" We played it for a good five minutes—*doo do da da*, *do da de da*—over and over until they did, in fact, chill. A great piece of theater. When they were finally quiet, Dylan sang the lyrics to them: "Something is happening here, but you don't know what it is, do you?"[2] It was almost as if he'd written the song knowing full

---

[2] "Ballad Of A Thin Man," © 1965 Warner Bros. Inc.; © renewed 1993 Special Rider Music (SESAC). Used by permission. All rights reserved.

well that the moment would come when he'd sing it to a crowd like this one. Just like "Baby Blue" at Newport. It was lovely. We then segued into "Like A Rolling Stone," which was number one on the charts that week. Everyone sang along and then booed when it was over!

Dylan pulled his customary vanishing trick, leaving Harvey and me to make our way out into the chilly Forest Hills night unaided. People, recognizing our shirts from the stage, reached out to grab us, and believe me, they could have had anything in mind. We eventually escaped and stopped off at my apartment to shower before driving into New York for the postconcert party at Albert Grossman's apartment in Gramercy Park. Neither of us had the slightest clue as to what Dylan had thought of the concert. All we knew was that we played what we were supposed to play, and that the sound had been excellent. (There is great coverage of the sound-check, the backstage area, and the concert itself in Dan Kramer's photobook *Bob Dylan*.)

Harvey and I walked into Albert's apartment, and Dylan bounded across the room and hugged both of us. "It was fantastic," he said, "a real carnival and fantastic."

He'd loved it!

The following weekend we were scheduled to play the Hollywood Bowl with the same repertoire. Not only had I never been to California, I'd never even seen the inside of an airplane. The band was supposed to make that journey in Grossman's private plane (the Lodestar), but I pleaded to fly commercially for my first flight ever. Harvey took the Lodestar, but I had visions of Buddy Holly and Ritchie Valens.

I sat between Dylan and Neuwirth coast-to-coast, and they staged the best horror show they could dream up for my benefit. Every time the plane would dip or move the least bit awkwardly, they'd look at each other with blatantly pessimistic frowns and say, "This is the worst flight I've ever been on." Dylan would grip my arm and stammer, "I think this is the big one, Al." And Neuwirth would cradle his head in his hands and whimper "No, no, no." They'd be ringing for the stewardess every ten minutes, telling her I was very ill and could they please have yet another air-sickness bag. This drama had me just about ready to blow the emergency hatch until I looked around and saw everybody else on the plane calmly enjoying their cocktails and conversation. I quickly caught on and relaxed. When the plane landed, Neuwirth handed us pull-on wrestling masks to get through the crowd. The three of us ran through LAX with these stupid masks on till we got to the limo. Our baggage was "looked after" as we sped to the hotel.

While in Los Angeles, Harvey and I shared a suite at the Hollywood Sunset Hotel down the hall from Dylan's suite, which was the hub of activity for the week. We got there about two days before the concert, and I went the goggle-eyed hip tourist route all over L.A., which, in 1965, was approaching the zenith of its glory. I went shopping and saw all the clothes that I'd ever wanted to own. Incredible brightly colored shirts featuring big polka dots and floral patterns; the kind of mod look that had been imported from London to Los Angeles but hadn't hit New York yet. I immediately blew my entire wad on shirts.

One day a bunch of us were congregating in Dylan's room: Irwin Levine (he came along for the ride), Michael J. Pollard, P. F. Sloan, who was the most blatant West Coast Dylan imitator, and a few hangers-on. Dylan loved meeting lower-echelon, mirror images of himself; and it was sorta like giving them the Bad Housekeeping Seal of Approval. "Get P. F. Sloan," he'd scream. "Let's have P. F. Sloan up here."

Dylan was in the midst of modeling a new suit he'd just purchased when the phone rang. It was obviously someone Bob didn't want to talk to, because he was trying to hang up almost as soon as he took the call. As he was talking, room service wheeled in an elaborate cart of sandwiches and desserts that Bob had ordered for everyone, and he grabbed a sandwich. Now at this time it didn't particularly matter whether Bob was lighting a cigarette, reading a book, or talking on the phone; he was the center of attention. He tried to explain to the guy on the other end of the line that he had to hang up, that they just brought lunch in, but evidently the guy was holding on hard. Dylan nonchalantly took the egg salad sandwich he was eating and started grinding it into the mouthpiece of the phone, all the while explaining that it was lunchtime. The guy must have been getting the message, because everyone in the background was loudly in stitches. Dylan's parting shot was to pour his glass of milk into the phone as well, saying, "Well, so long, thanks for having lunch with us." Totally oblivious to the milk and mayonnaise all over his new suit, he just strolled into the other room and took a nap. End of audience.

The Hollywood Bowl concert was in sharp contrast to the Forest Hills show, in that it defined the essential differences between the two coasts. The audience (and what an audience: Gregory Peck, Johnny Cash, Dean Martin, The Byrds, and Tuesday Weld for starters) listened attentively to the new Dylan and, after polite initial applause, got caught up in the electric feeling. Soon we were getting thunderous ovations. In the middle of the encore, my ulcer began to go haywire. I didn't have my pills with me, so the most logical plan of action was to try and latch on to the coattails of Dylan's escape at the end of the song. This part of the evening was as well planned as any military maneuver, so it was a matter of pure timing. I didn't know what the plan was, but I figured that if I followed Dylan, I couldn't go wrong. Boy, that little fucker could run! By the time he was halfway down the back ramp, the car, driven by his old friend Victor Mamudes, was already moving. "Wait

The view from behind the organ at the Hollywood Bowl soundcheck: Robbie Robertson and Bob Dylan warm up. Los Angeles, 1965. (Photo: Al "Instamatic" Kooper.)

for me, wait for me," I yelled, as they pulled Dylan into the car.

They yanked me inside barely in time. We were doing about ten miles an hour already, and when the door closed behind me, Victor quickly accelerated. Because of the tremendous amount of sweat Dylan and I contributed by our presence, all of the windows in the car became fogged. When I glanced up, the speedometer said eighty-five, and the girl in the front seat beside Victor was screaming, "You're going the wrong way! We're headed for a brick wall! Turn around, Victor!"

She was perfectly correct, and Victor executed a turn that would have given Evel Kneivel an ulcer to rival my own. Out of the Bowl we wheeled, making it to the hotel before the audience's demands for more had died away. I took a double dose of pills and crashed.

As no other concerts were scheduled, Irwin and I stayed on in Hollywood for an additional week. We were theoretically there to hustle our songs, but mostly we just let L.A. hustle us.

When I finally made my way back to New York, Dylan's office dropped the full itinerary for a major tour in my lap. Noting that the tour stopped in Texas, I began to give serious consideration to making my exit from this traveling circus. I mean, look what they had just done to J.F.K. down there, and he was the leading symbol of the establishment. So what was going to happen when Bob Dylan, the most radical vision of the counterculture, paid them a visit? I wasn't sure I wanted to find out. Besides, what musician enjoys being booed on a consistent basis?

This was actually good timing, because I was about to get canned anyway. It seemed that the remaining members of the Hawks were eager for the gig, not having been at all happy with their separation from Levon and Robbie.

One morning I called Dylan and asked him what he was doing.

"Eating a piece of toast and listening to Smokey Robinson," he replied.

"I'm going to have to leave the band," I said.

"Okay," he said.

"See ya," I said.

"Okay," he said.

And that was that.

The release of *Highway 61 Revisited* elevated me to the position of an organ player in demand. People I'd never heard of were calling and offering me sessions, talking to me as if we'd been friends since childhood. I'd get a call and they'd say, "Can you make it for 8:00 p.m. Thursday at Bell Sound Studios?" And I'd say, "Yeah, I'm free. Who is it for?" I had no money to speak of, so I should have jumped on any opportunity that came my way. But I just couldn't see sitting in some studio for three hours, being forced to play music that I found distasteful. I'd tell them up front how really inexperienced I was, that I didn't sight-read music (I did, but not well enough to make any claims for myself), and then ask if they were still interested. Without fail they were. I remember getting a call once for a session that I had absolutely no desire to do. The only way I can do this, I told the guy, is if you pay me triple scale. This was just a joke; my way of expressing my unwillingness to play the date. So imagine my shock when he said, "Okay, triple scale," without even stopping to think about it. It was a wonderful ego boost, but ludicrous all the same. They didn't want me, of course, they wanted the new "Dylan sound."

When "Like A Rolling Stone" hit number one, all the Mister Joneses might not have known what was happening, but they sure knew what to do about it:

Cover it!

Copy it!

The tip-off was when I'd tell them that my guitar playing was actually superior to my elementary grasp of the organ. "Oh no," they'd say. "We want you to play keyboards." They'd have a place penciled in for me, usually right in the spot where you'd find the organ on a Dylan record. Clever.

It was embarrassing. When I got to the studio, I'd be treated a little too nicely for comfort. There I was, surrounded by some of the finest players in New York City—Gary Chester, Everett Barksdale, Eric Gale, Frank Owens, and Chuck Rainey—and I was getting preferential treatment while they were treated like hired help. I mean, these were exceptional musicians; they had ears, they knew I wasn't shit. I was still new to the instrument; I practiced constantly and was getting better, but I still wasn't much more than adequate. It just happened that my simplistic style of playing fit the groove of Dylan's new approach. Taken out of context, it could be funny. Or worse.

For kicks, I'd go out and buy all the records that aped the Dylan sound. I'd take them over to Dylan's house, and we'd play them and laugh. The imitation Kooper organ was one of the the stellar attractions. I had a "style" based on ignorance. And then to hear these great musicians imitating my inexperience! Really.

When they hired Kooper, though, they got everything but the Dylan sound. I wasn't about to give them the easy carbon copy they were looking for; that would have been pure prostitution. (Not that I hadn't whored in my Tin Pan Alley days, but my moral fiber was becoming thicker.) Without Dylan, these guys would never have been calling me, so why put his trip on sale for chump change? I just went to those sessions and played what I thought the songs required. Take it or leave it.

In certain respects, my presence did add color to any session I was on. At this time I was trying desperately to grow long hair, and I was wearing the bizarre clothes I'd picked up on my West Coast trip. I wore a gold earring in my left ear (snap-on) just for good measure. All this was to affirm my mental departure from the old Al, and wardrobe weirdness has been a trademark of the new Al ever since. Well . . . that is, until I turned fifty.

I received a call one day from Al Grossman's partner, John Court, to do a session for the Simon Sisters, they being Carly and her sister Lucy, in an early performing incarnation. I arrived at the session and walked smack into jazz icon Gary McFarland, who was the arranger on the session. Then, as I glanced around, I recognized nearly half of Count Basie's band sitting there waiting to play. *Oh no*. How was I gonna get through *this* one?

I looked at the keyboard parts and, sure enough, they were far beyond my limited sight-reading capabilities. So I walked over to McFarland and did an instant confessional.

"Look, Gary, I'm a huge fan of yours and of just about everybody in this room. But I can't read the part you wrote for me, and I'm feeling real sick about all this, and who do I have to fuck to get *out* of this movie?"

He was tremendously reassuring. He told me to sit on the part and play what I felt like playing; that was why they'd hired me in the first place. I sat down at the organ and sweated through the run-throughs. But, by session's end, I'd played decently and had certainly not sabotaged the entire day as I had feared. Once I got through *that* session, I felt I could handle anything.

Sometimes session work could be great fun; prime examples were the sessions for Tom Rush's *Take a Little Walk with Me* album. What was happening musically at the time was an incredible cross-pollination effected by Dylan (folk) playing electric (rock). Former folk acts were playing the old rock 'n' roll songs of the fifties and considering that folk music. Chuck Berry was playing the folk festival circuit along with Muddy Waters and Jimmy Reed. Fifties' rock 'n' roll was now the darling of the folk set. Someday rap music will be performed at folk festivals. Rock was slowly taking over as the primary contemporary musical expression by simply incorporating everything in its path. Explosive as this takeover was, the development still caught most of the record company A&R men (for "artists and repertoire"—an early synonym for producers) with their backgrounds down.

At Elektra Records, Jac Holzman had fashioned a fortress of folk music, wielding the formidable talents of artists like Tom Rush, Judy Collins, and Phil Ochs. Marc Abramson and Paul Rothchild were Holzman's producers in residence, but they were comparatively inexperienced to handle the new electric music. This is not to belittle their talent, which was later proven to be immense (Rothchild, for example, went on to produce all of the Doors' big hits), merely to point out that their output had never been channeled in this direction before.

Tom Rush, however, had been performing stuff like Bo Diddley's "Who Do You Love" and the Coasters' "Shoppin' for Clothes," and was anxious to make a rock/folk album that would mirror his affection for this music. Marc Abramson called and asked me to put a band together for the project, and I readily assembled a tasty little unit composed of Bruce Langhorne on guitar, Harvey Brooks (né Goldstein) on bass, Bobby Gregg on drums, and yours truly on lead electric guitar (playing all the tunes I'd played, when they were new, with the Royal Teens) and keyboards. We went into the studio and just rocked our asses off, having one hell of a time and getting paid for it to boot. *Take a Little Walk with Me* was one of the most enjoyable recording experiences I've ever had.

There were so many sessions that my memory banks are too overloaded to recall them all. Once I played behind the daughter of the owner of one of the largest department store chains (which sold a lot of records) on the East Coast. Must have been her birthday, so Daddy bought her a recording session with the best musicians in New York. The only reason that I even remember this is that every couple of years she turns up on a different label, usually around the same month.

I played on Judy Collins' version of Bob Dylan's "I'll Keep It with Mine," for which Bloomfield was expressly flown in from Chicago. I cut a Spider John Koerner session produced by Felix Pappalardi, an electric version of "I Ain't Marchin' Anymore" with Phil Ochs, and David Blue's "Stranger in a Strange Land" for Jim and Jean, another Tom Wilson production. I played on a Dion album of blues and folk-rock songs. I did sessions with Peter, Paul, and Mary and the Butterfield Blues Band—just sessions every day for months and months all through 1965.

Quite a chunk of the above session work was for Elektra, and they returned the favor by asking me to participate as an artist on an album they were compiling called *What's Shakin'*.

They asked for two tracks, I cut four, they used one: "I Can't Keep from Crying Sometimes," a Blind Willie Johnson tune I adapted and arranged. I played both piano and overdubbed guitar, with the asistance of two young New York musicians soon to figure prominently in my future; drummer Roy Blumenfeld and bassist Andy Kulberg. The recorded quality of the track seems almost garage-level in retrospect, but there's a certain unselfconsciousness about it that the several subsequent versions, by myself and others, don't approach. In the accompanying booklet that came with the album, I was identified as a "New York legend." I thought that was nice until I read critic Nat Hentoff's review of the album where he said: "Al Kooper may be a New York legend, but based on this track, certainly not for his singing or piano-playing. . . ." Now *that'll* bring ya down to earth real quick!

Tom Wilson rang me up one day and requested my services on yet another session. I always gave Tom top priority because of the tremendous debt I owed him, and I gladly assented. I arrived for this date in my typical out-there fashion, earring and all, and was introduced to a roomful of my contemporaries known as The Blues Project.

1965-1967:

THE BLUES PROJECT,

BLONDE ON BLONDE,

JUDY COLLINS,

JONI MITCHELL,

A NERVOUS BREAKDOWN,

CALIFORNIA,

GROUPIES,

BRIAN WILSON,

MONTEREY POP, AND

A SHEEPISH RETURN TO NEW YORK

Up to this time, *The Blues Project* had been Elektra record number EKL-726, "a compendium of the very best on the urban blues scene." Which was a nicer way of saying "this record contains the performances of twelve middle-class 'white punks on dope,' who have for the most part successfully achieved the ambience of twelve 'black bluesmen on booze.'" I had no idea that there was a band walking around with the same name and identical values. One of the performers on that album, a guitarist named Danny Kalb, had appropriated the name (with Elektra's blessing) and, with the assistance of four friends, had assembled a New York Jews for Electric Blues crusade.

To wit, Danny Kalb was an established sideman/singer on the New York blues scene, having gained his measure of prominence from appearances on recordings by Dave Van Ronk, Judy Collins, and the aforementioned *Blues Project* album. Danny's love of blues was shared by Roy Blumenfeld, a neighbor of his from Mount Vernon, New York. When no one sensitive enough to play drums could be found in

Blues Project '65 (early period). (Left to right) Tommy Flanders, Danny Kalb, Steve Katz, Roy Blumenfeld, Andy Kulberg, Mr. Polka Dots. (Photo: Al Kooper Collection.)

the Village, Roy taught himself to play and joined the group. Steve Katz had appeared on a similar Elektra white blues album, *The Even Dozen Jug Band* (which also featured the recording debuts and talents of Maria Muldaur, John Sebastian, and Stefan Grossman). Like Danny, Steve was a student of Dave Van Ronk. He signed on as second guitarist, replacing a not-very Happy Traum. Andy Kulberg was a classically trained flautist from Buffalo, New York, whose professional experience had been limited to a few polka bands in his hometown area. He was overjoyed at the prospect of being able to leave his heritage behind and become the group's bass player. Tommy Flanders, a refugee from the Cambridge, Massachusetts, rock 'n' roll circuit, was designated the group's Mick Jagger in an effort to increase its commercial potential.

When I walked in, this session was just one more entry in my appointment book, but for these guys the experience was probably terrifying. It was not only their audition session for Columbia Records, but also the first time that the band in this line-up had been inside a recording studio. I was surprised to find that they'd chosen an Eric Andersen song, "Violets of Dawn," to hang their futures on, as this was not your standard blues band fare. But as I soon discovered, this was not your standard blues band.

The two guitarists were fingerpicking a weaving construction of the chord sequence, and I made the mistake of attempting to weave with them on the piano for the better part of an hour. I kept trimming my part until there was almost nothing there, but what little was left seemed to do right by the arrangement. All this time I had no idea whether what I was doing was even vaguely what they were looking for, which was making me more than a little paranoid. But we finally got a good take and everyone was all smiles. When the session ended, they invited me to lunch the next day. Feeling relieved, I accepted. At the appointed time I met Danny, Andy, and their manager, Jeff Chase, at the Keneret Restaurant in the Village, and we sat down for a pleasant meal. I assumed that they wanted to hire my hands for the rest of the album, and that the purpose of the lunch was to fatten me up so they could bargain me down. All of a sudden they were asking me to *join* their band, which caught me so completely off guard that the best initial response I could muster was a "Huh?" It took me about thirty seconds of silent mulling to sort out all the pros and cons of joining their band: The Dylan trip was definitely over, the studio work was getting a little samey, and here was a chance to practice and improve on my "new" instrument, and maybe even make a couple of bucks. "Sure. I'll do it," was my response. And that was the beginning of a three-year whirlwind that changed my life forever. This whirlwind, however, had modest origins.

First of all, I had to be initiated into the Mystic White Knights of Da Blooze. B. B. King, Muddy Waters, Son House, Blind Willie Johnson—these were names I'd seen but music I'd never heard. Danny would play me these treasures for hours on the guitar and the phonograph until he was satisfied that the sound had been strummed into my head permanently. It was a loving assimilation because the music appealed to me emotionally as well as intellectually. While I was growing up with R&B and gospel, traditional blues had somehow escaped me. In New York, R&B and gospel music were readily available on the radio, but it required some fancy dial twisting to scare up a Muddy Waters or Howlin' Wolf record in the fifties or early sixties.

Then, of course, there were band rehearsals. When no one will hire you, you can't really do anything but rehearse. Unless you could play the entire Top Forty or you had a hit single out, club work was nonexistent. Plus, we had no matching suits or other related all-American paraphernalia. (This is not to say that there weren't a few $39.95 tux jackets from The Royal Teen days in my closet right next to the skeletons.) Everyone else in the band was far more advanced in the area of rejecting middle-class values, while I was still living in Forest Hills and taking in at least a few hundred dollars a week from sessions. But I respected their dedication, and slowly began to make that move myself.

My first rehearsal with the band took place at the apartment of a friend named Julie on Grove Street in the Village. I still couldn't tell Steve and Andy apart—all I could see were noses and work shirts, but I knew Roy was the tall one, Danny was . . . err . . . well . . . *Danny*, and Tommy was the one with the Rolling Stones haircut. Kalb and Flanders ran the band and that was fine with me. Tommy the singer would tell Danny the guitarist how he wanted his backgrounds painted, and Danny would attempt to assign the proper brush strokes. Each player, however, had his own style and it quickly became a magical musical melting mixture.

We rehearsed about four hours until the neighbors called the cops. It actually was not very intelligent to have a rock band in the living room of a cramped Village brownstone, but what did we know? We were *crusaders*. Rehearsal space was at a premium because it cost money. (The Lovin' Spoonful were rehearsing in the foul basement of the run-down Albert Hotel at this same time for the same reason.)

Somehow we managed to scrape together enough cash to rent rehearsal space at 1697 Broadway and move the crusade uptown for awhile. The Tokens and other people I knew in that building would come down to see what Al was up to, but it wasn't the kind of music that paid the rent, so of course none of them understood or were the slightest bit impressed. But the juxtaposition of images involved in The Blues Project rehearsing at 1697 Broadway was like a symbolic farewell to a set of values that no longer applied. I knew which side I was on *now*.

By this time, I was hooked on the blues crusade. I began to really understand the cultural potential of the band, and how important it was for younger fans to find out about Muddy, B. B., and the whole blues scene in general. They had probably OD'd on Bobbies Rydell, Vinton, and Vee, and I came to see what a positive alternative blues was.

Obviously we were not a traditional blues band in the sense that Paul Butterfield's group was. They played the tunes almost exactly the way they sounded on the original records, like a Top Forty blues band. We'd change *all* the arrangements, never doing a tune like someone else had done it. This is not to say that we didn't do other people's songs; we just did 'em our way. We also did folk-rockier things than Butterfield's scope allowed for, like Donovan's "Catch the Wind" and Bob Lind's "Cheryl's Goin' Home."

Meanwhile Butterfield was out there proselytizing and making his contribution to the crusade; and as long as we're owning up, he was probably responsible for starting it. His band had built a strong following in their native Midwest, and their much-acclaimed first album on Elektra, along with Al Grossman's high-powered management, was causing the ripple of interest to swell into a wave. The three B's—Butterfield on harp and vocals, and Mike Bloomfield and Elvin Bishop on guitars—created a powerful three-pronged attack, aided and abetted by the unflagging rhythm section comprised of Sam Lay on drums, Jerome Arnold on bass, and the later additions of Mark Naftalin (his pop was the former mayor of Minneapolis) on keyboards and Billy Davenport replacing Sam Lay on drums. They were a kick-ass group, and it was dangerous for any lesser band to share the stage with them.

Not long after I joined the Blues Project, Tom Wilson left Columbia Records for MGM-Verve. Columbia waived its claim to us, so we moved with him and signed with Verve-Folkways, MGM's answer to Elektra. It was also around this time that our manager was able to secure a week's berth for us at a Village jazz joint called the Cafe Au Go Go. This club had gained fame for hosting the likes of Stan Getz and Lenny Bruce (actually what it gained was *infamy*—the owner, Howard Solomon, was brought to trial on Bruce-induced obscenity charges but was later vindicated) and for being the location of Stan's popular *Getz Au Go Go* live album. I don't think the place had ever booked a rock band (that's us) before, but business stunk and Solomon was desperate. God knows, he must've been!

To put it diplomatically, we were green. Our hair was somewhere between short and growing long, nobody but me thought to "dress" to go onstage, and, most of all, we were still learning. Hardly headliner material. Hardly even support band material.

Then a funny thing happened. After we played the week, he hired us for three more. I don't think it had anything to do with the business we did (there wasn't any); he was probably just fascinated because he was so unaccustomed to seeing acts survive. We'd take each night's proceeds and adjourn to the bar across Bleecker Street called the Dugout. In an hour we'd be as broke as we'd been earlier that evening, but too drunk to care. The ironic part was that all through the early stages of the band's career, I waived taking a salary, due to my outside income. And, because of my ulcer, when the take was squandered on alcohol I didn't get to participate on that level either. (Another illustration of the band's poverty was that Tommy would show up at your house, ask to use the bathroom, and then tie it up for an hour or two by taking a shower. He could only get away with this once at each band member's apartment!) As our Au Go Go residency wore on, a few brave faces reappeared. Fans! They helped us gain a little confidence, and I think, experience aside, that's what we really needed.

Meanwhile, Tom Wilson and Verve were trying to figure out how to record (or relate to) us. They didn't know whether we were Paul Revere and the Raiders or the Mothers of Invention. Neither did we, really. Based on our emerging local popularity, Howard Solomon was planning a Thanksgiving holiday all-blues show that would feature some of the more accessible blues greats. Looking to subsidize his advertising campaign (that means get somebody/anybody else to pay for it), he turned to Jerry Schoenbaum, then president of Verve-Folkways.

The original concept Solomon had envisioned was to get some money to promote this potential Thanksgiving turkey starring his house band, Verve Folkways great white hope, The Blues Project. Schoenbaum took it five steps further by having Verve underwrite the *entire* week in exchange for the recording rights. Because the majority of the artists were either signed to Verve or unsigned altogether, this was a way of assuring at least three or four albums to amortize the initial investment.

"The Blues Bag," as it was so trendily baptized, was advertised extensively both over- and underground for Thanksgiving week of 1965. It featured Muddy Waters, Big Joe Williams, Otis Spann, John Lee Hooker, and the band of white Jewish kids who taught them everything they knew, The Blues Project. Prior to this, nobody had been adventurous enough to bankroll a blues package in a small club on the white side of the tracks. However, Solomon and Schoenbaum (attorneys at law?) found themselves with sold-out, standing-room-only performances for the entire week. And twenty minutes after Muddy Waters had brought each capacity house to its feet, The Blues Project would take the stage.

I think they picked us to close the show strictly by virtue of the fact that we were unquestionably *louder* than anyone else on the bill. It was embarrassing, our heroes having to warm up for us; the first few shows we used to go in their dressing rooms and apologize to them! Someone recently interviewing me asked why we played so loud on a bill with Muddy Waters and John Lee Hooker, who were masters of dynamics. "Probably to compensate for our penis sizes . . . ," I honestly replied.

While we were hanging out in Muddy's dressing room the first night, I took Otis Spann aside. I had a plan that was even ballsier than my first Dylan session: "Maybe one of these afternoons you could teach me some stuff. I think you're the greatest pianist who ever lived, and it would be an honor to learn from you." He miraculously agreed to meet me the next afternoon. *What a sweet man.* We were scheduled for four o'clock. I got there at three-thirty, he at four-thirty. My "lesson" lasted two hours, and we adjourned to the Dugout, the restaurant across the street, where I bought him dinner. This went on for two more days. Piano lessons paid for by dinner and drinks. What a bargain! Now I had the blues piano playing basics

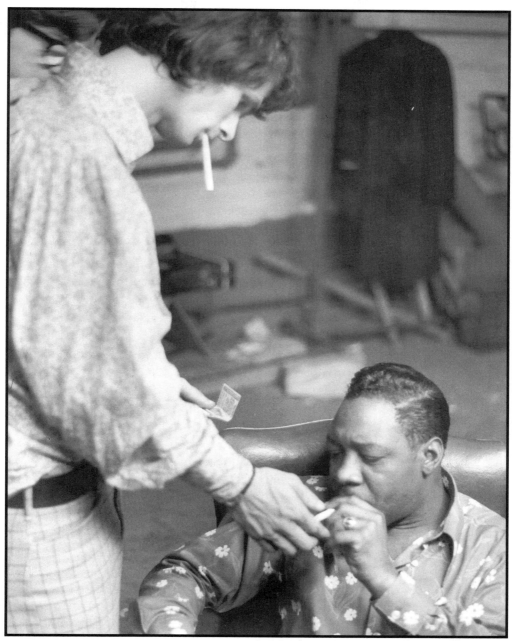

Backstage at the Cafe Au Go Go, 1965: Inadvertently and sadly aiding and abetting mentor Otis Spann toward an early grave; he died of lung cancer shortly thereafter. (Photo: Don Paulsen.)

down I so desperately needed, as taught by the master!

These days it's not unusual for B. B. King to play a sold-out show with nary a black face in the audience, but in 1965 it was quite a novelty. We looked out into a sea of faces that we had all seen in the next room in the college dorm, ahead of us at the draft board, and sitting behind us in temple. These kids were just younger versions of us, and not much younger at that. And they knew it. We were theirs! We didn't have the cool assurance of a Muddy Waters, the natural instincts of a John Lee Hooker, or the sheer talent of an Otis Spann, but now we had an inkling of what *they* felt like when they faced a packed house at the Apollo or the Regal.

In later years, I had an interesting experience. I went to see The Cars at the dawn of the eighties, when their star was just beginning to rise. They were headlining at Universal Amphitheater and I went backstage to meet them. Turns out they were *huge* Blues Project fans, especially guitarist Elliot Easton. They regaled me with stories about different gigs they had attended that even I had forgotten. Then it was time for them to go onstage. I was actually growing quite fond of them and I had enjoyed their album as well. I stood in the wings and watched the first half-hour of their show. For the life of me, I couldn't see *any* Blues Project influence in what they were doing, and their musicianship was far inferior to their album. Why did they like The Blues Project? I stood there perplexed and then a bolt of thought-lightning hit me: This was probably the way Muddy Waters felt when he saw The Blues Project the first time. "Why do they like me so much? I can't hear any of *my* music in there!" I groaned to myself and walked away. It was a troubling realization.

Returning to the sixties, our band came out fightin', trying to stay alive and get our point across any way we could. It wasn't like we sat down at a conference table one day and said, "OK, Danny is gonna jump up and down and make all these faces, and Al is gonna wear a cape and a taxi-driver's hat, and Steve, you get a Beatles haircut, and Tommy you do splits while we're playing solos." We were real in our own way, McLuhan's media children flexing their newly acquired muscles. We may have borrowed our music, but our demeanor was strictly our own.

In the face of all the talent and roots that surrounded us, *we stole the fucking show every night*! In retrospect, it's easy to see why. It was our audience's equivalent of when we sat in dark theaters watching the knife fight and the chickie-run in *Rebel without a Cause*. We sat in those seats and we *squirmed*; relating even though we weren't always able to duplicate. When we left the stage, the audience was sweating as heavily as we were and was probably just as exhausted. Our idols played with dexterity and dignity. We got 'em with energy and volume. The music would catch up soon enough.

The whole time Verve's tape machine was rolling, getting our first album down.

Robert Shelton, the staid *New York Times'* music critic, applauded our efforts in print, and when The Blues Bag reached its delirious finale, it was only natural we should remain in residence at the Au Go Go and fill the joint ourselves. This little, unkempt, former jazz club came into its own right then and there. In later years I found out that Al Pacino, Peter Boyle, Rob Reiner, and Peter Riegert, to name but a few, were regular faces in the front row. There was an actor's studio around the corner, and the fledgling thespians would check us out after class. Procol Harum, Moby Grape, Jimi Hendrix, and every up-and-comer felt obliged to serve time at the Au Go Go. I remember nights when, just as we finished our last song, Dylan and Neuwirth would lunge out of the darkness, grab me by the arms, and drag me across the street to the Dugout for some late-night hi-jinks. This would usually leave the audience with something to chat about on the E train home.

It was a small fame we had achieved, but it put spending money in Howard Solomon's pocket. The band, of course, was still starving because we maintained the same overhead, and the money hadn't improved dramatically enough to affect our paychecks. And we had our problems. We needed new equipment; so it was decided that we'd pool each weekend's take for that purpose, leaving the rest of the week's gross for rent and food.

Tommy didn't go for it. He felt that he was a separate case in that he was the singer and we were the band. He paid for and looked after *his axe* (his throat) and would we please pay for *our own* instruments because he didn't know how to play them, so why should he be party to buying them? Also, Tommy didn't happen to be Jewish, and that was the *only thing* the rest of us had in common. Whatever the reasons, there was a showdown, and Tommy, bless his heart, stood his ground. The man had the courage of his convictions, and I respected that. It cost him his gig, though, and it shook us bad, because a lot of charisma walked out the door when he did.

Tommy's departure automatically consigned Steve and me to singing chores, whereas previously only Danny had shared Flanders' field. We weren't gonna pick up any new charisma with this plan, I thought. I picked a Chuck Berry tune, "I Wanna Be Your Driver." Steve took over a song he'd written that Tommy had been singing, called, strangely enough, "Steve's Song." I took a gospel song I knew and rearranged it for a Jewish blues band, and that's how we started doing "Wake Me Shake Me." One night, Roy broke a bass drum pedal in the middle of a show, and Steve pulled out Donovan's Top Forty folker "Catch the Wind" and did it percussionless while Roy fixed his pedal, so we kept that in the show. Little by little we fashioned a new repertoire. Danny, however, remained the chief lead singer and band leader. Soon after, Jeff Chase signed us up with the William Morris Agency (ta-da). An international booking office saw potential in, of all things . . . us!

We cautiously stepped outside the confines of the Cafe Au Go Go to test our stuff in other locales. Our first out-of-town gig was as opening act for Stan Getz in the gorgeous vacation retreat of Pittsburgh, Pennsylvania, in the dead of winter. We had no cars, trucks, or roadies, and certainly no money to rent any of the above. So we self-schlepped all our amps and equipment down to Pennsylvania Station and hopped the train.

Boy, it was surreal. Dirty hippie kids lugging all these guitars and crap onto a train populated primarily by old ladies and sailors on shore leave. And, of course, the train was delayed and we got there real late; Stan Getz had already gone on and was pissed off that he had to. The audience was there for one reason only: Stan Getz. It was actually quite considerate of them to wait a few minutes after he'd finished while we set up. Halfway through the first number, however, they unanimously agreed it was *too loud* (not enough rockers present, too many jazzers) and most of them left. We played with all the gusto a train ride to Pittsboig can inspire, and, mercifully, it was over. Once again, we packed up our stuff, headed for the train station, and caught the late flyer to New Yawk. God, it was depressing. No reward, no relief, no standing ovations, no encores. Just old ladies and sailors.

Our next "road trip" was different: We had *two* gigs booked. The first was a Friday night at Swarthmore College, the second Saturday night at Antioch College. This time we tried it with two cars and one roadie, the band in one car and the roadie and all the equipment in another.

Swarthmore's a neat little school tucked somewhere out of my memory in rural Pennsylvania, and it was holding its first Annual Rock 'n' Roll Festival, so we knew that volume would not be a problem. Swarthmore was probably the breast at which rock journalism suckled. It was here that the first rock mag of fairly intelligent criticism was born. A mimeographed two-sheeter called *Crawdaddy*, completely authored by student-journalist (not the singer) Paul Williams, made its way around the campus and eventually matured to press. This was a good two years before *Rolling Stone* debuted its first issue.

As we pulled into Swarthmore, the students welcomed us with open arms. We were surprised; they actually knew who we were! We availed ourselves of their dorm showers after the grueling drive and hit the stage only ten minutes late. It was no contest. The Energy-plus-Volume Machine trampled 'em and, two encores later, we piled into the cars and began our comparatively long trek toward the hinterlands of Ohio and our next victims.

In the car, there was exhilaration (and opium). We had carried our sound out of New York, made it portable, and it had worked on 'em out-a-town. Our enthusiasm soon gave way to tedium as we plowed toward our destination. We drove all night and it seemed that we hadn't even put the slightest dent in our mileage. We drove all the next day as well, but by sunset we were still hours from Antioch. Finally, at who knew what time, we staggered into Yellow Springs (that's what we felt like), Ohio, and pulled up in front of the auditorium.

Talk about cuckoo. No sleep, lots of drugs, and a few of our women (allowed to come along for the ride out of inexperience; road virgins complaining and misunderstanding all the way). It was two hours after we were supposed to have played; but was the audience uptight? No way. They were just glad we were there. The auditorium was jammed with people who wanted to, as they used to say, "boogie." We made it to the now-familiar dorm showers and mounted the stage on by-then shaky legs.

Antioch was one of a handful of "progressive" institutions that was totally into psychedelics at the time. The entire first two rows were watching us through kaleidoscopes! No one in the band felt much like being awake, much less playing, but there wasn't even time to vomit. Because of the epic proportions of our journey, we did not play well. But did they give a shit? *Could they even tell the difference?* Not two, not four, but *five* encores! I couldn't believe after each one that we were going up there again.

This was one of the major weirdnesses of being on the road. Sometimes you could play the best music you'd ever played, and they'd just sit there on their hands; no encore, no nothin'. And then, as on this particular occasion, you'd shovel an hour's worth of elephant shit on 'em and get standing ovations and twenty encores. This usually helped to temper our respect for the people we played for.

They put us all up at the school and we slept like rocks for the first time in two days. Sunday afternoon everyone woke up refreshed and the plan was to fly back to New York; fuck this stupid driving shit! Monday afternoon, however, I was committed to be in Nashville to play on some Dylan sessions (for the album *Blonde on Blonde*); so I had planned in advance to stay over at the school one more night and fly directly from Columbus to Nashville. I tagged along while some school kids drove the whole entourage to the airport, gave the boys five, said, "See ya in a week," and hopped a ride back to the school with two women on the concert commitee.

They were the first "dedicated fans" of The Blues Project (it being too early to call them groupies). I never made it to the school. I just barely made the plane the next morning. It was the first time I had ever been with two women at once and only the clarion call of Bob Dylan could've got me to that airport on time. Well, almost on time. When I got there, the plane was taxiing toward the runway and it was snowing like in *Dr. Zhivago*. All of a sudden the plane stopped and this tiny jeep pulled up carrying yours truly, looking a little worse for the previous night's shenanigans. They dropped the stairs down and I, unaware that the flight had originated in New York City, boarded the plane only to be greeted by much laughter and fingers pointed in my direction. Many of the passengers were music business people that I knew from New York: Al Gallico, the publisher, Bob Morgan, the producer, and Bobby Vinton, the Polish person. And they couldn't understand what I was doing in a jeep on the runway during a snowstorm in Columbus, Ohio, at nine o'clock on Monday morning. And I wasn't tellin' either. I believed in the magic of rock 'n' roll!

Bob Johnston, a Southerner, who had replaced Tom Wilson as Dylan's producer at the time, suggested that Bob try cutting his next album in Nashville with some of the best musicians that town had to offer. Bob agreed, but stipulated that Robbie Robertson and I join whatever cast was assembled. I had never been down south before and was not particularly looking forward to it based on various accounts I had perused in the papers. However, Johnston met me at the airport and had secured the services of one of Elvis's bodyguards for the duration of the visit just in case Nashville folk weren't "ready" for Dylan, Robbie, or myself. Mr. Lamar Fike was introduced to us, and he spent the two weeks we were there telling us what life was like with Elvis. Actually, Lamar was a great guy with a *nasty* sense of humor.

The great Lamar Fike story, as Bob Johnston told it, started with Elvis' love of throwing darts. Lamar would sit to the side and read the paper while Elvis threw the darts. On a few occasions, the darts would bounce off the target and stick in various parts of Lamar's anatomy. He wouldn't even look up from the paper as he pulled the darts out and handed them back to El each time. Not even a grunt.

One day, with some time off, I ventured out of our protective web on a shopping expedition to Buckley's, the largest record store in town. I decided to make it on foot from the hotel, as it was a nice day and it was just a straight walk down the main drag about three-quarters of a mile from the hotel.

About halfway there, I spotted a bunch of kids hanging out on the corner looking for trouble or me, whichever came first, I thought to myself. They were about eighteen-nineteen years old, but real mean looking; about three of 'em. I didn't even have what you would call long hair then; I actually looked straight. Had on black Beatle boots, black pants, shirt and tie for good measure, and a black leather car coat. This was my basic uniform in that era.

I decided to cross the street so as not to even walk past their line of vision. I was running across the street to make the light and right off they were imitating my run as they spun off after me. I should've continued running, but I didn't know if it was early enough to commit myself to my paranoia. *It was.* All of a sudden, there was a hand on my shoulder.

Now, it was midday in downtown Nashville, there were lots of people and traffic in the street, and we were on the main drag, but inherently I knew that if these guys started wasting me, nobody was gonna pay much attention, 'specially if they heard me say "Ow" with a Yankee accent. Also, in case you didn't know me in those days, let me explain that I was never a contender for the Golden Gloves. I was about six-foot-one and weighed about 145. In short, a meek, walking stick of broccoli.

So a hand was on my shoulder spinning me around, and the reality hit me: If I didn't nail this first guy first, I'd be going straight to Baptist Hospital. Just as he was about to say something funny at the conclusion of the spin-around, I uppercut my fist into his groin. He hit the dirt groaning. His friends, deciding that valor was the better part of punkdom, stood their ground, and it was sort of status quo for a second there, but we all turned into cowards. I started tear-assing down the boulevard looking for sanctuary and a telephone. About two or three blocks down, with the boys hot on my trail, I found a well-populated bookstore and barreled into the phone booth. I called Al Grossman (Dylan's manager) in his hotel room and told him what was happening and where I was. He said sit tight, they'd be there in a minute.

I hoped so, because the punks were now outside the store. They spotted me in the phone booth inside and set up guard outside the front door, figuring I would have to leave at some point. (Better some point than gunpoint!) After about five minutes of mock-chatting, I edged out of the phone booth and pretended to browse around the bookstore.

Mistake.

One of the punks entered the shop and was heading right for me. I could see it all happening: books flying, jail cells, death notices. Concurrent with the guy entering the shop, Lamar arrived in a fat Caddy, screeching to a halt in front of the store. He jumped out of the car, spotted me through the window, then casually strolled into the store. The kid headed right for me, and my adrenaline was at the bursting point. I grabbed him by his collar and said, "Look, you motherfucka, you and your friends get the fuck off my back or I'm gonna get MAD!"

He looked at me incredulously just as Lamar rounded the corner and pulled me off the punk. "Al, you better stop picking fights, "Lamar said."I'm tired of bailing your ass outta jail every other day!" All the while we're edgin' outta the shop. The kid was probably still thinking "What the fuck?" as we dove into the Caddy (probably a gift from Elvis) and headed back to the hotel, laughing hysterically.

The combination of Dylan, his current material, and the Nashville musicians was near perfect. There was me and Robbie, Charlie McCoy, Henry Strzelecki on bass, Wayne Moss, Jerry Kennedy, and Joe South on guitars, Hargus "Pig" Robbins on keyboards, and Kenny Buttrey on drums. They were extremely flattered to have Dylan in their midst and gave him every consideration they could. The janitor emptying ashtrays at the sessions in later years turned out to be a young, struggling Kris Kristofferson.

We worked at Columbia Studios. Dylan had sketches of most of the songs, but he completed the bulk of the writing there in Nashville, most of it in the studio. When he felt like writing or rewriting, everyone would repair to the ping-pong tables in the canteen. Sometimes, in the case of "Sad Eyed Lady of the Lowlands" or "Visions of Johanna," he would sit in there for five hours without coming out and just play the piano and scribble. The atmosphere was as if clocks didn't exist. The musicians were truly there for Bob and if it meant sitting around for five hours while he polished a lyric, there was never a complaint. I was not used to this, being raised as a three-songs-in-three-hours New York kid, and I preferred this ambience much more. It relaxed everyone, especially Bob, and the results are obviously there on my favorite Dylan album of all time.

Bob had a piano put in his hotel room, and during the day I would sit and play the chords to a song he was working on, like a human cassette machine, while he tried different sets of lyrics to them. (Incredibly, cassettes hadn't been invented yet!) It was good 'cause I got the jump on learning the tunes and was able to teach them to the band that night without Dylan being bothered with that task. My favorite of the lot was "I Want You," and each night I would suggest recording it to Bob, who saved it as the last song recorded, just to bug me.

There were some little things about the sessions that were funny. There was this keyboard player named Pig. He looked like your everyday plumber or executive (late thirties, well-scrubbed WASP look) except that he was blind. He was so unuptight about it, that after awhile *you* would forget it.

Dylan had this problem with him. He couldn't talk directly to him because he couldn't call this sweet guy Pig. So he would say to someone else (usually yours truly): " . . . and tell the piano player to play an octave higher." Then he would look in Pig's direction and sorta smile, 'cause that way he avoided calling him Pig.

The definitive Pig story is told by Bob Johnston. Seems that Pig and the boys tied one on one night after a late session, and they were driving home when this uncontrollable urge came over the inebriated Pig.

"I wanna drive. You so-and-so's move over and let me navigate this Cadillac!" he erupted.

His buddies, bein' drunker than Pig, pulled the car over and put Pig in the driver's seat. In a moment they were goin' down the highway with a blind driver and a car fulla drunk rednecks. The guy ridin' shotgun was sayin', "A little to the left . . . good . . . uh, now a little to the right . . . a little faster . . .," and they're actually pulling it off until they see a red light flashin' behind 'em and the familiar siren of the Tennessee Highway Patrol. They get Pig to pull the car over, and that's where the story usually ends. The rest is left up to the listener's imagination, if he can imagine. Usually, he's laughing too hard.

One night I was sitting in the control booth while Dylan was in the studio unmoving, writing again. Al Grossman had made a habit of pitching quarters into the soundproofed ceiling, and now everyone was doing it. I just knew that when we left town some enterprising engineer was gonna turn up a bass track to full volume and all them quarters were gonna rain down on the control room like a Las Vegas jackpot. Anyway, Grossman, Johnston, and I were pitchin' quarters in the ceiling, and this local newspaperman had somehow gotten in the control room. To his credit, he didn't say a word. He was in there about an hour and a half just staring at the motionless Dylan through the glass when he finally said, "Damn! What's he on, anyhow?"

Grossman, not wanting the facts to get distorted in this guy's potential scoop, tells him, "Columbia Records and Tapes, actually." The guy was ushered out shortly thereafter.

Dylan was teaching us "Rainy Day Women #12 & 35" one night when Johnston suggested it would sound great with a brass band, Salvation Army style. Dylan thought it over and said it might work. But where would we get horn players at this hour? "Not to worry," said Charlie McCoy and grabbed the phone. It was 4:30 a.m. when he made the call. Now I am not exaggerating when I say that at 5:00 a.m. in walks Charlie's friend, a trombone player. He was clean-shaven, wearing a dark suit and tie, wide awake, and eager to please . . . and . . . he was a helluva trombone player. He sat down and learned the song, Charlie played trumpet with him, they cut three takes, and at 5:30 a.m. he was out the door and gone.

Charlie McCoy blew my mind several times that trip, but my fondest memory was when we were recording "You Go Your Way and I'll Go Mine." There was a little figure after each chorus that he wanted to put in on trumpet, but Dylan was not fond of overdubbing. It was a nice lick, too. Simple, but nice. Now Charlie was already playing bass on the tune. So we started recording and when that section came up, he picked up a trumpet in his right hand and played the part while he kept the bass going with his left hand without missing a lick in either hand. Dylan stopped in the middle of the take and just stared at him in awe. It's on the record with no overdubbing two takes later; bass and trumpet! This guy is everything great you ever heard about him. That's him playing the lead acoustic guitar on "Desolation Row" on *Highway 61 Revisited*, as well. If it makes music, he can play it.

The credits are vague on the *Blonde on Blonde* album. Maybe I can fill in a few holes for the reader. Joe South is playing bass on "Visions of Johanna." He has a very special style of playing bass, sort of hillbilly funk. His unique guitar style is most discernible in the mix on "Memphis Blues Again." He and I have some nice organ-guitar trade-offs in that one. Wayne Moss plays the cool sixteenth-note guitar parts on "I Want You." The other amazing thing about cutting that album was the firsthand knowledge that you were making history. After I cut the *Highway 61 Revisited* album, I heard those songs everywhere. I will probably hear them all my life, anywhere I go. They were instant classics because they are prime Dylan. Imagine how it felt playing on a session where, by virtue of the fact that you had already done it once before, you knew that whatever you played would last forever. That's a heavy responsibility for a punk from Queens. Thank you, Bob, for giving me that opportunity.

Verve was wavering about releasing the first Blues Project album. Tommy was so much a part of the live recordings, Verve felt that since he had left, to release the album in its present form would misrepresent the band. It was hurriedly decided to return to the Au Go Go and record some additional material with Steve and me singing lead. Back to the beginning, almost. We booked a week *during the afternoons* (the nights, unfortunately, were taken already) and announced on the radio that we were recording live, and lots of kids came for free after school. It was weird gettin' it on at three o'clock in the afternoon, playing a whole set, then going outside while it was still light out.

Anyway, we got what we needed, and shortly thereafter our first baby, *The Blues Project Live at the Cafe Au Go Go*, was delivered to record stores all over America. Although, in retrospect, the sound quality was not unlike playing a shirt cardboard on your turntable, it more than served its purpose. For one thing, it was the first rock album to appear on the charts without benefit of the requisite "hit single." This made the industry look up from their ledgers and take notice.

At the same time, adventurous FM stations (based on the successes of WOR in New York and KMPX in San Francisco) were switching their normally staid formats to progressive rock programming. Many kiddies were rushing out to buy new radios so they could be "with it." The FM stations took The Blues Project to their hearts and played our album vociferously at a time when the AM stations completely ignored us. The record actually sold. I remember Verve's first ad, which was placed in all the trade publications (*Cashbox*, *Billboard*, etc.). The headline read: "This Album Has Already Sold 22,000 Copies/That's 18,000 More Than the Street

Thought It Would!" What they failed to tell you in the ad was that it was also 19,000 more than Verve thought it would sell. Times have changed. Can you imagine a company today bragging loudly in a full page ad that their new group has sold 22,000 CDs? Preposterous!

Nevertheless, Verve began to show some confidence in the band. They flew us to L.A. to appear at the MGM annual sales convention. The high point of that trip was when five starving hippies and one starving manager invaded Trader Vic's restaurant and ran up a two hundred dollar dinner tab and charged it to MGM with a belch and a satiated smile. Our appearance at the convention was well received, and the record company pencil-pushers caught a glimmer of the potential in what we were doing. We made our L.A. debut at the Troubadour, but not many showed up to notice. Fucking snobs!

While we were in L.A., we also went into the studio to work on our next album. Jack Nitszche, who wrote arrangements for Phil Spector and The Stones, came down to produce us, but we were so into it that I'm afraid we ignored him (fucking snobs!), and he left the studio throwing his hands up in frustration.

I don't remember this, but Andy Kulberg says that Nitszche brought us a demo that night of a song he wanted us to record. We all sat there as it played over the speakers, and Danny looked at him like he was crazy when it ended.

"We don't play music like that, Jack . . . ," Danny said and basically turned down the chance to record "Wild Thing" before The Troggs or Hendrix did. In essence, he also turned down Jack's services as he was out the door later that same evening.

Billy James, a friend of mine from the Dylan days and also head of public relations for Columbia Records West Coast, helped us cut a few tracks, but for political reasons he was credited as Marcus James, his eight-year-old son—probably the youngest producer in record biz history. We cut a song I'd written called "Fly Away," and a Chuck Berry tune, "You Can't Catch Me." Then we hit the road. Or actually it seemed that the road hit us.

In the mid-sixties long hair on males was only regarded as commonplace in New York City, Los Angeles, and San Francisco. Everywhere else it was as life-threatening as it appeared in that *Easy Rider* film. We took our by then long hair and ridiculous clothes out into Middle Amerika and she bitterly retaliated:

- In Cedar Rapids we were hissed and booed as we deplaned.
- In Boston some guy tried to run me over as I crossed the street.
- In Canada they threw whiskey bottles at us as we left the stage.

- In Maryland we were refused lodging in two hotels.
- In Detroit we were refused service at an airport coffee shop.

Not being into martial arts, we retreated into the sanctuary of drugs. I mean, we tried to keep ourselves as incoherent as possible at all times so we wouldn't realize what indignities we were being put through. It was real lonely. I realize that you're probably slapping your head and saying: "What a fucking cliché!"

Wait a second. Let me explain.

It's 1966 and we're playing in your small college-town gym. Everyone has brought a date to the show and consequently there are no "singles," if you catch my drift. (There was an unspoken double standard in rock at the time. Musicians were expected to have dalliances with the various groupies that were proffered to them. It didn't impinge on any emotional ties to your wife or girlfriend. It was therapeutic—like a massage. But God forbid that a neglected woman at home should seek the solace of a companion for a physical tryst—she'd be thrown out in thirty seconds. With all the indignities of touring at this time, if some camp follower smiled and offered *anything*, I admit I took it.) You've arrived, after driving all night, at your Holiday, Days, or Ramada Inn room, where the staff lets you know that you are most assuredly *not* welcome. You rush out to a soundcheck, where a skeleton college crew is totally unprepared, and the simplest matters wind up taking hours. You've got maybe enough time to return to the hotel and shower (lunch, dinner, forget it—they wouldn't serve you in the restaurant even if you *had* the time to eat) and then race back to the gym. Then it's wait around while the first act goes on late, plays twice as long as they're supposed to, and makes the audience really irritable just in time for you to go on:

Your big hour.

Now that was *golden*.

It was, for sure, the only enjoyment in the entire schedule. God forbid you played a lousy show; then suicide seemed like the logical alternative to the boredom, frustration, and futility. After a quick perusal of the premises for a smiling female (nope!) it's back to the hotel where the kitchen is (you guessed it) closed and it's 11:30 p.m. and all you can pick up on the TV is waving American flags and priests.

So practically all of us got high a lot. I'm surprised we weren't junkies. It's probably a miracle of sorts that no one in the band was inclined that way, but mostly we smoked hash, grass, and opium, and took some occasional mescaline. Imagine being revered on stage for that wonderful hour and then being rushed back to your hotel cell. You felt like some talented animal in the circus after they tore the Big

Blues Project '66 (middle period). (Left to right) Andy, Steve, Danny, Dutch Boy Al, Roy.
(Photo: Linda Eastman—Al Kooper Collection.)

☜☞

Top down. It made us closer to each other, 'cause we were all in the same boat. If deep down we hadn't *really* dug each other, we could never have pulled it off (we did that a lot, too; but in separate rooms!).

With our record out and on the charts, our modest level of fame spread out of the general Eastern area and across the Great Divide. The agency booked us heavily and we went out and got 'em all. Sometimes for convenience we would charter small aircraft (five to eight seaters)—Buddy Holly Specials, I called 'em. The first pilot to fly us in a charter was Stanley Pell, the brother of famous West Coast arranger Dave Pell. He owned a STOL (Short Take Off & Landing) Aero-Commander Number 68 Romeo that sat six plus pilot and copilot. We had an afternoon appearance at a college in Waterville, New York, and an evening's engagement at Steve Paul's Scene in New York City. William Morris suggested we rent a plane and turned us on to Stanley, who flew Dionne Warwick and some of William Morris's other clients.

Everyone was a little uptight as we climbed aboard that first day, but Stanley had an excellent planeside manner and, placing Danny in the copilot's seat (he was the most nervous and Stan figured if Danny could *see* everything was OK, he'd be cool), he taxied down the runway and took off directly into a huge blizzard. The plane bounced around the sky like some crazed pinball, but it's different somehow when you can see the pilot, hear the radio transmissions, and see out the front window. There's no element of doubt, no matter how bouncy the ride. Suddenly, Stanley pointed off to the right side and announced we were in the area. "There's the runway," he said, and we all looked down. It looked like a teenie black magic marker line on a huge sheet of fluffy white paper. He swung around and headed straight for it. The plane was swaying from side to side but he was dead on it and he landed smoothly to a standing ovation (well, half-standing). We never thought twice (well, maybe once) about flying with him again.

Sometimes we'd take turns sitting in the copilot's seat, and Stanley would let us take the wheel and steer the plane. I had it once and was supposed to maintain an altitude of 7,000 feet. I held the wheel steady as a rock for forty-five seconds until Stanley nudged me, saying, "You better bring it up a little; you've just dropped 1,500 feet." It's a good thing he never passed out or anything. That wheel is so sensitive— don't believe those movies where the stewardess ends up flying the plane!

Once we had a show in Canada and we couldn't get Pell. It was the opening of Montreal's Expo, and we were playing in Place de Nations, which held close to 100,000 people. Everything converged on this boxing ring (!) that was used as a stage in the center of the arena. You'd think they would've erected a real stage or something for the fucking Montreal Expo. No way. So it was with great trepidation that we stepped through the ropes and addressed this mostly French-speaking, short-haired audience.

It took us about five seconds into the first song to realize that the "sound system" for our concert was also the same one that the announcer would use to say, "And in this corner, weighing 215 pounds. . . ." We looked at each other, somehow made it through one more instrumental (singing was impossible in a room that size with a tin-horn PA system), and then departed rather ungracefully through the ropes in the general direction of the dressing rooms, dodging a hail of bottles as we went.

Andy went to the bathroom and didn't return. Our roadie rescued him from a slicing at the hands of a couple of young punks. The climax of all this bad feeling was a short but genuine fistfight between Steve and myself. Both our nerves were short and shot, and somebody said something dumb to somebody and that was it; flailing arms everywhere.

Like I said, we were with a new pilot on this trip. The pilot, it seems, had inhaled a few drinks at the gig (which is against the law, by the way) but no one got on his case. He still had to fly us home, after all, and nobody wanted an *angry*, drunk pilot, did they? We got back on the plane real shaken. He taxied to the runway; so far so good. Fingers crossed. He revved up the engines for takeoff and then his haughty voice came over the intercom: "Fasten your seat belts, kiddies, it's time to cheat death once again!"

Danny was especially terrified during this two-hour jaunt and, as we thankfully began our descent over New York, Kalb began howling in pain. It seems that his ears were bothered by the pressure drop, an affliction that can sometimes befall anyone who flies, and he was in terrible pain. We made three separate descent attempts courtesy of our polluted pilot. Finally, with mostly green faces and Danny locked in Roy's arms howling away, we dropped down to terra firma, grateful to be alive. For the most part, however, flying was a commonplace thing to us, and I never thought too much about it. It was like getting on a subway or a bus to go to work in the morning.

Limousines also found their way into our lives at this time. We got a big kick out of the incongruity of it all; chauffered Cadillacs picking us up at our slumboxes in the Village. Danny's place was the most urbane, to put it politely, of all our abodes, and it was real cute picking him up on Welfare Avenue while he glanced nervously from side to side to make sure no one saw. We were all really poor at this time. I think our take from the band was an individual salary of $150 a week. It was embarrassing to get caught by our contemporaries in the limo, 'cause it was contrary to our image (De Blues Project Gets Down Wit Da Peoples, Right On). But if anybody stared in the windows at us, they'd find five third-fingers raised skyward for their trouble: the Blues Project salute.

The first night I rented a limo on my own tab, The Blues Project was headlining at Town Hall in New York City. I was separated from my wife and wanted to celebrate the show afterwards with my new girlfriend, Joan, and damn the cost. My wife had asked for four comp tickets to the show, for her and three friends. I found this quite unusual. After the show, they came backstage, and one of her "friends" served me with a divorce subpoena! I had to let the limo go and return home to call my lawyer. I was furious!

I remember the destruction of one of the last bastions of our collective sanity; the crack that caused the dam to burst. It was the day that Steve, who wore his hair combed straight back, came to rehearsal with a genuine Beatle haircut. God, we gave him so much shit, but at the same time we were proud of him. He had sacrificed his previous image (which wasn't shit, anyway) on the Scissored Cross of Rock 'n' Roll. *Actually, it was his mother who cut his hair.* With this one great transformation to her credit, and the fact that she came cheap, Mrs. Katz became the official Blues Project barber. There were no hip barbers or haircutting establishments in those days (1965); even in the Village you took your chances.

Naturally, it would soon change. But for then, Steve's mom was the Vidal Sassoon of our world.

Steve lived at home but he was unusually tight with his parents; so tight that he even used to bring girls home after gigs. I couldn't relate to it. I mean, a gal schleps all the way to the suburbs so she can bed this rock star, and next morning wakes up to the mother making pancakes and the father pulling out the family album. If I'd been his date, I couldn't have handled it. But Steve made out OK, so what did I know? Andy lived with his wife, Phyllis, in a tidy little apartment on Perry Street. Danny, as I implied before, lived in a place that would give *any* parent nightmares. For a kitchen he had a two-warmer hotplate. That was it, no refrigerator or even a sink. After visiting his apartment once, I never questioned Danny's right to sing the blues. Roy lived on the Lower East Side in a little pop-art cubbyhole where he collected fabrics and presidential seals. I think I was only there once; we used to room together on the road, but off it Roy kept pretty much to himself.

I lived in a six-flight walkup on Lexington Avenue at 35th Street. I was living with Joan, a woman-child who was soon to become the next in my procession of marital mishaps. My first marriage had gone bad with all the changes in my life. Judy remained the same person she always had been, while I popped out of the Dylan cocoon a completely new person. This new butterfly barely knew his wife and all our little differences widened into an irreconcilable chasm. I knew it was over but couldn't find the right moment to confront the situation. She became accidentally pregnant and refused to have an abortion, which was illegal and slightly dangerous at the time. I saw myself in the near future, trapped in a marriage with our new baby as the jailer. My twenty-two-year-old mind decided to bail before that cute baby-face snared me in for the next eighteen years. We split early in her pregnancy. It was an ugly confrontation and I'm not proud of it. Fortunately, at the age of eight, our son came back into my life where he remains today, close to my heart. But my abandonment of Judy during her pregnancy was perceived by her as an act of selfishness on my part for which I may never have been forgiven.

Everyone was a serious pothead by this time except Danny. In 1965, I'd had a Thanksgiving party at my apartment in Queens and Danny got loaded with us and we loved it. He confessed that the only other time he'd gotten high was during the Cuban Missile Crisis, because he thought we all were gonna die and he wanted a headstart to heaven. But I was high *all* the time. Before I went to sleep I'd stash a joint under my pillow so I could get loaded before my feet touched the ground in the morning (which they seldom did). And, of course, we were influenced by the sensibility of the Beatles in *A Hard Day's Night*. *Our* movie, which was never realized, had some fabulous footage in it. I'll recount to you a random scene from our true-life screenplay:

In mid-1966 there was this huge one-night blues festival at the State University of New York at Stonybrook, on Long Island. We were the headliners. This is where *The Blues Project Live at Town Hall* was actually recorded, but Town Hall sounds much better than SUNY at Stonybrook, so don't tell anyone, and I won't either.

Anyhow, it was an important night to us. We went out there early in the afternoon to check the recording balances and make sure everything was A-OK. It took all day, and we finished just as they let the people in to take their seats. The line-up was Chuck Berry, Muddy Waters, Richie Havens, John Lee Hooker, Dave Van Ronk, David Blue, and us. While the rest of the band watched the show, I escaped with a newly acquired female "special friend" in search of a place to get better acquainted. We ended up consummating our mutual feelings for each other on the indoor handball court. Just as we were concluding, our roadie burst in. "Al! Where the fuck have you been? Everyone's looking for you," he shouted, glancing at his watch."Holy shit! You got forty-five seconds before we're announced!"

Blues Project '67 in its final throes; on the Upbeat *TV show, Cleveland, Ohio. (Left to right) Roy, Andy, Al, Danny, Steve. (Photo: George Shuba—courtesy of David Spero Collection.)*

1965-1967

Well, you know the bit where you're running and pulling your pants on at the same time. I mean no time for a fond farewell or even a kiss goodbye. I made it backstage just as they're announcing the band. In full gallop I leapt onstage half-dressed. Danny was already into the intro to our opener, "Goin' Down Louisiana" (*I had been Goin' Down Linda myself*). I had pants and a white tee shirt on, that's it. No sox, no shoes. (Usually, I took the opportunity of appearing onstage to indulge my taste in sartorial splendor. There were kids who'd come to see us just to laugh at my clothes.) So when the spotlight hit me for my solo and the band saw me for the first time in just a tee shirt with a huge hickey on my neck (which I, of course, hadn't seen), they could barely keep playing, they were laughing so hard. It was wonderful.

The time came to complete *Projections*, our second album, and to get it out as soon as possible. Pressure again. It was always rush time when we were supposed to record. In those days ('66) the artists did not have anywhere near the control they do today. They had no say in what studio was used, had no concept of the stereo mixing processes, and were seldom consulted regarding the cover art. Sometimes (as with the Byrds on "Mr. Tambourine Man") they didn't even *play* on their own records. We just played and prayed. At least we got to play on our records (maybe that's what our problem was).

We used to get the spare time The Animals weren't using. Verve would call us the day before and say, "OK, tomorrow from one to six you're at Regent Studios and we need to get three tracks cut." Tom Wilson would be there. Since he produced both us and the Animals, I'm sure he didn't know who was gonna walk in the door at one o'clock; he just sat there and ground 'em out. They'd set us up and we'd play our little hearts out. Three takes a tune was all we were allowed, due to time restrictions. But we didn't know any better. I was always amazed when I heard other records that were so precise; I thought *everyone* made records the way we did.

One day we were recording "Two Trains Running," which was ten minutes long and one of our live cornerstones. There were many tempo changes and subtleties in it. We were halfway through it and no one could even see anyone else 'cause they had all these partitions and isolation screens up, yet we were playing it better than we ever had. Danny was singing it live and doing an incredible job and I was ecstatic. We got to a real quiet spot in the song and suddenly Danny's saying, "Stop the tape. Hold it. I can't go on!" We put down our instruments and looked at each other. I could see in everyone's eyes that, yes, *everyone* thought it was the best we'd ever played it.

Not Danny. I guess the isolation and the fact that he was having trouble hearing his guitar and keeping it in tune threw him. So we took a break for awhile and then started from the beginning again. And we lost that whole take. Nowadays, they would keep it and have us start where it broke down, finish it and splice it all together; we could've been heroes, but it was not to be on that day in 1966. So we were playing it again and all of a sudden magic happened: We got to the same spot, a place where the band just stops cold for four beats. One of Danny's strings slipped a half-tone out of tune, and he used that space to play a riff incorporating the necessary tuning back up of the string. Clever. We all kept going and finished the take. When we played it back, the one lick was so incredible that it warranted keeping *that* take for the album. Listen for it.

Two of my new songs, the first I had ever written all by myself A.D. (after drugs), were included on the new album. "Fly Away" was a transition song; like a lyrical bridge between my two marriages. The other was "Flute Thing," the song that changed Andy's life. Andy was primarily a flautist, but aside from a lick here or there he had no vehicle to showcase that skill in our band. One night in Cambridge, Massachusetts, on the floor of Jill Henderson's apartment, while Danny was cooking beef stroganoff for everyone (God, what a stickler for detail that Kooper is!), I composed a little instrumental on Danny's acoustic guitar. It was based on a cadenza played by Barney Kessell at the conclusion of some jazz tune.

In those days, Andy carried his flute everywhere. Not that he would play it all the time, but it was his last link with the classical world, and I guess he needed some reassurance. Well, out it came and he quickly digested this bit of pap I had dashed off. Soon we were rolling all over Jill's apartment with our new song. Two days later we were playing it on stage with extended solos by everyone except poor Steve, who was relegated to playing the bass in order to free Andy up to play the flute. Later on, Andy, frustrated at not being.able to be heard over our OV (oppressive volume), surprised us by matter-of-factly drilling a hole in his precious flute and installing an *electric* pickup. There was no looking back now; the Buffalo Philharmonic would not have stood for any of *this* tomfoolery. Andy's flute, along with Steve's slicked-back hair, both were now casualties of the rock 'n' roll revolution.

The electrification of the flute was added, unfortunately, *after* we'd hastily recorded "Flute Thing." However, this was just the beginning for Andy, who appears to have been, chronologically, the first electric flautist of note. Not satisfied with that distinction, he concocted a complex and expensive set of pedals and effects for his instrument, which he was always primping and improving in his spare time. It used to sound incredible (he incorporated time delay, fuzz tone, wahwah, and echo effects), but it pissed the rest of us off because we ended up spending more money on that one damn song than for anything else on stage. Not to be outdone, I started collecting weird percussion instruments (Pakistani bells and toy pianos, styrofoam blocks, and Indian clappers) and integrating them into the freer sections of the song just to bust Andy's balls.

Projections was released in mid-1966. Its initial sales surge was almost three times that of our first album. We were movin' on up. This time out I'd written four of the nine songs on the album and was becoming more than the "piano player in the corner" that I'd initially envisioned myself as. I was being consumed by an inner drive to do more than that.

This, of course, caused tremendous conflict in the band. The group, once entirely Kalb-driven, was now up for grabs. And it was a knock-down, drag-out battle for control, to say the least. Danny was, is, and always will be a traditional bluesman. I was, am, and always will be a rock 'n' roller. It was a battle between the purist and the bastardizer.

I used to carry around a cane "for effect" until one day, in an argument, I realized I was capable of bashing Danny's head in with it, and threw it away. But I don't wish to mislead you. It was all of us. We had nothing in common other than music and being Jewish and maybe that is why the band was so strident and energy-filled. It certainly didn't do much for our mutual communication. But, as I mentioned before, somewhere down there was the deep love we had for each other and the musical Frankenstein we had created together. Once, in an effort to confront all the inner demons, we sat down together in a psychiatrist's office and had what was probably the first rock group therapy session. It was like an emotional Fourth of July. Everybody got their deep-seated animosities out and the air was charged with discontent and the psychiatrist's fee. We realized that if we had one more session, we could grow closer as people, but the band would have to die. That was the finale of rock group therapy. Everybody came out of the hostility closet all at once, and the fur began to fly. Danny didn't like this about Roy, Steve didn't like that about me, etc. *One session.*

It was around this time that we made a shift in management. We had outgrown Jeff Chase, who was basically Danny's and Roy's high school chum. When Jeff was handed his pink slip, he ran to the attorneys. We ended up negotiating a $20,000 settlement with him. This financial setback eventually killed us. We were never able to overcome it.

At any rate, we went manager shopping and, let me tell you, I'd rather comparison shop for diarrhea. Only rodeos have more bullshit than we encountered in our quest for our next career guide. After a month of eeny-meeny-miny-mo, the burden of our future success fell into the soft hands of one-time concert promoter Sid

Bernstein. Sid, who was a serio-jolly fellow and claimed to believe in the blues crusade, also managed The Rascals, who were doing quite well at the time. Our performing price soon doubled, but our salaries remained the same due to Jeff's management settlement and our increased overhead. In retrospect, I figure that getting any richer might've corrupted the music, so maybe it was just as well.

We were out there playing, too. We played at the San Francisco State College Folk Festival with Richard and Mimi Farina, Mark Spoelstra, and Malvina Reynolds. We drew quite a few people to the Newport Folk Festival of 1966, as well. That was a weird gig for me. Just prior to my departure for Newport, I was feeling particularly awful and went to the doctor. He took some tests and said, "Son, you have mononucleosis. I heartily recommend that you enter the hospital."

We were playing at the Scene in New York until the Newport gig, and right after that we were booked into an important new New York disco called the Phone Booth. I made a deal with the doctor to take lots of medication, rest as much as possible, and not to kiss anyone above the waist, and as soon as the Phone Booth gig was over, enter the hospital (they'd probably carry me in).

All through Newport, of course, I was running a fever and having to keep a low profile. Miraculously, I made it through reasonably intact. The night we opened at the Phone Booth, the band had installed an army cot outside the dressing room. It was a good thing they did, 'cause toward the end of the first show I passed out cold.

I was rushed to the hospital (I told ya they'd carry me in) and was glad to be there. Paul Harris, a friend from Queens who had been the recipient of all my studio work when The Project became too time-consuming, was called in to replace me at the Phone Booth on two hours' notice. He fit right in and saved the gig. After a few weeks of hospitalization, I was good as new (which was just to the left side of healthy compared to normal people).

Because of our insecurities about not having a charismatic-type lead singer, we hired on a young lady named Emmaretta Marx, who could sing quite well. Emmaretta was not Jewish, but she was black. She would bound onto the stage halfway through the show and liven things up a bit. She also brought along her own "roadie," a Jean Shrimpton-ish mod delight named Gail. This meant we had to carry *two* extra people and pay higher hotel bills, so Emmaretta was definitely *on trial*.

Gail caused a little friction in the band, 'cause everyone fell in love with her at the same time and didn't bother to tell the others (or Gail, for that matter) about it. A few indecent proposals from a bunch of emotional cripples sent Gail fleeing straight into the arms of Frank Zappa. She soon became Mrs. Zappa, eventual mother to Moon Unit, Dweezil, and Ahmet Rodan. Emmaretta turned out to be a passing Project performer and, after missing more rehearsals than she could afford to, was returned to from whence she came.

We were packaged on blues shows quite often, and ended up becoming friendly with those performers whom we had once revered from a distance. Muddy Waters, B. B. King, James Cotton, Otis Spann, and Howlin' Wolf became close friends of ours. Usually, if we played on the bill more than one time with these people, they would drift into the dressing room to find out what we were all about. All except Chuck Berry. Early in our careers, we backed up Chuck Berry at his first New York solo concert. He was a scary guy and a tough leader, and *never* did he encourage any friendship. He was strictly professional:

"All you do is watch my foot. When it go up in the air, get ready. When it hit the ground, if you playin', stop. If you ain't, start."

That was his mantra.

It's A Mod, Mod, Mod World. Gail and Al backstage somewhere in America. (Photo: Alice Ochs.)

৩৩

When we were in town, we hung out mostly on Bleecker Street. A few of us would make the journey uptown to Steve Paul's Scene or Max's Kansas City, but that was mainly for whoring. Usually, it was the Au Go Go, the Dugout, or the Au Go Go's competition across the street, the Bitter End. But for laying back, about two blocks down Bleecker was Alice Ochs's apartment.

Alice was Phil Ochs's ex-wife, and she lived with a girlfriend in a cozy apartment that overlooked all of Bleecker. Every folkie and folk-rocker hung out there, and Alice would sit in the corner with her Nikon and snap away as 1965, '66, and '67 rolled by. We used to get a few extra bucks from Verve and take Alice on the road with us so she could keep on takin' all those pictures, many of which enhance this book.

While in San Francisco, we played at the first concert thrown by a hippie cartel known as the Family Dog. They had rented out a huge ballroom on Sutter Street called the Avalon and booked three rock groups for Friday, Saturday, and Sunday nights. We headlined over two local bands, The Sons of Adam and The Great Society (which at the time contained the talents of future Jefferson Airplane co-pilot Grace Slick and her brother-in-law Darby). It was April 12, 1966, and the weekends that followed gave local rockers an alternative to Bill Graham's shows at the original Fillmore. Eventually they went the way of all hippie business ventures, and Graham resumed his stranglehold on rock in Northern California.

Back in New York, The Blues Project finally had its big showdown with the Butterfield gang from Chicago. It was on our home turf. They muscled in on the Cafe Au Go Go, and, frankly, *what could we do?* We had to face 'em head on. So from July 1 to July 3, 1966, we were on the same bill at the club. It was the first time we had ever squared off against each other on stage. We were primed and they were primed. We alternated headline status each show.

Town Hall, '65. Chuck Berry: "You see my hands? When I play this G chord, so do you!!" Blues Project: bewilderment. (Photo: Don Paulsen.)

After our first set, Bloomfield came into our dressing room. "We heard you guys were shit and played real pussy. Well, it ain't true. You kicked ass out there and we just wanna acknowledge that." We still tried to get up there and kick *their* ass, but it was completely evenly paced throughout the entire gig. It was amazing. We would get up and play a hot set and they would play a burner. We would slip and play a fucked-up one, they would go out and die. The weekend culminated in a massive jam during the last set on the last night. The gunfight was over and no one had been injured.

By then, we were at our peak. We were New York's most beloved underground band, the toast of Cleveland, Ohio, *les enfants terribles* of Cambridge, Massachusetts, and invaders from Mars to the rest of the country. We would often need good security to guarantee trouble-free exits from concert appearances.

My favorite memories from this time period were from a ten-day stage show we did for Murray the K. It was over Easter vacation and began March 25, 1967. Murray the K's Easter Rock Extravaganza featured The Blues Project, Cream, Wilson Pickett, The Who, Jim & Jean, The Chicago Loop, Mitch Ryder, The Mandala, The Hardly Worthit Players, and The Jackie the K (Murray's wife) Dancers. It was the American debut for The Who, Cream, and the Canadian rock group Mandala, all relatively unknown commodities here, and it was convenient and inexpensive for Murray to fit them into the framework of this fifties-style rock 'n' roll revue. I had played many shows like this with The Royal Teens. You play your one, two, or three hits and get off quick. Five shows a day, shuffle, shuffle, etc.

Ludicrous, huh?

You bet.

Murray tried to media it up by shooting film on each of the acts and running the clips during set changes. But in order to make a profit, he had to keep the time of each show down, so many of these trailers hit the cutting room floor. A nice idea, though.

We shared a dressing room with Cream and got friendlier with them than with anyone else in the show. It was their first U.S. trip, and diving directly into this show must have given them a more than distorted look at life in America. I remember the first day they showed up. Ginger Baker walked into the dressing room. We were introduced, and trying to make conversation, I said: "So what do you think of America so far?" He looked rudely at me and replied: "How the fuck should I know? I've only been 'ere thirty-five fucking minutes, 'aven't I?" Our relationship went uphill from there, and by the last night of the show, we were throwing eggs and whipped-cream at each other, that old American rock 'n' roll ritual that denotes mutual respect.

The show took place at the now defunct (an oft-used phrase in this book) RKO Fifty-Eighth Street Theater in Manhattan. On Easter Sunday, in between shows, Jack Bruce, Steve Katz, and I strolled over to Central Park, where New York's First Annual Be-In was taking place. It was the counterculture's free Easter party, and we thought we'd have a looksee. Everyone in the area was attired in glorious flower-power finery; women were passing out wine, candy, popcorn, cakes, and dope. As I stuffed a few handfuls of popcorn into my mouth, it occurred to me that perhaps some folks might've combined dope into the food (San Francisco style), and maybe discretion was in order for any acceptance of free handouts. I mentioned this to Steve and Jack, but they hadn't eaten anything.

After we got back to the theater, I discovered I had shut the barn door after the horse was loose. Boy, was I gooned out. It's hard to pinpoint what I was experiencing, but I do remember it was positive all the way. The band wisely decided to play the next show without me. Our roadie took me out into the audience and, for the first time in my life, I watched The Blues Project play. A pleasant trip.

One afternoon, Eric Clapton, Steve Katz, and I ran out between shows to Mannys, the local music store. We dallied a little too long and were nervously checking our watches as the return cab pulled up at the stage door. I got out first and ran for the door. Steve was right behind me and as he left the cab he accidentally slammed the door *right on Clapton's hand*! Eric began to scream in pain, and Steve turned around, ran back, and opened the door. Miraculously, Eric hadn't broken any bones or even punctured his skin for that matter. Steve felt like a jerk, however. Can you imagine that kind of guilt?

Cream was having a time of it. For a band that later became known as the stretch-out group of all time, fifteen minutes to do three tunes was a bit restrictive. They did "I Feel Free," "Spoonful," and alternated closing with "Traintime" or "Crossroads." It was uninspired compared to the shows they would later whip on people. (*Wheels of Fire* is playing in the background as I'm typing this, and I'm grinning.)

The Who were another story. I had read all about them in the imported English papers, so I knew what their story was. I'd seen pictures in the English import rags *Rave* and *Disc*, and was looking forward to seeing their guitar-smashing climax firsthand. They were chosen to close the show, and wisely so.

At the first show everyone in the cast stood in the wings to see what all the fuss was about. Well, they launched into "My Generation" and you could feel it coming. Keith Moon flailed away on these clear plastic drums, and it seemed like he had about twenty of 'em. It was the first time any of us colonists had seen the typical English drumkit. There are usually six to eight tom toms of various sizes as

Two guitarists of varying degrees share more than secrets backstage: (Left) Eric Clapton and Steve Katz, 1967. (Photo: Alice Ochs.)

compared to two or three in most American drumsets. And huge double bass drums, one of which said "THE" and the other, of course, "WHO." Moon just beat the shit out of them for fifteen minutes nonstop.

Pete Townshend ("He's a God in England," Eric Clapton said to me before they went on) leaped in the air, spinning his arms wildly and just being the most generally uninhibited guitar player ever seen in these parts. Roger Daltrey broke a total of eighteen microphones over the full run of the show. And John Entwistle would just lean up against his amp and take it all in.

They reached the modulation part of the instrumental, and Townshend spun his guitar in the air, caught it, and smashed it into a placebo amp. No cracks in his Strat, so he aimed for the mikestand. *Whackkkkk.* Crack number one. Then the floor. *Whommmpppp!* The guitar was in three or four pieces and he still got signal coming out of it! All of a sudden, Moonie kicked his entire drumkit over, and the curtain rang down in a cloud of artificial smoke. Just then I realized my heart was beating three times its normal speed. I figure that, as a critic of the show, my electrocardiogram would have been the best testimonial I could have offered.

Between shows, The Who's roadie, Bob Pridden, would glue drums and guitar bits together in the dressing room, all the while constructing smoke bombs and signing microphone repair bills. He had his hands full to say the least. For The Who it was business as usual, even if it was at fifteen minutes a clip.

Wilson Pickett was a strong figure in the R&B world, racking up one hit after another and creating many classics ("In The Midnight Hour," "Mustang Sally," "I'm A Midnight Mover," "I Found A Love," and later a great version of Free's "Fire And Water"). He was interested in alternative music, and this was the first time he had encountered it firsthand, so he hung out with everyone as much as he could.

Mike Bloomfield and Barry Goldberg came down to catch the show one night. Mike had just quit Butterfield and was scouting new musicians for a concept he had in mind for a band. While listening to Pickett's set, he became hopelessly infatuated with the playing of Wilson's eighteen-year-old drummer. Bloomers took a shot and stole that drummer right out of Pickett's band. For young Buddy Miles it was a gamble, but a relief from the chitlin' circuit that had occupied most of his eighteen years.

So many incestuous things were going on. Little did Buddy know that years later, when he would front his own band, he would call upon Jim McCarty, the guitar player who was with Mitch Ryder at the show, to join his group. Little did Mandala know how they would divide and make a name for themselves individually (Dom Troiano joined The James Gang, Penti Glan and Josef Chiriowski would later provide powerful backup for Lou Reed and Alice Cooper).

It was during the run of this show that I received a call from my ex-wife Judy's family that our son was being born. March 29, 1967. I rushed out to Long Island Jewish Hospital and ran up to Judy's hospital room. She was asleep and looked like a girl who had crossed the line to womanhood and *was* the worse for wear as a result of it. I stood in the room solo, staring at her, and wept. I had been a bastard for my timing in leaving, but that's why it's incorrect to marry at age 21. Still, the guilt poured out of my eyes. I walked to the nursery and stared at the Kooper baby. This was one of the roughest moments in my life. Judy's family glowered at me and did not speak a word. I got back in a cab and began my return to Murray's show with my head in my hands. The dark, humorous part of this was that over the next few days people kept handing Joan cigars and telling her what a great recovery she had made.

After Murray's last show every night, those of us who could still stand up made it over to Steve Paul's club and jammed all night. Many incredible nights of music went down during that week. It was the memorable Spring before the impending Summer of Love.

One night I was sitting in my favorite bar in the Village, the Dugout. It was the best place to kill a summer's night, and I always ran into a few friends I would miss while I was on the road. I was living platonically at folk-singer Judy Collins' apartment on the Upper West Side in between my own apartments. Judy, the number two female folk singer behind Joan Baez, was a wonderful, generous woman. Her apartment was the folk music salon of the mid-sixties. People like Dylan, Leonard Cohen, Phil Ochs, and others would make the pilgrimage to her digs and enjoy her hospitality and earth mothering. This particular night in the Village I was sitting with a new girl in town. She had a crush on Roy Blumenfeld, the drummer from The Blues Project. Unfortunately for her, Roy had a girlfriend who was on to her and extremely jealous. So, this gal is crying in my beer for about three hours, and I don't mind 'cause she's kinda easy on the eyes and nothing else is going on anyway. So they're closing the bar and throwing us out and I offer to walk her home. It was about a fifteen-minute stroll, and it was a beautiful summer's night. Since I was covered in the ashes of my failed marriage, this was a pleasant diversion.

When we got to her door, she invited me in to hear some of her new songs. She was a folksinger. Canadian. Half of a duet with her recently divorced husband, they had achieved a mild popularity and a cult following in various American border cities. She, being real pretty, had me bounding up the stairs like a hound dog, figuring if the songs were lousy, maybe I could salvage the evening some other way. In a few minutes that became the furthest thing from my mind.

Her songs were incredible and totally original, which was a surprise in those days, but quite refreshing. She would finish one, and I would say more, more. And she had enough to keep going for hours, most of them brilliant. One song especially killed me, and I thought it would be great for Judy Collins—that a nice way to pay her for her hospitality would be to turn her on to it. Being impulsive, I asked my host if I could use her phone, and I called Judy up. It was 5:30 a.m. by now, and Judy was pretty pissed off.

"I have to get up soon and drive all the way to the Newport Folk Festival, and I wanted to get some sleep for a change. I can hear this song when I get back from the festival, Al," she said diplomatically.

Bang! A great idea hits me. "Judy, why don't you, room permitting, take this girl with you to the festival. She could play the song and others for you on the way up and make your trip that much more pleasant. Then, being that you're on the board of directors, you could see if maybe they could fit her in the schedule somewhere to play, huh?" Silence at the other end. "Judy?"

"Kooper, you bastard. Yeah, I'll do it. Gimme her number. Bye."

Just to make sure, I gave the woman Judy's number and told her to call Collins in a couple of hours. I split immediately 'cause I was exhausted and never made it to Judy's place, preferring to crash on a bench in Washington Square Park in the steamy, summer morning rather than get hell for waking her at 5:30 a.m.

Well, as the saying goes, the rest is history. The girl (Joni Mitchell, of course) played at the 1967 festival, thanks to the last-minute urgings of Judy Collins, and stole the whole show. Judy eventually recorded the song I thought she would like, "Michael from Mountains," and also had a huge hit with "Both Sides Now," another of Joni's songs. Joni never thanked me, but when I heard the album *Ladies of the Canyon*, that was thanks enough. Maybe I should thank *her*.

I was expanding my horizons and growing in many directions. For one thing, I couldn't understand why we couldn't make records that sounded as good as those other ones on the radio. I knew it was just a matter of concept and time spent in the studio. I'd just written a Top Forty-type song that I knew the band could do in a way that would endear us to those 45 rpm-buying teenies out there and give us the exposure we needed. I convinced Tom Wilson to let us take a *whole day* just to record this one song. To his credit, Danny was docile, and though he hated this kind of musical gesture, he played what was required and even pitched in on the background vocals.

We were in the studio from 11:00 a.m. to 7:00 p.m. We worked out the arrangement beat by beat, bar by bar, until it fit the confining time limit of the pop single. Wilson would let us go for awhile, then come in and channel us if we got on the wrong track. It was a key day for me. I was thinking Motown when I put on my organ part, Beatles when I played the synthy solo, and I was trying to imagine myself as a freaked-out Mark Lindsay (lead singer of Paul Revere and the Raiders) when I sang the lead vocal. That oughta cover all the bases, I thought. But most of all it was liberation day in the studio, and from then on no one could ever rush me through three takes again. The song we cut, "No Time Like the Right Time," came out and actually made the singles charts (a first for us and, unfortunately, a last) and *soared* to Number 73 on the Top 100. But mainly, it was the beginning of the end for the band because Danny hated it as much as I loved it.

Joan and I moved from East 35th Street to Waverly Place in the West Village. We had a pretty crummy place in a better location. We were on the ground floor, which made it a lot easier for the rats to come and go as they pleased.

Progress, dammit, that's what I was into. I wanted to augment the band with three horns, and got turned down cold by everyone. Danny said we hadn't scratched the surface of what we could do in our current configuration, so why add people and raise our overhead even more? I had no comeback for his financial argument, but the die was cast. I had been writing songs that I knew were best expressed with horn backups. Danny was on my case for trying to sing like a black man. Sort of hypocritical, being that he was as guilty of that as I was.

Rehearsals were becoming apathetic and nonproductive. The other guys were, in my estimation, getting lazy and fat musically. I realized I couldn't play somebody else's blues anymore. I had my own music now, and it was time to sing *my* song, not Jimmy Reed's or Muddy Waters'. All this pressure was building up inside me with no outlet, compounded by my usual high drug intake. Something had to give.

One night, in the middle of a blistering argument with Joan, I all of a sudden shut up and became catatonic. I didn't say a word for four days. It was like a dam cracking, except that it was me cracking (up). I actually felt a snap inside my head and then relief at not having to speak anymore. It scared Joan. I mean I just sat propped up in bed all day, staring at the wall, real quiet.

I remember they sent Sid Bernstein around to see me. He put his infamous, large, soft hand on my hand and talked to me, almost oblivious to the fact that I wasn't replying.

"Rest up, kiddo," he recited. "There's absolutely nothing you have to do this week, so there's no pressure if you just lay back and take it easy. By next weekend, you'll be fine and we'll play that Chicago gig."

I couldn't believe him. I wanted to jump up and scream, "*It's over, you mother-fucker! It's over! Look what's become of me. I can't stand another minute of this shit. Go away!*" Of course, he had no way of knowing this; he just thought I was tired. Sid was so busy keeping us afloat businesswise that he couldn't see the heavy emotional drama going on in the band. But it *was* over. The "leave of absence" I was about to take would be the first step in the end of the band as it was.

When I finally started talking, I called up my dad and borrowed two thousand dollars from him. First time I ever asked him for anything. Blew his mind. He did not fail me, even though he had to borrow it from someone else 'cause he was a little short at the time. Not much, mind you; about 5 feet 6 inches. Joan and I quickly packed it up and caught the next plane to California to "rest."

Los Angeles had always seemed to me a kind of mythical place where that magical "it" was always happening first, whether it was sun-baked beaches in the pages of *Life* magazine or bands like The Byrds and Buffalo Springfield that were providing the freshest American alternative to the English stranglehold on rock 'n' roll. The music business had begun its slow migration from Broadway to the Coast, and residence in L.A. was becoming a symbol of affluence. Sort of like, well, you've graduated from New York High School, now four years in the Los Angeles College Of (not so) Hard Knocks, and then maybe we'll ship you to London for your post-graduate work.

The paradox was that I found the thought of residing in that California "paradise" depressing and more than a little like giving up. The New York sensibility has always regarded California with suspicion. If your system is geared to New York's nonstop adrenaline rush, the relaxed California life-style can seem as if you're playing a 45 rpm record at 33⅓. Usually, if New Yorkers want to follow that slow a pace, they retire to Florida. My impression was that it was almost too easy to get by in Los Angeles and, although my overloaded mental and emotional circuits definitely needed the rest, I couldn't really feel comfortable about a move that I subconsciously equated with retiring to a condominium in Boca Raton. Nonetheless, I'd barely gotten it together to where I could roll out of bed before Joan had us winging our way westward.

We checked into the Hollywood Sunset Hotel (then the most favored pop hotel and now a retirement apartment complex) and fanned our address books in search of anyone who might put us up. Joan had a friend in Oakland named Anne, who was gracious enough to offer us lodging for as long as we needed it. So off to Oakland we flew, only to be confronted with a scene that we weren't even remotely prepared to cope with.

What Anne had neglected to mention was that her house was the number one crash-pad in Oakland. Joining us in our Northern California holiday retreat were every speed freak in San Francisco, an eccentric rock band and their various women, and Anne's old man, whose sole claim to fame was that he had once managed The Chambers Brothers. Talk about horror shows? This scene was like a distillation of all the negative stereotypes that the media was then promulgating about the hippie phenomenon. If this was the wave of the future, get me back to 1650 Broadway!

In order to get to our sleeping quarters, we had to stand on the kitchen table, then boost ourselves up through the kitchen ceiling and into the attic (which had just enough space to allow you to walk around in a small circle hunched over). Our newlyweird suite came furnished with a single blood-stained mattress that had no sheets, compliments of the management. Well, I admit that it wasn't the Beverly Hills Hotel (no matter what hallucinogenic drug you were on) but, I mean, *they didn't even ask us to chip in for food*!

God, it was depressing. I'd use up the days making small talk with the endless procession of wasted faces that passed through the house, At night I'd sit up in that attic and crumble into Mr. Hyde. It was *de rigueur* to cry oneself to sleep; it seemed to suit the environment. When they film this part of the movie, it'll be in black and white.

One day, in an effort to relieve my boredom and depression, I went to Mill Valley to visit my old friend Mike Bloomfield. We spent the day playing records and talking, and soon it was dark. Mark Naftalin, a buddy and playing mate of Mike's, dropped in, and the three of us sat in the kitchen trading stories about old blues players. Michael's dog was lying on the kitchen floor, crying the whole time we were sitting there. We were real stoned, having smoked the required fifty-seven joints that California people do in the course of a day (higher tolerance than New Yorkers). Maybe that's why I didn't notice right away that the "cookies" Michael was munching on while he talked about Howlin' Wolf were Fives, a popular California brand of kibble for dogs and cats. I called this to his attention, secretly hoping his sense of *something* had been dulled temporarily by his stoned state.

"Oh no, man, I eat these all the time. 'S good. Want some?" *His father was a fucking billionaire and he was eating dogfood?*

"Sure. I'll try some. . . ."

When no one was looking, I snuck my handful down to the dog, and he stopped crying. Yikes!

The Oakland/cockroach side trip was getting us nowhere, and was not exactly the kind of rehabilitation I'd had in mind when we fled to California. I mean, it told me everything I wanted to know about a certain kind of life I *didn't* wish to lead, but in that respect was just another addition to an already crowded list. I certainly wasn't doing too much to straighten out my considerably twisted brain. Each day I'd twist it a little more in an attempt to find an escape from my escape. My address book had burn marks on the pages from all the time I spent staring at the names and numbers in it over and over again.

Finally, we lucked out. I chanced a call to David Anderle, an old acquaintance in L.A., and he consented to have us as his Hollywood houseguests. Relief! David was a music biz person I'd met while in The Blues Project. He had been a promotion man for MGM in L.A., and during the convention at which we'd played, he was kind enough to take me to his doctor for a much-needed (feel free to use your imagination) penicillin shot. What I needed now was a shot of privacy, and his home was the welcome syringe.

At various times since the MGM days, David had managed a singer named Danny Hutton (who almost made it big with a local hit, "Roses and Rainbows," and later went all the way as a member of Three Dog Night), babysat for Brian Wilson of The Beach Boys (taking care of *him* as opposed to his kids), encouraged Van Dyke Parks, and painted fabulous portraits of the people who moved him. David's first love was painting, and anyone who's ever seen his work comes away wondering what strange allure the record business could hold for a man so artistically gifted.

David and his wife Cheryl resided in a lovely façade up in the Hollywood Hills, replete with a neat fake waterfall in the backyard. It was a vast improvement on our Oakland digs, and we were *almost* happy. But I was still running blind, and David picked up on that right away. He took me down the hill to an office on Sunset Boulevard where all these people were engaged in the planning of a pop festival to be held in Monterey in four weeks' time. Quite a crew: Lou Adler, Ben Shapiro, Alan Pariser, Guy Webster, Tom Wilkes, Derek Taylor, and the familiar face of Edward Herbert Beresford (Chip) Monck.

I'd known Chip from the Dylan days in New York. He always did the lights and staging at the Newport Folk and Jazz Festivals. He put in the Tiffany lamps at the Derby Steak House in the Village (his first New York gig) and redesigned the Village Gate jazz club. He was a welcome slice of East Coast reality. I sat down to chat it up with him and he was soon asking my advice on what kind of instruments and amplifiers to rent. In short order he had me on the phone making calls and assisting him. David ducked out the door, and before you could say, "I've never engaged in this kind of thing before," I'd become the Assistant Stage Manager of the Monterey Pop Festival.

The Monterey job channeled my insanity. I would arrive at the office every day, get on the phone, and order and attempt to cut rate equipment. The fever, dedication, and enthusiasm of those present hit you in the face the moment you walked through the door. Derek Taylor, fresh from a P.R. stint with the Beatles, was on hand as a general antidote to any unnecessary stress. Lou Adler and Alan Pariser took his shots straightfaced—I guess 'cause they were immune to him—but he could reduce anyone else to instant giggles if they got too far into a jam. He made a living out of that in the sixties and saved a great many people from falling into that dreaded abyss called seriousness. A transplanted fixture on the L.A. scene, it would have been impossible to pull the festival off without him. And for me his presence was just what the doctor would've ordered if I'd had the sense to see one.

Tom Wilkes and Guy Webster handled the graphics and put together a memorable program book. A classic time capsule of that period, it was unfortunately not made available after the festival. The only surviving copy I know about was on Steve Katz's coffee table, but his house burned down, so maybe even that copy isn't around anymore. I wrote a poem that was included in it; they encouraged off-the-wall contributions of that sort. I used to fantasize about putting out a book of poetry, so I carried a notebook around on the road and free-associated my way through The Blues Project in its pages. Only two of the poems were ever published: "Paramount As Abc" (in the Monterey program book) and "*Line* Her Nodes" (as the notes to my first solo album; more about that later). After my untimely demise, I'm sure you'll be able to pick up a copy of the rest of those poems; I've left strict instructions.

Lou Adler was real surprised to see me, as he'd booked The Project for the Festival:

"What are you doing *here*?"

"I quit the band."

"But I've got them booked."

"They'll be there."

"Are they any good?"

"Of course they are. I was only one-fifth."

Lou was easily persuaded to keep them in the show. (I was curious to see what they were gonna do, anyway.) Chip and I were snowing Fender and Hammond in an attempt to convince them to lend us equipment free of charge in return for credit in the program book and on the TV show (in the early stages ABC -TV owned the rights to the festival). We were in touch with the road managers from every group to make sure that their specifications would be met. In other words, no surprises for anyone except the audience. This was gonna be a smoothie even if the prefestival madness was anything but smooth.

Back at the house, meanwhile, it was midway through the six-day Arab-Israeli War, and David was locked into the TV, cheering his race on to victory. Joan was trapped in the house by her inability to face reality and take a driving test. Suffice it to say I wasn't paying enough attention to dear Joan, and she was getting madder each day. I was so caught up in the festival that I was oblivious to everything else, including her anger. But at least by this time my insanity was manifesting itself functionally. When I was working, I was totally coherent. When I wasn't, I was simply a lunatic. (People have since told me that's how I've always been.) Bad luck for Joan.

One day I had lunch with Jac Holzman, the president of Elektra Records and a close friend. Elektra was making a brave plunge into the new music that was in the air, and Jac asked if I knew anyone suitable to run his West Coast office and studios. I flashed on a great way to pay my rent and immediately suggested Anderle, who I was certain could handle the job admirably. Soon Jac and David were deep into discussions about how Elektra could conquer the world. David put his paints away, and in the course of running the office he wound up producing a few gold albums for Judy Collins. I felt I'd repaid the kindness David had shown me.

The weeks flew by until one morning we woke up and it was the day before the festival. The management had rented a Lear Jet in which to ferry the staff and notables from L.A. to Monterey. Joan and I somehow lost track of the schedule, and late in the day we got a frantic call from the airport.

"Where the hell are you? The plane is waiting, it costs money, blah-blah-blah."

So we raced for the airport in David's car and ended up tear-assing onto the tarmac just like at the end of *Casablanca*. Life imitating art.

Ever flown in a Lear Jet?

Real exciting.

It was a five-seater, and its passengers on this shuttle were Alan Pariser, John Phillips, me, Joan, and Brian Jones (late of The Rolling Stones). Brian had just endured a flight from England. Pariser met him at the gate and whisked him through customs and straight to the Lear Jet. He appeared to be convening in the neighborhood of Jupiter.

We all strapped in and the plane took off immediately. Almost straight up. The flight was outrageous. I was at this time already a veteran of the skies, but no commercial flight really prepares you for your first Lear Jet ride. The thing goes so fast that you don't believe it even as it's happening.

When we landed in Monterey, Brian spoke to me for the first time that evening: "Hi, Al." I don't think he was aware that our introduction had taken place some forty-five minutes before.

And High Al I was. The flight velocity, altitude, or something had stoned me good, and I tripped along quietly as we drove into the fair city of Monterey. At the motel we ran into some friends we hadn't seen in a while, and stayed up all night partying. It was a fitting beginning to the festival weekend.

I made it over to the fairgrounds early the next a.m. Chip, who'd been there for five days doing advance work, had it together as usual. I just got on the phone and confirmed everyone for the soundchecks and so forth, filling in the small details. The show began with a set by Canned Heat, and from there it was three days of paradise. And, from an Assistant Stage Manager's perspective, it worked like a charm. By now reams have been written about Monterey Pop, so you'll excuse me if I don't detail it act by act at this late date. I do have a few pleasant memories, however:

There were several artists and friends that I was especially looking forward to seeing. While sitting around David Anderle's house that summer, we spent a great deal of time listening to this English album I'd borrowed from Aaron Schroeder—an act Aaron had recently signed for stateside publishing. The trio was fronted by a guitar-playing American expatriate that I'd often marveled at when he was a part of John Hammond Jr.'s backing band at the Cafe Wha! in New York, and I was anxious to see how he would do in his debut American performance since becoming a European sensation. His name was Jimi Hendrix.

In later years, when Hendrix became a worldwide legend, he invited me to play on his third album, *Electric Ladyland*. For my efforts, he rewarded me with one of his personal guitars. The day after I played on his session, it was delivered to my apartment in New York City. More about that guitar appears in a following chapter.

Also on the bill were my old friends from the Murray the K disaster, The Who, and even older friends, Paul Simon and Artie Garfunkel. It was also an opportunity to take in the whole spectrum of West Coast music, from the Los Angeles bands that I already knew and loved (The Byrds, The Buffalo Springfield, and The Mamas and the Papas) to the surging San Francisco wave that, for the most part, I'd only heard about (Jefferson Airplane, The Grateful Dead, and Big Brother and The Holding Company, which had a singer named Janis Joplin that *everybody* was raving about; I soon found out why).

To digress a bit now that we've mentioned West Coast music, David Anderle had also been responsible for engineering a meeting between me and one of my idols, Brian Wilson of The Beach Boys. David took me up to Brian's house, a sprawling, Spanish-style mansion in ultraposh Bel-Air, one evening about a week before Brian

Checking Hendrix out at soundcheck: Monterey Pop, Summer of Love '67.
(Photo: © Jim Marshall. Used with permission.)

unleashed *Pet Sounds* on the world. Brian played a test-pressing of the record, jumping up and stopping cuts in the middle and starting them over to emphasize his points. He was very proud of his accomplishment, maybe even a little show-offish, but I wasn't about to argue. Do you remember the first time *you* heard "God Only Knows"?

Then Brian sat down at the piano in his living room (which featured a full-on soda fountain where the bar should've been) and gave us two uninterrupted hours of possible variations on "Trees"—you know, the "I think that I shall never see a poem lovely as" thing—which he hoped to have The Beach Boys record. I'd brought along a copy of *Music of Bulgaria*, my favorite album at the time, and he got blown out by that. Then he shattered me completely by playing a track he was working on and singing along to it live. The song was "Good Vibrations." 'Nuff said. He also played me a rough tape of "Heroes and Villains," which had evolved, I believe, from a Wilson revamping of "You Are My Sunshine." In all, it was a great evening; one of the few that really captured all the California magic the rest of the country only imagined from a distance.

Through all of this, I had been sort of planning my next move. Deep in the back of my mind was a band that could put dents in your shirt if you got within fifteen rows of the stage. Like Maynard Ferguson's band from the years 1960-1964, I wanted a horn section that would play *more* than the short adjectives they were relegated to in R&B bands; but, on the other hand, a horn section that would play *less* than Count Basie's or Buddy Rich's. Somewhere in the middle was a mixture of soul, jazz, and rock that was my little fantasy.

I confided this concept to David Crosby one day, and he sent me to a local club to check out a guitar player he thought would be great for it. I loved the guitarist, introduced myself, and explained this concept to him. He thought it was a good idea, but insisted that he was committed to the band he was in. His name was Danny Weiss, and his band was Iron Butterfly. He left soon after we met anyway and joined the great but doomed band Rhinoceros.

I was then turned on to Jim Fielder, who had just been booted out of The Buffalo Springfield, and had played with Frank Zappa and Tim Buckley before that. He was a Texas-born mother of a bass player, and we jammed a lot over at his house in Laurel Canyon with a drummer friend of his named Sandy Konikoff. We made pretty agreeable music.

Mike Bloomfield was concurrently putting together a horn-type group up north that sounded in rumor exactly like my fantasy. This group was closing the big afternoon show at Monterey, so you *know* that's what I was most interested in. Bloomfield had kidnapped Buddy Miles (from Wilson Pickett's band at that Murray

Simon & Kooperfunkel—together again!!! (Photo: Gerald Jacobsen.)

ʕ๑ʔ

the K show already described), and together with Harvey Brooks (finally in a name band) on bass, Barry Goldberg on keyboards, Marcus Doubleday (a descendent of the inventor of baseball, Abner Doubleday) on trumpet, Peter Strazza on tenor sax, and Nick Gravenites on vocals and percussion, they had rehearsed for two or three months up in Marin county, just outside San Fran.

Monterey was their first gig, and they were terrified. Buddy Miles had a suit on fer chrissakes; one of those jobbies like James Brown wore, with no lapels and a shirt and tie! Bloomfield came out and gave one of his great speeches about how we (the audience) were all one and it was peace, love, and incense, and here's some music by the way.

Heavy drama. But they played great. The crowd went nuts. I was standing backstage with Susie Bloomfield (Michael's wife), and she was crying tears of joy and relief. Buddy Miles came off after playing to his first large, predominantly white audience, and he was sweating and crying. And, caught up in the thrill of it all, I was crying. But I was smiling at the same time, because my idea was still intact. Bloomfield's band, soon to be called Electric Flag, was sticking to tradition. They played their tunes in a faithful Stax-Volt tribute to the Memphis sound, and while it was overpowering and gorgeous to see and hear, it was flagrantly derivative. It was exactly like the differences between The Blues Project and The Butterfield Band. The band I was hearing in *my* head would not sound like any other band that had ever been.

After Monterey folded up its petals, I bummed a ride to San Francisco to waste a few days. Joan had fled back to the Big Apple, in a rage, on the last day of the festival, giving my self-absorbed ass a much-deserved stiff boot. Joan Baez was throwing an annual party known as the Big Sur Folk Festival, and I drifted in that direction. I'd played at the previous year's show as a solo act, and had been invited to perform once again.

The get-together, held on the grounds of the tranquil Esalen Institute, had maintained a low enough profile to insure that it would be full but not overcrowded. It was as if they'd simply shifted the party from Monterey to Big Sur. Simon and Garfunkel donated their much-in-demand services for free in order to partake in the surroundings and get their hip cards punched one notch further. It was especially nice for me, 'cause I schlepped Jim Fielder and Sandy Konikoff along and took the opportunity to debut some of my new songs. "I Can't Quit Her" and "My Days Are Numbered" went down well with the crowd, adding fuel to my fantasy of a new band.

Owing to future politics, this is the last we will see of Sandy Konikoff. I should thank him profusely for working for insulting wages, loving the music, and inventing the sphincterphone.

The *what*? Ah, a good story. . . .

Elektra Records West, under the direction of one David Anderle, had opened a secluded recording ranch on the Feather River in Northern California so that embryonic talents could have a relaxed environment in which to record and then, the script goes, think kindly enough of Elektra to sign with the company if the corporate faces smiled on their tapes. Sandy was the drummer in the ranch band. One night, bongos or congas were desperately desired for a particular song they were recording, but none were to be had, and it would've taken days to have anything shipped to their far-flung location. In a spectacular effort to please, Sandy took a pencil-thin snare drum microphone and inserted it into himself anally, beating out the required rhythm on his belly, after the engineer had jacked up the level and added appropriate echo. Not having been present on this historic occasion, I can offer only second-hand information, but I'm told Sandy didn't miss a beat. That was the birth of the sphincterphone. I've heard of putting your ass on the line for a gig, but Sandy, you're ridiculous!

Back at the Big Sur Folk Festival, they were offering Simon and Garfunkel, The Chambers Brothers, Judy Collins, yours truly, and Joan Baez and her sisters Mimi Farina and Pauline Marden (The Baez Brothers, as I was fond of calling them). The three-day hang-out climaxed with the afternoon of the actual performances, which attracted scene fixtures as diverse as Ralph J. Gleason and Bobby Neuwirth and tied it all together with a peace and love ambience that was much easier to believe in in those days.

The only loose end was Al "Not Quite the Life of the Party" Kooper, who wandered off into the woods to have a catatonic flashback. I must've been giving off rank vibes, because Judy Collins followed me into the woods and asked what was wrong. When I proved incapable of a reply, she took me by the hand and steered me back to my hotel room, where she then endured an all-night crying jag on my part. To her credit (and, I've no doubt, extreme discomfort), she was able to talk me down to a somewhat functional frame of mind—just another of the many Big Ones I owe Judy Collins. (I've glossed over the depths of my emotional traumas because, as I said before, that stuff is best left to soap operas. And besides, how can you take *anything* seriously scant paragraphs after reading about the sphincterphone?)

The next day I caught a ride to San Francisco and proceeded on to Berkeley. Sally Henderson (the sister of Jill, in whose Cambridge apartment I'd written "Flute Thing") was running the Jabberwock, the club where I'd first met Joan, and she booked me in and gave me room and board. I played solo for the first time since I'd joined The Blues Project; I almost felt like calling myself Al Casey.

Opening the show was another man in limbo at the time, Taj Mahal. I was familiar with Taj from an L.A. band he'd been in called The Rising Sons. He had a National steel guitar and he had the blues. He dispensed them in such a forthright manner that the stage would be smoking each night after he'd come off, and it took some severe rising to the occasion for me to hold my own on the bill with him. There was no Energy + Volume to save me or Blues Project to surround me to blast my way through this confontation. I played my Blues Project favorites and the new songs I was developing and, in retrospect, it was probably one hell of a show, historically speaking, for $3.50.

A nice gesture for history, perhaps, but monetary rewards from this venture weren't enough to sustain me for more than a few days. It was clearly time to face the music, both personally and professionally, back in New York. I caught the first available plane east. I had been gone ten weeks, and had pissed away in excess of

Backing up lovely Baez Brother Mimi Farina at the Big Sur Folk Festival.
(Photo: © John Byrne Cooke.)

two thousand dollars. I had barely enough money in my pockets to get myself home from the airport . . . *and I didn't even have a tan.*

1967-1968:

I arrived in New York, as best as I can recall, during the first week in July of 1967. On the plane ride home, I had constructed a scheme of complex proportions for:

1. Changing my environment
2. Getting some cash together for myself, alimony, and child support
3. Putting my dream band together

I got home and took inventory: no money, no Joanie, no gigs. My rat-infested apartment (I walked in the door from California, only to be greeted by the scurry of little feet) was a depressing base of operations. The one thing I had going for me was friends (not the furry, rodent kind, although some turned out to be more like that later on).

I got on someone's phone and called all my friends who were musicians. I talked Howard Solomon, the owner of Cafe Au Go Go, into giving me two nights there so

I could throw a benefit for *myself*. In retrospect, *this was even ballsier than crashing the Dylan session!* Then I called Judy Collins, Paul Simon, and Eric Andersen, among others, to ask them if they'd play for nothing as a favor so I could raise enough money to at least function for a couple of months. Well, everybody agreed to play and soon we had us a show. We advertised, peddled tickets at reasonable prices, and sold out in advance.

I decided to get a pickup group together 'cause now I'd gotten the fever and wanted to play at my own show. I got an advance from Howard Solomon and flew Jim Fielder in to play bass (he was all I had to show for that hunk of time spent in L.A.). Steve Katz knew of a good drummer, his close friend, Bobby Colomby, who had been playing backup for Eric Andersen and Odetta. Steve came to the first rehearsal to watch and ended up joining on guitar. We rehearsed about five days and worked up most of the new material I had written, plus my "hits" from the Project.

My plan was to take the proceeds from the gig, buy a one-way plane ticket to London, and put my band together there. I thought the change of scene would do me good, England was musically charismatic at that time, and I found it romantic to consider myself an "expatriate." Not a bad scheme, I thought; it looked great on paper and it had worked for Jimi Hendrix, P. J. Proby, and Scott Walker.

The shows went on, and it was incredible seeing Judy Collins, sweat pouring off her (as Howie's air conditioning rudely bit the bag the night she played), appearing in a small club again, showering her rekindled intimacy and perspiration on a loving audience. Everybody in the Village came down to play; there were jams and too many acts to even fit in at each show. It made me very proud and thankful that people can be so thoughtful and philanthropic. We stretched it out through a third night and then it was over.

Six sold-out shows: July 27, 28, and 29; two shows a night. That's eighteen hundred people at four dollars a head. You figure it out. So the next day, I'm sitting in Howie Solomon's office and he hands me a check for five hundred dollars. He says the rest went to expenses—paying the help, advertising, free admission to many "friends," and a thousand miscellaneous etceteras.

My shot was blown. I didn't even have enough for the *plane ticket*. I was stuck in New York, my lady had run off with another man, and after what everyone did for me at the benefit, there was no way I could dial a number in New York and say "please" or "could you" or even "what's happening?"

I was sitting in my apartment, well into a state of shock, when the doorbell rang and in marched Katz, Fielder, and Colomby. "Al, we heard what happened. But why don't you add horn players to our existing rhythm section? We already know how good it can sound, and Jim's offered to move permanently to New York."

Hmmmmmmmmm.

"Well," I said, mulling this one over. I couldn't realistically imagine rising to any great heights with Steve, who had tagged along and was, at best, an adequate guitarist. But there was virtually no choice. Right now, it was them or starve-o. "There is only one condition," I said. "I know exactly what I want to do, and in The Blues Project I was prevented from doing it because of majority rule. It's got to be set up in front that I'm the leader and will define the band's repertoire and arrangements and anything else to do with musical policies."

No hesitation.

"Oh yeah! Right on, Al baby."

I should have known better.

Bobby was the only one who had any links to horn players, because they hadn't played a role in the rest of our musical lives up to that point. Bobby said there was one guy from his neighborhood who was a local legend and had been Bobby's boyhood idol. His name was Fred Lipsius, and Bobby set about attempting to contact him.

Fred showed up at rehearsal a few days later, and I couldn't believe it. Sam Straight. Short hair, square clothes, the whole bit. Then he unpacked his alto and started playing and that was *it* for me. I didn't care what this guy looked like, he could play the fucking saxophone and make it cry f'chrissakes! We played him all my tunes, and he said he was in. Freddie was as sweet and innocent as anyone could possibly be, and a corruption process was essential. He'd *never* listened to rock 'n' roll; he was a hard-core jazzer, but had soul in huge doses. We used to force-feed him marijuana and make him listen to James Brown with headphones on. He got the picture, and pretty soon we had us a rockin' alto player.

Freddie was put in charge of recruiting the horn section and we devised a strategy for choosing the right members. Freddie and I wrote the initial arrangements together and purposely overwrote them. That is, we had the horns playing practically all the way through each song, and executing difficult passages a player might normally confront once in ten songs, in *every* song. We decided that anyone who could play these charts and still have any desire to be in the band (thinking he would have to do this every night) was OK in our book.

We held open auditions and went through quite a collection of characters. Schoolteachers, junkies, real old dudes, pimps, winos—it was an assortment of people we didn't normally spend a whole lot of time around. Horn players had been sadly neglected in the white rock 'n' roll business. Little did I know that this band would change all that.

While we were trying to find the right guys, I took the rhythm section into the studio and cut three demos to play for record companies in order to sell the band. I hired two trumpet players (studio musicians) and overdubbed them so that the final sound was us and four trumpets. We recorded "I Can't Quit Her," "My Days Are Numbered" (which are both featured on our first album), and "I Need to Fly," a song I cowrote with a friend named Tony Powers. The overall effect was surprisingly close to our goal, and certainly indicative of what someone could expect to get if they purchased us.

We needed $40,000 to keep the band alive while an album was in progress, and a humanistic relationship with our next corporate fathers, unlike the lack of affinity we initially got from MGM-Verve with The Blues Project. The forty Gs turned off Jerry Wexler at Atlantic (they were not known for gambling large sums of monies on embryonic talent), although I must say he was into the music. Mo Ostin of Warner Brothers came over to (or should I say braved) my ratpad to listen to the demos, but his follow-up from California seemed apathetic.

Bill Gallagher at Columbia and his soon-to-be successor, Clive Davis, were real interested. They had attended the Monterey Pop Festival and were now turned on to the dollar potential of the alternative market. Clive set up a luncheon date for the two of us. I met him in his office at CBS. I was real scruffy, rather wild-looking, and a true test of any executive's desire to sign the band was if they would dare to appear in public with me. Clive seemed unfazed by the prospect, and we adjourned down the block to the Hickory House, a pencil-pushers' steak haven on West 52nd Street. I had asked that we go somewhere where I could order eggs, because, although it was *his* lunchtime, it was *my* breakfast time. We were ushered in and seated immediately. Along came one of those inevitable waiters-with-an-accent cartoons, who handed us menus and waited for our order. I didn't see any kind of eggs on the menu, and I could immediately see that this was gonna be trouble. I mentioned as much to Clive and suggested going somewhere else, but he must have had a piece of the place or something 'cause he wouldn't budge.

"Just tell the waiter what you'd like," he said.

Here goes nothin', I thought to myself.

"Can I have three eggs over medium, buttered whole-wheat toast, and a large milk?" I said to the waiter.

"*Escargot?*" he says, trying to figure what this long-haired weirdo is talking about. I recited the order slowly once again, and he was even more confused. I flashed an "I told you so" look Clive's way. Clive, ever eager to sign a new band, leapt from his seat and, while I was wondering if I could quietly slip under the table, he grabbed the waiter's jacket collar with both hands and screamed, *"He wants three eggs over medium with buttered toast and a glass of milk!"*

I didn't get the whole-wheat toast, but we signed with Columbia anyway.

During this time period we were all burdened with the number one teen crisis in America—the draft. Uncle Sam was extremely interested in quite a few of his musician nephews and a Master Plan needed to be concocted. At this time, approximately one out of every five "visitors" to an army physical was attempting to get out of serving, and as the war escalated and more bodies were needed overseas, the recruiters became wiser to the "tricks of the afraid." The most important ammunition for a draft-dodger at a physical was a letter from a psychiatrist that waxed imperative about the lack of mental stability of the person presenting the note. This was an essential plank in the Master Plan. Then one had to begin a transformation that began a week prior to said physical:

- If you were thin, it was important to eat as little as possible that week. If you tilted toward obesity, gluttony was suggested.
- Changing clothes (including undergarments and socks) was verboten that week, as was actually removing said garments. This exempted bathing, tooth-brushing, use of deodorants, etc. Judicious use of hair-spray was encouraged, however.
- Sleeping was frowned upon and drug intake was expected to increase from one hundred to three hundred percent in that week.

All these instructions had to be carried out to the letter if the inductee was to have *any* chance of escaping Uncle Sam's long arm. The final phase of the Master Plan took place the night before your physical. This was a tradition that supplanted the bachelor or stag party in the mid-sixties.

The victim would hold open-house that night and all his concerned friends could gain admittance by drug contributions or expert advice. If you had ten joints, three hits of speed, or had taken the physical more than twice and knew special stuff, you were most welcome. Our operation was smooth, professional, and, finally, claimed a one hundred percent success rate. Not one of our enrollees had served in the military and all had been classified 4F except yours truly.

My first instinct had been to take my preinduction physical with my psychiatrist's note only. I figured my ulcer would get me out because it definitely would have recoiled in horror from a typical day's cuisine in said Army. So I followed my first instinct and forwent the excessive drug-taking and nonchanging of clothes, etc.—and wound up with a plump 1A classification, fit for service and ready to ship overseas! This meant that at any moment I could receive my orders to report for an induction physical. That's the one where you show up with your toothbrush and a picture of your gal, and if you pass, you're on a bus to Fort-Something-or-Other that very afternoon without benefit of actually going back home again. *Big difference from a PREinduction physical.* Soooo, needless to say, when my notice to report for my induction physical arrived, I was shitting in my pants.

Now let me qualify my comments: I was against the war in Viet Nam, but also felt that, if someone wanted to be patriotic and serve their country, it was their privilege to do so. For the rest of us, though, I was against being forced to attend these Asian festivities. After all, that's what freedom is all about. Time has shown that it was a morally bereft war, and that our country gained nothing but a body count as a result of it. I look at it as the end of an era, and a black mark on America's already blemished record. Nowadays, wholesale aggression may still go on as a matter of foreign policy, but many more questions are asked before we commit the lives of our young men and women to some battleground halfway across the planet.

Okay—those are my politics, for better or worse, and we now continue on with our story.

The government was calling my bluff and wanted me to go to Viet Nam. No way. Not even on a USO tour. I wanted a scarlet letter and number 4F tattooed on my forehead, so there was no question about my stance. So I began the Master Plan in earnest. I got my shrink note, and chose my wardrobe for my morning of reckoning. I selected black boots, black socks, black pants, a nice black shirt, black underwear, and a bulky New Jersey police officer's jacket (as a nice touch of irony) for my uniform de jour. I slept in the coat with all my clothes on for the prescribed week (it was cold in my apartment, anyway). The night before Draft Morning we all convened at Steve Katz's apartment in the Village (he had finally moved out of his folks' place and was ready to host social gatherings).

This was, as a unit invoking the Master Plan, our first *induction* physical and a serious, urgent note hung in the air. I think it was F#. Seriously, I smoked about forty joints that night, chainsmoked a few hash-oil bombers, and at 5 a.m., one hour before I was due to report, dropped a massive amount of speed. The intended effect was: totally incoherent and yet completely wired.

The sun had not even risen as Bobby Colomby's car came to a halt in front of the induction center on Whitehall Street in lower Manhattan. Suddenly, after a night of sincere bonding camaraderie, I found myself incredibly alone in front of this federal monolith. It was cold, dark, and scary.

I walked inside to the main gathering room. I sat down on a bench and I must say that, as the room became more and more crowded, that bench remained entirely mine.

Preparing for my army physical while predating Richard Ashcroft by thirty years for the "Best Scooped-Out Cheeks" award. (Photo: Alice Ochs.)

☺☺

The stench on that bench repelled all sects, religions, and lifestyles. Nobody got within ten feet of me without altering their course, pronto.

So far, so good.

An officer called out everyone's name and dispatched each contestant to various testing rooms. I ignored my assignment and headed straight for the psychiatrist's office on the second floor. This was part of the Master Plan. Immediate disobedience. There I sat waiting for my man. It was now 7 a.m. and a first had occurred. The shrink was *not in.* This scenario was *not* in the Master Plan. I would have to improvise now.

Various brass would come over to me from time to time and say, "You can't sit there all morning, son. You've got to take your physical sometime today!" I just stared at them wide-eyed and speedy and, along with my bouquet, I felt no words were necessary. I sat there for *three* hours dodging removal requests left and right. Finally, the shrink arrived.

"Message for you, SIR!" I said snapping to attention and saluting smartly after handing him my psychiatrist's note. I gave him the envelope and he didn't even read it! He kinda held it up to the light to make sure something was in it.

"Alright son. While I'm reading this, go and take your physical," he said, then walked into his office and slammed the door.

By then the speed was beginning to wear off, and the lack of sleep in the last week was catching up with me. I was viewing everything through a kind of yellow haze. I was completely vulnerable and gooned out. I would've joined the Marines if they put the proper papers in front of me to sign at that moment. Some sergeant type walked me through the physical and I couldn't believe I was participating without screaming and making a scene. In fact, I was being a nice guy! My twisted mind could only see the end of the physical and a nice warm bed somewhere. I had lost sight of that toothbrush and the bus that was gonna take me away. I walked through the physical and ended up back at the shrink's office. I finally snapped back to the reality and urgency of my situation. A pivotal scene:

> **Shrink:** Sit down, Mr. Kooper [he does]. I am none too fond of your appearance today, Alan. You know that reporting to an Army physical is akin to showing up for a job interview. You wouldn't show up for a job you wanted dirty and unshaven and dressed like this, would you, Mr. Kooper?
>
> **Mr. Kooper:** Ah . . . well, uhh . . . fact of the matter is, uh, sir, that I was out so late last night I had to come right down here without the luxury of returning home, sir, to shower and shave. I didn't want to be late or anything like *that*, sir. . . .
>
> **Shrink:** [Caught in Mr. Kooper's game now and doesn't even know it] Well, if you were truly responsible, you wouldn't have stayed out so late last night, would you, Alan? [Pause for effect] Yes . . . uhh . . . I've read your doctor's letter here. Are you currently being treated by this Dr. Schmutz [not his real name]?
>
> **Mr. Kooper:** Oh yeah—three times a day . . . errrr . . . a week, I mean. Sorry, sir.
>
> **Shrink:** Well, if you continue therapy with him, perhaps we can see you

in a year and see how you are doing then. . . .

Mr. Kooper: [Incredulous that it was this easy; getting more than a little uninhibited and nuts] Well, sir, point taken. But ya know, I'd really like to go over there and kill all those bastards for ya, I really would, ya see. It's just that. . . .

Shrink: [Sighing loudly now]

Mr. Kooper: [At full speed] Seeee, I just don't have time to go over there now. I'm in a band and people are just starting to like it. I've been working all my life toward this, ya see. It's my big chance. After we make it and make all the money and fuck all the women, I'll be back here. You just wait and see. [Patriotic music begins in the background] You won't have to remind me by mail either. [Raising voice] WITH A CLEAN SHOWERED APPEARANCE, SIR! A SHAVE. A SUIT. A TIE. I'M NOT FUCKIN' AROUND EITHER, SIR. . . . YOU CAN. . . .

Shrink: [Interrupting; red-faced] MR. KOOPER!!! PLEEEEEEASE!!! I said we won't take you at this time but we WILL recall you. [Rises] Thank you and good afternoon!

Mr. Kooper: [Rising fast and snapping to attention with a smart salute] Thank you, sir!!! [Continuing as he heads toward the door] I won't forget this, sir. We'll put your name on the album, sir [we didn't]. I'll send you a copy, sir, I won't forget [I did]. God bless you, sir!
[Fade in]:

Mr. Kooper: [Skipping the light fandango down the street, doing cartwheels 'cross the floor with a *huge* grin on his face looking for a pay phone. Finally finding one, dials and delivers sotto voce] Bobby??? I'm at the corner of . . . uhhh . . . Grand and Whitehall. Come and take my exhausted ass home. It was a real close call. I'll tell ya when ya get here. HURRY!!!!!
[Fade out]

After myriad auditions, the lineup of the band was firm: Steve, Bobby, Jimmy, Freddie, and me, plus Randy Brecker and Jerry Weiss (trumpets and flugelhorns), and Dick Halligan (trombone).

The experiment even had a name. One particular night, Jimi Hendrix, B.B. King, myself, and an unidentified drummer and bass player were going at it all night at the Cafe Au Go Go. (The Go Go, Steve Paul's Scene, and Generation—a new club on Eighth Street—were all in competition, even over who would have the best after-hours jams.) At daybreak, when we finished playing, they put the house lights

Passing the buck in the original BS&T, 1967. (Left to right) Steve Katz, Jim Fielder, Jerry Weiss, Fred Lipsius, Bobby Colomby, Dick Halligan, Randy Brecker (accepting buck), Mr. Flower Power. (Photo: Don Hunstein—Al Kooper Collection.).

on and somebody observed: "Christ! Look at the organ! There's blood all over the keyboard!" Sure enough, I had cut my hand playing, and in the state of bliss induced by my compatriots' sound had not felt a thing. What a great album cover, I thought. No. What a great name for a band. *Blood, Sweat & Tears*—and *that* was *that*.

We then began serious rehearsals in a two-platoon system. I would rehearse the rhythm section, and Freddie would put the horn players through their paces at separate workouts. Every three days we would rehearse the whole band together, see how the pieces fit, and polish it until it shone. After six weeks of intense preparation, we were ready to whip it on y'all.

On November 18, 1967, we debuted at the Au Go Go, opening the show for Moby Grape. The horns had not yet fully memorized their parts, so our roadies built a giant music stand to set out in front of them. A first for rock, no doubt. The place was packed with press and Moby Grape fans. I've always felt that some people are sitting there just itching for you to fall on your ass, and that's where the *real* drama comes from. Not whether you're good, but rather whether you somehow trip and stumble in some hopefully dramatic fashion. Whatever they expected, we played a burning set right down their throats. No mistakes. And all new material that no one had heard before. That's hard for an audience to digest, but we pulled it off. After it was over, I was *not* the only one with tears in his eyes backstage. The band was off the ground and it looked like it was gonna fly! We went uptown a few nights later and played at Steve Paul's Scene club for Thanksgiving week and tightened up enough to get rid of the music stands.

I decided to ask John Simon, the guy who produced *Bookends* for Simon and Garfunkel, to produce our album. I had played "I Can't Quit Her" for John when I first wrote it, and he said if I ever recorded the song, he'd like to produce it. Well, I was ready. We needed a producer who knew *music*, and unfortunately there weren't too many around that fit that description.

John came to hear us live, loved it and signed on. We had a producer, and we were almost ready for the studio. John took us in one day and had us cut all our material live, one take each, just to use as reference. (Portions of that session are available on the Sony gold disk version of the first BS&T compact disk—number CK 64214.) He and I then spent the next two weeks at his house, playing the tape and editing the material in such a way that it would make some kind of sense on a phonograph record. He would say, "That trumpet part there is shit. It's gonna have to go." I'd say, "Well, what have you got that's better?" Then we'd kick it around until the right part developed. When it did, we both knew it.

John picked what songs went on the album. They weren't necessarily the ones I would've picked, but I needed to step outside of the situation anyway. I was not keen on "I Can't Quit Her" (which turned out to be one of the most popular) or "My Days Are Numbered," which were both taxing to my limited vocal capabilities, but John got them on the record and coaxed the best vocals that were possible out of me.

Meanwhile, I was churning out newer material. One night I finished a song that knocked me on my ass. Where most of my songs were blues-influenced and drew on fairly obvious roots from my background, this new one was strangely original. It had its own feeling and owed nothing to anything in my record collection. I called every-one in the band up and urged them over to my house to hear the new composition.

When my audience was assembled, I played it to them and they loved it.

"What are you gonna do with it though, Al?" said Bobby Colomby.

"I wanna put it on the album. It says a lot about my growth as a writer, and I'd like people to pick up on that," I responded with typical naiveté.

"But the band can't—I mean horns and drums would fuck that song up. We can't do it on the album," countered a quasi-diplomatic Colomby.

I got trouble here, I'm thinkin' to myself.

"I want to do it by myself. Maybe with ten or twelve strings or something. It'll give the record some variety and a change of pace."

Pause. Then Bobby again. "But that wouldn't be *the band*, Al. It's not what *the band* is."

That was it. I lost my temper and my cool.

"Look. We made a deal, or did you forget? It's my band. But that's not even what I'm talking about. I'm a member of the band. So if I step out on one track out of eleven, it's still the band 'cause I'm *in* the fucking band. If Randy played some incredible improvisations with just a string chart behind him, I'd put it on our album. The only difference would be that we couldn't perform *one* song from the album live. Isn't 'Yesterday' credited to the Beatles? Big fucking deal."

Now Bobby was mad.

"There's no way that song is going on the album and that's it!"

He exited with the band members at his heels. The next day it was dumped into John Simon's lap for mediation. He slept on it and two days later called to tell me it was thumbs up in my direction. We would use twelve strings, and in the interest of budget, John would write the arrangement. The song was called "The Modern Adventures of Plato, Diogenes, and Freud." It was a stream of consciousness lyric about this disciple of Timothy Leary I had encountered who was a psychatrist, used drugs in his sessions, and had sexual relations with his women patients. The decision to include the song on the album was the first step in my departure from the band, only I wasn't aware of it at the time.

Another song which I had just finished, "I Love You More Than You'll Ever Know," was a split tribute to Otis Redding and James Brown. (The lyrics were a nod to Otis's song "I Love You More Than Words Can Say," and the melody was "reminiscent" of James Brown's "It's a Man's World.") On December 6 ('67), Otis died in a plane crash and it really fucked me up. The next night we began recording the album. I insisted we record "I Love You" first. Nobody objected. We put down a blistering track, and it looked like this was gonna be an easy album to make. We overdubbed Freddie's solo and Steve's fills, and then it was time to put a vocal on it. Everyone was real jumpy 'cause on the reference tape, where I sang live while the whole band played, my vocal performance had been a little shaky (to put it mildly). Now, everyone (including me) was concerned that the addition of my nickel throat might fuck up this hundred-dollar track. I was prepared for this tension, however; I had learned the first few lines of the song in French. So they lowered the lights, and everyone was hanging out in the control room. I was out in the studio with headphones on ready to sing. They started recording, and the room was all tensed up. It came time for my first line, and I sang it in French: "*Si je te quitterais.*"

Everyone was hysterical and they stopped the tape.

"Ohhh, you wanted me sing it in ENGLISH??? Ohhh . . . sorry . . . okay then, take two."

That loosened everybody up, and we started again. Now my eyes were screwed shut, and I was thinkin' about Otis and this sounds clichéd as hell, but it's true. I was saying to myself, "This is for you." And I was singing. One take. They called me into the booth for a playback, and everyone was smiling. I listened to it. It wasn't great and it wasn't awful, but no one could say it wasn't *real*. The one thing I had going for me was that I *believed* the words of every song I had to sing. If I picked somebody else's song, it was because I was moved emotionally by it.

I sang Randy Newman's "Just One Smile." I got that from *Gene Pitney* of all people; it was on one of his early albums. (He did a great job on it.) I picked "Without Her" by Harry Nilsson, my favorite "outside" song at the time. I had a 45 of it that was just about worn out. I had no idea who the guy was, but the baroque arrangement and superb voice did me in. The words were entirely relatable. I turned it into a bossa nova. Later, the song would become a standard, and such hippies as Jack Jones and Herb Alpert would record their own renditions of it. "So Much Love" was a Carole King-Gerry Goffin tune that I'd heard covered by Percy Sledge and Ben E. King. I did a lot of rewriting on it (changed the words in the second verse, left out half the bridge, and changed the melody to the second half of the bridge), and my arrangement was considerably different from the original. Amazingly, at the same time we were recording in New York, Dusty Springfield was in Memphis and by chance cut "So Much Love" and "Just One Smile" on her album *Dusty in Memphis.* That album was produced by Jerry Wexler, who had previously heard our band's repertoire and passed. Coincidence? Perhaps. . . .

Steve needed another song to sing, so I suggested Tim Buckley's "Morning Glory." Freddie and I wrote a Bob Dylan-Curtis Mayfield (not-so-strange bedfellows) arrangement, and Steve loved it. He wrote a little ditty called "Meagan's Gypsy Eyes," which was about his *brief* relationship with Mimi Farina, though he named it after Alice Ochs's daughter. Freddie, Steve, and Bobby wrote the arrangement of that one. John rented this weird organ (an Allen Explorer) from Carroll

Music for me to play, and it gave this song quite an individual sound.

When Steve was putting the vocal on, we convinced him to hold his Adam's apple between his thumb and forefinger and shake it up and down to simulate fast tremolo on a guitar amp. In truth, it was mostly just to see him standing in the studio all by himself shaking his Adam's apple up and down and singing. We were all in hysterics in the control room. So much laughing, in fact, that I had a lunatic flash and quickly snuck into the studio on all fours and tackled him from behind in the middle of one of his vocals. He didn't think that was too funny.

I wrote another song which was sort of a tongue-in-cheek paean to life in the woods called "House in the Country." I wrote this in Bucks County, Pennsylvania, on the set of a movie in which I was making my acting debut. The film folded after six days of shooting, but I got a good song out of the experience.

The horn introduction to that song was extremely high-pitched. It was difficult to record as the boys had to contort their faces to hit some of the higher notes, but they got it inside of an hour. A few days after that, we were overdubbing percussion on that track, and working with an assistant engineer who was filling in for our regular guy, Lou Waxman. Part of Lou's job was to run the tape machines, making sure the right tracks were in record and playback. So Bobby was in the studio with headphones and a tambourine, and John said "OK, roll it." The tape started rolling, but we didn't hear anything. *Not a good sign.* All of a sudden this middle-aged engineer jumped up and slammed the machine off. Like a deranged player out of *Othello*, he paced up and down screaming, "Oh my God! Oh my God!"

John and I were looking helplessly at each other, trying to figure out if he had erased the whole song or what. John played it back to check and it turned out the engineer had erased the horns from that really hard beginning part. The guy was having a nervous breakdown all the while. It was a drag, but it wasn't a disaster. It just meant an hour's work some other day. Once we established this fact, you'd think the guy would cool out or somethin'. Nope. He was going bananas. By then, all John and I could do was laugh at this guy. He phoned for a replacement and went home in a state of shock.

As the album neared completion, we brought in a string section to spice up some of the songs and put the backup on my solo song. We decided to have an overture on the record, and John and I wrote a satiric medley based on themes from all of the songs. I'm not sure, but I think we had the first rock record with an overture. It was certainly the first with an underture.

We recorded the overture and it sounded legit, which was far from our intentions. John asked Bobby, who had this ridiculous laugh, to laugh all the way through the tune (one minute and thirty-two seconds), so people would know for sure that we weren't serious. Bobby went in, started laughing and discovered that it's not as easy as it might sound. His peculiar laugh was very high-intensity, and he could only get about fifteen seconds on tape at a time. So we kept backtracking until, about an hour later, we had a complete track of Bobby's insane laughter.

After laughing hysterically for over an hour, he walked into the control room out of breath. His face was sort of an iridescent green color as he sat down on the couch. We listened to the playback and everyone was howling along with his laugh track. As the playback ended, Bobby leaned over and threw up, then fell asleep on the couch for the rest of the night. He had OD'd on laughter. Probably the first such casualty in recording history.

To get atmosphere for the opening and closing of "House in the Country" we needed some down-home ambience; a pastoral setting to complement the song's theme. We took a poll and found out that, among ourselves, we could imitate a number of woodsy animals! We filled up eight tracks with Bobby the frog, Freddie the bird, Al the goat 'n' goose, and Steve the horse. It actually achieved that country feeling, but it was hard to keep from breaking up while we were doing it. I kept thinking to myself, "Grown men are doing this!" Then we got a bunch of our friends' kids to sing at the end, highlighted by Bobby Colomby's nephew, who looked at everyone coaxing him to sing and blurted out, "*I don't wanna!*" We kept *that* on the record. From the first note of "I Love You More Than You'll Ever Know" to the last mix of "So Much Love" took a grand total of two weeks. On December 22, 1967, exactly two weeks after we began, we finished our first album just in time to take a break to celebrate the holidays.

Still we had no title and no cover idea. Initially, we wanted to call it *How I Spent My Summer Vacation*, and even went so far as to shoot a cover in various summer-fun regalia. It proved too silly for the album's contents, however. I racked my brain for weeks until I came up with an interesting idea. There was a semifamous poster of a Telly Savalas-looking fellow with a freshly lit cigarette sitting with a young boy in short pants on his lap. The lad has his exact face, a minor photo retouch, but extremely effective in that setting. The photo was shot by one of my idols, Alfred Gescheidt, one of the deans of darkroom technique in trick photography.

At my insistence, Bob Cato, Columbia's art director, put in a call to Gescheidt, but he was unavailable. What we did then was to duplicate the poster idea of the man and boy using the members of the band sitting with little children on our laps. Later each child's face was replaced by the face of the person whose lap they occupied. The album was then called *Child Is Father to the Man*. Bob Cato shot the cover himself, but the credit on the album reads: "Cover Photo by Bob Cato apres Al Gescheidt." Credit where credit is due. In later years, the Man/Boy Love Society used the . . . oh, just kidding!

By this time, after surviving many personal crises, Joan and I had decided to marry quietly at City Hall. The clergyman who performed the ceremony lisped, and I confess I laughed through the entire vows. Not a good start. The deed was done, however, and life chugged on.

The album came out to fairly good reviews, and Columbia sent us on a ten-city promotional tour. We played to the press of each city and talked on countless radio stations about ourselves and our new album. In San Francisco, Bill Graham put us in Winterland trapped in a staggering show: Jeremy & The Satyrs, James Cotton, and Cream. We held our own and got good reviews. The Family Dog headlined us the next week at the Avalon, with John Handy and Son House as support, and we did good business. *Rolling Stone* covered the gig and gave us a three-page spread with photos.

I remember one night in Boston we'd finished gigging early and had all returned to the hotel. Joan had joined the tour that day. It was only 11 p.m. or so, neither of us was tired, and we were in a mischievous mood. Bobby Colomby's room was across the hall, so I walked across and listened at his door. He was sweet-talking a young lady in his inimitable fashion, and I silently laughed as I listened to his secret persuasions. After awhile, it became quiet. I gave them about ten minutes to develop their new relationship before bludgeoning Bobby's door.

"Who's there?"

"Police. Open up in there!!" I gruffly hollered, as Joan strolled across the hall with her new Polaroid camera.

"Just a minute," Bobby stalled, to the sounds of intense rustling from inside his room. Finally, the door opened and Bobby appeared in his shirt, with one leg in his pants and two out. FLASH! went the Polaroid. Hysterical went Joan and I as we collapsed laughing in the hallway.

Bobby took it pretty well until I recited his seduction rap of the past hour verbatim. Red-faced, he pulled me into the bathroom.

"*This* is the only way I can show you how embarrassed I am," he said, plunging his naked foot completely into the toilet and flushing it continuously.

After he regained his composure, he decided it was a great joke, and shouldn't we try it on Steve? This time Bobby would call ahead to Steve's room and warn him that the police were ransacking everyone's room. Then I would hammer on his door. Give it a little more credibility.

Bobby on the phone: "Steve. I'm glad I got you. I can't really talk much but the cops are going through everyone's room, and they've got search warrants and they're being really vicious and I don't—"

Mr. and Mrs. Samuel Kooper were proud to announce the marriage of their son, Alan, to a Fender Telecaster covered with decals. The honeymoon was soon to be over. BS&T, Winterland, San Francisco, 1968. (Photo: © Jim Marshall. Used with permission.)

BAM! BAM! BAM!

Steve on the phone: "Oh my god they're here, gotta go!"

Steve must have been *truly* terrified, because he was rooming with one of the horn players who was the biggest doper in the band. He must have flushed half of Mexico down the toilet in about three seconds. He then came to the door, opened it, and FLASH! Another shot for my growing Polaroid collection. This time I was in tears I was laughing so hard, crawling down the hallway, leaving Steve talking to the wall: "That's the meanest shit I've ever seen. . . ." It was, actually.

Flushed with our success, we sorted out the vulnerable ones in the band for our caper, and all of them got their pictures taken that night. If the Polaroids hadn't faded, they would have made a great album cover.

Just to balance out the karma, the band repaid me the next day. We were flying from Boston to Chicago, and the group was gathered at the gate half an hour before departure time. I was sitting there in the cheap faux fur coat I had bought for the winter and this weird moustache I had grown for the tour. The stares were a little heavier than usual, it being proper Boston and all that. Bobby came over with his carry-on bag and asked if I'd watch it for him while he went to the magazine stand. Sure. Then came Steve with the same request. Pretty soon I was surrounded by everyone's luggage, all by myself in this stupid coat and moustache, and everyone walking by was breaking up that this weird looking asshole was traveling with twenty-seven pieces of luggage. They were now *even* with me.

In St. Louis, we had to cancel the gig 'cause I lost my voice, and Columbia wanted me in shape for the more important San Francisco and L.A. dates. We signed some autographs at the place we were supposed to play and made it back to the hotel. Don Johnston, our roadie, Jerry Weiss, and I were in my room, spacing out on how boring St. Louis was at 11:00 p.m. on a Tuesday night.

"Let's escape!" I hoarsely suggested. "We're gonna fly to 'Frisco in the morning, so why don't we just fly out tonight and not tell anyone."

We called the airport and, sure enough, there was a 2:45 a.m. nonstop with three empty seats calling our names. We packed our shit and snuck out without anyone in the band seeing us. A definite caper.

There was only one other passenger on the flight, an old lady in first class. The stewardesses turned out to be hip and not at all hard to look at. It was not long before we were getting high and necking. It was surrealistic. These things do not happen on commercial flights (and never will again, if I'm any judge).

We landed in 'Frisco about 5:45 a.m. and deplaned, carrying (concealed) about half the equipment, cargo, and miniature booze bottles they had on board, courtesy of our new "girlfriends." The prize possession was the battery-operated emergency bullhorn, which Don Johnston won from his fair damsel (and which was later to get us nearly kicked out of our hotel for disturbing the other occupants when Don called the band to quarters at 4:00 a.m.).

While we were waiting for our real luggage, Jerry Weiss was leaning against the wall trying to adjust to this new life-style. Quite a difference from pushing up a horn in the back row of Larry Elgart's dance band like he used to do before he met Freddie Lipsius. Jerry just kept saying over and over, "It didn't happen. I can't believe it!"

The bags came and we jumped in a taxi and headed for the hotel. No sooner did we pull away from the curb than the driver turned around and asked, "Anyone want to get high?" That was it for Jerry. New Yorkers aren't used to such mellowness, especially in the traditional armored attack vehicle known as the taxi. He didn't ever wanna leave California.

Back in St. Louis, meanwhile, "the great escape" had been easily ascertained. Noting the absence of our luggage, no one was uptight; they knew we were in California. But they sho' was jealous when they got there and heard about our pie-in-the-sky!

We returned from the tour with a developing reputation and an album entering the charts. It was decided that we needed to tighten up, so we took up residence at the Garrick Theater (adjoining the Cafe Au Go Go) following The Mothers, who had concluded a *six-month* stint there. I was hoping we wouldn't stay quite so long as they did. The Mothers moved downstairs to the Au Go Go, and The Electric Flag moved in across the street at the Bitter End. B. B. King opened a week at the Generation Club, and you'd best believe the Village was jumpin'. In between sets, along with the Flag, we would catch The Mothers. The Flag weren't able to catch our show and vice versa as we were all on the same schedule.

When our last show ended, however, B. B. King's started. We used to finish up and catch the tail end of his set. I sat in his dressing room after the show, renewing a friendship with one of the most sincere, incredible human beings ever to set foot on the planet. I told him about the new band, and we figured out that his schedule made it impossible for him to catch us. He was real interested in hearing us, though, so I put on my thinking cap.

The next night, when B. B. finished his last set, BS&T was "in the house." They closed the club doors and we hopped onstage to play an after-hours set for B. B. and the employees of Generation. We played about forty-five minutes and before our closer began, I invited B. B. to join us onstage. It was "Somethin' Goin' On," a tune I'd written in the style of B. B. King. We played up to the guitar solo and then dropped the volume way down and B. B. played, building slowly to his inevitable climax. As the horns eased in behind him, he took a step forward and *really* began to play.

Obviously inspired, he played things I had never heard him or any other guitar play-er play before. He was rocking from side to side smiling, and as each verse ended, I yelled out, "Don't stop now, Bee," and he was up and away again. After ten minutes he took it down, and the band and the audience went nuts. Even if we had had the foresight to record it, I don't think anyone would've believed it. Elvin Bishop was in the audience and he later concurred that, indeed, it was the best he remembered ever hearing B. B. play. It was ten minutes of sheer ecstasy I will never forget.

The seeds of discontent, however, had been sown, and it was only a matter of time before they blossomed. In The Blues Project, we had done everything togeth-er. Knowing such behavior did not solidify group unity, I attempted the opposite with BS&T. I only hung with the band at rehearsals or gigs, preferring the confines of home and the company of Joan, wife number two. The formation of the band had a stabilizing effect on my previous mental aberrations, and my subsequent abandonment of drugs made me the straightest one in the band (although certainly not the straightest looking).

I thought all this would improve my relationship with the various members of the band, hopefully delaying overkill for at least a year. But while I was busy keep-ing to myself, the band was forming into various little political pockets (the Colomby-Katz faction most notably), and musical revolution was in the air. The failure of my voice to endure on the tour had caused concern and, unbeknownst to yours truly, plans were afoot to change all that.

One of my founding concepts was that Freddie Lipsius and I would write an arrangement, and the band would be asked to play it in its entirety one time to my satisfaction before any suggestions were offered. At that point I could take sug-gestions, and usually did. I will admit I ran my dream a *little* Hitleresque (witness Jeff Lynne and ELO), but I was trying to prevent it from becoming a disorganized nightmare.

The true beginning of the end came at rehearsal one day. Freddie and I had writ-ten an arrangement of Stevie Winwood's "Dear Mr. Fantasy," to be played for the first time that day. I double-checked the parts as I handed them out and was sur-prised to find they had been altered from what Freddie and I had arranged. Bobby had taken the liberty of changing the parts without bothering to ask anyone. Freddie and I had spent at least six hours on that arrangement, but our work had been erased and there was no way we would be able to hear it. I walked out of that rehearsal, furious. I suppose Bobby was trying to show me what life was like under *my* rule, but I didn't get the hint. Also, I couldn't help thinking back to the day we decided to form the band. My contingency for going along with it was that it would be under my guidance and leadership, and Bobby had readily agreed.

I suppose the final spark that incited the mutiny was my growing dissatisfaction with Steve's progress as a player. I felt he was holding the band back from some incredible musical pyrotechnics. I went around to each member separately and suggested that Steve be replaced. To a man I was turned down cold. Of course, I wasn't aware that *my* offing was in the cards; I just assumed they didn't want to upset the delicate balance that was holding the band together. So I could keep basically honest, I approached Steve and told him what I had done. Instead of calmly taking it in, or interpreting it as a rather crude instructional criticism of his playing, he went nuts.

The next day a band meeting was hastily held at our lawyer's, who happened to be Steve's brother (nepotism I was too blind to consider). Before we could even come to verbal blows, Randy Brecker took the floor and announced he had been offered the trumpet chair in Horace Silver's group, and he thought he was gonna take it. Silver was a top-flight jazz pianist and composer, who led an extremely influential quintet at the time. Bobby freaked out and filibustered in an attempt to talk him out of it. Randy's loss to the band would be a heavy one. Even so, I defended his position on a growth basis. Horace had never hired a white trumpet player in his group before, and so Randy would be participating in history. What an honor!

Horace had been one of my boyhood idols, and I also knew Randy would be happier with the comparative freedom of expression he could find in that situation. Randy was a genius player, but you can't force a man one way when his mind is made up the other. Bobby sat down, exasperated. There were cracks in his ship even *he* hadn't anticipated.

Then the shit hit the band. Bobby said he felt we should hire a lead singer because of my limited voice capabilities and my voice's lack of tour endurance, and I should be relegated to organist and composer/arranger. He was totally prepared in his support. I was certainly aware I was not one of rock's trendsetting vocalists, yet I was at least as good at what I did as Steve was at what he did. But I guess they wanted a new singer more than I wanted a new guitarist. I was heartbroken as I left the meeting, 'cause I knew the dream was over.

It was heavy drama at the Garrick that night. All of us knew it was over, but we didn't know when it was gonna come to final blows. We played a tense first set, culminating in Jerry Weiss telling me, "Go fuck yourself," right in the middle of the encore. It knocked the air out of me. I called everyone into the dressing room as soon as we got offstage.

"OK," I said, "you don't want me in the band, you don't want to play the tunes I choose, and I don't want you to suffer working with me. I'll go away and make

Canadian singer David Clayton-Thomas finds out he's been accepted to replace Kooper in Blood, Sweat & Tears. (Photo: Alice Ochs.)

my music elsewhere. Anybody who wants to join me is welcome, because you win—I quit. I'm sorry it had to end like this." And I was out the door.

As I rounded the corner, I heard Bobby saying, "Can't you see what he's trying to do . . .?" and I realized that it would be impossible for me to be in a group again. Because, simply, I wasn't trying to do *anything*. I just did what came naturally to me, and to be resented for it caused me to retire from participating in the world of bands until 1991, when I hesitantly put The Rekooperators together. That band has outlasted both The Blues Project and BS&T by four years and still counting.

Returning to 1968: I ran into Freddie in the men's room. He was real down and disillusioned. He said he was gonna go back to school. "No," I said. "Stay with 'em. They need you to hold the band together if it can, indeed, survive me and Randy leaving."

Freddie did stay on, and everyone knows the rest of the story. With David Clayton-Thomas to replace me as singer, and Dick Halligan to cover my organ playing, with half a new repertoire, a new horn section, and a new producer (James William Guercio), they went on to set trends and records in the music business. I was proud when their next album hit number one. Even though I received no financial interest, I knew where it had all begun. God bless you, Maynard Ferguson. I had lived in my musical Camelot. It only lasted eight months, however, shot down from a grassy knoll by "Lee Harvey" Colomby.

In an interview on the Web recently, like one of the characters in Akira Kurosawa's *Rashomon*, Colomby imaginatively recalled the origins of Blood, Sweat & Tears. Quoting Bobby directly:

> "Steve (Katz) and I discussed the merits of Al's songwriting (thieving) and I asked Steve to ask Al if we could use some of his material in a band we were going to start [AK: I guess Bobby liked "thieving" in his choice of material!]....I received a call from Steve telling me that not only did Al agree that we could use his songs...BUT that Steve asked Al to join the band as its lead singer...."[1][AK: *Steve Katz* would even refute that!]

Bobby also states (a) that I came up with the name of the band from the title of a Johnny Cash album (!!!!), (b) that Jerry Weiss left the band to form Ambrosia (it was actually Ambergris that he started), and (c) that Randy Brecker joined his brother Michael in Horace Silver's band. (Michael didn't join Horace's band until nine years later.) So this is just a small example of the misinformation that just one person can put out there that will be picked up by researchers and used as the truth.

Shortly thereafter Bobby copyrighted the trademark Blood, Sweat & Tears in his *own name* (something I never would have dared to do even though it was I who christened the band). I know that, when Columbia Records sent any royalties for *Child Is Father to the Man* (which eventually earned a gold record) to Bobby's Blood, Sweat & Tears, my portion never got mailed to me. I find Bobby's version and Steve Katz's version (that I left The Blues Project because they wouldn't perform "This Diamond Ring"?—ludicrous!) of the origins of the band silly revisionism. They ousted me from the band I had envisioned like the monster who killed Dr. Frankenstein, regrouped with a singer of *their* choice, and made millions of dollars (in addition to my share of the royalties). Wouldn't you say that if they had a war with me, they *won*? So why come up with these stories? They won. I left, as they desired, they made an embarassing amount of money, traveled all over the world, won Grammys--and secretaries everywhere thought they were the greatest thing since sliced bread for three years. So why attempt to discredit me after thirty years? They got everything they ever dreamed of. You know, it doesn't really matter anymore. If they can live with "Lucretia MacEvil" and their Las Vegas desecration of "God Bless The Child," then God bless them.

Okay. It's off my chest forever....

---

[1]Interview with Bobby Colomby, April 2, 1998. Appears on the World Wide Web at address http://www.rdrop.com/users/rickert/bobby.html. © 1998 by Jeremiah Rickert.

1968-1969:

A&R AT COLUMBIA RECORDS,

SUPER SESSION,

MIKE BLOOMFIELD,

LIVE AT THE FILLMORE,

BILL GRAHAM,

NORMAN ROCKWELL,

THE ROLLING STONES, AND

THE FIRST SOLO ALBUM

At this time, Columbia Records was headquartered in the CBS Building on Sixth Avenue between West 52nd and 53rd Streets in midtown Manhattan. Creative Services were on the tenth floor, A&R was on the eleventh floor, Publicity was on the fifth floor, etc. They occupied a nice chunk of the building. The building was commonly known as "Black Rock" because that's what it was made out of, and partly because of the film *Bad Day at Black Rock*.

The day after Jerry Weiss told me off on stage, I found myself in Clive Davis's office at Black Rock, trying to explain to him the changes his $40,000-plus investment was putting itself through.

"Well, they don't like me, they don't want me to sing anymore. I mean, what would you do? I quit and . . . uh . . . I really had no choice."

Clive suggested I stay with the band until a suitable replacement could be found. Concerned with my personal safety, I flatly dismissed any such notion (as I imagined the band certainly would), and that brought me to the other reason for my visit that day.

"Clive, I've decided to produce records full-time now. I'm in no position to record a solo album, join, or much less form a band at this point. Being that you have me signed individually as an artist, I felt you should have first refusal on my services as a producer. Let me know what you think within a week." He was still wondering about his investment as I bade my bye-byes out the door.

Four days later Walter Dean, head of the CBS Business Affairs division, called to say that I had a job as staff producer in the A&R department at Columbia Records. I was bouncing off the peeling walls of my ghetto cell with joy. Columbia had called my bluff, but I was (sort of) ready to deliver. I felt this was an important decision on Clive's part for two reasons:

1. I was sure there would be other people with plights similar to mine in the near future and, if my test run proved successful, perhaps large companies would open their doors to them.
2. It was something of a precedent at that time for a major corporation to hire a long-haired freak on staff.

A contract was to be signed and, being that I had no manager, I wound up representing myself. To a hippie busting his guts to hold down $150 a week, doubling that amount and adding an expense account, an office, and a secretary seemed like moving next door to Howard Hughes. Later I found out that they got me for comparative peanuts, and that they were deducting that salary from my future royalties, but for the time being I was joyous.

Before I started my new job, I took a cash advance and went to London for the first time to see first-hand what all the fuss was about. I had a wonderful time (except for the food) and met some great people. I bought about forty albums, ones you couldn't find in the U.S., and couldn't wait to hear them when I got home. One of them stuck out from all the rest in its brilliance of songwriting, production, and focus. The first day I went to work at CBS I took it with me. I made an appointment with Clive Davis and put the album on his desk. "I really think we should purchase the master rights to this album for the U.S.," I aggressively suggested. He took one look at the cover and replied, "We already own this album. I was just about to sign off on our option to release it domestically."

Now, it got good to me—

"I think that would be a huge mistake Clive. Why there's at least two hit singles here." He told me he would sleep on it and thanked me for bringing it to his attention. Two weeks later I got an interoffice memo saying they *were* gonna put it out, with instructions to rewrite the liner notes and pick a single. Cautiously, Clive released it on a little subsidiary label CBS had called Date Records, in case I turned out to be wrong. But my lucky streak was goin' strong and that is how the single "Time of the Season" by The Zombies came to be number one. The album *Oddesey* [sic] *and Oracle* had been out quite awhile in England. (In fact, the band had already broken up and metamorphosed into a new band called Argent that CBS had signed before "Time" was released.) A buncha Zombies crossed the ocean to take photos and get gold records. No one at CBS thanked me for this; I received no gold record or cash recompense. But The Zombies, who knew what really happened, made sure to come to my office and thank me profusely. That was worth it all to me at that time.

In those days, I was *very* un-money conscious. When you are, the sharks can smell it and move in for the kill. I had no concept of the Big Picture. The music business is a very youth-oriented business, and we all get varied windows of opportunity that usually shut down tight on us before we are ready for them to do so. The idea is to have all your ducks in a row, so that when a particular window does shut on you, your royalties, residuals, and savings from your previous body of work will cover you for the rest of your life. I was twenty-four years old and didn't think *anything* like that. So long as I had a roof over my head, food to eat, and enough petty cash to buy records, magazines, and flashy clothes, I was quite content. I moved my wife and our belongings to a rat-free apartment house on the edge of the Village (which also, ironically, housed one-time Blues Project manager Sid Bernstein, Au Go Go magnate Howard Solomon, and Verve Folkways' Prez Jerry Schoenbaum; talk about living in your past!). I bought some new clothes in England, got a haircut, and began the next phase of Al in Wonderland.

I sat in my office the first day and just beamed. My secretary had previously worked for someone who recorded original cast albums of Broadway shows, and she was downright terrified of me. I didn't know what was going on in this weird-ass building, and she certainly wasn't gonna clue me in. Next door to me was my old friend Wally Gold, Aaron Schroeder's assistant throughout my writing career, who was also just starting work there. That was reassuring. Wally, however, was their easy listening great white hope, and was soon extremely busy producing Peter Nero, Jerry Vale, and Barbra Streisand.

On my right was the office of John Hammond, Sr. He was a certifiable legend in his own time, having discovered Benny Goodman, Billie Holiday, Aretha Franklin, Dylan, Bruce Springsteen, and Stevie Ray Vaughan in the course of his career. His son, John, Jr., was an established blues singer and a good buddy of mine, and it was easy for his dad and me to establish a rapport. John Sr. was a sly guy. He kept to himself, so folks weren't sure *what* the ol' gent was ever up to. John knew what he liked and he never lost his ears. He had no use for business by the book, which used to freak people out up there, but I related to *that*! In essence, he was the original Columbia Records hippie. John Sr. had married William Paley's sister many years before. Bill Paley was Chairman of the Board of CBS and Columbia Records. John was well-placed there. Here's a story that was told in those days:

Every Thursday night, Hammond, Paley, and a bunch of corporate heavyweights had a standing card game at Paley's home. One Thursday they were gathered there in the middle of a hand and Paley asked: "What's new at Columbia Records nowadays, John?"

Keeping his poker face down in his hand, Hammond answered: "I got fired today."

The room exploded into laughter and disbelief. Paley couldn't stop guffawing. "Who on earth fired you, John?" he asked with tears of laughter in his eyes.

"The new guy, Dave Kapralik," John answered.

"Well, don't empty your desk just yet," Paley blurted out in between howls of laughter. The card game continued as usual.

The next morning, *Dave Kapralik* was the one emptying out his desk drawers. John Hammond was just *not* to be trifled with, no matter *how* quiet he was.

Across the hall from me was David Rubinson, who produced most of the alternative albums recorded at Columbia Records. I found out later he was instrumental in getting me hired, and I owe a great debt to him for that. David produced and signed Moby Grape, The Chambers Brothers, Taj Mahal, Tim Rose, and an avant-garde group called The United States of America. I first met him when I sat in on the Moby Grape *Wow/Grape Jam* album (the *real* first rock jam-session album). David later realized the promise he showed early on, by producing and managing some of the finest acts on the scene in those days, including Herbie Hancock, Santana, and The Pointer Sisters.

The interior design of the floor I worked on was Fellini-ish. It was designed by some guy who had probably always dreamed of doing doctors' offices in Italy, but got stuck with a record company in New York instead. This development evidently didn't deter him. The color scheme was your basic chiaroscuro (black and white) with a lot of light beige and grey thrown in for good measure; you could wear a faded referee's shirt to work and blend right in with the environment. The part that killed me was that the walls to each office were prefab and the more important you got, the wider your office suddenly became. I had your medium-sized shot, an uncommonly lucky debut. One guy in Artist Relations (I *still* don't know what that job means. Is he/she the person the record company hires to surreptitiously fuck the

What's wrong with this picture???? The 1969 Columbia Records convention in San Juan, Puerto Rico, gathers its A&R staff for a family photo. (Far right, in more ways than one): John Hammond, Sr., and your nattily atttired host. (Photo: Al Kooper Collection.)

artist? My experience leads me to believe the answer is "yes.") had the tiniest office, barely large enough to accommodate a desk and two chairs. He had to beg the use of someone else's office if he had a meeting with more than one person.

You were not allowed to bring your own wall hangings to your office; framed paintings of someone's choice had arrived long before you did. They were permanently fastened to the prefab walls, so you couldn't even adjust their position, or swap 'em like baseball cards. I had a pretty nice George Gershwin portrait, so I didn't mind. Oh. I mustn't forget my plant. I inherited a plant; medium-sized, nice 'n' leafy and all that. Every day at 6:15 p.m., some nondescript guy would come around and water everyone's plants. I mean, he wouldn't care for them or even look at them for that matter, just pour the prescribed amount of H_2O in the pot, yawn, and stumble on to the next one. When I left CBS, I replaced that plant clandestinely late one night with a plastic one that looked just like it. Wanna bet that guy's still watering it every night???

The eleventh floor housed the pop A&R staff, the studio booking department, the classical department, and the exec offices (relative lower echelon). Clive Davis and Walter Dean were here, but the biggies, William Paley and Goddard Leiberson, were somewhere else. The only time I ever saw Goddard Leiberson was at the annual conventions, where he would circulate quite a bit and display an engaging sense of humor. He was big-time, and Clive Davis reported to him. He had been with Columbia for decades (produced the original cast album of *My Fair Lady* fer chrissakes!) and was well liked. No executive has come close to replacing his charisma or integrity at Columbia since his demise in the seventies.

After the first week of staring around, meeting everyone, and getting a new secretary, it was time to get down to business. The problem was that there was *none* to get down to. I hadn't found or discovered any great bands (except for that Zombies album!), I wasn't ready to make a solo album, and nobody from the company suggested I cut any acts that were already signed to the label. I was full of piss and vinegar; I was ready to *produce* someone, something, the plant in my office, anything, I didn't give a shit. I just wanted to get turned loose in that studio!

I was also aware of the fact that I didn't have any up-to-date experience in the production area, but I had watched John Simon like a hawk as he produced that first BS&T album. My influences were most notably Simon, Phil Spector (king of the sixties' producers in sound innovation), Jerry Ragovoy, and George Martin. But having good taste in the records you listen to doesn't necessarily qualify you to create them. (Not true in the '90s unfortunately.)

One day, an absurdly simple solution popped into my cranium. Why not get a bunch of proven rock players into the studio and just jam in a relaxed atmosphere? This modus operandi was a staple of jazz recording, and maybe it could lend a bit of respectability to the rock genre. CBS would pay for it (hopefully) and I could finish up my post-grad record producing course. Possibly the result would sell enough to pay for itself. I decided to call Mike Bloomfield in San Francisco and find out what he was doing.

Mike Bloomfield was the son of an amazing businessman who created one of the most lucrative businesses in the history of America. Included in his father's giant restaurant supply arsenal were patents for the hexagon-shaped saltshaker with the steel circumcised top and the Jewish star pattern of holes, the cut-glass sugar canister with the steel doggy-door top, and the classic coffee-maker later appropriated by Mr. Coffee for home use. The coffee-maker still bears the Bloomfield name today. Mr. Bloomfield sold his business and patents to Beatrice Foods at its peak, and retired to a life of horseback riding and golfing while his two teenage sons went about the business of growing up in his extremely large shadow. My origins were comparatively humble in comparison.

However, there had been an amazing parallel between Mike Bloomfield's career and mine. We were both Jewish kids raised in big cities who were drawn to urban musicologies. We both came into the public eye from our playing on Dylan's *Highway 61 Revisited* album (where we met). We both served apprenticeships in pioneer electric blues bands (Paul Butterfield/Blues Project). We both started relatively embryonic horn bands (Electric Flag/BS&T) and both eventually got kicked out of of them. It seemed like destiny was throwing us together whether we liked it or not. *We liked it.*

I got him on the phone and it turned out he was not doing much of anything. "Why don't we go in the studio," I proposed, "and just jam? I don't think your best playing is on tape yet and this might just be the best way to get it there. Columbia will pay for it and release it and . . . ya know . . . big deal."

"Okay," he said, "let's just do it in California."

We picked the sidemen (I chose bassist Harvey Brooks, Mike's recent bandmate from The Flag and my boyhood buddy; Bloomers chose Eddie Hoh, The Mamas and the Papas' drummer, known as Fast Eddie) and set the dates. I got all the proper permissions, filed all the correct paperwork, and away I went.

To make sure everyone was comfy, I commandeered a rent-a-house in L.A. It was a nifty joint with a pool that fellow producer David Rubinson had been using while recording blues singer Taj Mahal. It had two weeks to run on Dave's monthly rental, and it seemed like a drag to just waste it. I got there a few days early and swam my New York ass off 'til Harvey and Bloomfield hit town.

Michael always had some *problem* that he carried around with him; it's like a cross he enjoyed bearing (part of his American-Jewish suffering heritage). This time around he arrived with an ingrown toenail, which he kept insisting was gangrene. As soon as he walked in, he took the most expensive crystal bowl from the kitchen cabinet and soaked his big toe in it for an hour. His injured toe is immortalized in a photo on the back of the album for all you blues purists and foot fetishists.

That first night in the studio, we got right down to business. Barry Goldberg, also late of The Flag, came down and sat in on piano for a few tracks. We recorded a slow shuffle, a Curtis Mayfield song, a Jerry Ragovoy tune, a real slow blues number, and a six-eight fast waltz modal jazz-type tune, and in nine hours had half an album in the oven.

Two Jews Blues: The barefoot boys discuss the finer points of jammin': Alan and Michael recording Super Session, *Los Angeles, 1968.* (Photo: © Jim Marshall. Used with permission.)

Jim Marshall and Linda Ronstadt came down to visit, and Jim snapped away on his Nikon documenting the evening on film, while Ronstadt quietly sat in the corner watching. There was a real comfortable feeling to the proceedings, and while listening to one of the playbacks I noted that I *had* gotten the best recorded Bloomfield and, after all, that was the whole point of this exercise. We piled in the rent-a-car and made it back to our palatial surroundings, crashing mightily with dreams of finishing the album the next night.

What happened next is one of those quirks of fate that you can't explain, but you never question in retrospect. The phone started jangling at 9:00 a.m. and it was some friend of Bloomfield's, asking if he'd made the plane 'cause she was waiting at the airport to pick him up.

"Huh? Michael's fast asleep in the next. . . . Hold on," I said, doing a gymnastic hurdle outta bed into the next bedroom to find . . . an envelope? And, inside: "Dear Alan, Couldn't sleep . . . went home. . . . Sorry."

Shit!

Raced back to the phone.

Nobody there.

I got half an album, studio time, and musicians booked, and this putz can't sleep in the $750-a-month dungeon with the heated pool and the crystal toe-soaking bowl.

My first corporate hassle.

"Well, Clive, of course I'm aware of the costs, but he couldn't sleep. I mean, haven't you ever had insomnia?" No way *that* was gonna work.

It was 9:15 in the morning and my mind and ulcers were havin' a foot race for the finish line. I was actually on the verge of packin' it in myself, but a cooler part of me fortunately prevailed. I methodically made out a list of all the guitar players I knew who lived on the West Coast. At noon, I started callin' 'em—Randy California, Steve Miller, Steve Stills, Jerry Garcia. By 5:00 p.m. I had a confirm on one player and left it at that. Once again, fate stepped in to save my ass, this time in the persona of Steve Stills, also unemployed by the breakup of *his* band, Buffalo Springfield.

Steve was primarily known as a singer-songwriter, and mainly on the West Coast, but I knew he was a hot guitar player and I was more than willing to give him a try. (Besides I didn't have a choice, did I?) At 5:00 p.m. I tried Ahmet Ertegun in New York, but it was three hours later there and Atlantic Records was closed for the night. Steve was signed to Atlantic, and you just don't make records for other labels without permission—another corporate hassle. Steve was one of my favorite singers and to have his voice on the album would've upgraded it two hundred percent, but at that point I felt it would've endangered the release of the album by tying up Atlantic and Columbia in one of those red tape battles that pencil pushers are so fond of. It's bad enough he's gonna *play* without permission, I thought. Let's leave it at that and cross our fingers, hoping Atlantic will let us just use his fingers. In retrospect, the negotiations included a swap so that Graham Nash (signed to Epic/Columbia as a member of The Hollies) was allowed to record for Atlantic on the first Crosby, Stills, and Nash album in exchange for Stills appearing on our album. Steve had just gotten his first stack of Marshall amps and was chompin' at the bit to blast his Les Paul through 'em.

At seven that evening Steve, Harvey, Eddie, and yours truly sat down at our instruments and stared at each other.

Now what?

One of the songs I wanted to do was inspired by an English album I had recently acquired. It featured the performances of a spectacular young organist named

Brian Auger and a trendy jazz singer named Julie (Jools) Driscoll. The album contained their version of Dylan's "This Wheel's on Fire," which was a top single in Europe, and a rambling version of Donovan's "Season of the Witch" that I had heard coming out of every shop on Kings Road when I had recently visited London. I thought it would be nice for us to do it, 'cause it provided a lot of room for improvisation and everyone already had the basics of the song down. We did two takes straight off, and the version we kept was edited from the two. Since this was the first big-time record I'd ever produced, I was kinda green in some areas. Editing was one of them. During "Season of the Witch" there are a few edits between takes 1 and 2. The problem is that the two takes were different tempos. I didn't care. I just hacked away and got the bad parts out and the good bits in. So at every edit point the tempo changes. Either you hear those edits or you think we were musicians so attuned to each other that we sped up and slowed down perfectly together. *Not!*

When I'd played on *Highway 61 Revisited*, we'd cut some songs two or three times with different arrangements each time. One such song was Dylan's "It Takes a Lot to Laugh It Takes a Train to Cry." We originally recorded it as a fast tune, but Dylan opted for the slower version cut a few days later as the keeper for his album. I pulled out the fast arrangement and taught it to everyone and we had song number two.

A staple number in Buddy Guy's and Junior Wells' repertoire was Willie Cobb's "You Don't Love Me." It was usually done as a shuffle, but I found it lent itself well to a heavy-metal eighth-note feel. Later, when I mixed the album, I put the two-track mix through a process called "phasing" that gave it an eerie jet-plane effect.

It was 3:00 a.m. and we had three tunes under our belt, leaving us one or two tunes short of an album side. We racked our brains, but to no avail. Then Harvey said he had just written a tune that we might like, and played it for us on the guitar. We did like it and that became the final tune on the album. It was called "Harvey's Tune" at that time, but was later included with a lyric on an Electric Flag album as "My Woman Who Hangs around the House." *Nice title, Harvey.*

I left for New York a day later with the tapes and continued working on the album there. I put on all my vocals, added some horns for variety, and mixed it slowly and deliberately. After all, this was my debut as a producer, and I wanted it to be as competent as possible. I played it for the big boys at CBS and they thought it was okay enough to release. Bruce Lundvall, a kindly V.P. (later to become president of Blue Note Records) named the collection *Super Session*. Six weeks later, it was in the stores.

Fully aware that this was just a furthering of the *Grape Jam* concept, and considering the relative infamy of Bloomfield, Stills, and myself, I didn't delude myself that the album was going straight up to number one or anything. It was

The gentle grizzly bear watches the funky cowboy consult with the neo-foppish producer. With Harvey Brooks and Stephen Stills recording Super Session, *Los Angeles, 1968. (Photo: © Jim Marshall. Used with permission.)*

merely something for me to do while I learned my new craft. I was back in L.A. the day it was released, and ambled into Tower Records to see the initial reaction. I swear they were sailin' 'em over the counter like Beatles records!

In a matter of weeks, it was in the Top Twenty and finally peaked at number eleven. But that was plenty. This was a first for me. It only cost $13,000 to make, and soon it was a gold album (for sales exceeding 450,000). I found this particularly ironic. All my life I'd busted my ass to make hit records. Now me and these two other goons went into the studio for two nights, screwed around for a few hours, and boom, a best-seller.

In retrospect, I think that's what sold the record. The fact that, for the first time in any of our careers, we had nothing at stake artistically. Also, we had brought another ounce of respectability to rock 'n' roll by selling a jam session as "serious" music, something that had only been done in jazz circles up 'til then. All of a sudden, I had the respect of the CBS shorthairs. Shortly thereafter, because of the tremendous success of Blood, Sweat & Tears' second album, my BS&T album turned to gold, and then there were two (gold albums, that is). In retrospect, I might add that as of this writing, I *still* have not received one cent in royalties for these albums that sold millions of copies.

With *Super Session*'s success, things became a lot more comfortable around the corporate HQ. Instead of being just the company freak, I was the company-freak-with-the-number-eleven-LP-on-the-charts, an important distinction. I had already been through three frightened "straight" secretaries (who quit or asked to be transferred), and I still didn't understand the ramifications of the "paperwork system."

As *Super Session* began making its way down the charts, I needed some product on the street. I got a bad case of commercial fever and decided to cut a follow-up to our quasi-hit. One of the only criticisms of *SS* was that it was a studio album and, therefore, "uninspired." Always one to want to shove it up critics' asses, I decided to cut a live jam album, possibly at the Fillmore in San Francisco. I called Bloomfield and he said sure, I owe you one (for when he snuck out of the first album).

This time he chose his friend and neighbor, John Kahn, on bass, and I selected Skip Prokop on drums. Prokop had just quit The Paupers, a Canadian group I was friendly with. I couldn't get Steve Stills because of prior commitments on his part—but mostly on instructions from my higher-ups, who evidently were still embroiled in the legal aspects of our last venture.

I called Bill Graham and asked if he would book us in for a weekend at the Fillmore, and could we record it? He said sure. We scheduled it about five weeks in advance, and I began making arrangements. I figured on ten days of rehearsal in Marin County, where Michael lived. I booked Wally Heider's remote truck to record the proceedings, and got a budget OK. Things were lookin' good. Skip arrived from Toronto, and we were scheduled to begin rehearsing the next day.

I left rehearsal arrangements up to Bloomfield, 'cause it was his home turf and he had all the grease in town. He booked us into this strange place called the Mill Valley Heliport. Actually, it's the upstairs to the waiting room and repair shop of the heliport. For some reason, bands had been renting out the top floor and rehearsing there for quite a few years.

When we arrived, we found the band that had loaned us their room and equipment had got a last-minute gig out of town, and the place was padlocked. Peering through a crack in the door, I noticed that the lion's share of their equipment was gone as well, so efforts to obtain a key were abandoned. After a few frantic phone calls by Michael, we piled into the rent-a-wagon and drove thirty-five miles into the woods to a house owned by a friendly bunch of freaks who called themselves The Anonymous Artists of America. They were a band that played "avant-garde poetic music" and featured a topless female bass player named Trixie Merkin. They had just returned from a weekend's work (can you imagine where?) and we all pitched in unloading their equipment to facilitate the beginnings of a first rehearsal.

Soon we were jamming away, and the combination of musicians seemed to work very nicely, considering we had never played together before. Everything went real smoothly but, at the end of the second day's rehearsal, we were pleasantly evicted in deference to The AAA's rehearsals. I was starting to sweat it, but Rock Scully, The Grateful Dead's manager, lent us their place for three days.

All of a sudden it was Thursday, and we were to open that night. We were half ready. We had six tightly worked-out tunes and about ten frameworks for jam situations. The last few days of rehearsal Michael's infamous insomnia had returned, and he had not slept at all in that time. He was reeling around the dressing room, and I couldn't believe he was gonna get up there and remember all these songs and play his ass off like me and Columbia Records were counting on him to do.

Well, here goes, I thought.

We mounted the stage (show business is so sexual) and tuned up. Just as Bill Graham was about to introduce us Michael grabbed the mike away from him and delivered his own introduction (and I quote):

Uhhh . . . listen here now, here's the thing of this gig and here's . . . I'll tell you about it now. Uh, awhile ago my friend Alan Kooper [AK: It always struck me as weird that Bloomfield always referred to me as Alan, and I referred to him as Michael, as we were commonly known as Mike and Al.] called me on the phone and said, "Let's make this gig, an LP in Los

Angeles, and we'll jam together and we'll see what will happen!" So we went and I played, and I played one day in the studio with Alan and I went back to San Francisco where I live [AK: Very good, Michael!] and the other day Stephen Stills played . . . and they put out an album called *Super Session.* [AK: I wish it had been that easy.] And then Alan said, "OK, that's a groovy thing, let's play a super session, you know, let's do a session and play somewhere!" [AK: Yeah, those were my exact words.] So I said, "Awright man!" Now this is exactly what's gone into this thing, I'll tell ya about it now—Now we played together once on the LP session, that was the one time, and then we practiced together the three days, the four of us: that's John Kahn, and Skip Prokop, and Alan. Now, I've jammed with John a few times, never with Skip. Alan, I guess, has played with Skip, never with John. [AK: Okay, so now you guess—who fucked the boss's daughter?] And altogether we've played four days and so it's half a session, you know, half a session because we're gonna jam because WHAT THE HELL—HOW MUCH DO WE KNOW, and the other half is numbers. But I want you to know this is the truth of where we're playing. See? Now you know where it's at . . . OK!" [AK: If Bloomfield had written George Bush's speeches, he'd still be President!]

That little monologue reduced me to gales of laughter, and I relaxed and played a real comfortable set. Everyone in the band was calm, and it worked. This is not to say that we didn't make mistakes and fuck up every now and then, but like the man said: "WHAT THE HELL—HOW MUCH DO WE KNOW?" and after all, it's nice to let people know you're human beings and not preprogrammed machines vomiting out somebody else's music. Right? That was our whole concept. We were the anti-band band. We felt anybody had the right to play with anybody for as long as they wanted to, no commitments, no image, just music.

Anyway, the first two nights went smoothly enough, and I had roughly enough material for an album already. The third morning I got a call from Michael's wife, Susie, saying, "He's in the hospital being sedated to sleep; he couldn't stand it anymore." (I presume she was talking about not sleeping as opposed to the gig.) Well, he'd done it to me again. So I moseyed on down to the Fillmore office to tell Uncle Bill Graham the good news. I think I'd rather cut my dick off than tell Bill Graham half his show ain't gonna be there that night. As expected, he went ballistic, screaming as if I'd murdered his best friend. "What the fuck do you want from me?" I responded. "I'm not in the fucking hospital! I'm in your office at *noon* offering to call everyone in town and you're chastising me. I'm here ready to play.

And the other guy ain't runnin' out on your contract. It's just that he hasn't slept in a week."

All Bill knew was that it said Mike Bloomfield on the poster, and Mike Bloomfield wasn't gonna be there. He called up Michael's house and started screaming at Susie; telling her how unprofessional her old man was. She'd just got back from taking Mike to the hospital, and she let go with a barrage that leveled him. He was screaming and she was screaming and . . . sometimes I truly hate show business.

I got on the phone and called Carlos Santana (a local hero not known outside San Francisco at the time), Elvin Bishop, Steve Miller, Jerry Garcia, and others. Once again San Francisco responded, and every musician in town showed up and offered his/her services. It was a helluva show that night. Steve, Carlos, and Elvin all came up and did three or four songs apiece, and we ended playing way past closing time. The audience was happy. Graham was happy. Columbia Records was happy.

And I was confused. Should we include the playing of the "guest artists" on the album? I mean, it was the essence of the whole concept and it would certainly spice up the record. It would also make it a double album, however, which was not nearly as marketable because of the cost factor.

Somehow, I was able to convince CBS to release the album under its KGP pre-fix (two records for only a dollar above the price of one). I think the money boys must have thought long and hard because they were narrowing their profit margin by cost-cutting the follow-up to a Top Twenty album. We were not able to get Capitol Records' permission to include Steve Miller's performances (he played great; I still have the tapes!); but Elektra gave us permission to use Elvin Bishop's stuff, and Carlos, who was a year from releasing his first album, was unsigned at the time and available to be included on the album.

I must tell you what kind of a guy Elvin Bishop is, because I love him dearly to this day. The track that is included on the album with him is sort of a contest between me, trying to end the song because of curfew, and Elvin, lost in some blues half-dream playing through at least five obvious endings. I thought it added a great touch to the record, and I even explained what was happening in the liner notes so folks could enjoy it.

Well, late one night after the album had been out a month, I ran into Elvin in a bar. "Hey, Kooper, how ya doin'? By the way I hate you for putting that piece of shit out on your album. It's terrible and embarrassing and [before I can reply] ah, fuck it! It's out anyway, nothin' we can do about it, lemme buy ya a drink!" And off he goes laughing into the night. Now that is a guy *at peace with himself.*

After looking through twenty rolls of film shot at the gigs, I couldn't find any-thing suitable for a cover. We considered a shot that would be doctored up to look

A rare photo of the "Norman Rockwell Experience," a power trio from Nutley, New Jersey, who made one album and then mysteriously vanished off the face of the earth. (Photo: Al Kooper Collection.)

like me and Michael jumping off the Golden Gate Bridge, but that got tired *fast*. One Sunday, I was lying in bed watching Joe Namath and the New York Jets sock it to the Denver Broncos. I'm thinkin' to myself: "Yeah, ya got long hair— Yeah, ya play rock music for a living— But on Sunday afternoon, just like every other average Joe in America, you're chillin' and watchin' the football game, aren't ya? Like a Norman Rockwell painting!" All of a sudden it hit me. Norman Rockwell! Let's get Norman Rockwell to paint a portrait of me and Michael. Is that fucking beautiful or what? I raced for the phone and called Bob Cato, the CBS art director, at home. Is it possible? Can it be done? He said there was actually a good chance and he'd check it out first thing in the morning.

A week later Michael and I were sitting in a photo studio at CBS waiting for Norman to photograph us so he could paint our portrait. In he strolled, right on time, and Bloomfield, a closet-Rockwell-groupie, just gushed all over him. As it turned out, Michael was wearing his brother's coat, found a pill in the pocket, and popped it. It was STP (superacid) and he gooned out all over Norman: "Oh man, you're the best. You should come to San Francisco though, man, you would see such sights there to paint. You wouldn't believe it. People in robes in the street, mothers suckling their young, I tell you it's just like *Jerusalem*, Norman, so whaddaya think?"

Norman, who was listening intently, just puffed on his pipe and was . . . together. He took our pictures and chatted amiably with Michael, thanked everyone, and then was gone like a cool breeze.

Two weeks later, after Michael had returned home to Marin County, Norman sent me an invitation to his opening at a ritzy New York gallery. First one he'd had in years; I was honored. The missus and I dressed up in the finest rock-star regalia 1968 had to offer (satin pants, Nehru shirt, two-thousand-bead necklaces, embroidered jackets with fur cuffs, etc.) and we trucked on down to the gallery.

Now, we were about as out of place as Beavis and Butthead would've been at a New Age convention. Rock stars at this time did *not* mingle with society, and these folks, well, they weren't shy about looking down their noses as we perused Norman's great works. And I must say he had an impressive collection of art there. Just when it was getting really uncomfortable, Norman and his *great* wife came flying in the door, and who did he come over and hug? Not the Vanderbilts, the Rockefellers, or the Von Furstenbergs, but Mr. and Mrs. Beavis Butthead, which caused the black sheep of the party to become the "*Who-is-that???*" of the evening.

He yanked us off to the office, where he relaxed and said, "I hate this stuff. I can't wait to get back home. It's so nice to see you again. I'm glad you could find the time to attend." His wife was mostly silent but she had that Norman-is-a-dear-old-guy-isn't-he look on her face, and this lady was obviously so much in love and God knows how long they'd been married. Did my heart good, I tell ya. My last words to him that night were, "Paint me a little heavier. It'll make my parents happy."

The painting arrived at CBS seven weeks later (Rockwell was painting Nixon's portrait at the same time, and it threw him off schedule, not to mention point of reference) in a cheap frame with this note: "Here is *The Blues Singers*. These boys were the most interesting looking people I've ever painted. Thank you. Norman." Well, except for his portrait of Bertrand Russell, I think he was probably right. If you notice, my face was a little fuller than in real life at that time. My parents were *thrilled*.

The painting hung in art director John Berg's office at CBS for many years. I must confess I tried to steal it on a number of occasions, but only half-heartedly. Now, I regret it. For some reason that has nothing to do with justice, John Berg kept the painting with him when he left CBS. I once found his home number and called him up: "Don't you think Michael or I deserve that painting? How can you justify keeping it?" His answer was quick: "I've considered leaving it to you in my will, but then I know you'd just have me killed." Well, as Joe Walsh is fond of saying, you can't argue with a sick mind. Five years ago, I did an interview at a radio station and the disc jockey informed me that *his brother* now owned the painting. He got him on the phone and his brother told me that he didn't buy the painting from John Berg. So Berg sold it a long time ago and that's just how life is.

A photo of Norman Rockwell's painting of Bloomfield and myself used as the album cover for The Live Adventures of Mike Bloomfield & Al Kooper. *Rockwell dubbed us* The Blues Singers. (Photo: Al Kooper Collection.)

ଚ୨

Shortly thereafter, Columbia released the double-album set *The Live Adventures of Mike Bloomfield & Al Kooper* with the Rockwell portrait on the cover. It began with a version of Paul Simon's "Feelin' Groovy," featuring Paul singing overdubbed harmony with me on the third verse. Included within was an instrumental of The Band's "The Weight," Booker T.'s "Green Onions," Traffic's "Dear Mr. Fantasy," and the usual assortment of blues tunes. Guest appearances were credited to Carlos Santana (still unknown) and Elvin Bishop. The record made a handsome profit but never did duplicate the phenomenal success of *Super Session*. It covered me for awhile, though, as I finally began work on my first solo album.

Around the time I finished the *Live Adventures* album (as it came to be called), I was feeling overworked and was sick of being in a studio day after day. *Live Adventures* was the fourth album in a row I had worked on, and I was burned out. I called my close friend, Denny Cordell, producer of Joe Cocker, Procol Harum, and the legendary Move, who lived in London. "I wanna come over for awhile with Joan to rest from the studio. Please pick us up at the airport and don't tell a soul that we're coming. It's escape time!"

Denny was an incredible character and deserves a chapter all his own, but that's for another book at another time. He picked us up at the airport and informed us that The Stones' office had called him and "did I feel like playing on a few sessions with them?" *Oh, no.* Not the studio again! I mean it was really an honor and all that, but why did Claudia Schiffer wait until I slept with every woman in town before she slipped her room key into my hand, if you catch my drift.

We got dropped at our hotel and we just crashed from the flight the whole first day. How did The Stones know I was coming to town? I lay in bed and wondered. The next day we were shopping on Kings Road, and we bumped into Brian Jones in a shirt store: "Are you gonna play the session, Al?" he asked. *How can you say no to these people?*

The Stones wanted me for two sessions. I decided to do one and if it was really fun, rock on; if it wasn't I'd get an ulcer attack the next night and beg off. I think the reason they called me was that their regular keyboard player (Nicky Hopkins) was in the States at the time.

As usual, I got to the studio early. Charlie and Bill arrived next. I had met them before with Dylan. First-rate, no-nonsense guys. It was good to see them again. I was sitting at the organ sort of nervously doodling around 'til everyone was there but Mick and Keith. Jimmy Miller, an American, was the producer. We exchanged amenities.

Just then Mick and Keith came exploding in through the door. Mick was wearing a gorilla coat, and Keith had on this sort of Tyrolean hat with a real long feather in it. It was gonna be party time, and they were the party from the moment they arrived. Everyone sat around on the floor with either an acoustic guitar or a percussion instrument, and Mick and Keith played the song they wanted to record until everyone had the chord changes and the rhythm accents. There was a conga player there who could play congas and roll huge hash joints without missing a lick. It was decided I would play piano on the basic track and overdub organ later.

I got into this groove I had heard on an Etta James cover version of "I Got You Babe" (of all things!). It really fit their song well. Keith picked up on it right away and played a nice guitar part that meshed right with my piano part. While they were getting the sounds they wanted on the instruments, Jimmy Miller was showing Charlie a certain accent he thought would work well on the drums. Charlie just couldn't seem to get the part and stepped down unhappily to take a break. Jimmy Miller sat down at the drums and remained there playing drums on the take! Charlie was not happy, but remained graceful about it. Mick and Keith played acoustic guitars, I played piano, Bill was on bass, and Brian Jones lay on his stomach in the comer reading an article on botany through the entire proceedings.

When a proper take was gotten, Keith overdubbed an electric part and I overdubbed the organ. After about four hours of recording, two men showed up with long folding tables and set up a veritable beggars' banquet of racks of lamb, curries, vegetables, rices, salads, a large selection of wines, and lots of different desserts. Quite a change from a cheeseburger break in the States. I was so full after all that, I almost fucked up the organ part. I had a great time playing, and I was treated regally, so I was actually looking forward to the next evening's session.

The song we recorded the first night was "You Can't Always Get What You Want," which later appeared on the *Let It Bleed* album and was also the flipside of the single, "Honky Tonk Woman." I told Jagger that if he ever wanted to put horns on it to call me 'cause I had a great part for it. Almost nine months after that session, an eight-track master of the song arrived at my office one day at CBS. There was a note which said: "Dear Al, you once mentioned you could put some great horn parts on this. Well, go ahead and do it and send us the tape back. Love, Mick."

What a memory that Jagger had. I wrote out a horn chart, leaving a spot in the intro where I could play a French horn solo. The intro itself took me three hours to get 'cause I'm not the world's greatest French horn player, and I wanted to sound like I was. I could never have done it at all without the coaching of one of the best horn players in the country, Ray Alonge. Thank you, Ray. Then I put the rest of the horns on with a studio section. It was a bad night in the studio for me, and the part didn't come out nearly as good as I thought it might. I crossed my fingers and sent Jagger back his tape. A year later it came out, and they had ditched all the horn parts except my little French horn intro. It sounded fantastic on the radio. You could hear the piano and the organ, and they actually gave me credit on the single. Nice guys.

Back in London, the next night as I was getting ready to leave the hotel for the studio, the phone rang. It was Mick. He and Keith were down in the lobby. *They came to pick me up!* That night we cut a track from the film Jagger was currently working on, *Performance*. The song was called "Memo from Turner," but was not the version used in the film or on the soundtrack album. I believe it was issued on a later album of outtakes. I played guitar with Keith on that one.

I played one other time with The Stones a few years later at a birthday party for Keith at Olympic Studios in London. They were working on the *Sticky Fingers* album. After the party, they cleared away the debris and set up to record. They cajoled Eric Clapton, myself, and Bobby Keys to join them in a previously unheard tune called "Brown Sugar." George Harrison, who was among the partygoers, was invited to play but declined. I read somewhere in an interview with Keith that it came out great and that they would release it someday, but the version on *Sticky Fingers* is another one entirely.

I must take this opportunity to say that, over the years, The Stones have always been honorable, great people to hang out with, and the best people to play after-hours music with.

Before I started my first solo album, I ended up waiting out Blood, Sweat & Tears to see what tunes they were going to do so there would be no duplication. From my original set, they kept "You Made Me So Very Happy," "Smiling Phases," "More & More," and the jam portion of "Somethin' Going On," now called "Blues Part IV." I wrote some new tunes, chose a few others, and took one we had been doing with BS&T that they had opted not to record. While I was working on other projects for Columbia, I would chip away at my solo album in spare moments. I also experimented profusely by using Columbia's recording facilities in Nashville and Los Angeles as well as in New York.

I didn't know what to do for the cover, so I dumped it in Art Director John Berg's lap. He came up with putting my face on the Statue of Liberty. I thought it would be hysterical to see this freak representing Amerika, and made them add a shot of me up in the torch laughing just so everyone got the joke. The inside was a photo collage, the track information, and a poem I had written when I was in The Blues Project that miraculously explained why I was recording a solo album.

The album, *I Stand Alone*, was released to mixed reviews, but a much more negative phenomenon took place at the same time. Coinciding with the release of the album, BS&T had thrown some quotes out in the press about why I had left the group, and they depicted me as some demonic egomaniac with whips and chains who kept them all in cages. Prior to all this, I really had no press image; I was neither black nor white, just a grey type of fella. When critics wrote about me, there was no personality mentioned. It would just say here's a good record by Al, or on this one Al turns in a mediocre performance, or would just comment about the musicality of it all as opposed to the person himself. This was fine with me, 'cause that's all I was selling. I mean, you can hate or enjoy my music, but me the person is usually not revealed, except through the lyrics occasionally. Somehow, probably because of BS&T's meteoric popularity and the release of my solo album, I got nailed with one of those unfortunate press images. Then everything I had done was tied into the ego thing. People said: "When he says 'I Stand Alone,' he means there is no one comparable to him, that he's got an ego as big as the Statue of Liberty," etc. Reviews were taken up with this Downtown Julie Brown gossip shit instead of talking about the music itself.

Not being a thin-skinned person, I was surprised this stuff got to me. *But it did.* I hired a public relations firm to try and set up interviews where members of the press could meet me face to face and decide for themeselves what I was like. I remember words from one article about me from that time period: ". . . In the studio, joking around and at ease, he doesn't seem like the monstrous prick others have made him out to be. . . ." There's a left-handed compliment for ya. So this was the beginning of my interest in stepping permanently into the background. As Orson Welles once said in the middle of doing a frozen-food commercial, "No money is worth *this*!" I had achieved many of my goals, and now I felt like blazing new trails.

I was twenty-five years old, had been in two successful bands, and now held a respected A&R position at one of the top record companies in the world. I was drawing three hundred dollars weekly plus expenses, and on the weekends was making between five and ten thousand dollars per gig playing personal appearances. I had four albums in the *Billboard* Top 200, but I was looking for something new to do.

1969-1972:

SCORING A FILM,

LOSING A WIFE,

ELTON JOHN,

ADDICTION,

TOURING,

DEEP PURPLE,

NEW MORNING,

SMOKEY ROBINSON,

MILTON BERLE, AND

BATTLES WITH CLIVE

Hal Ashby, who had been famed Canadian film director Norman Jewison's Academy Award-winning film editor, had just directed his first film. For some reason I never quite understood, he felt that I was the perfect person to write the musical score for his cinematic debut. I guess he was a fan, and so I was flown to Hollywood to screen a rough cut of the film. It was called *The Landlord* and starred Beau Bridges, Lou Gossett, Jr., Lee Grant, and Pearl Bailey. It had an interracial theme and plenty of room for good music. I really enjoyed the screening and felt that I could conceivably do a credible job scoring it, although in that capacity it would be *my* debut as well. I recounted this to Ashby at the screening's conclusion. He told me that someone else was competing with me for the job, and asked that I indulge him and stay another day while he made his decision overnight. I told him that was aces with me and called up some friends to spend the evening with.

Denny Cordell, as you recall, was a close friend from London who had recently immigrated to Hollywood. Teaming up with session pianist Leon Russell (who had arranged the Gary Lewis record of "This Diamond Ring" in his younger days), they formed a new label called Shelter Records. Leon was to be the first artist on the label and they were currently embroiled in recording his debut album, tentatively titled *Can a Blue Man Sing the Whites* or something like that. Denny invited me down to Leon's session that night, and I was glad to see some old friends and just kick back. They asked what I was doing in town, and I told them about the movie and how I had to wait for Ashby's decision in the morning. I quietly watched Leon work on one of his tracks and just generally enjoyed the company. I bade my farewells about 2 a.m. and drove back to the hotel for a good night's rest.

I arrived at Hal Ashby's office about 11 a.m. the next morning and was greeted warmly and told that I did, indeed, have the job. I was ecstatic, but curious.

"Hal, can you say who the other person was that you were considering?" I asked.

"Oh sure," he said. "It was *Leon Russell*."

That fucker! I told Hal how I had spent the last evening and we both were hysterical laughing. *I had to get to a phone*. I called Denny and told him that I had gotten the job. He sheepishly congratulated me and then I read him the riot act for playing dumb the night before and not telling me about Leon's involvement. In fact, I was convinced that if they had told me, their karma would have shifted and I would have been the one sheepishly congratulating *them* this morning. Anyway, we did laugh about it and no harm was done, though somehow I think Leon wasn't too thrilled about it. Frankly, this movie was set in modern-day New York City, not Tulsa, and that was my town, buddy!

Meanwhile I had just agreed to score a major Hollywood motion picture and I didn't have the slightest idea even how to begin. *I needed help; that much I did know*. I enlisted one of my favorite gurus—Charlie Calello. Charlie was the arranger on all The Four Seasons and Lou Christie hits, and had been involved on *I Stand Alone*. We had a wonderful working relationship, and most of all, *he knew how to score films*! I went off to Los Angeles and rented a bungalow at the very bohemian Chateau Marmont (a big movie-star hideout in the forties; the bungalow I chose would later serve as the location for John Belushi's last night on earth) for a month. I wrote music there every day and had access to a screening room to make notes and refer to the film for reference. There were no VHS machines in those days! I then returned to New York to record the score. After all, the film took place in New York City. The music was to be organically extracted from musicians who had that "New Yorkness" in their approach to playing. Paul Griffin on keyboards, Chuck Rainey on bass, Eric Gale on guitar, and Bernard Purdie on drums were the core members of the band.

I had written a song about the sociological changes in America at the time that seemed appropriate for the film. The song was called "Brand New Day" and I thought it would be wonderful if it were sung in the film by the Staple Singers. A family group formed in the late fifties by patriarch Roebuck Staples, they embodied the power and honesty that brought them to the top of the gospel world in a short time period. Initially signed to Chicago's famous Vee-Jay Records, they passed uneventfully through major label Epic, and then found total crossover acceptance on Memphis' Stax label in the late sixties and seventies. Initially led by Roebuck's velvet tones and his pioneeering tremoloed guitar sounds, he was complemented by daughter Mavis's powerful lead vocals. I had a casual friendship with them, and when I called to ask if they would participate, they were happy to oblige.

On my way to New York from Los Angeles, I stopped in Chicago to visit them at home and teach them the song. I had a four-hour layover at the airport, so a limousine was charged to the film budget, and I was whisked to their home on Chicago's South Side. The limousine was to wait and then speed me back in time to catch the New York leg of my flight. Unbeknownst to me, they had a home-cooked soul food dinner waiting when I arrived. It was so thoughtful that I didn't have the heart to tell them my ulcer precluded me eating practically anything they had prepared. I just politely filled up on stuff that I could eat (cornbread), and we laughed our way through dinner anyway. About ten minutes after I arrived, the phone rang and Pops went to answer it. He came back moments later, in tears, laughing.

"What's so funny, Pops???" we all inquired.

He could barely speak between guffawing spasms, but managed to reply: "Mr. Lincoln, the neighbor from across the street, saw Al's limousine parked out front . . . and called to see if I had died!"

He hadn't. But we did. *Of laughter.*

Borrowing Pop's guitar after dinner, I played them the song, and just as I had anticipated, they assimilated it in five minutes as if they had been singing it all their lives. Mavis sang the verses and Pop sang the choruses. It was wonderful. Off I went, back to the airport, full of too much cornbread, with a huge smile on my face.

Recording the score went quite smoothly with Charlie's help. We decided to time the cues with a stopwatch, and specifically not record with the picture screening in the studio so that the musicians could concentrate on the music and not be distracted by the film showing. The detailed on-the-mark cues would be completed later on a soundstage in California. For some source music cues (radios and records blaring out of ghetto windows and car speakers) I decided to use one of my favorite singers, Lorraine Ellison. My friend and mentor Jerry Ragovoy had produced one of the great soul records of all time with her ("Stay With Me Baby"), and I had always wanted to work with Lorraine. Since we were working at Jerry's studio (Hit Factory), it was an easy task to bring her into the fold. This brought parts of my life full-circle. When I was in The Blues Project, I learned our signature song, "Wake Me Shake Me," from a gospel record by the Golden Chords that featured lead singer Lorraine Ellison. Now here I was producing her. This was a good life, it was.

While recording background vocals one day, an amusing incident occurred. One of Lorraine's tracks needed backup singers, but neither Charlie nor I could come up with any ideas for specific parts. We asked the backup singers, Tasha Thomas, Carl Hall, and Melba Moore (three fabulous African-American artists in their own right) if they could work with the track to see if they could develop any ideas, while Charlie and I took a break for a few minutes. When we returned to the control room, they were ready to go. Showing complete confidence, we recorded them immediately without even hearing the parts they had created. Needless to say, the parts were wonderful and they got it in one take. When recording was done, Charlie pressed the talkback button:

"Hey! That was fantastic! You guys are the best, and I really appreciate you getting us out of that jam. That's a wrap and thanks again. You were brilliant!"

Tasha stepped up to the mike on that 1969 afternoon, and without missing a beat replied: "*Why, thank you, Charlie. We'll remember that when we come burning houses down!*" A prophetic and yet humorous capper to another day in the studio.

The score was completed, the film mixed, and United Artists allowed me to host my own screening in New York. I remember that I was sitting behind Clive Davis, then-president of Columbia Records, and anticipating some fun. In one scene in the film, I had created a radio commercial for ". . . 200 current underground hits for only $14.95. Yes, incredible as it sounds, 200 underground hits as played by the exciting, dynamic, Ca-live Davis Band. . . ." Well, when this snippet came over the speakers, he stiffened up as if a steel rod had been inserted in the base of his spine, while his cronies cracked up and slapped him on the back. I shrank down in my seat and did my best Claude Rains imitation. His reaction did *not* prevent me, however, from including that commercial in the soundtrack album on United Artists Records, of which he was *not* the president. The film came out to mixed reviews, but for Hal Ashby, Kooper's reverse curse prevailed. Every film Hal directed after *The Landlord* was a box office smash or a classic: *Harold & Maude*, *Shampoo*, *Being There*, etc., etc., etc.

Hal was an interesting guy. He was rail-thin, had shoulder-length white hair, seemed like he married a new woman every time he made a film, and smoked pot incessantly. Once, I got two front-row tickets for a Band concert in Long Beach. I invited Hal as my guest, provided *he* would drive, as I did not know the way there.

Film Director/Editor Hal Ashby and I pretend he is editing The Landlord *for the benefit of the camera.* (Photo: Al Kooper Collection.)

When we arrived, he parked his Ferrari illegally in the backstage parking area and we went in and enjoyed the concert. Hal sat to my left and sitting on my right was a portly gentleman I had never met wearing a beret. He nodded out on my left shoulder shortly before the end of the concert. After the show he was introduced to me as Mac Rebbenack, and that is how I first met Dr. John. Asleep on my left shoulder.

Hal and I exited the concert through the backstage door, and the moment we stepped outside, he fired up a joint. I was a little nervous.

"Hal," I said, "there are cops all over the place and we're illegally parked here. You think it's a wise decision to walk around getting high?"

Just as he sucked in a lungful of smoke, he replied, "Well, what's the worst that can happen? They'll beat the shit out of us and throw us in jail."

I guess you really can't argue with logic like that. We motored back to Hollywood unscathed and with our freedom intact, so I guess he made his point. Still, that train of thought never rubbed off on *me*.

Recently, I was introduced to Lee Grant at a party. She had been nominated for best supporting actress for her role in *The Landlord* back when the film was in release. I told her I had done the music for that film, and her eyes lit up. "You know," she recounted, "that was my favorite film appearance *ever*, largely due to working with Hal Ashby. He was an incredible director." We concurred on that and spent the evening trading Hal stories. I told her this book was coming out and that Hal was mentioned a few times. When she asked the title of the book, her eyes lit up again. "I'll definitely pick that one up when I see it!" she laughed.

Back in New York, I got a call from Dylan to meet with him at his house on MacDougal Street. He had been asked to write the score for a Broadway musical production of *The Devil and Daniel Webster*. He was going uptown to meet with some of these people and wanted me to come along for some reason (sometimes I thought he regarded me as *his* Charlie Calello). Bob was usually interesting company, so I tagged along. After the meeting, in the cab going home, he confided to me that he was considering yanking the songs from the show and making them into a new album right away. His last effort, *Self-Portrait*, had been mutilated by the critics, and had only been out two months. He asked me to help him with this project. I really liked the songs he had played me, so I was completely into it. This was the album that came to be known as *New Morning*.

For the project, Bob Johnston, Dylan's producer, assembled a cast of players at the studios in New York including Ron Cornelius on guitar, Charlie Daniels on bass, and Russ Kunkel on drums. But after about two or three sessions, Johnston stopped showing up. Just like that. When things were disorganized in the studio, I used to jump into the fray instinctively in hopes of pulling a runaway session together. And that is what I did here. I called some more musicians in, rearranged some songs, and even had one sweetening session with horns and strings (never released). I brought in Buzzy Feiten and David Bromberg on guitars, Harvey Brooks on bass, and Billy Mundi on drums. I also hired my usual female backup singers, this being perhaps Bob's first recorded instance of using this type of accompaniment.

Unfortunately, poor Joan was in a hospital nearby, miscarrying, while these sessions were going on. I would cut a few tracks, go to the hospital, come back, cut more tracks, go back to the hospital, etc. I was pretty stressed out. One night after the sessions ended, I was booked to play a high school prom in New Jersey. I ended up crawling inside the piano and playing the strings with a guitar pick during a thirty-minute version of "La Bamba." I think we actually cleared the house. As I said, I was *very* stressed out.

Bob had this kind of beat poetry number called "If Dogs Run Free." I suggested having Maretha Stewart, one of our backup vocalists, scat-sing in between his recitations to give it a fifties' jazz-beatnik feeling. Maretha stepped up and did a fantastic job, while the rest of us pretended we were wearing berets and goatees. I especially enjoyed playing lounge-type, tongue-in-cheek piano on that song. Bob played some terrific piano on "Sign in the Window." When we had recorded everything, Bob pulled out some random tracks he had cut in the last year and added those to the oversupply we already had from the current sessions. Then we began to select and sequence. He changed his mind daily and the weeks began to drag on. *This drove me nuts.* We had a final title and cover artwork, but we had a new sequence and songlist every day.

Finally, I said: "Look, Bob, I am done here. There's nothing else I can really do. When you decide for sure what you want, put it out!" and exited the proceedings. Soon after he called to ask: "What credit do you want on the album? It can't be producer because of a contractual hitch with Johnston and CBS."

Oh great. All that work and no credit. . . . (This was back in the days when I still coveted credit.)

"How about Special Thanks?" I said.

"That sounds fine. See ya, Al." And that was that.

For the time being.

Three days later, Bob called back.

"The album is supposed to come out on the tenth, but they screwed up and left your credit off. If they put your credit back on, it won't come out until the twenty-fourth. What should I do?"

Boy, was I angry. "Put it out when they get the credits right," I growled.

That was the last Dylan album I ever got involved producing. It was one of those situations where you have to place your friendship ahead of working together so closely. You give up one to save the other. While I have never produced another Dylan album, I've played on many others and . . . we're still friends today.

Around this time period, I spent a lot of time recording in London. This was precipitated by a fortuitous meeting with Elton John. I had worn out his first American release (the one with "Border Song" and "Take Me to the Pilot"), and on one occasion noticed that he was only playing two U.S. dates: Boston and L.A. Living in New York City at the time, I hopped the shuttle to Boston and, bunking with my in-laws, proceeded to the club where he was appearing. Prior to showtime, Elton and I were introduced and shared an instant rapport. This is the coolest thing about the rock music fraternity. We all have heard of each other. We all enjoy and suffer the same perks and indignities that come with the lifestyle. So when we actually meet each other, we can cut right to the chase and not hem and haw like you might when meeting a normal person. *I love that.*

I invited Elton and his lyricist Bernie Taupin to spend the next day with me, and I rented a limousine. We went visiting the historical sites around Lexington and Concord, where my ancestors vanquished many of their ancestors. We stopped at this one area and Elton read the inscription from a brass plaque aloud: "The Tomb of the British Soldiers—they travelled 3,000 miles to die here."

Elton reflected for a moment. "The thing is," he quipped, "this has happened to so many British bands lately."

They played me some new tracks they had just cut and I was overwhelmed, especially by the bass playing. "Who's playing bass on these tracks?" I inquired.

"That's Herbie Flowers, mate. He's a god in England. And before you ask, here's his phone number!" they thankfully offered.

Back in those days, it was my habit to find great sidemen, and then travel to wherever they were and record in their particular indigenous environment. And so it was off to Blighty and the very musical Herbie Flowers Experience. Elton was extremely helpful in securing various musicians for my sessions, and graciously made his office staff available to me. The first record I made in this situation was my solo album *New York City (You're A Woman)* at Trident Studios (right next door to a bordello).

Herbie's contributions were fantastic. A lanky, loony potsmoker, he was in a class by himself as a musician. I still learn things today by listening to his older bass tracks! He had previously played on Bowie's "Space Oddity," was rumored to have played on "OO Bla Di-OO Bla Da" by the Beatles, and had been a member of

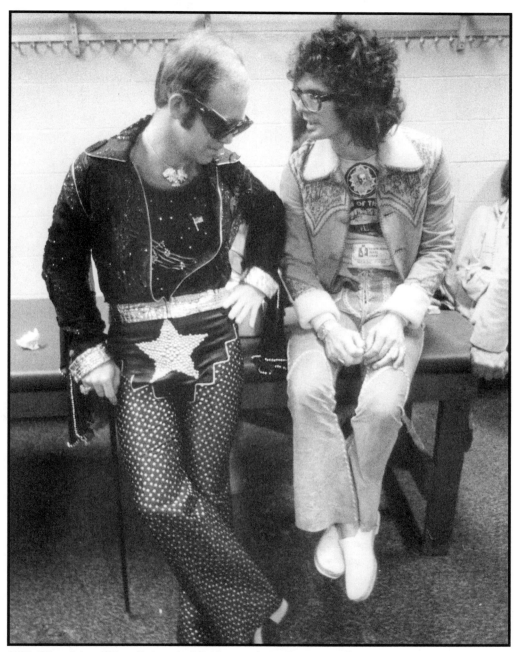

With Elton John. Elton: [Interestedly] Nice package there, mate!!
Al: [Tactfully] Uhhh. . . . If you'll look a little harder, you'll . . . uhhhh . . . notice that the
package, although addressed to the right, uhhhh . . . is not actually addressed to you, per se.
(Photo: Bob Gruen.)

Herbie Flowers was, like, a-rollin' . . . stoned. (Photo: Al Kooper Collection.)

the successful London band Blue Mink.

When artist and producer friends Harry Nilsson and Richard Perry visited one of my sessions, they asked: "Who's that bass player?"

I answered: "That's Herbie Flowers, boys. He's a god here. And before you ask, here's his phone number!"

Harry and Richard used him *all over* their stuff (specifically the *Nilsson Schmilsson* album they were working on at the time), and then there he was, on "Walk on the Wild Side" by Lou Reed. The next Elton album (*Tumbleweed Connection*) contained perhaps his best playing of all time. "Burn Down the Mission" and "Country Comfort" are still confounding and influencing bass players everywhere today.

Once, during one of my sessions that Herbie was booked on, we went into the booth for a playback, and there was a particular passage where the bass seemed to be out of time. I stopped the playback and said: "Herbie, do you want to redo that bit there?"

He looked at me incredulously. "No. I do not want to *touch* that bit there. Ten years from now you'll understand it. Just leave it be."

Embarrassingly, he was right. Well. . . . Maybe it was nine years.

Things were tense in the marriage department at this time. Now my wife Joan was a great gal (still is, I imagine). She will always own a piece of my heart for two incidents:

1. At one point in our chronology, we were living in this un-air-conditioned rat-trap on Waverly Place in Greenwich Village. I would come home at night, strip down to just jockey shorts, and read the *New York Post* while Joan dear would cook dinner. So this particular night, as I was regaling myself with the daily murder count, she ran into the barely-living room and announced that the stove was on fire and could I do something about it. So macho Al sauntered into the kitchen, opened the oven door, and a huge fireball shot out and singed my eyebrows and hair. I hurriedly shut the oven door and the two of us looked at each other in a we-don't-own-a-fire-extinguisher panic. "Let's just split!" she said.

2. Same scenario: me reading the paper and Joan cooking. Add to the participants Magoody, a new sheep dog puppy that we were currently unsuccessfully house training (don't ask). I was really engrossed in the paper but I did hear Joan scolding the dog: "Magoody! NO! BAD DOG!!" Then Joan walked into the living room, with a newspaper full of apparent doggie-doo, and flung it off the newspaper, across the room onto my bare, sweat-drenched chest! I stared in disbelief, while she collapsed in laughter across the room.

   "I can't believe you just did that to me," I said with righteous rancor. "Oh cool out, will ya?" she said as she walked over to me, picked up one turdlet in her bare hands and took a bite out of it! I thought I had married John Waters' ex-wife until I realized that Joan had just cooked chocolate fudge and was pushing the envelope of my sense of humor. What a gal, huh?

While I was cavorting around London, our marriage was crumbling. In a nutshell, it was the basic scenario of the musician-marries-pretty-girl-who's-left-at-home-way-too-many-times-and-doesn't-have-a-career-of-her-own movie. We separated and I found myself living in a hotel room in the city I resided in. The irony was painful: I'd come home from touring to yet . . . *another hotel room.*

The Beast & the Beauty: Al and Joan, New York City, circa 1969.

૭ઝ

Finding an apartment in New York City is a perilous task. It can take months. I was incredibly depressed, and emotionally weak; the perfect profile for a drug abuser. I had quit all drugs in 1967 while I was putting BS&T together, but now I suddenly crumbled and fell victim to the world of painkillers. I hesitate to document this part of my life (sound the *serious alarm* here for the next few paragraphs), but I feel perhaps it may help someone out there to see a foolishness of choices and light the way out of the tunnel for them. Back then, there were no rehab centers, and one had to take matters into one's own hands. At any rate, I'll be concise.

Percodan was the choice I made. Favored by doctors for migraines and dentists for post-op relief, in my eyes it was a chicken-shit, Junior Miss heroin substitute. Not forlorn enough to punch a needle in my arm, I chose these convenient little escape tablets to cope with my problems. Completely unaware of the addictive features, I went hog-wild. With the help of inspired tale-telling to various East and West Coast "Dr. Nicks," I built up a formidable stash. Behind my back, the members of my performing band would take bets on how many times I would walk into the microphone during each performance. My friends from Dr. Generosity's (an Upper East Side rock star hangout in Manhattan that had become my clubhouse) would literally carry me home on occasion, when I nodded out past closing time. Cute. And into this potentially lethal chemistry, I added the purchase of my first automobile: a brand-new dark blue 1972 Corvette with two tops. Putting that car into the equation was the closest I had ever come to inadvertent suicide so far.

One night, I was performing at a college in New Jersey. I had dated a woman twice before who was the sister of an actor who would become famous in two years on a television sitcom. I called her from the college and asked her if she wanted to spend the night together when I got back from New Jersey. The plan was that I would pick her up at her place on my way back from the gig and we would "hang out" at my hotel for the rest of the night. I had driven the Corvette to Jersey since the gig was so close. As I headed back to the city with the top down, I realized I was starting to nod out. I drove faster toward her apartment and stumbled to the buzzer when I got there. *Some Romeo.*

This was a dangerous game I was playing. She came downstairs and got in the car.

"Can we get something to eat?" she said. "I'm starving!" Just what I needed.

I answered: "Michelle, I'm seriously nodding out here. Let's just get something delivered to the hotel, OK?" She agreed, and I told her to call for food wherever she wanted and handed her a wad of bills.

"I have *got* to take a nap for two hours," I went on. "Order some food, make yourself comfortable, watch TV, and before you know it, I'll be up."

Another great date with Al. This was fine with her, however, so I headed off to the bedroom. It was 1 a.m. and I crashed instantly and awoke at 4 a.m., refreshed and randy. I sashayed into the living room, and the little doll was attired in nothing but one of my shirts (quite oversized for her). She was out cold with a drinking glass still in her hand. How cute, I thought. I kinda settled down next to her on the couch and made a few moves. I got zero response. I shook her gently to wake her up. No response. She began drooling.

Oh shit, am I in trouble, I was thinking. I tried the mirror trick, and to my relief she was still breathing.

I gave her one last tentative shake and said to her: "Okay, this is your last chance! If this is some method acting tour-de-force, now is the time to 'fess up 'cause I'm about to call an ambulance." No response.

I was really scared now. I called the hotel doctor and dressed her as best I could while waiting for him to arrive. He examined her and called for an ambulance. Suspected overdose. My world is just filled with irony, I was thinking. *I'm* nodding out a few hours ago and now I'm taking *her* to the hospital!

She was rushed to an emergency room, where I paced around. The cops took her handbag and emptied it onto a gurney, looking for whatever had felled her. It was a moment out of a Woody Allen film. An incredible amount of stuff tumbled out: hairbrushes, makeup, cigarettes, magazines, address books, tampon holders, scraps of paper, and loose tobacco, for starters. The cops looked incredulously at each other and began the task of weeding through all this feminine paraphernalia. I was actually able to grin for a moment until I started imagining the headlines in tomorrow's *New York Post:*

DEAD NUDE GROUPIE FOUND IN ROCK STAR'S HOTEL ROOM

This sobered me up rather quickly. About an hour later, some doctor arrived with the news: "You got her here just in time. If you had slept through the night, you'd have awakened to a corpse in your room. She overdosed on something or other, and we were able to pump her stomach and save her. You're a lucky guy." Somehow, I didn't *feel* like a lucky guy.

Around lunchtime, she was discharged from the hospital, and I took her in a cab to her soon-to-be-famous brother's place. We walked into his soon-to-be-better-decorated apartment.

"She's all yours, big brother," I announced as I quickly took my leave. As I headed out the door, he looked at me with the look of a weary man who had done this before. *Whew! Close call, kids. . . .*

Part of me took this as a sign from above (or below). A heavenly (or hellish) warning to curtail my chemical activities. Shortly thereafter, the clouds parted and I found an apartment. Situated on the Upper East Side on 84th Street between Park and Lexington Avenues, I was close to my clubhouse (Dr. Generosity's) and this fabulous New York institution called Papaya King (amazing juices—nectars of the gods). It was then that I realized that this was my first apartment on my own. I had gone from my parents' house to my first marriage, from my first marriage to my second marriage, and now finally, I Lived Alone. I was happy.

I decorated the joint like a stoned-out rock star and then realized, hey!—*I don't have to take these pills anymore! I'm cured!* So I just stopped dead cold—a brave gesture at the least. The next day, I got this wicked flu and then the truth hit me like a ton of bricks: *I am actually physically addicted to the Percodan!* And I was booked *solid* for the next six weeks with only two or three days off a week. I made an appointment with this doctor that I saw for actual physical ailments. Now this was no Dr. Nick. He was a serious, older man, who knew more than most doctors. He was so good, in fact, that I went to him despite Kooper's Medical Law, or KML: If you can't make them laugh, get rid of them.

On this occasion, I went in on some unrelated pretense (maybe an ingrown toenail) and asked him: "By the way, I have a friend who is addicted to Percodan and wants to end his horrible addiction. Is there some drug that can ease the pain and effects of withdrawal?"

The doctor paused maybe eight and a half seconds, and then, with only the most incredibly subtle trace of a baby smile, said: "No."

Of course he realized the true story. How stupid of me. He knew there was no friend.

That doctor was my only hope. As I mentioned before, in 1971 there were no rehab centers and I knew I would need more than three days off to end this curse myself. The really twisted part was that I was ready to stop taking the pills, but didn't have the time frame to do it in. So now I had to take a daily dosage just so I wouldn't get sick. This did not appeal to my intellectual side.

For a month and a half, I lived this horrible life of preventive drug maintenance until the time I had booked to kick the addiction arrived. I told everyone I was going on vacation to an undisclosed place and stocked my apartment for the inevitable onslaught. I should have had someone help me, but I was simply too embarrassed to share my horror with anyone else. That first morning I took my stash, which was quite formidable, stared at it for a full five minutes, then quickly flushed hundreds of pills down the toilet.

This was it. No turning back now.

I knew I had a day before the withdrawal would set in, so I went to the market and bought supplies, and began reading one of the books I had naively set aside for this trip. The next morning, the flu began again. I woke up bathed in sweat with a temperature that was raging. I cursed myself for flushing my stash as I spent most of the day retching into the very toilet down which the stash had exited.

Ever wonder what happens when you take ten Percodans a day for a few months and then suddenly stop? When I wasn't bathed in sweat, I was suffering incredible chills. Tylenol was the medication I had allowed myself, and I'm surprised I didn't just down the whole bottle. All the demons I had avoided for 27 years were in that apartment alongside me running wild. Eating was impossible as nothing really stayed down. I drank as much water as I could to keep from dehydrating and replaced meals with frozen fruit bars, which were all I could get away with eating. This went on more or less for five days.

On the sixth day, I began to feel the stirrings of the first minor victory. I had periods of normal body temperature. I was so thankful that I eschewed reading or watching TV. I just sat there and marveled at feeling human again, albeit a shell of a human. I wondered how Jerry Lewis had gotten through this (another book-confessed Percodan addict). The soundtrack for this nightmare was provided by Stevie Wonder's *Music of My Mind* and Rory Gallagher's self-titled solo debut. To this day, when I hear any music from those two albums, memories of all kinds flood my soiled synapses. They were my only companions on that unguided tour through hell.

Week two began weakly. I needed to get my strength back and develop a new daily regimen. The food I had foolishly bought on the first day was all spoiled. I ventured outside for the first time in a year unaddicted. Words basically fail me here. Breathing the fall air, seeing the birds—I took nothing for granted. The people who worked at the market that knew me were kind enough not to comment on my appearance, and I headed home with my new supplies. That next week began the *mental* rebuilding. I knew one thing. I would eventually have to leave New York City. The demons were waiting around every corner. *It would never be the same again.*

Touring was pretty much a way of life for me in this era. I had a four-piece combo of childhood friends, and I often would take my best friend, Michael Gately, along, who would play court jester. We gigged about four days a week and usually returned home on the off days unless we were doing a full-blown tour.

Around '71, I was rounding out a nationwide tour with a few dates in the New York area. One concert was booked out at C. W. Post College in Greenvale, Long Island. The last time I played at old C. W. was for their homecoming weekend of 1962-1963, which I mentioned before, when an unknown Paul Simon and I played twist tunes as part of his dad's society orchestra!!!

Anyway, here I was back at C. W., and at $5,000, I think they were paying me one hundred times what they paid me last time. Not bad for seven years' work. We were headlining this show with Long John Baldry and The J. Geils Band in support. I had seen The Geils Band play a week earlier, and there was no way I was gonna follow them. I never dug headlining anyway. In a three-act show, it's hipper to go on second 'cause you get the audience in their prime. By the time the third act comes on they've sat through at least three hours of god-knows-what, and they're tired. Also, if you headline, you gotta hang around all night long, and that is the lowest. It's strictly a matter of ego and management, but let me get in there, play, and go home, I don't care if I open the damn show.

I strolled on down to The Geils' dressing room while Baldry was onstage. Peter Wolf, their lead singer, was an old friend of mine (used to interview me when he was a DJ in Cambridge, Massachusetts), and we said hi and all the amenities. I then asked them if they minded closing the show and they were glad to do it. It also let the show make more sense in terms of energy buildup. Baldry was into his last song, so I made it back to my dressing room to get ready. My folks had made one of their infrequent pilgrimages to hear their "darling son," and I wanted to get up there and "kick a little ass" for Mom and Dad.

Well, I was just slipping into my rhinestone-studded pants when the Man entered. Cops in the dressing room didn't bother me much, 'cause I had just kicked drugs and was not getting high at the time, and I didn't have a police record (they didn't even start recording till the late '70s). Usually cops were just nosing around for dope, so I'd ask them real complicated questions about their guns or boots until they'd get bored and leave. That night we had the chief of police of Greenvale, Long Island, and the head of security for C. W. Post College both in my dressing room at one time. I was honored.

Said the chief: "Mr. Kooper? Ah, yes. Well, it seems that someone has threatened to do you bodily harm tonight during your performance. They phoned headquarters to warn us, so I wouldn't put much credence in it, but nonetheless, what would you like to do about it?"

I told him I would like to get the hell out of there as soon as possible. However, it was a sellout concert, I was the advertised headliner, and it was probably just some coked-up guy whose girlfriend bought an Al Kooper album that day.

The chief informed me he had thirty policemen (that was probably the entire Greenvale force) outside to assist if anything might occur. I told him to dismiss twenty-six of 'em; all we needed was four pall bearers. Heh, heh.

We were all yukking it up when I realized I had go onstage in five minutes. *Target time*. Not only that, but there were probably only *two* people not smoking dope in the audience (my parents), and a surprise appearance by thirty uniformed policemen would not endear me to the crowd, if you catch my drift. And the ol' chief, he didn't wanna start a riot for a few joints, bless his heart. Well, I said, let's put four plainclothesmen in front of the stage ready to rock, and do a quick-escape-motorcycle-escort right after the last song, and we'll basically just roll the dice.

"Great. Thank you, Mr. Kooper," the chief said, and the two men were gone.

My sidemen at the time, John Paul Fetta on bass and Roy Markowitz on drums, were more scared than I was. And I was gettin' *kinda* scared. As we walked out . . . no . . . *edged* out on stage, I realized that my parents being out there somewhere gave it a kind of a John Frankenheimer reality. (Imagined *New York Post* story the next day, *". . . and as his horrified parents Samuel and Natalie watched in helpless horror, a volley of bullets caught him in the chest right in the middle of 'Season of the Witch,' toppling him to the stage floor. At first the crowd thought it was part of the show, but when thirty police officers began to. . . ."*)

Well, we didn't play too well. I got distracted, though, and played for a long time. A half-hour over my prescribed set time. The Geils Band were pissed off, but they never saw me after the show. Three cops immediately grabbed me and "escorted me to an already moving vehicle" (shades of Dylan) with a motorcycle escort to the Long Island Expressway.

Obviously, I didn't get killed. I didn't even get shot at, not a stab wound or any wet noodle marks.

The booking agency I was with paired me with many of its other clients in various package shows. Consequently, I spent a lot of touring time with mostly Cactus, Rory Gallagher, and Badfinger. The only time I played Carnegie Hall was on a package tour with Badfinger. They were also managed by the same company I was. They couldn't cope with the financial shenanigans going on around us as well I as I could, and two of them—Peter Ham and Tom Evans—hanged themselves within a few years of each other. They had a financial picture painted for them that was rosy and cheerful. But when the porous layers were peeled away, they found that they were rich only in their dreams and all their money was "gone." For some people this can be just too much to bear. Ham and Evans couldn't live with the deception and so they checked out. Ham allegedly left a suicide note that named Stan Polley—the principal of the agency—as the cause of his suicide. Polley denied the existence of such a note. This was horrible stuff and I don't know how I rationalized my way through it all, but blindly I did. I was making a great deal of money. My rent and all the rest of my bills were paid for me, lucrative deals were struck when necessary, and I always felt flush. So, even as everyone dropped away from Polley one by one, I stuck it out.

As I said, Stanley Polley was the principal of the company. Its other clients were Lou Christie, Bob Lewis (a top New York DJ and voice-over king), my friend Charlie Calello (who had recruited me into the firm), Irwin Levine (my old writing partner who was reaping wild success with Tony Orlando & Dawn songs like "Knock Three

Times," "Candida," and "Tie a Yellow Ribbon" sans me), The Tokens (a fifties' doo-wop group who were extremely successful producers in the sixties), and Badfinger. Polley was incredibly bright and had some bona fide original business plans. His downside was that he was incredibly devious and, in my opinion, had zero regard for the human condition. The latter was, I believe, the reason we lost the two lads from Badfinger. Polley reminded me of Dr. Lechter from the Thomas Harris books. An acknowledged brilliant doctor, but one who just happened to eat a few of his patients. That was Polley, figuratively speaking. Take my own case: My royalties always used to be mailed to him, and of course, after he stopped representing me, he stopped sending any rightful money or royalties to me. It took me twenty-five years of legal wrangles to stop those royalties from being mailed to him. A detailed look at the above-mentioned situation can be found in Dan Matovina's thorough Badfinger biography.

I went out with Badfinger on a tour that lasted three months. The last date was in Chicago. There were bets I couldn't finish the tour because of my previously annotated condition. I had a lot of money and faith riding on this tour. The final two dates were in Chicago with a day off in between. We played the first date, and on the day off my band and I had a celebration dinner. I had a huge prime rib entree and retired to my room with a Hawaiian female acquaintance. About 3 a.m. I became incredibly ill, and had to call the guys in the band. Food poisoning was determined to be the culprit as all the lads were afflicted—but none as bad as I, the ulcerated contestant. The hotel doctor gave me a strong sedative and advised hospitalization. I told the guys to book flights and get us out of Dodge pronto. I had them call my parents and have an ambulance meet us at the airport. I got off the plane, got into the ambulance, and checked into the hospital. I lost the damn bet and it hadn't been my fault. I told everyone to put "Felled by Roast Beef at the Albert Pick Motor Hotel" on my tombstone. I was in incredible pain most of the time and was being fed intravenously. Ironically, morphine was being administered for the pain. This is a no-no in twelve-step programs, but I had graduated from the two-step program.

The next day, a visiting friend was sitting there eating pizza just to bug me. The nurse came in, gave me my pain shot, and departed. An hour later, soon after the nurse-shift changed, another nurse came in to accidentally give me the same shot.

"You're early," I slurred, "The other nurse got me just a few minutes ago." This alleged angel of mercy was not interested. "Just you roll over and don't give me any of your lip!" she ordered, as nurses do. I began to wonder just when that last shot *was* administered as her needle jabbed me painlessly.

A few minutes later, I started rushing like crazy. My pizza-eating friend looked up and happened to notice I was turning blue and ran to get help. "Oh, great!" I thought to myself, "They've just overdosed me by accident in the fucking *hospital.* Who is going to believe *this*? I'm gonna spend eternity as a junkie who killed himself. Fuck all the irony *before* this. *This is the ultimate irony!*"

Everything went cool and black like a dark, air-conditioned room except that a feeling of swift motion accompanied the other feeling, as if the room was a vehicle moving at hyper speed. Finally, a clearing came and I could actually look down from above at *me* with doctors and nurses working away to save my life. This lasted a very short time. Back to the cool, dark, speeding room and then groggily awakening in the real world. I'm told this is called an "out-of-body" experience. The whole thing was incredibly clinical and smooth. So was the removal of the nurse who had OD'd me.

Two weeks after I got out of the hospital, my agent called me.

"You have got to help me out of a jam," he pleaded. "I have a million-dollar tour booked for Deep Purple starting in two weeks and Ritchie Blackmore [lead guitarist] just went in the hospital with mononucleosis. Can you go down and audition with them tomorrow afternoon?" I was dumbfounded. Firstly, I was now a keyboard player, a fair one at that, who only dabbled on guitar. Richie Blackmore was a guitar *god*—light years ahead of what I could ever assimilate. Secondly, I did not know any of their songs, and most of all, I had just finished a tour that had put *me* in the hospital. *There was no way I was gonna do this*. I told him so but he begged me to go to the audition anyway just to buy him some time to secure someone who really *was* capable. I owed him that.

I packed up my trusty Epiphone Wilshire guitar and went to the rehearsal studio where they were practicing. I knew some of the Purples from the circuit and we exchanged happy hellos. They started playing something pretty simple and I joined in. Having spent many years as a studio musician, I was able to learn things quickly, on the spot. Everyone was smiling and, frankly, I was amazed. They played a song next that was *really* fast and I waved off the guitar solo. It was simply too fast for me to play a solo.

"That's OK, Al," the lead singer, Ian Gillan, said to me. "We'll just have a longer organ solo there. Not to worry."

These guys really think I'm gonna do this, I thought to myself. Incredible.

I finished playing with them and everybody was smiles. The road manager walked me to the door. "That was great, Al. You passed the ultimate test. The roadies all loved it. And in that first song, you even started the solo on the same *note* Ritchie does. See ya tomorrow."

On the cab ride home, I actually considered it for five minutes, but common sense prevailed before I arrived. I called Jeff Franklin, the agent, and berated him.

I had fulfilled my end of the bargain, and he had to tell them I really couldn't do it.

Franklin was actually in tears on the phone. "What am I gonna do? Who can I get to do this? Please at least suggest someone!" he said.

I pulled out the name of one of my favorite guitarists, Randy California, who played with the group Spirit. Franklin thanked me profusely and that was the last I heard of it for a month. Then a third party told me that Randy had rehearsed with them and it was magnificent. The first date of the tour was in Hawaii. The night of the show, I'm told, Randy barricaded himself in his hotel room and refused to come out and play. The tour was canceled. Guess it was jinxed and there was nothing *anyone* could do about it.

Mike Bloomfield and I played a few live gigs and mini-tours together. Mike was full of surprises. Like not showing up until 8:05 for an 8 p.m. gig. His brother Allen lived in New York and we became friends. He was slightly younger than Mike and there was more than a passing resemblance. My manager hired him as an assistant and occasionally Allen would come along on gigs to settle accounts with the promoters. And so there he was, one wintry eve, as we arrived at the Boston Garden to play a soldout show. I was excited; home of the Boston Celtics, etc. It was no mean feat to sell out the Boston Garden. Buddy Miles' Express was opening for Bloomfield and me. So, Buddy Miles went on and still there was no sign of Mike. Don Law, the promoter, came in the dressing room and noticed there was no Bloomfield.

"Is Mike showing up?" he asked, visibly upset.

"Yeah, yeah, Don. He's here. He just went out to listen to Buddy's set. Not to worry."

Buddy Miles played his encore and Don left, not totally convinced—and neither was I.

I looked at Allen: "We are up Shit's Creek here, bro. I can't believe he still does this to me!"

Allen gave me this commiserating look and a light bulb went off in my head. "Allen, take off your coat. Hurry!"

I slipped a guitar and strap over his head against his heavy protestations.

"Just come out on stage with me and tell the audience you have a high temperature and can't play and that the band will play without you," I said, half-smiling. "Then duck and run!"

Now we were actually walking to the stage when Mike finally showed up. He gave me a big hug and then saw his musically untalented brother with a guitar strapped on him. Grabbing the guitar out of his brother's hands, he looked deep into Allen's eyes and said: "What are you . . . *fucking NUTS*??? Gimme that!!!"

It was also around this time that I had a short fling with Quincy Jones' daughter, Jolie. My ex-wife Joan actually fixed the two of us up, and I believe I unknowingly stepped in between Keith Richards and her. But Jolie was a wonderful woman and we got along quite well. I put pen to paper and wrote a song called "Jolie." I recorded it and gave it to her for her birthday. She loved it and insisted on taking me home and playing it for Dad. Now back then Quincy was not the megastar he is today, but I certainly knew who he was and I was a big fan. So we came into his home and Jolie introduced us and then put the tape of the song on. I was as embarrassed as I've ever been in this life as the tape played and Quincy listened real hard to my pathetic Al Green imitation. The lyric was personal and real, however. The song finished and he looked at the two of us holding hands and said, "I feel like I'm peeping in the keyhole!" Guess *he* was embarrassed, too. Our affair didn't last too much longer; geography was against us at the time. But I'll always have fond memories of her and Quincy. Oh, and by the way, Tony Orlando and Dawn, and Lattimore, also recorded "Jolie."

Whilst in the middle of some criss-crossed touring itinerary, I ended up on a red-eye flight from Detroit to Los Angeles, flying first class. It was around 1 a.m. I was exhausted, and collapsed right into my window seat and immediately shut my eyes. In a dream-state, I heard the occupant of the aisle seat sit down and the stewardess ask: "Mr. Robinson, can I get you anything before we take off?"

A gentle voice informed her that everything was fine and he wouldn't be requiring anything until after we were airborne. There was something about that voice. . . . My brain cycled through its voice files. Naaaah, it *couldn't* be. . . . Slowly I turned my head and ventured a peek.

Holy shit! *I was sitting next to Smokey Robinson!* This was incredible! All systems went into full wake-up. I opened my eyes, stretched, and gave out a casual "Hey Smokey, how ya doin? Al Kooper here. . . ."

He shook my hand and said, "Yeah—I thought I recognized you."

He knows who I am? I thought. I secretly pinched myself, and I was still there.

I had just recorded a song he wrote for my next album. I carried one of those three-piece-pre-walkman units that had a cassette player and two detached speakers in a pseudo-leather case. The player itself had a headphone jack. Unzipping the case, I offered: "Smokey? I just recorded one of your songs for my new album. Wanna hear it?"

He actually seemed interested! He slipped the headphones on, listening to my cover of "Swept for You Baby" from my album called *A Possible Projection of the Future* with a slight grin on his face. And we hadn't even taken off yet! I was in heaven.

Then, it got good to me. "Have you heard that new guy Al Green's version of your song, 'My Girl'?" I asked. Back on went the headphones, and I produced a pre-release cassette of Al Green's new album with Smokey's song on it. Again, he listened intently, smiling slightly.

The plane finally took off, and we had a great time. Even got a little shut-eye before landing. Exchanging phone numbers, we shook hands, bade our farewells, and wished each other luck. He wouldn't actually be needing *my* good luck wishes.

So you can imagine my surprise when, a year later, the phone rang and it was Smokey Robinson. He was making his farewell tour with The Miracles, and invited me and a guest to see their show at the Apollo Theater in New York. I was honored and flabbergasted. I thanked him profusely and hung up the phone.

I was in the middle of producing three sides on Bobby Hatfield, the high-voiced-half of The Righteous Brothers, for Warner Bros. I invited Bobby to go with me to see Smokey, and since he was a little reluctant to venture into Harlem, we decided to go during the day to alleviate his fears. I hadn't been to the Apollo in quite a while, but I was usually oblivious to the black/white thing.

On the appointed day, we showed up at the backstage door, gave our names, and were ushered right in and up to The Miracles' dressing room. We were greeted warmly by all concerned and sat down to shoot the shit while various card games went on all around us. After about fifteen minutes, a valet guy stuck his head in the door and announced the classic five-minute call. I was jazzed. I was only hoping Smokey wouldn't call us onstage to sing cause Bobby and Smokey can really sing and I was . . . errr . . . still learning.

We walked down to the side of the stage and Smokey signaled for a monitor speaker and had it set down right in front of Bobby and me. I was really flattered. All this time there was a comedian onstage telling a long story about a black kid's first day at school. The valet asked Smokey if he was ready and Smokey said yeah. Right in the middle of this comedian's routine, the valet leaned out from the wings and stage-yelled: "That's it, muthafucka!!" The comedian was in mid-sentence. I'll never forget it. This is how it went:

"So, the little brother is walking to the classroom and he runs smack into the white kid. [Here the valet shouted, "That's it, muthafucka!!"] And the white kid. . . ." "IT"S SHOWTIME, LADIES AND GENTLEMEN!! SHOW-TIME!!! ARE YOU READY FOR THE STARS OF OUR SHOW? MAKING THEIR FINAL APPEARANCE TOGETHER, HERE ARE SMOKEY ROBINSON AND THE MIRACLES!!!"

The place went nuts. The audience really didn't care about the black kid's first day at school anyway, and no one was gonna remember they never heard the punchline to that story. All they knew right then was it was the last time they'd ever see Smokey Robinson and The Miracles live together onstage.

The sound in the monitor was perfect, and Bobby and I were having a great time. In the middle of the show, Smokey introduced us to the audience and we came out and took a bow, and thankfully, that's all we did. After the show, we went back to the dressing room to hang and forgot all about time. We were the token white guys. Before you knew it, it was five minutes before the *next* show and we'd definitely overstayed our welcome. We walked outside from the stage door and it was night time. Bobby was apoplectic. To the right was a completely empty, desolate alley. To the left was a street with guys all hanging out.

"Which way, Bobby?" I asked. "It's your choice."

Bobby opted for the empty alley, which we raced down till we hit West 125 Street. We got a cab instantaneously and Bobby handed the driver ten bucks as we got in, shouting: "Downtown! Quickly!"

And that's my Smokey Robinson story. . . .

Well, there's actually a Milton Berle story.

On a coast-to-coast flight in first class, some airline employee with a sense of humor sat me next to Milton Berle. Now, when I think of Milton, I think of the rumors I've heard of the comparatively giant size of his manhood. So sitting there next to him I was trying to work up the nerve to ask him about that topic, but I just couldn't. Besides, we were having a spirited debate about whether or not I'd paid my dues in show business as compared to him. Really! He was actually very nice and respectful to me, and I was really liking him. Then, in a total non sequitur, he said:

"Al, you think you know how to fuck?"

He had caught me a little off-guard.

"Well, maybe a little bit," I answered. "But I practice for hours on end every day, Milton." He smiled.

"Let me tell ya, Al—you don't know how to fuck till you get to be *my* age."

Yeah, Milton—but then what do you do with that information when you're eighty???

This was a stupefying thought to me. And to this day, I couldn't agree with him less. As in roundball, I think my best playing years are behind me. And the day he said that to me, I bet any woman on earth would've chosen me in head-to-head competition, if ya catch my drift. But me Mum taught me to respect me elders and if you're still alive and reading this, Miltie—I pretended that you were right, but in my heart I knew you were not.

Still another story: Some airline employee with a sadistic streak sat me next to an Army uniform-clad George Jessel on a long flight. After fifteen minutes, I changed my seat. And not because of the Army uniform.

Then there was the Miles Davis problem.

Miles and I were both signed to Columbia Records. Miles didn't like me. He wrote letters to Clive Davis and Goddard Leiberson urging them to drop me from the artist roster because I was "ripping off the black man." If only he knew that the white men were ripping me off. He would glower at me if he saw me in a store or a club. Around this time, Miles was into boxing, and he had many pictures of himself sparring in many publications. I was sure he was gonna knock me to the moon one day. I was always jumpy when he was in the vicinity.

One night, I was in the studio recording and Harvey Brooks told me that he would be in the building at the same time on a session on the second floor. I was at the soda machine and I asked some woman who walked by if she was on the session on the second floor. She said she was, so I asked her nicely if she could tell Harvey Brooks to come up and see me on the fifth floor during his break. She said she would, and that was it for about half an hour. Then the janitor walked into the control room with a note for me. On the outside it said: "Al Kooper READ THIS 3 TIMES!!" I unfolded it, and inside it said: "Don't you ever talk to my wife again in this life!! Miles Davis." Oh, great!!! I thought. Why didn't Harvey tell me whose session he had been booked on? More Miles trouble. Wish I'd saved that note, though.

This bad blood went on for about two years. One night I had just finished a show at the Bitter End on Bleecker Street in the Village, and Miles walked into the dressing room. My heart beat "like a hammer," as B. B. King once sang. Miles walked right up to me. "I really enjoyed your performance." He smiled, shook my hand, turned, and walked out. And that was the end of the Miles Davis problem. Why hadn't he come to one of my shows sooner??? I'll never know.

Charlie Calello did a lot of jingle work. He was always trying to talk me into turning those jingle tricks, but I noticed when I was a sideman on some of his dates how obnoxious the ad guys were, and frankly didn't think I could interface with that nonsense. Finally, one day, he broke through.

"They want you for an international Pepsi spot, Al," he said. "This is worth a fortune. Please take this meeting. I'll go with you. It'll be a cinch. Tell them what to do and collect a huge check."

After years of pestering, I relented and "took the meeting." So there's Charlie and I seated at this conference table with the ad guys. I had brought along some LPs of music I thought would be good for Pepsi ads. We watched the sixty-second spot, and I reached for that first Elton John album. I played them "Border Song," which actually *would* have been fabulous for the spot. This incredibly stupid anal debate began that I instantly tuned out. Frank Zappa said it best: "Talking about music is like dancing about architecture."

I sat in quiet horror and watched these guys completely misunderstand every-thing in the world. Finally, I could sit no longer. They were treating Charlie and me like we were hockey refs who had just thrown the puck in the huddle. They ignored us. I told Charlie that I was really sorry for what I was about to do and I hoped I wouldn't get him in trouble. He gave me that "oh no" look that he reserved for my worst behavior as I stood up to leave. The conversation in the room stopped dead.

"Hey, Al, ya thirsty?" asked one of the ad guys. "Ya want a Pepsi or somethin'? I'll have the girl get ya one."

I lost it.

"You know," I said, packing up my LPs and moving toward the door, "when you guys get up in the morning, you don't put your clothes on . . . you put yourselves on." And out the door I sailed, leaving Charlie with the dirty laundry.

I was told that the business changed shortly thereafter, when many more peo-ple my age infiltrated the ranks of ad agencies. I even tried again in 1997, but it was just as disastrous. Hey, you can't do everything!

As I mentioned previously, I was touring quite a bit at this time. One particular scenario comes to mind: We were in some town, early seventies, and I lost control and took some wild-looking-dreadlocked-ring-in-her-nose young woman back to my room that night. This was in the days when one in six hundred young women opted for this particular haute couture. We were scheduled to leave at eight the next morning and drive to the airport. I tried to sneak this young woman out without the other musicians seeing her, but it didn't work.

They were giggling like girlie-men!

As we got into the station wagon for the half-hour-haul to the airport, the gig-gling continued and I turned around to them and said:

"I don't want to hear *one word* from you guys on this trip, okay? And that includes that stupid giggling, too."

Silence.

For ten whole minutes.

Then, from drummer Roy Markowitz, way in the back:

"Hey! I thought you said her father was a *rich* doctor!"

Even I had to laugh at that one.

There came a time when I realized that, even if I recorded an album as great as *Sgt. Pepper's Lonely Hearts Club Band*, CBS would put it out, but basically ignore it. My contract had another two years to go and I decided not to record until I could sign with another label. I owed CBS one more album, however, and that would have to be done. I went up to Commander Clive Davis's office and asked for a release. Flat out. He smiled at me, saying: "Oh no, my friend. We have far too big an investment in you to just let you go." Well, *that* didn't work, I thought to myself.

Clive's reply was from a man who juggled company funds to remodel his apartment and pay for his son's $100,000 bar mitzvah (speaking of big investments). When the latter tidbits of information were uncovered, Clive was unceremoniously ushered out of his posh job to the relative discomfort of his newly remodeled apartment, while some of his underlings who also had wives and children went to prison on drug-related charges that Clive never had to face. After a few years, he was resurrected to run a new label, which he named Arista—ironically, a synonym for "honor society"—and to this day the world still wrestles with Whitney Houston and Kenny G as a result.

The week after this conversation with Commander Clive, I was scheduled to play Atlanta for a few days. Little did I know how much that trip would change my life.

1972-1974:

ATLANTA,

SOUNDS OF THE SOUTH
RECORDS,

LYNYRD SKYNYRD,

A MOVE TO L.A.,

DUSTIN HOFFMAN,

A MILLION DOLLARS, AND

SPEED IN MY SODA

My band and I arrived in Atlanta for a few nights' engagement at a club in the Underground. I had not appeared there since the Pop Festival of 1969, three years previously. *Things had changed.*

It was looser than I remembered it. It wasn't so . . . *Southern*. There was a sociological gentrification in attitude that had taken place that was tangible to me. The *rednecks* had long hair now. They were no longer the enemy. People got along better. I liked this. The women were beautiful and willing. We had a wild time that week. My penchant for womanizing during this time-frame was akin to sexual addiction. In fact, it *was* sexual addiction, in hindsight, if the truth be told. This lasted, without treatment or diagnosis, until around 1979, when it got more reasonable. That was also about the same time AIDS reared its ugly head, so it was just as well. For those of you who were born in the late sixties and seventies, I have detailed a few sociological encounters of the sexual variety further along in this text to illustrate that sexual activity was not always as it is now. My motive is sociological, not misogynistical (is this a word?): I won't be bragging about these trysts; I will just be reporting the way things were back then.

While in Atlanta, I called my friends who had been Roy Orbison's backup band, The Candymen. They were now called The Atlanta Rhythm Section and were busy making a new album. They had their own recording facility called Studio One, and they invited us down to jam one night. My band came in with me, and all of us just jammed away. I was quite taken with the sound they got in that studio. I was *extremely* impressed.

When I got back home, I made a deal with Warner Brothers Records for me to produce my backup band Frankie & Johnny. We booked time in Atlanta at Studio One for a month. This time when I set foot in Atlanta, I would never return to living in New York City again.

Our modus operandi was thus: We would start work each day at noon and quit around eight. The Atlanta Rhythm Section was the backup band fronted by Frankie (Frank Ribando) & Johnny (John Paul Fetta). The ARS consisted of Barry Bailey and J. R. Cobb on guitars, Dean Daughtrey on keyboards, Paul Goddard on bass, and Robert Nix on drums. The engineers were Rodney Mills and Bob "Tub" Langford. After each session, Frankie, Johnny, and myself would repair to Funnochios, a rock club, downtown on Peachtree Street. Some guy I had gone to summer camp(!) with was the manager of said establishment, and he gave us the red carpet treatment. Each night we were shown to the VIP Balcony, where we could sit and view the whole club. We had our own waitress and security guy. If we saw any young ladies on the dance floor that were to our liking from our catbird seats, the security guard was dispatched to invite them to our private enclave. Most women were happy to join us and get that "special treatment." It seemed like Paradise. What I didn't know was that this club was a traditional "bucket o' blood" establishment where shootings and stabbings regularly took place, and bodies were routinely carried out. Later, I would notice these things. But from where *we* sat, everything looked *beautiful*.

The first week we were there, a band named Boot was playing. Around midnight or so, I'd go down and sit in with them and play a few songs. This became an every night occurrence, as Boot played there for a whole week. The next Monday, Boot was gone and a new band took their place. The "tradition" immediately stopped as we sat and checked out the newcomers. The lead singer was blond and barefoot, and swung the mikestand around like a majorette's baton. The hair of both guitarists was so long you literally couldn't see their faces when they played. They looked like a coupla Cousin Its on stilts with guitars. And they played no cover tunes. It was all original stuff. They were really cool and I spent more time listening to them than I did searching for women. They had that sound I was looking for—that return to basic rock. The third night I worked up the nerve to sit in with them. They actually had heard of me and were flattered to have me join them. I strapped on a guitar and said: "*Let's go!!*" The lead singer called out "Mean Woman Blues" in C# and counted it off. *C#????*

In all my years of jamming, nobody *ever* called C#. It's a weird key between two relatively easy keys that would just as easily have sufficed. Later, I found out it was an intimidation process they dreamed up to keep jammers offstage. But I could play fine in C#. As Nigel Tufnel of Spinal Tap would say: "*It's just one more than C!*"

The rest of the week I sat in with them in C#. On Friday night after the club closed, one of the guitarists and I found ourselves at the same young lady's apartment. We ignored her and yakked all night. I was really starting to like these guys. They were playing a weird amalgam of blues with second-generation British band influences (Cream, Free, etc.). The resultant sound was unique and appealed to me. The one song that got to me every night was called "I Ain't the One." By the third night, I was waiting for them to play that song, although I did not know its name yet. The last night they played, I offered them a recording deal with me as producer. They said they would mull it over and discuss it with their manager. We said our goodbyes, and that was it. I hoped Lynyrd Skynyrd's manager would call me back.

Some nights we'd go to other clubs and see more bands that were quite good. The unsigned crew back then were Hydra, Eric Quincy Tate, Mose Jones, Kudzu, and a raft of other pretty good little groups. I had not seen such a fertile breeding ground and local scene since San Francisco in the mid-sixties. I had begun to make various friends from all this meandering, and I was growing very fond of Atlanta.

As we began the final week of working on Frankie & Johnny's album, I made a rash, crazy decision. I decided to send for my stuff, rent an apartment in Atlanta, and move there permanently. I never even went back to New York. Roadies back in New York packed all my stuff, and I settled into a little village of townhouses on Roswell Road. The first thing I noticed was that everyone had a handgun. I was not used to this mentality. You'd see them lying on coffee tables, on the bar, or even on the kitchen table. And many of the young ladies who lived in this development waitressed and tended bar but were not above turning a trick or two to pay the rent. Between the artillery and the hooking, it was quite a culture shock. Not that handguns and hooking didn't go on in New York City when I lived there; it's just that it hadn't been in my face there as much as it was in Atlanta. For example: In twenty-seven years of living in New York, I never witnessed a shooting. In three months in Atlanta, I witnessed two.

My business overview was thus: No record company except Phil Walden's Capricorn Records based in Macon, Georgia, understood that something was going on in the South. If Capricorn turned a band down, they were pretty much doomed, because no other label understood this phenomenon. I decided I would start *my own label* as an alternative to Capricorn and base it out of Atlanta. My agent had friends at MCA Records in L.A., and I flew out to meet with them. I painted this rosy picture and told them to surprise me with a visit so that nothing could be rigged and we'd go to a bunch of clubs and spontaneously see unsigned bands that were ripe for the picking. If they agreed with my evaluation, we had a deal. They came down soon afterwards, and we toured the town that night and saw a handful of great, unsigned bands. The next week we signed a deal. I would helm my own record company, and they would distribute its records. More importantly, they would bankroll the company, because I've always adhered to the first law of business: "Never spend your own money."

I rented a large house to live in and run the company out of in Sandy Springs, a middle-class (back when there *was* such a thing) suburb, and dubbed this new venture "Sounds of the South." The logo of the company was a photo of a one-hundred-fifty-year-old log cabin that was on my property.

Concurrently, I finally heard from Skynyrd's manager, who turned out to be Phil Walden's younger brother, Alan. This illustrated my case in point. These guys had the closest inside track to Capricorn (their manager was the president's brother!) and obviously Capricorn wasn't interested, or maybe some sibling rivalry was going on. None of the other labels understood what Phil Walden and I knew—and so here was Skynyrd at my doorstep with virtually nowhere else to turn; album-ready and leery of the Yankee slicker (that would be their nickname for me in their soon-to-be-written song, "Workin' for MCA").

Alan Walden and I pounded it out for two or three months until we finally came to an agreement. During that period of negotiation, Ronnie Van Zant called me about 2 a.m. one night.

"Al, our equipment van got broken into last night and we can't put food in our families' mouths without that gear. We have engagements to fulfill immediately and unless you can lend us five thousand dollars by tomorrow morning, we're fucked!"

I didn't even think twice: "Where do I send it, buddy?" He gave me the address and closed with: "*Al, you just bought yourself a band for five thousand dollars.*"

I never worried about that money. Ronnie was a gentleman and a man of his word. He ruled that band with an iron fist, and God help any band member who crossed him. Of course, that was impossible, because they all worshipped him.

Possessed of a unique talent for savvy songwriting, a rather pedestrian voice that had its own unique sound, and remarkable leadership skills, Ronnie was the mediator between the rest of the band and myself. As a producer, I offered my artists one hundred percent of my input. What percentage they chose to use was up to them. Of course, it varied from act to act. With Skynyrd, there wasn't that much to do. They were incredibly well rehearsed (they even composed their guitar solos beforehand), they were the best damn arrangers I have *ever* worked with, and their musical discipline was *everything* to them. They understood music organically, not by the book. What I brought to the table was comparatively small, but important. Basically, I showed them how to use the studio as another ingredient in their arrangements. I taught them about the relationship between the bass and the bass drum, and how, if used correctly, it could make certain grooves rock even harder.

I only had to show them once.

I introduced them to horns and background singers when appropriate. And because all the guitar solos were composed beforehand, I usually doubled them to give them more strength. I would try to argue out weak songs. When I was right, they were dropped. When I was wrong, I was overridden. It was that simple. One time, I was making a point about something, and they were all groaning. Ronnie said: "Awright. Wait just a second. I think that idea sucks too *but* I will listen to everything Al says. Maybe once in twenty times he'll have a great idea, but I will suffer the other nineteen times because that twentieth one will make us sound better, so go easy on the old guy!"

Yeah. The "old guy" was twenty-nine at the time!

The band that I signed was Ronnie, Allen Collins on guitar, Gary Rossington on guitar, Leon Wilkeson on bass, and Bob Burns on drums. These were all buddies who grew up in Jacksonville, Florida, and taught each other to play. It was that ideal situation that bands everywhere strive for: friends first, musicians second. *And believe me, they lived by that.* Between the time that I signed them and we went into the studio, Leon had quit the band. I think he was actually frightened of all the responsibilities that would be forthcoming. The band had played some shows awhile back with The Strawberry Alarm Clock and remembered what a great musician Ed King was. They called him and offered him Leon's bass spot on the recording sessions. Ed accepted and pretty much played Leon's composed parts on the record, but was able to add those little flourishes, slides, and grace notes that make the difference between bass playing and art. They also brought classical-whiz ex-roadie Billy Powell with them to play keyboards. This was a pleasant surprise for me. It added all the textures I loved to their guitar-driven sound.

Billy came right out of classical music, though, and tended to overplay with his left hand, causing the band's beautifully-constructed guitar parts to get lost in the mud. I took to actually *tying his left hand to the piano bench leg* to make my point, but he was pretty darn stubborn. By the third album, however, he was a grizzled studio veteran. There were many advantages to his classical background. Everyone remembers the intro to "Free Bird," and the solo in "Tuesday's Gone," which is a beautiful little sonata that he wrote himself. His solos throughout the proceedings were truly unique and he was a big asset to the band.

Allen and Gary had tremendous respect for each other's playing. Allen had an Eric Clapton-like approach to his playing, while Gary's was a curious mix between Ry Cooder and Paul Kossoff of Free. He had definitely appropriated Kossoff's vibrato and it became Gary's signature after Kossoff's untimely death. Bob Burns was not a great drummer, but he was one of the "gang" and he took direction well. The drum parts were always composed by committee, and Bob just did what he was told. Somehow, it all worked. But Burns was the least musical of anyone in the band.

On March 26, 1973, prior to recording their first album, I took them into the studio to record every original song they knew live-to-two-track, so that I could select what would go on the album. There was not a bad apple in the bunch of fourteen songs, so there were many tough decisions. In fact, many of the songs that did not make the first album were taken right off that demo tape and used as B sides for the first few singles and, later, as posthumous album filler. It's great stuff, and it's all live with no overdubs. If I were in charge, I would eventually put it all on one CD called *The Audition Tapes*, even with the demos of the songs that made the first album. It's a nice piece of history. Perhaps, one day this will happen. *Don't hold your breath.* . . .

The sessions for the band's first album went pretty well. We only clashed on a couple of points, but there was nothing we couldn't resolve with clear thinking on both sides. (I lost both arguments!) I had to mix the album three separate times in New York City to bring it up to *my* satisfaction. When I was happy, I played it for them, and they were happy.

My favorite story from those sessions:

One early morning, about 6 a.m., we were still doing vocals and Ronnie was out in the studio with headphones on waiting for us to change reels of tape. He began singing the Johnny Cash tune, "Hey Porter," a cappella to amuse himself. Unbeknownst to each other, the janitor had entered the studio through the back door and was preparing to straighten up. He hadn't seen Ronnie yet. As he walked in, Ronnie began singing "Hey Porter, Hey Porter, would you tell me the time?" He nearly died when this guy behind him yelled out "6:08 a.m., son!" Needless to say, those in the control room had a good fifteen-minute laugh as well.

I had also signed a local Atlanta band, Mose Jones. In my mind, stylistically speaking, Mose Jones were my Beatles, and Skynyrd were my Stones. My fantasy was that each band would sell in the 400,000-record range, which at that time was a good breaking point to do another album. That way, I could keep my house in the woods and earn a decent living. We went in and cut Mose Jones' album first. The material was not as good as Skynyrd's, but we had a nice, poppy, Beatlesque product and Sounds of the South's first release was the Mose Jones single "Here We Go Again." We got a lot of press and our little label was just about launched. I signed a horn band from East L.A. (hell, it was *my* label and they were from *Southern* California) called Elijah. And then there were three.

We hired Norman Winter Associates out of L.A. to do our press, and this woman named Sharon Lawrence was assigned to our account. She really got into it. Made friends with all the bands and really cared about our little operation. Sharon and I planned this huge launch party for the label. It was to be held at Atlanta's best rock club, Richard's. We were gonna fly all the important radio and press people in from all over the country, feed 'em delicious ribs, and have entertainment by Mose and Skynyrd. We actually pulled this off. The place was packed with the most important media people in the country. Hell, even Marc Bolan from T. Rex was our guest that night! Mose came out and played a great set. But Skynyrd stole the show. They mustered up all of their inherent discipline, and put together a show that *floored* these people. With their album due out in only weeks, they set themselves up brilliantly for press and radio support. The party was a huge success and I think MCA began to understand what great bands they had under their umbrella.

Early on I begged Skynyrd to change their name. It looked on paper like it was pronounced "Lie-nerd Sky-nerd." It didn't make any sense at first glance, and it certainly didn't conjure up what their music was about. I tried everything, but to no avail. They would not budge. So, I decided if I was stuck with it, I'd make the best of it.

They were also always getting in fistfights. If they couldn't find anyone to fight, they'd fight each other. I decided to paint a rough-house image for them. I designed a skull head and spelled their name out in a bones typeface. I proposed a teaser ad campaign to MCA that cost $100,000, a lot of money in those days. Because of the buzz from the launch party, MCA approved the campaign. It began six weeks before the release of the album with four quarter-page ads scattered throughout the music trade magazines and ten major-city alternative papers (i.e., *Village Voice*, *L.A. Free Press*, etc.). The ad said: "Who is Lynyrd Skynyrd?" And it used the bones logo. Each week, the size of the ad grew and a little more information was disseminated. The week the album came out, there was a huge two-page

Lynyrd Skynyrd being held captive in Al's home dungeon, Atlanta, 1972. (Left to right) Allen Collins, Billy Powell, Gary Rossington, Bob Burns, Leon Wilkeson, Ed King, Ronnie Van Zant (foreground). (Photo: Al Kooper Collection.)

ad. People were buzzing about them and radio kicked in three weeks before the street release. The first two weeks we were the most-added record on radio in the business. The album, intelligently titled *Pronounced Leh-nerd Skin-nerd*, began to sell nicely. Then our really big break came.

I ran into Pete Townshend of The Who and his manager Pete Rudge up at MCA. They were launching a huge tour for their *Quadrophenia* album (also on MCA), and I gave them Skynyrd's release and told them how well we were doing and what a great opening act the boys would be for them. Miraculously, the timing was perfect. The Who were looking for a young buzz act that they felt could sell whatever seat deficit was left over from their own fans. Skynyrd fit the bill perfectly.

I met with Skynyrd and we had this great pep talk. I knew they would rise to the occasion. They always did. So here was this young band from Jacksonville, which had never played to more than a thousand people at a time, and mostly to fewer than that in little Southern honky-tonks, who were now gonna step on stage in front of twenty thousand people every night to warm them up for one of the biggest bands in the world. I wanted this to be really foolproof and I kinda lost control. I insisted on mixing the house sound for the band on the tour. I just wanted it to be great, and while I trusted the band, I was uneasy about their crew. To Skynyrd's credit, they didn't balk. And neither did their sound crew.

And so there I was, mixing live sound on the tour. I used to say, "Let's see Clive Davis do this!"—referring to a record company president mixing live sound. The only problem was that, unlike normal bands that put the mixing console somewhere in the middle of the hall, The Who had to be mixed from the wings of the stage, so that if Townshend didn't like something, he could actually stroll over and whack Bob Pridden, their sound guy, across the head. This did not serve *me* in good stead, however, as I could only use a small pair of monitors or headphones and had to imagine what it sounded like in the house. With an ingenious system of good-eared runners, I eventually worked out a method of sending people I trusted out to various parts of the hall to report in by walkie-talkie. Somehow, it all fell into place, and Skynyrd began to do what no opening band for The Who had ever done—*they got encores*!

Pete Rudge stood in the wings with me the first night and was incredulous, saying: "I have *never* seen this happen with any Who opening band."

The boys rose to the occasion. And The Who took them inside their circle and treated them as peers.

The album took off, but we had no single to hang our hat on. We put out "Gimmee Three Steps" to no avail. The album's eleven-minute closing track, "Free Bird," garnered most of the FM airplay, and someone at MCA edited *that* down to four minutes and put it out, but no cigar. That was OK with me; slow and steady wins the race. Album sales were increasing as our demographics expanded. Radio embraced the album, and we were six cuts deep in formats that accepted them. Skynyrd became the favorite opening act of arena headliners because they sold whatever tickets were left over. ZZ Top, Savoy Brown, Eric Clapton, and even The Blues Project (at Philharmonic Hall in New York City) all enjoyed the benefits of Skynyrd's immediate fan draw.

Once, while not sympathetically billed as opening act for Black Sabbath, the audience came at them. I believe this was on Long Island at Nassau Coliseum. Leon had taken to wearing a London bobby's hat and a holster with a real gun in it containing blanks. Some vociferous fans approached the front of the stage.

"*You guys suck! Get the fuck off the stage! Ozzy rules!*" they screamed. Leon pulled out his gun and fired off a blank, but convincing, round right at them that caused a few wet pants in their crowd and an immediate cessation of catcalls.

My friend David McSheehy, who had managed my former clubhouse, Dr. Generosity's, in New York, got fed up with New York, threw all his stuff in his car, and drove to the Sounds of the South House to became my assistant. I bought a vintage 1960 Silver Shadow Rolls Royce from a friend in England for nine thousand dollars and had it shipped by boat to Jacksonville. David flew down and drove it back from Florida. It became one of the great toys. Evidently, there weren't a plethora of Rolls Royces in Atlanta in 1973, and so Governor Jimmy Carter's office used to rent my car to pick up visiting dignitaries at the airport. *I had a livery business going now, plus an open invite to the Governor's Mansion.* The car was European-style right-hand drive, and Skynyrd loved to pile into it and head for the local McDonald's just to mess people's minds up. *Life was good.*

By now, we had four albums released: one each by Skynyrd, Mose Jones, and Elijah, and a double live Blues Project album, *Reunion in Central Park.*

The Blues Project effectively broke up and split into two factions in 1967. I formed Blood, Sweat & Tears with Steve Katz; Andy Kulberg and Roy Blumenfeld moved westward and started Sea Train; and Danny Kalb was institutionalized for awhile as a result of a bad acid trip he took while on vacation. I had my own label and missed playing with the lads. I resurrected the band and booked a mini-tour that would be recorded for a live set. No matter that two out of the three albums in our discography were already live and featured many of the same songs we were currently performing—this was gonna be fun and great therapy for Danny. One of the shows we played on the tour was at an indoor venue in Washington, DC. This was actually the best show of the tour. By the time we got to the last show in our hometown New York's Central Park, a lot of the spontaneity was gone. But the audience was fantastic. When I edited the album, I used most of the Washington performances. taking the introductions and applause from the Central Park show. Besides, the title *Reunion in an Indoor Venue in Washington, DC* would not have been nearly as catchy as *Reunion in Central Park.* But catchy title or not, The Blues Project album sales, along with those of the Mose Jones and Elijah albums, were disappointing when compared to sales of the Skynyrd album.

After making myriad trips to L.A., I realized that moving there was inevitable as the only way I could stay on top of MCA. My work was done in Atlanta, and as idyllic as life was there, I would've been sticking my head in the Georgia clay like a redneck ostrich if I remained. I had given my word to these artists that I would do my best for them, and right then, it meant moving to L.A.

I located a rental house in the Hollywood Hills and started packing up. Then the day I arrived in L.A., the deal fell through for the rental house! I called the movers and told them to keep everything in storage until I located a place, and I checked into the Beverly Hills Hotel, virtually homeless. The first night I was there, I met Dustin Hoffman in the bar. We hit it off instantly, although to this day I'm convinced he thought I was Alice Cooper. He told me his parents were looking to get rid of *their* place and that I might want to check it out. The next day, on my way to a photo shoot, I met Dustin at his parents' house to scope it out. I arrived with Sam Emerson the photographer, who I was working with that afternoon, and Dustin arrived with his publicist Paul Bloch. His parents weren't home, and he had forgotten to bring the key, so he tried unsuccessfully to break into his parents' house. All this was documented on film by Sam. I thanked Dustin for his kind thoughts and left for the photo shoot.

Two nights later, Grand Funk Railroad were having a press party at the hotel for

Dustin Hoffman picks the wrong time to attempt eye contact with me at a Hollywood party, 1974. (Photo: Al Kooper Collection.)

their new album *We're an American Band*. I was invited and took Dustin as my guest to show him what record business parties were like. He hit the cocktails pretty hard and was feeling no pain as the president of Capitol Records, Bhaskar Menon, got up to make a speech. There were about thirty lifesize blow-up Uncle Sam dolls set up throughout the party area. When Menon got up and began speaking in his Indian accent, Dustin went around and let the air out of the dolls one by one, causing various levels of flatulent sounds to escape from each one, punctuating Menon's diatribe. People began laughing as they noticed what was going on, and I think Bhaskar ended his speech prematurely due to paranoia. We left the party shortly thereafter, probably just before we would have been asked to.

Three days later, a real estate broker found me a wonderful rental that David Cassidy had just vacated. It was owned by actor-restaurateur Nicky Blair, and it was the bachelor pad to end all bachelor pads. Stained glass, sunken living room, jaccuzzi, original Henry Miller prints, all included. I snapped it up and had my stuff sent over. This was the finest place I had ever lived in to date, and I did not take it for granted. Now I could get back to the business at hand in complete comfort.

By now, Skynyrd led the pack. With the exception of an ad campaign for the Blues Project album similar to the earlier one for Skynyrd, the company was paying less and less attention to the other acts. In fact, it seemed that MCA had decided to put all its eggs in Lynyrd's basket and let the other acts fend for themselves. I spent an increasing amount of time meeting with MCA to try and remedy this, but to no avail. We even recorded Skynyrd's sophomore release in L.A., so I could stay on top of MCA on a daily basis. I had a pretty good relationship with the president, Mike Maitland, and with the head of business affairs, Lou Cook. Everybody was making money, but I could see the inevitable future through MCA's eyes—and there was no Mose Jones, Blues Project, or Elijah in it. I was getting tired of apologizing to these acts for things that weren't my fault, i.e., pulled ads, no tour support, and invisible promotion. They had fallen behind Skynyrd, and that much was obvious to everyone in the other acts. But I was virtually powerless.

What to do????

The scene for Skynyrd's second album was the Record Plant in Los Angeles. Now I hope *words* are sufficient for me to describe *that* environment. Chris Stone, a businessman, and Gary Kellegren, an engineer and idea man, had opened a studio in New York that had become very successful. They took their winnings and moved to Los Angeles, where they opened a studio like none other that had ever existed. Previously, studios were kinda antiseptic and dentist-officey. But the Record Plant's design was futuristic and rustic all at once. Lots of different-hued woods and tie-dyes. There were three studios, a jacuzzi room, and three bedrooms. It was Gary's pleasure palace. Gary had become one of the hottest engineers in New York, and he was a wild man. The design and concept of the studio was his, and Chris' business acumen brought it to fruition. Rock stars immediately flocked to a place that had a jacuzzi, three bedrooms, *and* the finest studios in Los Angeles.

The personnel that staffed the place were trained to accommodate *every* whim of every client. It was literally like ancient Rome in its heyday. My best friend Mike Gately became the nighttime receptionist. He was the keeper of the gates to heaven and hell. Every night, in-the-know young women would come to the reception area hoping to be allowed access to this rock star nirvana where a machine-vended beer cost a quarter and the game machines were free. It was not uncommon to walk out of Studio B, which was adjacent to the jacuzzi, and see laughing women *clad only in towels* strolling down the hall.

It was here that we set up our tents and began work on Skynyrd's second album, eventually titled *Second Helping*.

"Sweet Home Alabama" had already been recorded in Atlanta. Ronnie had been real excited about it and wanted to record it ASAP. I added the background singers in Los Angeles. There's also a little secret hidden in there. Right after the line "Well, I heard Mr. Young sing about her," if you listen real close in the left speaker, you can hear me sing in my best Neil Young imitation, "Southern man, better use your head. . . ." It's nearly subliminal. Check it out. . . .

The lads had some great material, and they were chompin' at the bit to git recordin'. Tracks were cut pretty quickly. In retrospect, if one listens to the basic guitar parts on "Sweet Home Alabama," "Swamp Music," or "Needle & the Spoon" there is a musical knowledge and maturity far beyond their mid-twenties age range. No attempt was made to do "Free Bird II." This was just the natural evolution of a talented band. Horns were added on J. J. Cale's "Call Me the Breeze," and "Don't Ask Me No Questions." "I Need You" was cut late one night when Bob Burns and I had already gone home thinking the session was over. There are time problems in it, but the band loved the spontaneity and we left it as is. On each album I did with them, there was always one song that was an out and out tribute to Free (the band). "I Need You" was the one on this album. On the first album, it was "Simple Man."

While we were toiling away in Studio B, my friend Bill Szymczyk (pronounced "sim-zik") was in Studio C producing the Eagles album that would eventually be known as *Hotel California*. It was not uncommon for people to be dropping in on each other's sessions, and the camaraderie was excellent.

One night, in 1995, Bill and I were having dinner together in Nashville. "Hey Bill," I said, reminiscing. "It was almost twenty years ago today that we were both in the

Record Plant doin' *Hotel California* and *Second Helping*. So now it's twenty years later, and practically *all* of today's country music is founded on either one or both of those albums, and *nobody* calls *us* to produce anything while they just imitate what we did twenty years ago! Is that hilarious or what?"

We just cracked up and enjoyed our dinner. Seniority is your enemy in the record business. They think you're not cutting-edge enough if you've been around longer than twenty minutes. Fortunately, Bill and I can laugh about it; other people have turned to drugs or taken their own lives because of it.

In the midst of recording *Second Helping*, on my thirtieth birthday Skynyrd came over to my house unannounced around dinnertime. "Better take off your watch, Al," Ronnie said. "*You're fixin' to get a birthday baptism!*" And with that they all grabbed me and headed for the pool. A picture of this happy event adorns the back of the *Second Helping* LP (and its twenty-bit remastered CD). To my credit, I did not go in alone. I took that pesky Van Zant character with me. *Life was good. Everyone was happy*.

We finished recording pretty quickly, and the boys went back to Jacksonville while I mixed the album. I sent them the mix and they went bonkers. Too much cowbell here, not enough vocal there, etc. I booked time at the Record Plant's newer studios in Northern California. It was a beautiful location right on the water in Sausalito, Marin County's little flower just over the Golden Gate Bridge. This time, Stone and Kellegren also rented a couple of houses in Mill Valley, all equipped with many bedrooms and jacuzzis. Skynyrd dispatched poor Ed King to represent them in the remixing of three or four tracks. We had the run of one house. Ed and his wife occupied the downstairs, while my engineer, Lee Keifer, and I abused the upper level. The downstairs residents were playing heavy domesticity, which manifested itself in early retiring and early rising for them. One night, Lee and I were grooving hard on a Beatles album about 1 a.m. when Ed appeared out of nowhere growling, and using the time-honored Southern-style volume control, *ripped the arm right off the turntable*. Bummer, dude.

A friend of ours, engineer John Stronach, was living at the other house and working at the other studio with Dan Fogelberg. John would hang with Lee and me in the evenings. Much Peruvian marching dust (cocaine) was in the air (not for me, however—my insomnia and new good sense precluded it).

One morning about 8 a.m., Ed came walking up the stairs and stumbled onto this scene in the livingroom: In the hanging wicker chair was a completely naked woman posed as if for *Playboy*. As John manned a camera on a tripod, Lee was brushing makeup on her nipples, while I directed the remnants of this all night photo shoot. Ed just walked outside shaking his head. Somehow, we actually got those mixes done to Ed's satisfaction, and I returned to L.A.

At the Third Street Record Plant, Los Angeles closing party with (left to right) Leopard Man,
Chris Stone (owner), Tom Werman (producer; last name sounds like "Fuhrman"),
Bill Szymczyk (producer; last name sounds like "sim-zick").
(Photo: Ed Freeman—courtesy of Record Plant Archives.)

Second Helping came out to rave reviews. We all knew "Sweet Home Alabama" was gonna be a hit single, but we had nothing on the album to follow it. I decided to put out "Don't Ask Me No Questions" first, because if it hit, "Sweet Home" would be a great follow-up as opposed to the reverse. I remember the ad in *Billboard*. It said over and over again:

What is the name of Lynyrd Skynyrd's great new single?
DON'T ASK ME NO QUESTIONS!
What is the name of Lynyrd Skynyrd's great new single?
DON'T ASK ME NO QUESTIONS!
Etc., Etc.

Needless to say, it was a bomb, but I don't believe there was any harm done other than a few vinyls dying so that singles could be pressed. We then came with "Alabama" and it was a complete smash. It became their biggest track. "Free Bird" from the first album—and the capper to their live show—began to get *tremendous* airplay as well.

On a recent remastered version of *Second Helping*, some MCA underling named Ron O'Brien wrote in the liner notes that I hated "Sweet Home Alabama" and didn't want it on the album. Now I may have occasionally been a fool in my time, but I sure wasn't deaf or stupid. Anyone who heard that track knew it was a hit, and I was no exception. Mr. O'Brien was probably shitting in his diapers when we recorded that song. If I've fucked up in my life, I admit it. And I think that I've admitted many of those errors right here between the covers of this book. When I confronted this O'Brien character with the truth, he said that he got his quotes from band members via old magazine articles. I asked him if he had spoken to anyone in the band lately who was present at those sessions. He said no one he contacted would return his calls. I told him I could see why. In my opinion this was irresponsible journalism from a person whose only qualification for writing liner notes was that he was a fan. This is the person who is the current curator of the Skynyrd Archives at MCA Records. It's a sad time for the record business, folks.

I had my attorney call O'Brien's superior and threaten MCA with a libel suit if these notes were not withdrawn immediately and replaced with the truth. I even arranged for O'Brien to "interview" Ed King, who was happy to speak with him and kill off all this revisionism. After two tries, O'Brien wrote ninety-five percent truth and I accepted that. Will the real truth about the past ever be known to students of rock 'n' roll in the future? Not if "fans" like this instead of journalists with a passion for truth and research are employed by record companies in the future. This is some of the "new music business" I have to deal with today, whether I like it or not. I wish I were more like Keith Richards and could just laugh it all off, but alas, I can't. And now, back to our story.

Overnight, Alan Walden disappeared from the management fold and Peter Rudge (manager of The Who) took over. The boys opened for The Rolling Stones at Knebworth in England and for the Allmans at Atlanta Stadium. Things were *very* good. Everyone was *extremely* happy (except probably Alan Walden).

My label deal was up for re-signing. Stan Polley and I went into a meeting with MCA. They said they wanted to change this, this, and that in the contract. We said, "Fine; redraft it and send it to us." Weeks went by and no contract arrived. We called MCA. They said, "By the way, we also want to change this and this as well." We said, "Fine; send us the redraft." Weeks went by and no contract arrived. Polley sat me down and explained the following facts of life to me:

- Under the existing contract, Skynyrd was getting five points and I was getting ten, and it was time to switch that around.
- I had an exclusive producer contract with MCA under the SOS deal and could not produce for anyone else under the existing contract.
- MCA wanted to buy me out and were withholding payment of any royalties in an effort to force me to accept their buyout, which was as yet unstated.
- It would take MCA a year to realize that we were holding the points they needed to give Skynyrd and, if we just ignored them all this time, we could charge them an inflated sum for those points in retaliation for their trying to starve us out by withholding our royalties.
- Polley would bankroll me for the next year in order to cause his hypothesis to happen.

"Well, if I can't produce anyone else," I reasoned, "what will I *do* for a year? He countered: "Why don't you write that book you're always talking about doing?"

And so, for the next forty-nine weeks, we did not hear a peep out of MCA or Skynyrd. I sat by the pool each day and typed out the story of my life from 1958 to 1968. That story became *Backstage Passes*, published in 1977 and edited by my friend, Ben Edmonds. It's the first version of the book you're holding in your hands and hopefully enjoying so much now. Then three weeks shy of Stan Polley's prediction, MCA phoned up:

"We want to buy the extra points you're holding and dissolve the deal," they said.

"Fine, no problem. The price is *one million dollars and that is nonnegotiable*," Stan countered.

They said they'd get back to us. Well, they called back rather quickly and said we'd have to hand over *everything we owned of the label* for the one million; which meant our total of fifteen points and our production royalties from the first two albums that were in escrow.

The deal was signed and the money changed hands. Then, a curious thing happened. Skynyrd went back to MCA and said:

"We want Al to produce our *next* album."

So then MCA once again had to pay me royalties on the third album. Revenge is sweet in real life. If MCA had come to us straight and honest a year before, they could have saved a great deal of money. Later, I found out they charged the million to *Skynyrd's account*! In spite of that, a year later *it was paid off*!

The downside for me was that, despite any fantasies, I was *not* a millionaire. After Stan Polley, agent Jeff Franklin, and Uncle Sam took their ends, I netted $375,000. I figured in order to *really* be a millionaire, one would have to gross at least four million. That wasn't gonna happen to me in this lifetime unless Lot's wife turned both my parents into solid gold, so I decided to bank the $375,000 and just get on with it. The thought of clinging to a hostile contract just for the sake of a future large pay-off is best left to music business lifers. I prefer my life simple and friendly.

Like "Sweet Home Alabama" before it, "Saturday Night Special" was recorded way before the album it was featured on. Through some connections, I was able to secure the song for the soundtrack of a new Burt Reynolds film, *The Longest Yard*.

Skynyrd's drummer, Bob Burns, had succumbed to the rigors of the road and was replaced by Artimus Pyle. We rented a club in Atlanta for an afternoon to rehearse Artimus on "Saturday Night Special." The boys counted it off and began playing on beat 2 of the second bar of the count-off. The downbeat or pulse of the song kept coming on the second beat instead of the first. I yelled: "*Wait a second, guys! Hold on! You're coming in a beat late. Why are you doing that?*"

Ed King said: "It all works out perfectly when we get to the guitar solo before the vocal." This set off my warning light; there was probably a 3/4 bar in there somewhere and they were not dealing with it as such. I asked them to play it again and damned if the drum fill between the first two sections wasn't a 7/4 bar!

"Artimus, you're playing a 7/4 bar for your solo and that's what's throwing you guys off," I explained. "What in the hell are you talkin' about, Al?" said Ed. "You can't have more than four beats in a bar!" That's what I loved about those guys. They had no book knowledge of music—they were just instinctively brilliant. I explained how you could have any amount of beats in a bar and they looked at me like I was crazy. It was like telling Truman Burbank he was a TV star.

"OK, OK, count it the way you want. It all *sounds* the same anyway," I said, backing down from an argument I *knew* I could not win.

The same thing had happened back when we cut "Sweet Home Alabama," and I heard Ed play the solo. *I freaked.* "You're in the wrong key, Ed!"

He looked at me with this sly look on his face and said: "This song is in the key of G, Al. That's the chord we end the song on when we play it live."

They actually ended on the IV chord (G) live as opposed to the root, which was D, the key the song is *actually* in. In *their* book of music theory, whatever chord you *ended* on was the key the *song* was in.

I listened again to the solo, which was in another mode, not unlike John Coltrane's work. "It's very progressive, Ed. I can live with it if that's what you want," I said, once again backing down from any kind of music theory debate.

By the time I mixed the song, I *loved* the solo, but I'll always know *why* he played it that way. Ed felt the opening chord of the song (D) was the V chord. *And he still does to* this *day.*

Al's advice: Don't stand in the way of genius!

This third album was gonna be completely different from the other two. The recording took place back in Atlanta again, but this time at Bang Studios instead of Studio One. I opted to use the engineer that came with the studio, one Dave Evans. This later became the bane of my existence, but I had no way of knowing that in advance. The atmosphere was already tense. Consigned to the road for the latter part of a year, there was no time for the usual Skynyrd modus operandi. No rehearsals, no planned-out guitar solos, and, in fact, *no songs!* I don't mean they had bad songs, they had *no* songs! They arrived believing they could combine the entire process into one month because they had no choice but to do that. After one month they were scheduled to be out on the road again. It was the first album with Artimus, and I spent the entire first day meticulously getting a drum sound. Finally, at 11 p.m., I felt we were fifteen/sixteenths there and called it a night. Imagine my horror when I walked in the next morning, *and all the microphones had been pulled back from the kit and they were starting again.*

"Dave says he can get a better drum sound so we let him have a go," Gary said.

I was *furious.* It is incredibly unprofessional for an engineer, especially one who is brand new with the client, to override the producer's instructions. In fact, in ninety-nine out of a hundred scenarios, the engineer would be rightfully *sacked.* The band was siding with Evans, however, and I let it go. This was a very bad foot to start off on. I decided right then and there that I would just step back and let *him* make any mistakes that were going to be made in that area. All engineering decisions would be *his.* The band would be happy, he would be happy, and I would live with it and pray I could correct any overt lapses of sound judgment on Evans' part in the mix. There was incredible tension between him and me from that point on. As the first couple of days unfolded, it became obvious that things were proceeding at a snail's pace, and we would never finish by our deadline.

I took Ronnie aside and said: "Listen, I know you and how you work. I'm gonna gamble on that and leave you alone for two weeks to write this album here in the studio. I trust you, and I believe in you, and I know you can do it. I'm gonna go to New York, and I'll call every few days and you tell me how you're doing. But remember, we'll only have *two weeks* left to record everything after that, so you *must* be done writing and arranging everything in the first two weeks."

He thanked me profusely, we shook hands on it, and I left for the airport shortly thereafter. I really *did* trust him. Ronnie Van Zant was a man among men and the rest of the band followed his direction. That is how we had gotten to *this* point. I knew that two weeks from now it was gonna be the worst hell *ever* trying to finish that album replete with an overambitious engineer who could not conceal his desire to replace me. I spent my whole time in New York partying my ass off, 'cause I knew of my impending prison sentence. I checked in periodically with Ronnie and he claimed they were making good progress. When the two weeks were up, I bit the bullet and clambered aboard that jet straight to Hell.

When I arrived, everyone was in good spirits and anxious to show off what they'd done on their summer vacation. I saw immediately that we had our Free tribute song with "On the Hunt," perhaps Ronnie's most misogynistic lyric ever.

So we had "On the Hunt." We had "Whiskey Rock-A-Roller," a nice shuffle with some great mood change-ups in it. There was a song Ronnie wrote to Bob Burns called "Am I Losin'" that was the mellowest, most country thing Skynyrd had ever cut, and "I'm a Country Boy," a great groove with really great Ronnie lyrics, which was one of my favorites. Ed and Ronnie had collaborated on "Railroad Song," which lyrically traced their country roots with a nice Beatles-inspired track. With the addition of "Saturday Night Special" in the can already, we had six songs. I needed two more, but somehow, I wasn't worried; they were three-quarters done with the writing and ready to rock. We set about cutting the basic tracks. and other than my distaste for the drum sound (which the band did not share), things began to coalesce.

For the first time since I began to work with these guys, there was room for my input on arrangements, and they were open to it. I patched up some holes, and we began to move along, albeit in sixteen-hour increments. I was having a hard time keeping up with the excruciatingly long hours logged each day. I bitched about it and continually ended the sessions before the band was ready to quit. Believe me, folks, great work rarely gets done after 2 a.m. if you've started at noon that day. But they were getting fed up with my early shutdowns, and somebody actually slipped some speed into my can of soda one afternoon. About midnight I was naively shouting: "I feel good tonight. We can go as late as you guys want!"

Little bastards. Next day I was sick as a dog, figured out what they had done, and gave them massive shit for it.

We spent one whole day, out of the fourteen left, creating the song "Cheatin' Woman." Ed and I wrote the music together, and Ronnie, of course, wrote the words. I played piano and organ because there simply was no time to teach it to Billy. This third album was a lesser Skynyrd work due to time constraints more than anything else. On the first album we had done a kind of jug-band song called "Mississippi Kid." Ronnie wrote another one real quick this time around, and we cut it jug-band style with marching-band bass drum, mandolin, dobro, harmonica, synthesized tuba, and piano. It was called "Made in the Shade," and it's the only Van Zant song I've ever covered on any of my albums. Jimmy Hall, lead singer of Wet Willie, came down and played harmonica on that one and "Railroad Song." I played piano on "Made in the Shade," while Barry Harwood, a friend of the band, played the mandolin and dobro parts, and David Foster played piano on "Whiskey Rock-A-Roller," overdubbed in California while I was mixing the album.

As the last day of recording approached, it got a little meaner and uglier. Ronnie was overdubbing the vocal to "On the Hunt," and the chorus was actually pitched about half a tone too high for his voice. He was out there straining at the seams to hit the notes and barely getting them. He was as angry (at himself) as I had ever seen him. Finally, in one take he hit every note right and knew it. Dave Evans, however, had employed the equipment incorrectly, causing Ronnie's voice to distort on various sections of the choruses. I pointed this out to the band 'cause I didn't want it blamed on me, nor for there to be any surprises later on. Ronnie said just to keep it anyway because he couldn't possibly perform it any better. On the record (in case you ever wondered), I had to bury his voice a bit on those parts because of the distortion. After the album was finished, I didn't see Dave Evans again until Ronnie's funeral. *He was the presiding clergyman! All dressed in robes.* And I thought I had a well-rounded résumé!

On the very last day of recording, their tour bus and Peter Rudge arrived. We had finished, and we were all thankful to be out of each other's hair. They had to go right out on tour. I had to go back west and mix this mutha. There were hard feelings. As we all gathered around for goodbyes, I spoke honestly:

"Guys, this is my last album with you. We've all made money together, but we damn near killed each other on this one. In the end, I would rather remain your friend than your producer. I still love you guys, and I'd rather not be put in this position anymore. It's too much of a strain on our friendship."

We all hugged and laughed, and I knew that I had made the right decision. Three weeks later, under cover of night and on the first leg of their tour, Ed King snuck away to the airport and left the band. Things were weird. *Nobody* was happy.

1974-1979:

After *Nuthin' Fancy*, as Skynyrd's third album came to be called, I was free to produce other people for the first time in three years. My first choice was a new band called The Tubes.

Two years prior, Irving Azoff, The Eagles' manager, had played me a tape of The Tubes that was circulating around. I loved it. He told me that no one was brave enough to sign them. So, one day in 1975, I was chatting with Dorene Lauer, one of my contacts at A&M Records, to find out what artists were looking for producers.

"We just signed this band called The Tubes but can't find anyone to produce them," she offered.

"Connect me to the head of A&R, quickly!" I responded.

A tape was dispatched to me, and I must tell you, it was *way* over my head, musically speaking. I told A&M I wanted to do it, but that I had another commitment that would take me about a month and asked whether they would wait for me.

Recording The Tubes' debut album—Studio B, Record Plant, Los Angeles, 1975. (Left to right) Lee Keifer (engineer), Rick Anderson, Kooper (producer), Fee Waybill, Roger Steen, Vince Welnick, Prairie Prince, Bill Spooner. (Photo: Al Kooper Collection.)

What I actually needed was time to figure out what the hell these Tubes were *playing* on their demo tape. Musically, they were incredibly ambitious, but unlike Skynyrd, the arrangements needed a lot of editing and fixing. If I, as a producer, suggest changes to anybody's work, I feel I must always have an explanation why I ask for those changes. And I certainly can't look a musician in the eye and say, "Change this chord here," and if he asks *which* chord, not be able to answer him. That's why I studied The Tubes' tape for a month—so I would have the answers to any and all queries. A great deal of reconstruction would be necessary to translate their vision to vinyl. And I would be the contractor for that reconstruction.

Their live show was even more ballyhooed than their music. I decided *not* to see their show until the album was finished. We began with two weeks in a rehearsal studio. As we set to work, I ripped and tore through their arrangements, and not a discouraging word was heard! They took to the editing and changes like ducks to water. They did not question *one edit*! And they were *great* musicians.

Bill Spooner was the musical leader of the group and a fine guitarist and singer. Roger Steen rounded out the guitar section in good stead. Fee Waybill, their former roadie when they were called The Beans back in Arizona, now fronted the band as lead singer. Vince Welnick, later of The Dead (Grateful, that is), played keyboards, and Rick Andersen played bass, while Mike Cotten (who played synthesizers) and Prairie Prince (who played drums) supplied the artwork for the various skits in the show. Prairie, a dead ringer for a young Robert Mitchum, was an *amazing* drummer.

My approach to this album, based on the material and what I had heard about their live show, was to make an original cast album of a Broadway show, the likes of which had never been seen on Broadway yet. And might *never* be seen there! The album began with an overture that wasn't an overture, titled "Up from the Deep," that had groove changes every few bars. This then segued into "Haloes," an interesting Marlboro commercial sound-alike that had a bombastic ending. Spooner played an incredible guitar solo that was mutated through Mike Cotten's synthesizer, while Prairie's double-bass-drum sixteenth-note playing pushed the ending to a musically orgiastic climax. Prairie's Keith Moon imitations throughout the song are spot-on as well.

To augment the band and make it Broadway-sounding, we enlisted strings, horns, and choirs. To save time, I felt I should hire an arranger, but the regular rock arranger would *not* have understood what was afoot here. So I took a chance and called film composer/arranger Dominic Frontiere. Dominic wrote "Hang 'Em High" for Sergio Leone, and scored the original *Outer Limits* television series. He came to the house and I played him the basic tracks and explained to him what I was looking for. "This is good stuff," he said. "I'm glad you called me. I know *exactly* what you want here." He was the right choice and we set to work writing the arrangements.

"Space Baby" was a mini-opera goof on David Bowie. This was one of our true Broadway show numbers. Dominic's augmentation really set this one off.

The boys had a tape from a Mexican radio station of "Malaguena Salerosa" and had learned it note for note as an exercise, I guess. It had become one of their best numbers on stage and they decided to record it. They really wanted Herb Alpert, president of A&M Records and famous trumpeter, to play the mariachi trumpet parts on it. I put in the request, but alas, was told: "Mr. Alpert is out of town and won't be back until [the day after your sessions end] further notice." We were crushed, but Lee Kiefer, our engineer, was friends with the guy who did the voice-over for the Juan Valdez commercials, and we got him to do narration on the track. A poor substitute for Herb, but funny nonetheless.

"Mondo Bondage" was one of the band's best arrangements and only lacked an ending that matched the rest of the song. I took care of that with the help of Dominic and some ideas I'd always wanted to try. But I'll always treasure the memory of the staid string section all yelling out "OWWWWWW!" in unison at the final coda. "What Do You Want from Life" was a fifties'-style, sociological comment on and paean to the TV game show, *The Price Is Right*. We spent the better part of an afternoon writing the script of possible prizes you could win, climaxing with "a baby's arm holding an apple," which some of you may recall as Lady Chatterley's description of her lover's "package." This survived censorship because not many DJs had read D. H. Lawrence at the time! "Boy Crazy" was the ultimate glam-rock send-up and one of the coolest instrumental tracks on the album. "White Punks on Dope" was an extravaganza. This was the finale, and cannons were heard, flags were waved, and confetti was every-where, until, to end the piece, Prairie's dad laughed at the top of his lungs: "Is that alright??"

One Monday night after work, we all went to talent night at the Palomino Club in North Hollywood. This was the major country & western venue in the Los Angeles area and The Tubes, operating under the pseudonym "Heifer's Dream," were out to win the talent contest. I had no doubt they'd be splitting up that $300 at the evening's conclusion. They performed Marty Robbins' "El Paso" replete with blank-loaded guns and animal blood. First shots rang out. And then—the horror as Fee, apparently truly wounded and covered in blood, fell to the stage floor. The stunned looks on the faces of these hardcore C&W fans are forever etched in my mind. Nobody could compete with those guys. The prize money was theirs!

We finished the album after two months of incredibly, hard, well-thought-out work. It was the first album I had ever recorded on twenty-four-track tape, patient-ly sticking with sixteen tracks until I felt that the new technology was state of the art. This made mixing all the more difficult and the band got nuts during the mix, so much so that I had to dispatch them home to San Francisco, at much peril to my tenure as producer. But an air of calmness was needed in the control room to mix this gargantuan property properly, and it was anything but calm with seven guys climbing all over the console, each wanting to make sure the listener could hear *his* part. We very carefully and methodically mixed the album, and the result was, in my opinion, the best record I have ever produced. The band was angry with me for asking them to leave, but at least they were happy with the mix. They asked that everyone's credits on the album be in their full given names. This became the only album ever produced by Alan Peter Kooper. *My parents loved it!*

With the album's release, major showcases were set up in various cities. I attended the New York and Los Angeles shows and they were the hottest tickets in town. A&M did a great advance job, and everyone wanted to see what all the fuss was about. For me, it was one of the best, most hilarious live shows I have ever seen and totally unique at that. Kenny Ortega, a young dancer from San Francisco, beginning a career that would see him end up as Hollywood director, invented incredible choreography and the three female dancers also doubled as backup singers, including the fabulous Re Styles. There were costume and set changes, and incredible between-song patter. No matter what your ticket cost, ya got your

A rare cameo appearance onstage with The Tubes—The Roxy, Los Angeles, 1976. (Left to right) Quay Lewd (Fee Waybill), Sputnick Spooner, Insect Kooper, and Reliable Roger Steen. (Photo: Richard Creamer—Al Kooper Collection.)

money's worth. In New York, during the finale of "White Punks on Dope," there must have been twenty-five people on stage (including yours truly and Lee Keifer). In Los Angeles, Fee started up a real chainsaw and buzzed through the tables at the Roxy, causing an embarrassed Clive Davis to hide a stain in the front of his trousers that might have been the result of unintentional urination. I'm just hazarding a guess here. I sat at a table with Ken Scott, an English producer who had engineered one of my early albums when he was a pup. Neither of us knew he would end up producing the second Tubes album. (Well, at least I didn't know. . . .)

A&M was happy with my work on The Tubes' album and asked me if I'd have a go with Nils Lofgren. I was a big fan of Nils, especially his guitar playing. I had first heard Nils a few years back when he fronted the band Grin. A track called "See What Love Can Do" came on the radio and the guitar solo took my breath away. Then I saw Grin live-opening for Van Morrison at Carnegie Hall in early '72. They were incredible. After four or five albums, they broke up. Nils cut a solo album for A&M that was quite good. And now A&M was asking me to work with him. It seemed irresistible.

Nils and I sat down and discussed a plan for this album. For personnel I suggested Jim Gordon, drummer from Derek and the Dominos (who would later murder his mom with a hammer following the instructions of "voices in his head"), and Paul Stallworth, bassist buddy of super-drummer Jim Keltner. Nils countered with his brother Tom on rhythm guitar, and I took the keyboard chair. I wanted to feature his guitar playing on this album. We were spending a great deal of time together planning, so I went to San Francisco with him to watch a live gig. The day after his gig we adjourned to the familiar Record Plant in Sausalito for a live radio concert. I sat in on keyboards as I had just about learned his show now. It was a great session, luckily recorded, and pressed in a limited edition for radio and promotion. It was a greatest-hits-up-to-then kind of thing, with a few Grin songs thrown in and a nice reading of King-Goffin's "Going Back." Be nice to see it on a legal CD someday.

Gary Kellegren had constructed a bizarre studio for Sly Stone at the Record Plant in Sausalito. The control room was in the center of the room with no glass or partitions around it. Different levels were built around it amphitheater-style for the various instruments, and it looked like something out of Thunderdome. It was here that we decided to cut the basic tracks for Nils' album. Add to this my new fascination with nitrous oxide. The studio was able to convince the Marin Gas Company that we needed nitrous oxide in the record-making procedure as a crucial tool, and tanks were dispatched to the studio weekly. I loved this. Unaware of the different mix between industrial and medicinal nitrous (cut with oxygen; as in the dentist's office), I plunged into each tank. I recall sitting on one of the levels in the studio playing acoustic guitar on one of the basic tracks, feet dangling over the side with my trusty tank right by my side. After each take, I'd slip the tube in my mouth and take a strong hit.

One night I was in the control room after the session, tank in tow. Nils came in and was about to shave in the bedroom in the back, before a dinner engagement. He took one look at me and walked over.

"Al? Hello, Al?" he said.

I knew he was right in front of my face but I was busy bouncing around the metallic valleys and nitrous canyons of my mind and his presence was peripheral at the very least. He took the can of shaving cream and started covering my face little by little. I watched from miles away, barely cognizant that my entire face was now covered with shaving cream. What a fun drug, huh?

It lasted only a few days, this nitrous binge. One morning I woke up so incredibly ill I wanted to die. The uncut nitrous had created little pockets of *hydrochloric acid* in my stomach, something that my already functioning ulcers did not welcome with open arms. Boy, was I *ill*. That was an instant panacea for nitrous usage. The next week, one of Gary Kellegren's friends died, alone with the tank. While in a dream world, the tank toppled over on him, the tube remained in his mouth, and his lungs froze, killing him instantly. And that was certainly the end of *that*.

I thought Nils showed great patience putting up with that nitrous episode. His album was, amazingly, moving along on schedule, no tanks to me. In addition to all this nitrous nonsense, my engineer was abusing cocaine very badly. This manifested itself in late arrivals, no-shows, and infection of band members. Warnings went unheeded, as they usually do when an insidious drug is in place. I called owner Chris Stone in L.A.: "I gotta fire my engineer. Where is that great assistant engineer that's usually up here? It's time for his big break."

At that moment, the man I was referring to—a young Bob Edwards—was crawling under the stage of the Aquarius Theater in L.A., laying microphone cable for a remote Record Plant recording. The call came, he dusted himself off, grabbed the next plane north, and began his first session as a full engineer. This is usually how it happens. Fortunately, my assessment of his talents was correct, and he was great from the moment he began. Sometimes you can be wrong. Not this time, though. Today, Bob runs the recording studios at George Lucas's Skywalker Ranch. He's a happy guy.

Please don't think that every record I produced was fueled by all kinds of drugs. This record was an aberration. I never allowed cocaine or heroin usage on any session I was in charge of—I just lost it for a brief moment in time with the nitrous and poor Nils just happened to be the victim. At any rate, this fall from grace only lasted a few days.

We went to Los Angeles for overdubs and mixing once the basic tracks were completed. On the song "Cry Tough," we had some wonderful textures. Emil Richards played tabla (Indian drums), I played Wurlitzer electric piano, and Chuck Rainey redid the bass part. I had left a long space for a killer solo and wanted to use a color other than just screamin' electric guitar.

"Can you play a National steel dobro, Nils?" I inquired.

"Play one?" he said, "I never heard of one!"

Now, I was smiling. I called Studio Instrument Rentals and hired one. A National steel dobro is a guitar made out of steel with an arched resonator on the front to propel the sound from the pre-electric days it was invented. It has a lovely, unique, tone when played with a slide. I handed it to Nils.

"You play it lap-style," I instructed.

Bob quickly set up a couple of microphones, and we went directly to the solo part of the song. "Let's try it, Nils," I said. "Record this, Bob," I told the engineer without Nils hearing.

And simply, in one take, as a young lad discovered a new instrument, we had one hell of a solo, with a sound that was quite refreshing.

As the overdubs and vocals wore on, Nils' vision began to take a turn that was divergent from mine. Maybe I should have kept doing the nitrous (just kidding), but by mutual consent I soon left the project. I had produced and mixed five tracks, and five tracks does not an album make. Nils went back and took some leftovers from his last album that David Briggs had produced and combined them with my five tracks. They were amazingly compatible. A listener could not tell the stories behind this album by listening to it. I was glad for Nils, because I was still a fan. In addition to "Cry Tough," the other tracks I was involved with on that album were "It's Not a Crime," a cover of The Yardbirds' "For Your Love," "You Lit a Fire," and "Jailbait." Some orchestral arrangements were employed using Dominic Frontiere once again. When Nils and I bump into each other today, we are still friends and can look back bemusedly at that time period. He certainly has some Al Kooper stories to tell. . . .

By now, I had moved into a luxury house in Coldwater Canyon I purchased for a mere $140,000. I put another $20,000 into it, hiring the carpenters who had done the space-age woodwork at the Record Plant, and giving them some designs that no one else would've understood. They moved in for two months before I even took possession of the house, and transformed the interior into a spaceship of sorts.

Lenny Bruce's daughter Kitty was in town with her mom, Honey, and needed a place to stay. I said they were welcome to stay at the house with the carpenters if they had sleeping bags. In no time, Honey and Kitty were painting the kitchen and the living room, and enjoying the pool and the view, not to mention the bare-chest-

Nils Lofgren counting how many days producer Kooper was incapacitated by nitrous oxide.
(Photo: Al "In A Haze" Kooper.)

ed young carpenters. The climax occurred one night while I was visiting and we all watched *Lenny* on HBO on the theater-sized screen in the living room. I can't begin to tell you how surrealistic *that* was. What I *didn't* tell the ladies was how, as a six-teen-year-old lad, I had gone to Carnegie Hall at midnight to see Lenny in his first legit appearance.

"Lenny Bruce at Carnegie Hall. Show begins at Midnight."

How could I resist going to see him all those years ago? The stately old hall was packed with jazz musicians, hookers, beatniks, and Manhattan-dwelling yuppies (the kind of white people who went to Harlem for "kicks"). At the stroke of midnight, Lenny strolled out onstage to a thunderous ovation. He walked up to the microphone, did a 180, unzipped his fly, and began to vent. And I mean vent. He had probably retained all day to achieve the effect, urinating nonstop for what seemed like close to five minutes. People went nuts. Some of the yuppies were literally nauseated and walked out on the more expensive seats (lest they should get wet). He shook off, zipped up, turned around to a standing ovation before he even spoke, and slowly shushed the audience. His first words?

"Okay! Now that we got ridda da squares, let's get down to business!"

But I digress. . . .

Back in seventies L.A., the house was an L shape that hugged a heated pool. Deep in Manson paranoia, I installed an electric buzz-in gate and intercom entrance. One of the intercom stations was built into the headboard of the bed, so that if I heard bumps in the night, I could immediately monitor the outside perimeter of the house. And the bed itself was built by two award-winning Australian carpenters who happened to be passing through L.A. on a sail around the world. The bed was modeled after Cleopatra's barge. The headboard area had a TV projection unit built in to it, as well as a stereo, and the latterly mentioned intercom. It was an *incred-a-bed*.

A partial look inside Free Bird Mansion—Coldwater Canyon, Los Angeles, 1976.
(Photo: Gary Nichamin/BOOM! Graphics.)

The bedroom closet had one of those automated thingies from the cleaners where you push a button and your clothes come around to you. Inexpensive yet functional, I thought of it as the silliest thing in the house. The master bath had a platform Japanese soaking tub, a sauna, and his and hers vanity stations. In the living room, a custom-made stone fireplace was framed by wooden speaker enclosures and a huge projection TV screen. A handmade horseshoe-shaped couch held up to eight people. The dining room set was carved out of driftwood and gave way to the centerpiece of the house—a huge, custom spiral staircase made out of all kinds of woods, with a handrail that turned into a huge wooden phallus at the upper landing. Custom murals were painted on the walls at the top of the stairs. *Enough, already*. This was Free Bird Mansion and the living was far beyond what I had ever fantasized for myself.

If I thought *Nuthin' Fancy*, *The Tubes*, or *Cry Tough* were tough albums to make, then I obviously wasn't prepared for my next two projects. It all started when I read that Epic Records signed Rick Nelson. I was a huge Rick Nelson fan and I knew exactly what to do with him: Reunite him with James Burton, his blazing guitarist from the '50s, and *stand back*! I went to Epic, and they said you can produce Rick Nelson, but first you have to produce this other artist for us. I said fine. It was a Nashville-based artist named Marshall Chapman. Marshall was a six-foot, extremely headstrong woman, with not much good material at the time, but with a lot of ambition and self-confidence. Without good songs, most projects are doomed. But she was so unapproachable, the subject could never be properly broached. To add to the problem, she came with her own studio-inexperienced band. I rehearsed them at my home for a week or two, but it was doomed.

Now *here's* an omen for you: One Sunday, while we were working in Studio A at the Record Plant in Los Angeles, the entire complex caught fire, and, if we hadn't hit the fire alarm instantly, it might have burned completely to the ground. As it was, we could no longer continue to work there. The studio assigned me its remote truck and crew, and we finished the album *at my house* with a remote truck parked in the driveway. I had James Burton booked to play a few solos on Marshall's album and warm-up for Rick Nelson. So at 10 a.m., here comes James Burton walking up the driveway at my house and sitting in my dining room playing the famous paisley Telecaster that he used on *The Ozzie and Harriet Show*! How *outrageous* is that for 10 a.m.? It was completely otherworldly.

Another day, I had male background singers booked. Now I had used these guys before and they were great. I had them go to the Record Plant for the session, where I met them with a limousine. I had gone to the store and bought four "blinders" (blindfolds you wear to sleep). I asked them if they could put the blindfolds on, as we were recording at my house, and I didn't want anyone to know where I lived. Used to weirder idiosyncracies than that, they got in the limo and put the blindfolds on. Did I mention that they were screamingly gay and very hilarious even without blindfolds on? I'll never forget that ride up to my house or the looks on people's faces when they looked in the windows of the limo and saw everyone blindfolded. The banter in the car ride up to my house should have been recorded. It would've sold more than the album we were working on! By the way, I really didn't care about them knowing where I lived; I was just trying to set up the funniest scenario I could think of. And when the recording crew saw the limo pull up and four blindfolded guys pile out, it was indeed hilarious.

We finally finished that record. I had done the best I could and so had Marshall. In retrospect, I think I tried to overcompensate on the arrangements and it is not my best work, nor, I'm sure, is it hers. *But* . . . Rick was next!

When James Burton worked for me on Marshall's album, I attempted to book him for Rick Nelson's upcoming sessions. "Only way I could see my way clear to do that, Al," said James flatly, "is if they give me two points on the entire record."

"I'll check and see, James, and I'll get right back to you," was all I could muster.

James had been largely responsible for the success of Rick's early work. His trail-blazing guitar work caused many, who might not have been customers specifically lined up for Rick himself, to fork over the cost of a record just to scrutinize James. I'm sure all he got were session fees, while Rick probably went on to to make a fortune. I didn't blame James for his stance, but Rick's management just laughed at his demands.

So there I was, poised to produce Rick Nelson, and my trump card had spontaneously combusted. I needed to come up with a Plan B by evaluating my pluses and minuses. Rick had a pleasant, instantly recognizable voice that had never been challenged much above or below an octave. I decided to follow the formula Linda Ronstadt had successfully employed at the time. I took her prescription for a hit album and matched it to Rick: one old song, rearranged in a modern way, plenty of California-sound writers, and some songs by traditionally great writers, all mixed together in a poppy brew, easy on the ears.

Rick knew this was the biggest departure he had *ever* made to date, but he accepted it with a completely open mind. I made him a cassette of fifty songs and told him that whatever he picked was already fine with me. He chose about five songs, so I made him *another* cassette of fifty songs and he was able to select the rest from that one. *There are some advantages to owning 14,000 records (with the exception of when you're moving).*

I assembled a crack (sharp; not drugged) studio band sprinkled with members of Rick's current road band. This was also a big departure for him as he had usually been recording with his Stone Canyon Band for years. We had Rick Schlosser on drums, Bob Glaub on bass, Michael McDonald on keyboards, and Jeff Baxter on guitar, while I played any utility parts that were needed on guitar or keyboards. No one had ever asked Michael McDonald to participate as a session *keyboard player* before, and he was actually nervous. He kept asking everyday: "Don't you want me to sing on a track or something?" I just laughed at him and said, "No, that's what everyone *else* does with you. You're doing just fine with what you're playing here." And he was. He played brilliant things that I would never have thought of and was a tremendous asset to the sessions. A shy, introverted guy, he never said much except with his hands when the red light was on.

Rick was at a strange point in his life. His marriage was very unstable. His wife Kris would show up at the studio unannounced, and have the receptionist announce her with another woman's name—say, Rebecca or something. If Rick allowed her in, she would be all over him in a jealous rage, disrupting the session. Once we went to Vegas, where Rick had to fulfill a contractual obligation at the Aladdin Hotel during the recording time allotment. I went along and played keyboards in his band to keep the male bonding together. Every night, when the second show ended about 1 a.m., Kris would call from L.A. and keep Rick on the phone for three hours, in her mind thwarting any dalliances.

One day, I just kinda blurted out: "Jeeez, guy—why don'cha just get a divorce??"

In traditional Beverly Hills style, he answered truthfully: "I can't afford it." And there is no rejoinder to that answer.

But Rick loved the accoutrements of his life. He drove a bright red Pantera. He doted on his kids, who would soon become successful themselves: Tracy as an actress, and the twins as the rock group Nelson. So he hung in this unhappy marriage.

At this point, I should explain how really different this album's content was for a Rick Nelson album. Included were ZZ Top's "Enjoy Gettin' It On," Little Feat's "New Delhi Freight Train," Allen Toussaint's "What Is Success?" Steve Alaimo's oldie "Everyday I Have To Cry Some" with an Andrew Gold-type arrangement, Dylan's "Mama You Been on My Mind" (perhaps the most traditional Rick Nelson number on the album), and two songs by favorite writers of mine: "Carl of the Jungle" by Randall Bramblett and "No Words of Love" by Fred Bliffert. Rounding out the festivities was The Atlanta Rhythm Section's "Conversation," and Danny Kortchmar's "Chump Change Romeo."

Singing-wise, it had to be the most versatile record Rick ever made. His voice

*Backstage at Universal Amphitheater, Los Angeles, 1978. (Left to right) Al, Hank Ballard, Rick Nelson, and Fats Domino. Fats's choice of neckwear eerily forecast the details of Rick's demise. (*Photo: Jan Butchofsky-Houser.)

was pushed and coaxed to do things he never dreamed it could do, and he was proud of it. To a Rick Nelson fan, it would probably have taken some getting used to, but it *could* have been a viable direction for him to have taken at that point in his career. At any rate, Rick's uncle, Don Nelson, and Don's daughter, Kathy (an exec at MCA Records), who were occasional cheerleaders at the sessions, both congratulated me when we finished.

At Epic, things were quite different. Lenny Petze, the man in charge, told me that it was the worst piece of shit he had ever heard in his *entire* life (this from the man responsible for "Girls Just Wanna Have Fun") and that they had no intention of ever releasing it. About six months after Rick's untimely passing in a plane crash, I called Epic to suggest they release it and they said: "We don't care if he's dead! We still hate it! Don't you understand? It's never coming out!" These are a few of my un-favorite things. Somehow, in later years, four tracks were released on a compilation CD. Perhaps, after *my* untimely death, it will be released.

My friend, photographer Gary Nichamin, called one day to ask if I could help him out. *Playboy* had hired him to shoot some photos for their "Sex in Los Angeles" issue. He suggested we adjourn to the Record Plant jacuzzi with two models and two bottles of Laurent Perrier Gran Sicle and shoot a little rock star decadence. I always liked to accommodate my good friend Gary, so of course I said yes. Gary shot about two hours of us cavorting around in flagrante delicto, and when it came time to hand it in, I decided to remain nameless in deference to my mom (*much to the chagrin of my dad*). So I'm just called a rock star in the 1979 issue with Raquel Welch on the cover. Just in case you ever get asked that question in a game of *Trivial Pursuit*, now you know.

During this time period, Bill Szymczyk, producer of the Eagles and others, had been surreptitiously recording the antics going on while recording *Hotel California* and *The Long Run*. At the conclusion of said recordings, he pressed up a select few of the edited foibles of Henley-Frey & Co. on his own Soul-Pole Record label and gave them out to engineers, Eagles, and crew involved with the sessions. I was lucky enough to secure a copy, and it set off a light bulb in the Kooper kranium. For years I had been collecting audio flotsam and jetsam; outtakes of the famous and infamous, and now I realized I could liberate all this stuff in a most philanthropic way. For Christmas, I pressed up three hundred LPs with color jackets and labels and sent them out instead of cards or gifts to people who understood recording studio humor. It was called *The Kapusta Kristmas Album* after an Ernie Kovacs character called the Kapusta Kid. The big hit on this LP was a tape I made of me calling my parents and disguising my voice by speeding it up electronically. My mom's comment was classic:

"Alan? Is that you? You sound like you're on LSD!"

This particular track got bootlegged all over the world. The next year's album "hit" was black keyboard player Donald Blackman spelling his philosophies out for Rick Nelson to hear. It is a classic.

I sent these out two years in a row: '77 and '78. Then the money began to run out. The house got sold and living large changed to living medium.

I banged out a new solo album in this time period called *Act Like Nothing's Wrong*. I stole the title from the inscription on Stevie Wonder's road crew's tee shirts (see more on this below). I had waited out my Columbia contract successfully, and not recorded since 1972's *Naked Songs*. *Act Like Nothing's Wrong* is one of my favorite solo albums—good songs, good covers, good arrangements, poor sales. I recorded my original arrangement of "This Diamond Ring" in an attempt to vindicate myself from the Gary Lewis record. Covers of Dan Penn's "Out of Left Field" and William Bell's "I Forgot To Be Your Lover" are on there, as well as some fine original new songs, especially one called "Turn My Head Towards Home," kind of a tribute to Thom Bell. John Simon, who produced *Child Is Father to the Man*, coproduced it with me and wrote some great arrangements.

John's sense of humor is quite dry. One of my fondest memories of making that album was during some lead vocal sessions. I was out in the studio singing my little heart out and John was in the control booth producing. The way they had it set up, we couldn't actually see each other, but we were in voice contact. I had just finished singing a long song all the way through, and personally thought that I had nailed it.

"So, John," I asked. "How was that? I thought it felt pretty good."

No answer.

I thought to myself: What if they just got up and left or something—went to dinner, etc. Just to fuck with me. "So are you guys there? Am I in this all by myself? How was the last take?" I asked further.

Finally! A reply from John: "Yeah, Al, that was pretty good. I'm gonna save that but I think you should sing it one more time and this time see if you can take that *quantum leap to palatability.* . . ."

I couldn't stop laughing for fifteen minutes. I still use that line today.

When it came time to shoot the cover, I was ready with a wild idea . There is a *Time/Life* photo of a young Jane Fonda sitting nude on the beach with her limbs positioned in a casual way so that nothing naughty shows. I engaged South African photographer Norman Seef to shoot me and my girlfriend, Linda Hoxit, separately, in the exact Jane Fonda pose. Then, with a few airbrushing miracles, I just swapped the heads on the two photos. So, there I am, on one side of the cover with ample cleavage and she's on the other side with hair on her chest. When it came time to title said album, I recalled a saying that was written in big bold letters on tee shirts worn by all of Stevie Wonder's road crew: "ACT LIKE NOTHING'S WRONG!" It really used to make me laugh, so we plopped those words as the title on the album and shipped it out.

I was so happy with what I'd done creatively on that album, I decided that, if it wasn't successful, I would stop making records for awhile, put my artist career on hold, and concentrate on other things like producing, writing, or playing live.

Earlier in the year, Denny Cordell hired me as musical director for a record he was producing of a new artist he discovered in Gainesville, Florida. We recorded about half an album and then the artist decided to go back to Florida and put his own band together and recut the album. His revised album was coming out at the same time mine was, so I invited him to open the show on my tour. It was to be his band's first national tour, and I was proud to have Tom Petty and The Heartbreakers as my opening act. Their keyboard player, Benmont Tench, did the best Al Kooper organ imitation I had ever heard (and still does). We all became fast friends over the course of the tour, and it's a friendship that is ongoing. Two tracks from that aborted first album I did with Tom are on his box set, *PLAYBACK*.

When it came time to tour the album, I put together a band from students at the Berklee College of Music in Boston augmented with some local pro Boston musicians. With Tom and The Heartbreakers in tow, we plowed across America in the winter of 1976. It was a huge band: Ted Lo on keyboards, Chris Morris and Les Kuipers on guitars, Vinnie Coliauta on drums (at the age of twenty, his first tour; later he made quite a name for himself with Frank Zappa and Sting), Tim Landers on bass, Stanton Davis on trumpet, Gary Valente on trombone, David Wilczewski on reeds, and Annie McLoone, Roz Bloch, and Meredith Manna on background vocals. Whewww! Quite a voluminous payroll at the end of the week.

At Paul's Mall in Boston, I put the head of my guitar through the ceiling as a musical exclamation point, and a dead rat fell on stage. In Nashville at the Exit Inn, we broke the club attendance record for the least people at a show. But the worst was the last. My agent had booked us into a club in San Francisco called the Old Waldorf with Mike Bloomfield as the opening act. I had great trepidation about this and insisted that the show not be billed as *Super Session* or anything resembling that. Well, needless to say, when we pulled into town, we saw *Super Session* '76 posters everywhere. The shows were sold out for two nights and I was furious. I knew that the paying customers would expect songs from that album and a set by the two of us together, and nothing like that was planned. It was a potential disaster. All I wanted to do was promote my new album and see my old friend. At soundcheck, Mike and I rehearsed a few jams with my band to approximate something we could get away with.

We played the first show, and it was shaky, audience-wise. Needless to say, they expected a night of live *Super Session* and we didn't even come close to their expectations with the little jam we worked up that afternoon at soundcheck. I had caught the flu and was running a high temperature. My road manager, Elayne Angel, had improvised a little healing room backstage with a cot and medication. The club owner, who was on the top of my shitlist for employing this whole *Super Session* marketing crap against my wishes, tried drunkenly to enter the dressing room. Elayne barred him at the door, saying, "Al isn't seeing anyone right now. He's quite ill and needs to rest." The club owner was right in her face: "I own this fucking club and

I'm going in if I want to!" he slurred. Elayne stood her ground and the guy actually took a swing at her, but missed. I saw this and jumped between her and the club owner, saying: "That's it, dickhead. You just canceled this engagement with that punch you just threw. We're outta here!" I put the whole troupe on the bus and turned my back on three sold-out shows. I never had a chance of winning anyone over the way he had set it up anyway.

That was how the tour ended. Despite some great shows in New York, Boston, Austin, Chicago, and Detroit, the album slipped into anonymity and I kept my word to myself. No more solo albums for awhile.

The L.A. clubhouse and training ground for female Record Plant recruits was the Rainbow Bar & Grill on Sunset Boulevard. Owned by Mario Maglieri, Elmer Valentine, and Lou Adler, this place has no equal in the universe. I think this is where George Lucas got the idea for the *Star Wars* bar. Opened in the early seventies on the site of the old Windjammer Restaurant, where Marilyn Monroe would take quiet dinners with prospective suitors, this place was an immediate hit. Ostensibly a sensibly-priced Italian restaurant and watering hole, it became a haven for rock stars, groupies, and wanna-bes of the former and latter. In the early days, it was also the clubhouse of Led Zeppelin, The Who, and many other famous bands as well as mine. I had met Mario Maglieri in 1965 on my first trip to Hollywood. An ex-cop, he had recently (1963) moved from Chicago with fellow officer Elmer Valentine and bought the Whisky A Go Go, which, under their tutelage (and with Adler's discovery Johnny Rivers in tow), was doing great business in 1965. We remained good friends as we were both Aquarians and he was exactly twenty years and one day older than me. He and I would hang out in the kitchen at the Rainbow, eying the waitresses and generally horsing around. Many a musician down on his luck was quietly fed gratis by Mario, who has a heart of gold.

So we'd be in the kitchen, and he would tell the waitresses that I was *gay* and attracted to *him*. I played along and little by little became friendly with all the waitresses. They really thought I was gay, and they would try and seduce me. I would eventually succumb to their seductions and make them promise not to tell anyone, as I was embarrassed by it. One by one, they all fell for it until I had "had" just about the whole staff. Eventually, Mario would tell each one the truth about my sexuality and just enjoy seeing the looks on their faces as they discreetly took in that information. These are just some of the shenanigans that went on in pre-AIDS California.

On another evening, a friend of mine called to say he was taking me to a party and that he was supplying a date for me. Knowing this guy's taste in women, I

Al plants a wet one on Mario Maglieri as Mrs. Maglieri smiles nervously.
(Photo: Al Kooper Collection.)

accepted this blind date and hopped in his vehicle at the appointed time. We drove to a parking lot on the edge of Beverly Hills, and then transferred to a mysterious RV that took us and others who had parked in the lot up a long, winding road to a huge mansion. My friend, David, went up to a clipboard-holding guard, slipped him some money, and we were in. This house was really something. It had a an indoor-outdoor heated pool that ended up in the living room. My date Jessica (not her real name; in later years, she married a big rock star and had a lot of kids, then divorced him; some clue, huh?) and I wandered off to look at this wild place. On the lower level you could see underwater in the pool as you walked down the hall-ways. In one of the hallways was a doorway that you had to kneel down and crawl through as it was so small and low. This caught our curiosity, and so we knelt. As we looked through the doorway, we were definitely not prepared to see about fifty or so writhing, naked bodies, all tangled up while lights flashed and New Age music slithered in the background. In all my years, I had *never* really witnessed this on such a grand scale. There we were, *at an actual Hollywood orgy*! Truthfully, the combination of being rendered speechless by what I saw, and my hardly know-ing this woman I was with, prohibited me from actually jumping in, but my voyeuristic tendencies kicked in, and we spent the rest of the evening visiting the various rooms and just . . . well . . . looking. This place was actually interior-designed to house these parties. I soon found out that this went on *every* weekend, and it cost $20 per couple to attend if you had the phone number and placed a reservation. *I knew what I'd be doing for the next few weekends!*

I've always been fascinated by subcultures, and this was what they called the "swing" crowd. The most amazing thing to me was the sociological breakdown. There were fat people, skinny people, pretty people, ugly people, hip people, straight peo-ple, single people, married people, old people, and young people all with one thing in common. And this was most assuredly a subculture; it had its own laws, magazines, and credos. There were probably four or five other similar houses operating in the Los Angeles area at that time as well. I don't know what the book law was on it, but there were no drugs allowed and it took place in private homes with no police around.

Anyway, the rules were pretty straightforward:

- Couples only—you had to arrive as a couple and leave as a couple.
- Absolutely no drugs.
- No meant no. If someone refused your advances, you had to honor that decision. No exceptions.
- Men were discouraged from walking around by themselves. Evidently, some guys would bring nonparticipating women, leave them in the living room,

and take off as single guys. This was frowned upon, and the offending couples would be asked to leave.

- Male bisexuality was frowned upon, but female bisexuality was common and encouraged. I have no comment for this; it's just the way it was.

Obviously, I got into this for awhile. The worst part of it for me was the exhibitionist side of it. I didn't particularly enjoy being naked in rooms with many naked people; it wasn't my thing. But I did enjoy the "zipless" part of it: no dinner, no movie, no pretenses. Little did we all know that this sort of behavior would be fatal in just a few years. Well, I'm glad I got to experience it in my lifetime while dodging the bullet as well. In later years I can recall my son saying: "Why do I have to be twenty-three *now*?"

On New Year's Eve '78/'79, The Doobie Bros. were headlining the Forum in Los Angeles. Jeff Baxter, their guitarist at the time, and I were great friends. We had plans for after the show, so I went along and hung out backstage. I can't remember today who the poor woman was, but she was both our dates for this crazy evening. She and I chatted while the Doobies played their set (one I had seen many times that year because of my friendship with Jeff). On the closing number, "Listen to the Music," I was invited to come out and sit in, which I did, albeit on guitar. Après show, a limo whisked the three of us back to Jeff's place in Brentwood, where my car was conveniently pre-parked. On the way to Jeff's, we all downed tabs of Demerol, the evening's entertainment. Demerol is a class A narcotic, sort of a synthetic morphine. We all had quite a buzz going as we hopped into Jeff's hot tub to wash off the tensions of the previous part of the evening's engagement. The next thing I remember was waking up sluggishly, still tub-bound, in nearly cold water, as the sun streamed in the windows. All three of us had passed out and it was a miracle none of us had drowned. I woke the others and hurriedly dressed to begin the drive back to Hollywood.

At this time, Kitty Bruce worked for me. She would come in for an hour every day in the morning and tidy up the house—a necessity for a seventies' swinging bachelor. She had a key and was already there with a girlfriend in tow as I stumbled in the door that day.

"Out of the way," I commanded. "Shower alert!"

I got in the shower and tried to wash off the Demerol as best I could. This took almost an hour, and I *still* had a wicked drug hangover. I walked into the living room, where the two gals were toiling away. "I wanna die!" I complained as my bathrobe-encased body hit the couch. Now just at that very instant, a rather formidable earthquake began, and scared the living shit out of the girls. They were screaming at the top of their lungs.

"Please don't yell!" I begged. "Let's just stand in this doorway here like they say on TV." The three of us huddled there as the quake wound down after twenty seconds or so.

This was *not* a great way to start the day, I remember thinking. God sure has a bizarre sense of humor to do this on the morning after New Year's Eve. I was sure I was not the only person in L.A. having trouble standing when the quake hit. After about five minutes of calming, an aftershock shook us at about the same intensity and started the girls squealing again. It's a privilege to live in Los Angeles. Really!

I had built up a very strong following in Japan over the years, but had never really done anything about it in terms of appearing there. It was primarily the twenty-hour plane trip that held me back. I just couldn't imagine, short of temporarily freeze-drying myself, what on earth a guy like me would do on a commercial flight for twenty hours nonstop. In 1968, when I was voted the number one recording artist in Japan, I just turned down all the offers that came in. In retrospect, that was probably a bad idea. In 1978, Jeff Baxter and I were offered a two-week "clinic" tour of Japan by Roland Corporation (a musical instrument manufacturer Jeff and I endorsed at the time). I accepted the offer, while I was still young and strident. At this time they had quasi-sleeping compartments in first class on planes, and that appealed to me. I took a heady sleeping pill dose after the plane took off.[1] The "sleepers" were up the spiral staircase and were really just bastardized versions of three seats together without armrests. Nonetheless, I quickly lopped six hours off the flying time with a fitful, drug-induced nap upstairs. I repeated it for about three hours without drugs toward the end of the flight, and when we landed I hit the ground runnin'.

The people from Roland met me at the gate and introduced me to our interpreter, whom I immediately dubbed "Ike," which is what his real name Akira sounded most like. In the days of no political correctness, I said to him, "Just tell me how to say 'Blow me' and 'Thank you,' Ike. That should get me started!" If this offends someone today, go pick on Rod Stewart or Kiss, who were fifty times worse than I was. Besides, it was a *joke*, okay?

We had a four-piece band for the tour. Jeff played guitar, I played Roland keyboards and a B3 organ, Keith Knudsen (from The Doobie Bros.) played drums, and we were aided by a local Japanese bass player, whose name now escapes me. Jeff complained about his marijuana withdrawal and wondered if the bass player would "score" for

---

[1] This was a lesson I learned once when flying from New York to London. A friend offered me a monster English sleeping pill, and I took it half an hour be before the plane was to depart. Fifteen minutes later, the flight was delayed two hours, and said friend ended up having to carry me on board! So after that incident I never medicated myself until half an hour after we were in the air.

him. Japan is a drug-free country. I don't know if you remember the mess Paul McCartney got in when pot was found in his luggage, but it's serious over there. Rick Danko picked up a Fed Ex package that had heroin in it and languished in a Japanese prison for months! So we didn't bring any marijuana with us.

Japan is a police state. The locals are truly frightened of the police. Uniformed officers are everywhere; at airports, streetcorners, etc., brandishing firearms and wearing deadly serious demeanors. So at about our third gig, the bass player took Jeff and me into the corner of the dressing room. He took out a packet of folded paper that usually contained cocaine or heroin. This packet had pot in it. First time I ever saw *that*. He had rolling papers, and Jeff twisted one up. He walked over to the window and opened it. "I'll just smoke it out the window so it doesn't stink up the joint," Jeff offered. The bass player freaked! "No! No!" he cried. "Police watching EVERYWHERE! Close window and pull shades, PLEASE!" He put three towels under the door, opened the windows just a crack, and lit up. He was truly careful—*and* brainwashed. American law enforcement should take a lesson from Japanese fear tactics today.

I had brought a prescription bottle of Quaaludes with me. Naturally, the prescription made them legal. We dispensed them one at a time to some of the ladies we met, and to a one, they all passed out cold! No drug experience. We soon ascertained we only had to dispense a quarter of a pill to get the desired effect. While arriving at this dosage, we left about six unconscious bodies in various hotel rooms, sleeping off our unintentional overdoses. Don't tell me, I know I'm going to hell.

I met a beautiful girl at a department store we visited. She came to see us play, and I brought her back to the hotel. She spoke virtually no English, I spoke virtually no Japanese. We handed a translation book back and forth as I tried to seduce her into spending the night. It should have been a scene in a movie; it was hilarious. She ended up paying for her own room at the hotel. A wise choice, in retrospect (for her).

After about a week, Ike's girlfriend joined the tour. He hadn't seen her in awhile, and we took him aside. I broke a 'lude in half and gave him the two pieces. "When you get ready for bed tonight, you each take half," I said. "You'll have a great time." He smiled and asked, "What do you call this stuff?" I said, "They're called gorilla biscuits," and gave him a big smile. The next morning Jeff and I were having breakfast in the hotel coffee shop and Ike came walking in. He had a huge grin on his face. "Did you have a good time last night?" Jeff asked. "Uhhhh—you have more gorirra biska?" he inquired. We cracked up and kept him in 'ludes for the rest of the trip.

That has been my only Japanese journey so far, but it was action-filled. All the while, kids trailed behind us and asked for our autographs constantly. They were sooo polite it was a pleasure. I will always remember and treasure my brief time in Japan.

As that seven-thing decade came to an end, my life was in turmoil. Reagan was sure to be elected President, and I began to question the sanity of continuing to live in the United States. I began to fantasize about conquering England. *"The heralded American producer moved to London and enjoyed hit after hit as the Britons stood in amazement at his immediate success"* was my little fantasy. I was living in a rented house in Sherman Oaks at the time, with a very talented airbrush illustrator, Patti Heid. My landlady was Rene Russo's mom. Through my music publisher overseas, I made some inquiries, and found that English lodging for us could be secured by phone. They had an apartment there that they would be happy to turn over to us.

I took one more stateside producing job to insure that we had enough moving money. It was a strange one, too. Ronnie Van Zant's little brother, Johnny, had put a pretty decent band together in Jacksonville and was ready to follow in Skynyrd's footsteps, according to Stu Fine, an A&R guy at PolyGram in New York. This would entail me going to Atlanta for a month to rehearse and record the band, and mixing would commence in England shortly thereafter. I said okay, and a deal was struck. Patti and I began to pack. Things were changing rapidly all around us. The Record-Plant-as-Rome scenario had peaked and was virtually over, luckily concurrent with the dawn of the AIDS epidemic, and music was going through one of its many metamorphoses. The Sex Pistols, The Clash, and The Ramones were spearheading a "punk-rock" movement that didn't leave much room for *my* producing skills.

I was thirty-five and scratching my head. The combination of the move *and* the production forced me to rethink the choreography, and the entire project was moved to Los Angeles. The band came to L.A. for a month instead of me going to Atlanta. I booked into a nearby Valley studio that had just opened called Record One. Val Garay, who had engineered a zillion L.A. hits, was the head honcho there. It was five minutes from my house and state-of-the-art. We rehearsed for a week, and I got to know everyone in the band and was able work out all the arrangement kinks that I had heard on the demos. They were a good little band and more than a little reminiscent of Skynyrd. With engineer Bob Edwards in tow, we cut all the basic tracks at Record One and then moved to the more-affordable Larrabee Studios in Hollywood for the overdubs.

One of the things I hated about moving to England was giving up my phone number, which at the time was 213-PUT-IT-IN. I even used that gimmick for my production company. The credit on the Van Zant album reads: "Produced and Arranged by Al Kooper for Put It Industries."

I was especially hard on Johnny Van Zant when we did the vocals, but it was necessary to get the proper performances out of him. He had to make that quantum leap to palatability! We finished all the recording on the Van Zant record, took one last look around, and flew off to England. *The only tears in our eyes were from the smog!*

It was 1979, and the seventies were most assuredly over. . . .

1979-1981

LONDON,

EDDIE & THE HOT RODS,

DAVID ESSEX,

GEORGE HARRISON,

TEXAS FLOODS,

SRV, JOE ELY, AND

LOS ANGELES (SLIGHT
RETURN)

As the plane touched down in England, I could instinctively feel that good L.A. weather lingering eternally in the overhead bins as we exited. One of the people from my publisher's London office met Patti and me at the airport to escort us to our new apartment.

"It's a cozy two-bedroom place that's right over one of the most popular clubs in London." Great, I remember thinking. I hope you can't hear the disco music coming through the floorboards. Imagine our surprise when we arrived and had to take our voluminous luggage supply to the top of a five-flight walk-up. These were our new lodgings, where the only telephone service was a pay phone in the living room. And there is nothing quite like English plumbing. After all: *Why change something from the nineteenth century if it still works?*

Our middleman with the landlord was the maitre d' at Rags, the club downstairs. His name was Santos and he was not unlike Manuel from *Fawlty Towers*. He enjoyed our discomfort with *such* relish that he felt anything he could do to increase it was his new goal in life.

Now let us enter in some sociological factoids that were indigenous to 1979 London. Television: we had none in the apartment. Public transportation (buses and subways) closed down at 11:45 p.m. Food? Here's an interesting quality scale I worked out within our first week there:

London	**United States**
Bad food	Not legal in this country—no equivalent except for American dog food
Average food (most restaurant fare)	Equivalent to fast food (i.e., Wendy's or Burger King)
Good food (above average pricey restaurant)	Average restaurant chain (i.e., Red Lobster, Chilis, Hard Rock)
Top-of-the-line snooty joint	Good, casual restaurant—moderate prices

Fortunately, only a few mistakes were made working out the above equation, and hospital trips were avoided. The local "superette" carried the staples and was just around the corner, albeit at frightening, exclusive Mayfair prices.

Driving a car was not an option 'cause they drive on the opposite side of the street there, and the steering wheel is on the right side of the car. The first time someone like me came to one of those rotaries, I'd take out probably . . . oh . . . fifteen pedestrians and four cars before I figured out where I was really supposed to be. The laundry was a bus ride away. So one had to locate a Santa-sized bag, go down the five flights, walk three blocks to the bus stop, and then wait a half hour for a bus, travel fifteen minutes to the required stop, walk two blocks and there it was. Simple as that. Of course, reverse the procedure for getting home. I could go on and on. It was the humbling experience I deserved for being an American who was used to cable, Rolls Royces, and orgies. And it worked.

After a month, we bought a TV set. In England you're required (and I am not making this up, Dave Barry!) to purchase a *license to watch television*! Don't ask me! You should be required to have a license to buy a guitar amp there, if there *was* any justice! So I got the TV, I got the license, I got the TV up the five flights, and what did I really have? Two government-controlled stations (BBC-1 and 2) and that's it. There was no United States equivalent for most of the programming we saw: darts matches for hours, the sheep dog trials (I could write a chapter about just this), eighty-nine reruns of the English *Carry On* . . . movie series, snooker championships, etc. *Not to be believed*. And, of course, the television ceased broadcasting at midnight so American insomniacs could contemplate murdering it Elvis-style nightly.

The two TV highlights of the week were *Top of the Pops* and *Dallas*. *Top of the Pops* was a below-average pop dance show with a Top Ten and lip-syncing guests. *Dallas*, which is something I *never* would have watched in the States, was somehow engrossing and comforting here. This was the peak of the series; the year J. R. got shot. It was amazing how deep I got into that show.

One rare night, they broadcast a Popfest from Barcelona and it started at about two in the morning, live. *I was ecstatic*. I bought popcorn and ice cream and set the alarm in case I got engrossed in whatever book was taking up the slack that week. Sooo, I'm watching this show and the band The Police come on. Somewhere in the first song, they cut to an overhead shot from behind Stewart Copeland playing drums. He had four tom-toms and had written in big black letters using all four toms "FUCK/OFF/YOU/CUNT!" And there it was on BBC-2 at 3 a.m. on Wednesday night. I was beside myself. I'm betting that the Spanish director of the show did not understand English and that Stewart was betting on that too. I'm sure the affiliates rang the phone off the hook, 'cause we never did see that overhead rear shot again during the entire broadcast. But I'll always be indebted to Stewart Copeland for that.

A week after settling in, Bob Edwards flew over and we set about mixing Johnny Van Zant's album at a studio called Basing Street that I believe Island Records owned. This went pretty effortlessly, except for the studio cat, who left his bladder's trademark everywhere. The entire studio smelled of cat urine. Back home in America, Chris Stone of Record Plant would have killed that cat with his bare hands. Here in Blighty, they just giggled about it. We called it Pat's Kiss.

After we dispatched the Van Zant album, I began post-production with the band called Eddie & The Hot Rods. They were kind of a punky band with two assets: a really good lead singer, and a great drummer. Their area of expertise was second-period Who territory—four-chord stuff like "Happy Jack" with great Keith Moon-type drumming. Patti painted a great cover for their album and designed the entire package. Nepotism. The album was lacking in quality material, but there were *some* good songs. It was to be their last album, however, and I suspect they went back to Canvey Island from whence they came. But I enjoyed the time I spent with them; Barrie Masters was a great singer and Steve Nicol was a great drummer—*so let it be written*.

One night we went to the Marquee Club to see a band called The Photos. Patti and I were always checking out woman-fronted groups 'cause we were thinking of starting our own. It was really crowded and we had to stand at the bar without being able to see the band performing in the next room. Now we had gone and heard quite a few bands and not liked any of them. We heard great stuff coming from the next room and it wasn't The Photos, just some opening band from Ireland. For the first time since I had moved there, I got excited. "I gotta go talk to those guys," I told Patti, and pushed my way toward the dressing room. At the conclusion of their set I burst in and immediately inquired: "Are you guys signed to a deal?" Well, they were. They were signed to Island Records, this was their first gig in London, and they were called U2. In hindsight, I still had good ears!

What happened after that was extremely bizarre. Herbie Flowers got me a job producing David Essex. David was well known in America for the hit "Rock On," which he was never able to follow up there. I knew him best from Michael Apted's great rock film *Stardust*, which may be the best *serious* rock film ever made (the other obvious choice being not so serious—*Spinal Tap*). Anyway, I hooked up with David and we began going over material. His songs were marred attempts at serious subjects. His heart was in the right place, but his songwriting abilities weren't able to reach as far as his initial vision. I helped as best I could, but that flaw remained. We cut a techno version of "Be Bop A Lula" that was actually quite humorous. The basic tracks were cut at Pye Studios in London, and the overdubs and some other basic tracks were cut at Concorde Studios in Los Angeles. Many notables played on this album, including: Steve Lukather, Rabbit Bundrick, Herbie Flowers (obviously), Jeff Baxter, and Michael Boddicker. We mixed at Sunset Sound in Los Angeles. There were a few peripheral stories involved in the production of the album that are worth telling.

One night, David took Jeff Baxter and myself to dinner at one of London's more exclusive gentlemen's clubs. Jeff and David drank a few bottles of wine and were feeling no pain. Freddie Mercury and a chap called Paul came over to the table as we (David actually) were paying the check.

"Hello, darlings," he said. "If you don't have any plans, Paul, here, and I are going over to the Blank Club [can't remember its real name—a notoriously gay club a few blocks away], and we'd like you three to be our guests."

Jeff, who was unaware of any of the sexual proclivities of those assembled or the establishments involved, cast a drunken eye Freddie's way: "They got any great lookin' women over at that club, pal?" he innocently inquired.

And Freddie just looked pitifully at all three of us and went off in a huff to the Blank Club with only Paul in tow.

And I can't leave out this great story one of David's business associates told in the studio one day. It seems that Mike (not his real name) and his brother Jimmy (not important what his name is) lived in a lovely flat on the second floor in Belgravia (a very nice neighborhood). One night, Mike brought this "great-lookin' bird" home. In the morning, as Mike made the obligatory coffee, said bird was leaning on the window sill, looking out at the day, with only Mike's shirt on. This was a temptation that Mike could not avoid. He came up behind her and quickly shut the window down on her at the waist, so she was forced to look outside at the view while he had his way with her. Right in the middle of all this, Jimmy walked in the kitchen. Mike motioned for Jimmy to take Mike's place behind her. Meanwhile, she had gotten into it and was enjoying this morning much better. She could not see the switch that had just gone on, however. Mike raced into the bedroom, got dressed, hurriedly ran down the stairs, then casually strolled into eye contact with her, giving her a big wave and smile.

That's how Mike ended the story. But Bob Edwards, wiping tears of laughter from his eyes as he listened, said, "Oh, man! What did she *do*?" Mike used only four words to conjure up the real end of the story, so to speak: "She went fucking MENTAL!"

David was playing a live show in London one night, and Patti and I were invited along. There was to be a party for invited guests après show at some ritzy club. When the concert ended, David, Patti, and I were rushed by limo to the party site. David had just come offstage, and was still sweating. We arrived at the club in moments and, after David changed clothes, just the three of us were sitting around waiting for his friends to arrive. Patti gave me a wink, and then offered David some chewing gum, which he accepted. We had just bought the gum that very morning at a magic store. It turned the whole inside of your mouth dark blue. Now I myself would not have been this cruel, but Patti, bored out of her mind in London generally, couldn't resist. We sat there watching his lips, tongue, teeth, and gums all turn this horrendous purple. David was unaware of what was happening, but just as the first guests began arriving, Patti broke down and told him. A handsome, vain devil, he was incredulous. "You're kidding, right?" he said. He looked at me for support. I smiled and told him, "No. She isn't kidding. Your entire mouth is fucking dark purple!" He flew into the men's room, and we quickly left for home in a taxi, another job well done.

At the time there was a soul-revival band playing in the clubs composed of white-kids-obsessed-with-soul-music. They were called The Q-Tips and had a horn section and a great lead singer. I was quite taken with them. They were signed to Chrysalis Records, and I went up there and asked if I could get in the studio with them. They let us go in to see if there was any chemistry between us. I taught the horn section certain blending tricks. English horn players are almost *always* lacking in skills their American counterparts seem almost born to. With a little work, we were putting down some nice tracks. I also got the opportunity to record them live one night at the Marquee Club on Wardour Street in Soho. That establishment had a functioning studio right in the same building, with tie-lines laid right into the club. I read in the paper that Stax superstar Eddie Floyd was in town, made some calls, and invited him down to sit in. We recorded some great stuff that night, including a duet between lead singer Paul Young and Eddie Floyd on the Stax chestnut "Raise Your Hand." This live stuff was eventually released in Europe, but our studio sessions remain in the can, unfortunately. Paul went on to become a big star with such hits as "Every Time You Go Away" and "Come Back and Stay."

The English lifestyle was getting to Patti and me. On the weekends, about half the cinemas would show cult movies or all-night marathons which were called "the lates." A weekly listings mag called *Time Out* would list the lates and we'd venture out to all sorts of weird neighborhoods in search of bizarre film fare. Many's the Saturday night we'd be in Islington or someplace like that at 4 a.m., praying for a taxicab to materialize. At the apartment, Patti had painted all the walls a super-glossy electric blue, with a few flying bananas sketched in there as well, and we

The Al Kooper Look-Alike Contest: Paul Young (left) and The Q-Tips mock the Kooper "style" using sunglasses and electrical tape (actual Al Kooper second from right).
(Photo: Al Kooper Collection.)

secretly had the pay phone taken out and a real one put in. One day superintendent Santos came in while we were out, ostensibly to check for a gas leak (yeah, sure). He saw the blue walls, the bananas, and the missing pay phone, and we were quickly served eviction papers. It was just the impetus we needed. We found a little side-by-side house in the Jewish community of Golders Green. Now we could walk to the market and the laundry minus five flights, albeit in the dead of winter, which it now was.

Mike Bloomfield called and said that he was seeing a professional dancer (ballet) and that she was gonna tour Europe soon. He wanted me to book some gigs for us together in London to coincide with his girlfriend's itinerary so that he could "tag along" with her. I booked us into this intimate club called the Venue for an upcoming date about two months later. About three weeks after I had booked the gig, I was sitting home one evening reading the paper and I read that Mike had died. I guess that no one knew how to reach me in London. I was completely shocked and shaken. After sleuthing for a few weeks I pieced together the circumstances of his death. Michael used heroin, but he was a "chipper"—that is, he wasn't neccesarily strung out, but an occasional user. For a special occasion, he'd drive over to the connection's house, score, and do it up right then and there. He had recently claimed to me that he was clean and was working out every day. Michael could tell a lie every now and then for no particular reason, however. So I theorize that he drove to the connection's house, scored, did it up right then and there, and overdosed for whatever reason. The people in that house panicked, put him in his car, drove him to a remote location, and left him there in whatever condition to be found. Happens every day. Just not to one of the most brilliant blues guitarists who ever lived.

Mike Bloomfield's loss was immediate and unrecoverable. He left some mighty big shoes to fill. I wrote about it:

> ". . . Although I love to play and I love to sing
> I'm quite content to stand right here on the shore
> With a teardrop in each eye
> 'Cause I have watched most of my friends die
> And they just don't make 'em like that anymore
> No sir,
> They just don't make 'em like that anymore. . . ."[1]

Bye Michael. You were one in a million.

[1]© 1995, Rekooped Music BMI. Used with permission.

Herbie Flowers (who seemed like my agent in the U.K.) called to say he had gotten me booked on some George Harrison sessions that he had been asked to do. They would take place at George's home studio, and Herbie would drive us there. Then the night before the sessions the phone rang about 9:30 p.m.

"Is this Al?" a voice asked. "This is George Harrison. I was just calling to see if you wanted any special keyboards for tomorrow. I've gotten you a Hammond B3 organ, a Fender Rhodes, and a Wurlitzer piano. We also have an Arp Omni. Will those be okay for you?"

I really thought it was Herbie having me on. Something told me to answer normally though, *just in case.*

"Uhhhhhh, yeah, that sounds like everything I need. Thank you and I guess I'll just see you tomorrow. . . . Good night." I hung up praying that the phone would ring right back and Herbie's maniacal laugh would be at the other end, but there was just silence.

The next morning, after an hour and a half's haul from London, Herbie and I pulled up to a set of gates in the village of Henley-on-Thames. Herbie got out of the car and opened the gates.

"Pretty special for a pair o' blokes like us to be invited to a place like this, eh?" he said laughing as he got back in the car. You couldn't even *see* the house yet. We drove through some really gorgeous landscaping until there it was—Crackerbox Palace. It was a damn castle! I had read it was a Catholic girls school or something like that at one time. We drove up on the tarmac and George came out to greet us. He had incredible eyes that could look right through you. I had not met anyone with that powerful a stare since Dylan.

"You didn't think that was me on the phone last night, did you, Al?" he said, laughing. "No, I didn't," I admitted. "I thought it might be Herbie having a go."

"Well, that's all right then. Shall we go inside?" he offered.

The castle was beautiful, and it *was* pretty special for a pair of blokes like us to be invited there. I remember I had brown-bagged it that first day, bringing along a chicken sandwich, etc. When dinnertime came around, George had a home-cooked meal for all of us in the dining room. Absentmindedly I left that brown bag in the studio until George found it three nights later after we'd gone home.

The sessions were great: Ringo on drums, Herbie on bass, Ray Cooper on percussion, George on guitar, and yours truly keyboarding it. We even cut some tracks for a Ringo album as well. "Wrack My Brain" and the standard "You Belong to Me" were cut on those dates. But the standout tune had no title. George was still writing the words. After we cut the basic tracks, Herbie was dismissed and we did overdubs. Ray Cooper took over driving me back and forth each day in his Rolls Royce. The drives home were like something out of *Annie Hall* as we drove into pitch black

The Fab Four (for this particular afternoon) at George Harrison's home studio: recording Somewhere in England, 1980. (Left to right) George, Ringo, Barbara Bach, lucky Al. (Photo: Al Kooper Collection.)

∾

countryside while Ray hollered out his political manifestos, hardly watching the road.

On the fourth night, I got home about 3 a.m. and was reading with the radio on in hopes I could get a little sleep before Ray came again at 10 a.m. An announcement came on the radio that John Lennon had been shot. I woke Patti up and we huddled around the radio, probably two of the only people aware of this event in sleepy Britain. An hour later, his death was confirmed. I got chills. Should I call George and tell him? *No, I didn't really want to be the one.* At 7:30 a.m. I called Ray, and we decided to go ahead with the day's session. We thought it might take George's mind off his personal tragedy.

It was a cloudy day with that typical British mist-rain when we arrived at George's gate. There were actually about thirty press people just standing out there in the rain. It was pathetic. I got out of the car to open the gate and the jackals descended on me: "Who are you? How does George feel? Does George know? Is there a funeral planned?"

I got angry quickly and shot back: "Surely, you people have something better to do today than stand out here in the rain bothering a delivery man like me?"

Yeah—a delivery man in a Rolls Royce. . . .

George was in the kitchen, white as a sheet, real shook up. We all had breakfast. He took calls from Paul and Yoko, which actually seemed to help his spirit, and then we went into the studio and started the day's work. Ray and I kept George's wine glass full all day, and by six o'clock the fab lad was pretty soused. I had brought a tape of my project with Patti that was crying for George to play slide on. When we ran out of things to do on his album, I brought out the tape and we did that. Finally, it was midnight and our mission was completed. "I'm pretty knackered, lads," George confessed."Let's call it a night, okay?" While driving home that night, Ray was silent and kept his eyes on the road.

Eventually all of this work coalesced into George's album *Somewhere in England*, featuring that "standout tune" I mentioned before, now with lyrics which became the number one single "All Those Years Ago." This was George's tribute to John Lennon, featuring yours truly spankin' the Wurlitzer piano, especially on the intro.

One night, Patti and I were playing charades (!) in the house, and I looked at her and said: "We are playing fucking charades here in England. You know why? 'Cause we are bored way out of our minds, that's why! We have *got* to get out of here, the sooner the better. I don't wanna see one more darts match, greasy newspaper filled with food, or *Carry On* movie. We are MOVING! I don't know quite where yet. . . . BUT COUNT ON IT!"

Amazingly, I located someone in Austin, Texas, who was ready to put me on salary to help him with his budding music empire. That is all I really needed. David Essex bought the TV, a video game player and refrigerator we'd bought, and the left-over magic purple gum. We filled our steamer trunks again, shipped them off, and took off back to dear, young, un-tradition-filled America! When the plane landed in Austin, I got down on my hands and knees and kissed the ground. I ate a hundred cheeseburgers that first week back and had a perpetual grin on my face all the time.

The man I was working with was Michael Brovsky, an entrepreneur who was then handling Christopher Cross, Carole King, and Eric Johnson. He had a band he wanted me to develop called The Blame. I met the principals, Bill Carter and Ruth Ellsworth, the first night I was in town and we got along famously. People were pretty friendly, generally speaking, and I liked the whole feel of living in Austin. We rented a little townhouse a ways down the road and settled in. Patti hated Texas right off the bat, as our relationship had already begun to deteriorate. This was our third city together, and Patti's career was suffering as a result.

This kind of summer heat was brand new to me and I soon understood why every car had a crack in the dashboard. (If there had been a Weather Channel back then, I would have lasted ten minutes in Austin. Their alarmist programming for this particular geographic location would have basically frightened me to death.)

I worked with The Blame and helped them put some demos together. I assembled a four-piece band for *myself* and started to play around town and all around the whole state of Texas, once I got my T legs. I produced a live Joe Ely EP called *Texas Tornado* and began to become part of the musical community. One day, some guy I knew from San Francisco who used to work with The Grateful Dead, invited me to come hear this young guitarist he was handling. I was very impressed and offered to sign and produce him on the spot, but he kept me at bay. The lad's name was Stevie Ray Vaughan and he was damn good.

About three months after he and I met, and after I'd gone to see him play live a few times, he invited me to jam with him one night at the Steamboat Club on Sixth Street. I got there about 10 p.m. and there was no keyboard in sight. On his first break, I asked him about that. "Oh, shoot, I'll lend ya a guitar and we'll play later on," he said. "Later on" turned out to be 1:40 a.m., and the place had a 2 a.m. closing time. I was a little disgruntled sitting around all night, especially imagining being a guitar shill for his great playing. Well, I got up on stage with one of his guitars and he started playing an easy blues shuffle. Needless to say, he was murdering me, but I couldn't for the life of me figure out why he wanted to be in a cutting contest with a keyboard player. So I was grinning at the display of guitarness he was putting on, and then he put his guitar behind his head like Hendrix and kept playing. Well, shoot, I thought to myself, I can do that. So I put the guitar behind *my* head and started playing. I was laughing just thinking what this must look like to the audience when I looked over at Stevie Ray and, amazingly, he was *angry*!

He is taking this far more seriously than I am, I was thinking.

So when that song ended, with five minutes left to play, I put the guitar down, waved to all, walked off the stage, went directly to my car, and drove right home still none the wiser about what was on his mind. That was one weird night!

Another Austin evening, while Patti was out of town at her parents', a bunch of us went to the movies together. All the members of The Blame, a photographer, and yours truly caught the Sean Connery flick, *Outland*, at the Metroplex. It had been raining really hard when we arrived at the theater, and as the show progressed, water began pouring in from the middle exit doors on each side, slowly creeping up from the first row of seats until there was a river covering the first eight or ten rows. We kept moving back a few rows as the river approached us. I guess they were used to that sort of thing in Texas! Every fifteen minutes or so, another usher would walk briskly down the aisle to see what was going on, only to walk right into the water, and a resounding "OH SHIT!" would fill the auditorium, to the amusement of the audience. Each usher would then turn on his or her wet heels and go back to usherland or from wherever they came. It was hard to concentrate on the movie with all this going on.

At the conclusion of the film, we exited and found an amazing sight. Half the parking lot was *underwater*! Marc, the drummer from The Blame, found his station wagon in water up to the windows. I had come with Jan, the photographer, and her car was okay where it was parked. We helped Marc get his car out, but its insides had been totally flooded and were ruined. The theater was on the outskirts of town, and as Jan and I navigated toward downtown, we met with many surprises. The interstate was totally underwater! At each entrance ramp, we'd go to drive on, and little by little the ramp would head underwater. We'd back up and try some other route. Of course, Jan's radio was broken, so we had no help from broadcast advisories. It was pretty scary. Amazingly, we made it back into town. Where I lived was okay but the news on TV was not. Flash-flooding had done an incredible amount of damage. A graveyard was flooded and a bunch of coffins ended up on a supermarket's parking lot! A bunch of pianos from a music store were floating in the creek! Stuff like that was happening all over Austin that night. The next day the waters subsided almost as quickly as they rose.

A concert was soon planned to aid the flood victims. It was called *Tornado Jam* for some reason lost on me. *Flood Fiesta* would have been more appropriate. The line-up was: The Fabulous Thunderbirds, Joe Ely, Al Kooper, Stevie Ray Vaughan, Delbert McClinton, and some band from Australia that was passing through called Cold Chisel. It took place on a sunny Sunday afternoon and evening at Manor Downs, a racetrack just outside of town. Attendance was good, but it was hot as hell. I remember having Joe Ely's girlfriend cut my hair just before we went on, so that I could breathe on stage! Michael Brovsky set it up so that the show would be audio- and videotaped, and I was producing the audio part. A remote truck was pulled up to the site, and good ol' Bob Edwards and I sat in there making sure that things were going okay to tape. My version of "I Love You More Than You'll Ever Know" took so long in performance that it literally went from daylight to night time during the course of the one song! It was interesting to note that people were so used to seeing Stevie Ray play around town, they were pretty blasé during his performance. The Thunderbirds headlined, however, and brought the house down. The Vaughan clan was well represented that day, and "Texas Flood" was an appropriate song for Stevie Ray to play. The show was deemed a success, but the video production never aired anywhere I knew about. It would be an amazing artifact to see today.

As time went by, I began to go weeks at a time without a check from Brovsky. Bob Edwards' invoices went unheeded as well, and finally I couldn't afford to stay in Austin anymore. My relationship with Patti had dwindled down to nothing. I sold my stuff to different friends. Joe Ely bought my refrigerator. He got it home and found out the door opened the wrong way for his kitchen set-up. He turned the refrigerator *upside-down* and I'm told it's still working for him today! Inevitably, it seemed, I was doomed to head back to California—alone, with my tail between my legs, and believe it or not, *still with no tan.*

1981-1985:

Patti and I called it quits, leaving Austin separately but both headed for L.A. Stan Polley was able to secure a friend's condo for me at a reasonable rent because it was a bust as a "for sale" item. It was located in the heart of Hollywood, down the street from the Directors Guild. The furnishings were from hell and that sort of made it depressing because not only did I have to look at them everyday, but so did anyone else who came to visit. But I had a home, even if three-quarters of my possessions were still in storage. Patti took a guest house in Laurel Canyon, and we somehow remained friends.

The first thing that happened was Bob Dylan's office called my manager to offer me a spot in Bob's touring band commencing in a week for three months' duration. This was approximately the beginning of September 1981. Now, Bob and I had not spoken in seven years, over a disagreement the details of which are unimportant. I figured I'd had seven years of survival without Bob, and I was basically curious to see what would happen now. There was a rehearsal the next day, and I went along to see what his stance toward me would be. Well, it was like those seven years of falling-out had never existed. We just hugged and took up where we left off.

There were thirty-five songs on the set-list, and we played them all in a relatively short amount of time. The band consisted of Steve Ripley (now of The Tractors) and Fred Tackett (now of Little Feat) on guitars, Tim Drummond (he of Neil Young and James Brown fame) on bass, the ubiquitous Jim Keltner on drums, and a member of the road crew, Arthur Rosato, on another set of drums. Three female Baptist Church singers rounded out the cast.

I felt confident after the rehearsal that I could play the gig, but the business people were still haggling. The plane left in two days and they still hadn't come to terms. I told my manager that I didn't care if I went or not, and to make the best deal he could. With two days to go, I imagined his bargaining position was pretty secure. My suitcase was half-packed on the bed, and I calmly waited to find out if I stayed or went. Finally, the answer came, and I packed the other half of my belongings and headed to the airport. Later, I found out that Bob's keyboard player had quit at the last minute and Dylan happened to be talking to George Harrison at the time, who recommended me. I was on a plane to Milwaukee, with a man who sang mostly religious songs in his show. *Oh, boy.*

Backstage at the first gig, things were tense. The road manager came to get me: "It's time for the prayer, Al." Yeah, I'll say, I thought. But to my surprise, the entire band stood in the wings holding hands with heads bowed. Madeline Quebec, one of the background singers, led the prayer that went something like this:

"Oh Lord. Help us to remember all our parts and bless us tonight on our first show. You are an Almighty God and we love and worship You. Amen."

We then went out and played "You Got To Serve Somebody" and "I Believe In You." I was thinking to myself: *This is a Bob Dylan show??? Why am I here??? Why aren't we playing all the songs Bob and I recorded???* I yearned to do something about this.

The band and road manager Bob Meyers traveled in one bus, the crew in another, and Bob in his own bus. The first hotel stay was either the Hotel Milwaukee or the Hotel Wisconsin, I can't remember which. The memory is the second thing to go; I can't remember what the first is, either. But anyhow, it was the kind of hotel where an ambulance arrives every six hours or so to cart away another expired tenant. The blankets were made from that stuff airplane blankets are made out of, and there were *dial* telephones in the room. The only other place I knew that had dial telephones in 1981 was my parents' apartment! I found out that Bob picked the hotels. *Now he's a travel agent too*, I thought to myself.

After the first show, Bob invited me to ride in his bus to the next stop. I started in right away: "Hey, man—why don't we play more songs we recorded together? I thought that's why I got the call. . . . And next time, ya know, I only stay in hotels with residents under ninety years old and *touchtone* phones, OK?"

We laughed, and that seemed to break the ice. I think this began the second phase of our friendship where we looked at each other as people who had been through a lot together *and* apart, and had survived it all. It was easier to be with him now. Not many people who had been in the picture all those years ago were alive or in Bob's current phone book. Hell, *I* wasn't in that book until the week before!

We started adding the older songs, and they sounded great. "I Want You," "Like A Rolling Stone," "Just Like a Woman" were big hits with both the audience and the band itself. Even so, Bob still wouldn't show up at soundchecks. I thought it would be great because we could try out more older material.

"Oh, man . . . I can't come there . . . I got all these guitars to tune!" was his answer to why he didn't make it to soundchecks. The guy is admittedly hilarious.

New Orleans was a fun stop for me on the tour. I bought this bright red Afro wig and brought it to the gig that night. I had this nice suit on, shirt and tie and all, capped with this full-on almost-Bozo wig. The band was in tears laughing. I walked into Bob's dressing room with it on.

"Oh, man . . . that is *obscene*!" he said as he smiled, recoiling in mock horror. As we walked to the wings to prepare to go on, his mood changed quickly. The dynamics of our relationship precluded him telling me I *couldn't* wear the wig onstage, but he was very upset. We stood side by side in the wings, saying not a word. I was imagining Dylan trying to figure out how to sing a song about God with Bozo the Clown playing the organ to his immediate right. Bob Meyers yelled "House lights" to the engineer, the house lights dimmed, and the crowd erupted. I pulled the wig off as we walked out and tossed it to Meyers offstage.

"You know I wouldn't do that to *you*, Bob," I said reassuringly, enjoying the look of sheer relief on his face. I couldn't find the wig after the show until we were boarding the bus and I saw the driver was wearing it!

Another night, I walked out onstage forty-five seconds late, just as they were starting "You Gotta Serve Somebody," wearing a hotel waiter's outfit and carrying a room service tray in one hand and a towel on my other arm. *Three months is a long time to be on a tour bus.*

Early in the tour, Bob began "Like A Rolling Stone" so slowly, it felt like half an hour until we hit the last chord. After the show, I said, "If we play 'Like A Rolling Stone' any slower, we won't have to do any other songs in the show."

Bob knew it had been slow. "Maybe I should drink some coffee before we go on, Al," he suggested.

"*That's* a good idea, Bob," I replied. And every night, as we'd walk to the wings, the ritual would begin as I'd say: "How many cups, Bob?" and he'd pick a number between 0 and 122, depending upon what his energy level was that evening. That way I'd know whether Jim Keltner should count off "Like A Rolling Stone" or leave it to Bob.

One night, at the Meadowlands in New Jersey, my parents actually came to see the show. When Bob was introducing the band, he said: "I'd like to say hello to Mr. and Mrs. Kooper. Glad ya could make it . . . and greetings!!" I'd never heard him do that before and I kept a cassette of that show just for posterity.

I hadn't done the sideman thing in many years, and I quite enjoyed it. No interviews, no real responsibilities, just show up and play. The road crew was wonderful, and I never had to lift a finger. The last leg of the tour was a bunch of Florida dates. The night of our Atlanta show I asked Bob to introduce the band at its end. I had lived in Atlanta and conjectured that some people in the audience might enjoy knowing the dot they saw behind the organ was me. Bob hadn't been introducing the band lately anyway. So the time came and he said: "Anybody here ever heard-a Al Kooper? [Two beat pause.] Well that's him over there!" Nothing about anyone else in the band. I was *real* embarrassed. I never asked him to introduce the band again, which is why he probably did that in the first place.

The bus began a real long haul to Fort Lauderdale, right after our Atlanta show. I opted to take a plane the next day and stayed overnight in Atlanta. Everyone was really looking forward to the Florida leg, because we had begun to get the cold weather at the end of November and it was gorgeous in Miami then. I remember arriving at the hotel in Fort Lauderdale, late afternoon, and there was our entire band pool-side in Panama hats, sunglasses, tanning oil, and drinks with parasols in them. I dropped my bags and collapsed laughing.

While in Miami, I got to see my old friend Bill Szymczyk, and I talked to him about producing my next album. The tour ended, and I went back to L.A. and reality. Back to that horrible furniture. *How much can a man take?* Well, at least the condo had a laundry room!

Plans were now afoot for a new Kooper album, to be produced by Bill Szymczyk: a duet record with Jeff "Skunk" Baxter (I would find out soon why he was called "Skunk"). The package was put together and offered to CBS Records, and then-president Al Teller signed the deal. I had not made a record since 1976's *Act Like Nothing's Wrong* on United Artists (now owned by EMI). The concept this time was sort of a modern *Super Session*, with less emphasis on blues and more on rhythm and blues. I can't tell you how many times record companies have asked me to remake *Super Session*. I was sick of reading reviews about how my vocals were adequate or less than adequate, and for one of the only times in my life, I succumbed to criticism. Three guest lead singers sang two songs each, and two instrumentals were offered. I sang only two songs on the album; a Billy Boy Arnold blues tune called "I Wish You Would" and one of my new songs, "The Heart Is A Lonely Hunter." Valarie Carter, Mickey Thomas (pre Starship and post Elvin Bishop), and Ricky Washington (Bill Szymczyk's gardener!) did the singing. Backup musicians included: Elliot Randall, Bruce Gary, Neil Stubenhaus, Vinnie Colaiuta, Paul Harris, Joe Vitale, "Chocolate" Perry, and the Tower of Power Horn Section.

We toiled over this flawed masterpiece for a few months. Right in the middle of recording, that skunk Baxter nixed it being a duet record on his lawyer's advice. He still played, but dumped the responsibilities on me. When it was finished, Szymczyk and I were invited up to Teller's office to play it for him. At the conclusion of the playback, Teller, with an annoyed look on his face, complained: "This is not the record I expected you to do." I suppose there will *always* be that communications breakdown between musicians and businessmen, but it was still a heartbreaker for Bill and me. We exchanged the same glance that Warren Beatty and Faye Dunaway shared in *Bonnie and Clyde* just before they were pumped full of two thousand rounds of hot G-man lead. And that, my friends, is the story of the album *Championship Wrestling*, aborted in stillbirth by Al Teller, who released it anyway just to prove to Bill and me what a dud it would be if the company completely ignored it.

There was still one post-recording, memorable experience that came out of that album. I was playing the flagship show of the *Championship Wrestling* tour at the Bottom Line in New York City, and an extremely inebriated version of adult film star Sharon Mitchell, whom I had seen on the screen but never met, was in the front row. In the middle of a cover version of ZZ Top's "Fool for Your Stockings," she clambered onstage in a red leather coat and began to dance. My roadies were always instructed *never* to remove a woman from the stage unless she was carrying a lethal weapon, so she was left alone.

Now the place was packed with press and fans, and that must have encouraged her, because Sharon soon doffed her coat and was nude except for a garter-belt and stockings. (Does that qualify as a lethal weapon?) Luckily, I happened to be videotaping the show, and I silently prayed this was being filmed correctly. It was, by the way, and is one of the funniest video artifacts I own. Alan Pepper and Stanley Snadowsky, owners of said club, were having a shit hemorrhage over in the corner, because what Sharon was doing was basically *against the law* in their club. Regard-

Onstage with Sharon Mitchell. The Bottom Line, New York City, 1982.
Al: "Hey, Sharon . . . if you wanna jump onstage here, ya gotta entertain this crowd!!"
Sharon: [Trying her best]. (Photo: Ebet Roberts.)

less, no one had the good sense to take her off the stage as she crawled around while we played. Greg George, my sax player at the time, went into a solo of "Harlem Nocturne," a popular background tune for strippers, and we all followed him. I looked out into the audience, and all the women were completely horrified, while the men just had stupid grins on their faces. Flashbulbs and jeans buttons were popping everywhere. The song thankfully ground to a close and Sharon was escorted offstage. They still talk about that night at the Bottom Line!

For a couple of years after that, every time we played New York City various adult film stars would attend our shows. We became the favored band of that genre. No one attempted to equal Sharon's performance, thankfully; they all just sat and watched each show and then came backstage to pay "their respects."

Al Teller's reaction to the *Championship Wrestling* album pretty much left a permanent bad taste in my mouth about making Al Kooper albums (and about Al Teller!), so right then and there in 1982 I retired that aspect of my life. Now, mind you, it takes a great deal of discipline *not* to make a solo album, especially if you're the producer as well. It's too much fun and the ultimate masturbatory recording experience, but ultimately it's overkill. Still, if someone allows you to do it, it becomes addictive. They should offer a twelve-step program for artists who make too many albums. I know there are some fans out there who wish Van Morrison or Neil Young had used some restraint at various stages of their careers. On the other hand, how else would I have been inspired to stop if they *had* been restrained?

On my son Brian's fifteenth birthday, March 29, 1982, he came to spend the evening with his poor old Dad. I was planning on a night of clubbing, so he'd feel like the mighty stud we all hoped he would grow up to be. Bruce Gary, the drummer from The Knack, was along with us this night; in fact, we were in his vehicle. Bruce was driving, I was riding shotgun, and Brian was in the backseat with white-

Son and proud father. Los Angeles, 1986.
(Photo: Gary Nichamin/BOOM! Graphics.)

framed shades on! As we drove along Sunset, Bruce stopped and engaged a few hookers in conversation, teasing Brian about buying him one for his birthday. I nixed that. Then Bruce fired up a joint. Now, I never hid anything from Brian. I let him see the good parts of life tempered with equal doses of bad. Drugs had never come up because, as he plowed through his teen years, my drug years were way behind me. But here comes Bruce's pot being passed around. I took the joint and offered it to Brian. He vehemently and wordlessly shook his head no. "Listen," I said, "tonight's your birthday and we're gonna party like maniacs. I won't tell your mom and it's okay with me if you smoke this. BUT

ONLY FOR TONIGHT!" He smiled, took the proffered joint, and worked it like a pro. I laughed at myself for thinking he had never done this before. I could just imagine my Dad and I passing weed around. No way. My father would say things like:

"I sat down next to this dame, and let me tell ya, she reeked of the pot."

A Timothy Leary he was not.

The next few years featured some of the low points of my professional life. That "career opportunity window" one hears so much about came crashing down on my fingers. People didn't seem all that interested anymore. Work dried up in the record production field, and I started to tread water while I figured out what to do next. I moved into cheaper digs and scaled my whole lifestyle back to accommodate this sudden chill. I put bands together in New York and Los Angeles.

In New York, the best part of all this was the discovery of Jimmy Vivino. Making his move from New Jersey, Jimmy became a member of my band, gained my confidence and support, and has been my musical director for over fifteen years now. Because I didn't play too many gigs, he supplemented his income by putting bands together for other people from my era, among them Felix Cavaliere, John Sebastian, Johnny Rivers, Darlene Love, Johnnie Johnson, Laura Nyro, Dion, and Clarence Clemons. He was briefly in a band with Jules Shear called The Reckless Sleepers.

Jimmy is one of the most well-liked musicians on the East Coast, and I'm very proud of my long-standing association with him. His profile became much wider (and so did he) when he became the musical director for *Late Night With Conan O'Brien* under Max Weinberg's smiling leadership. People got to hear his great arrangements and guitar-playing on a nightly basis, and he began to get the recognition he so richly deserved from the general public.

In Los Angeles, I had a real ragtag band of old friends, who were, like myself, "between engagements." Hutch Hutchinson had left The Neville Brothers and moved to L.A., and I grabbed him on bass. He's currently having great moments in Bonnie Raitt's band. Richie Hayward was displaced when Little Feat initially broke up, and I snared him on drums. With the two of them as a rhythm section and the addition of two ancillary players, we played around the L.A. bar circuit just to keep our chops together, not to mention paying the rent, while we waited for the next career train to stop in our various stations.

After spinning my wheels awhile, I went to New York on a long shot to meet with Jerry Jaffe, president of PolyGram Records. Jaffe was looking for someone to helm PolyGram's West Coast office. I had to wait it out for a few months, and was lucky

A dashing young Jimmy Vivino prepares backstage to go onstage. New York City, 1985.
(Photo: Al Kooper.)

ତ

enough to be able to stay at Terry Southern's loft in SoHo during this period. I met some great people there, rekindled my relationship with Harry Nilsson, heard the best stories about *The Paris Review* from Terry, and got through some real emotionally and financially trying months with a lotta help from my friends. Finally, a deal was pounded out, and I became West Coast Head of A&R for PolyGram.

Although in the late sixties I had served in a similar capacity for CBS in New York and was familiar with "the drill," the job had changed radically in the ensuing twenty years. In 1968, it consisted of going to clubs all over the country scouting for talent. In 1983, it consisted primarily of having lunch with lawyers and managers. I found it difficult to combine eating food and keeping it down in the presence of most of these people, and I guess it was apparent, because the more aggressive of them would complain to Jaffe that their phone calls went unanswered by Kooper.

In between vomiting at some of the better restaurants in Los Angeles, I was miraculously able (with a lot of outside help) to get PolyGram to sign Richard Thompson, the English songwriter/Stratocaster hero, formerly of Fairport Convention. Through the years, he had put out solo albums and duet albums with and without his then-wife Linda, on Joe Boyd's Hannibal label. Richard had built up a strong, dedicated audience in England and the U.S., and Boyd decided it was time to increase Thompson's audience in ways he was not able to do. This called for the resources of a major label (i.e., marketing, publicity, and distribution all on a grander scale than Boyd himself could provide). Richard and I shared the same booking agent (Elizabeth Rush), and she really was the catalyst that brought the whole deal together. We got Jaffe to go see him live, I told Jaffe how great I thought Richard was, and Elizabeth came in and closed the deal.

One night I gave a lecture to a songwriting class in the Valley. A rather attractive woman from that lecture called me at PolyGram to ask me a few more questions. I boldly asked her out, and we began seeing each other. Her name was Vivien Bilbeaux. She was a legal secretary and an illegal songwriter. *Here we go again.*

Concurrently, purely by accident, I had found a very strange band to sign. Some group invited me to Club Lingerie to hear their set at 10 p.m. on a Tuesday night. I arrived at 9:50 p.m. to find I was not on the guest-list. I was just about to pay to gain entrance when some likable English guy waved me in. He managed the opening band, who were just going on stage, and so I sat down and politely gave them a listen. *They were incredible.* There were three synthesizer players, a bass player, and a drummer, playing great modern R&B, with *no* guitar player. How refreshing! The songs were quite good, and I couldn't believe my good fortune. I rushed into the dressing room after their set and said to the first band member I could accost, "Are you guys signed??"

"No, actually, we're not," came the reply, and a big grin lit up my face. Unlike many of my contemporaries who just sat in their offices, signed nothing, and picked up their check every week, I *wanted* to find a great band. Jerry Jaffe would be in L.A. in two days. *He had to hear this.*

I set up a showcase at a local rehearsal studio. The boys were great, and Jaffe gave me the thumbs up. The band was called St. Regis. They were made up of Greg and Marc St. Regis, two fraternal twins who played keyboards, wrote, and sang all the songs; Jeff Bahr, another keyboard player; Nick Tumler, the drummer; and James Neuble, on bass. We went into pre-production, polished all the material, tightened the arrangements, and got ready to record.

I wanted to take the band away from L.A. and all the distractions inherent there so we could concentrate on recording only. I chose Bill McEuen's studio in Aspen, Colorado, where Bob Edwards had done a few Dirt Band albums. It was fall and it was beautiful there. Till we got into the studio.

The two brothers would get incredibly competitive and contrary with each other in the studio, and each session quickly degenerated into shouting matches between them. Shades of The Kinks and Oasis! Bob Edwards set up a roll of flip-cards with chronological descriptions like "2 HOURS AND 15 MINUTES TO GO," "1 HOUR AND 45 MINUTES TO GO," etc., etc. Each day's session would last a mere four to six hours before it would just deteriorate into ugly name calling. Schedules fell by the wayside. The trip to Aspen only yielded a third of the amount of finished product it should have. Returning to L.A., we settled into Westlake Studios to complete the record at the usual snail's pace of four to six hours a day. I began to record the brothers' tantrums secretly on cassette, lest someone think *I* was responsible for the mounting costs.

The twins were uncontrollable, and I lost my control over them the second week in Aspen. I give credit to their manager Leslie Leaney (who had sank his life savings into the lads) for discreetly keeping all the ugliness away from the ears and eyes of PolyGram. Now I was aware that many of my contemporaries spent sometimes up to a year or more making a record, but that was just not *my* style. Prior to this album, the longest I had taken was two months on the extremely-complex first Tubes album.

As the record approached completion in its seventh month, the boys went particularly bonkers. They fought tooth and nail with me over the mixes, which were quite good without their histrionics. I finished the album under protest from the band. The brothers were so fanatical in their quest for power, they got their *parents* to bankroll a completely new mix of the album done by themselves. Then they made their fatal mistake. They fired Leaney, the only really likable thing about the band besides their music. I decided it was time to step down and cease standing between them and PolyGram. As much as I loved my version of the finished album for its musical content, I didn't feel the band would survive the day-to-day direct contact with the record company. That was a fate I felt the brothers deserved. And after they actually phoned their married-with-children PolyGram product manager at home at 3 a.m. on a weekday night, they were quickly dropped. Between recording, artwork, and grooming, a quarter of a million dollars had been spent on the band. *No one cared.* PolyGram now just wanted to be rid of this pack of pests I had unleashed on everyone—and wanted it done ASAP.

This ultimately cost me my job, which I wasn't very happy performing anyway. I had been with PolyGram for eighteen months, approximately half of which were spent producing St. Regis. Over the course of my tenure, I had been helpful in getting Richard Thompson signed (he was subsequently dropped). I had alienated many lawyers and managers by not returning their calls. I was able to afford a better apartment and meet Vivien, the woman who would soon become my third wife. I was also able to upgrade my standard of living so that I could afford Stouffer's frozen foods, not the cheap brands. That was all fine with me. So when Jaffe flew out to L.A., and we had breakfast the next morning, I said to him as we were seated: "Can you please fire me now so we can enjoy our breakfast?"

He looked at me incredulously and asked: "How did you know?"

"I didn't," I said sheepishly, realizing I would not be enjoying *this* breakfast too much at all. Fortunately, Jaffe and I remained friends. And, as we have seen repeatedly in this convoluted story, things have a way of happening for a reason that is not always apparent at first.

Patti Heid, whom I had lived with in England and Texas, was now happily married to Cheech of Cheech and Chong fame. She called one day and set up a meeting for me with a friend of hers who had just taken a job at a firm that represented composers for scoring work. The friend's name was Linda Livingston, and she signed me to a one-year representation deal with the Robert Light Agency.

For the next six months, the agency delivered me no nibbles or actual work. Then, Stan Polley, my manager of fifteen years, abruptly dropped me. He seemed to sense that it was over for me, and not smelling any more money, departed for greener pastures. He still continued to participate in my royalty-earning revenues, as—explained earlier in this tale—he had set it up so that all monies came directly to him. More than participate, in fact, *he kept all my royalties*, never sending me a check after he departed. It is an expensive, protracted, legal road one must travel to win back one's rightful royalties. As of this writing, I have finally settled with Polley and will begin receiving eighty-five percent of my current royalties from Lynyrd Skynyrd. However, all the royalties from the years that Skynyrd was *really* selling product are sitting safely in *Polley's* bank accounts, thanks to the statute of limitations. Please, guys and gals just starting out, *learn* something from my mistakes!

Prior to my landing the PolyGram position, an acquaintance named Debbie Gold offered to represent me and secure me an A&R job. She was a mover and shaker on the West Coast and had done publicity on the *Shot of Love* tour I'd done with Dylan, which is where we met. I thought this was a good idea, till I found out she was putting *herself* up for some of the same jobs. This infuriated me so I told her to back off representing me, and stopped speaking to her altogether. That's when

The infamous Stan Polley always knew how to get my attention. (Photo: Al Kooper Collection.)

I went to New York and got the PolyGram gig on my own. So, in my new phase of unemployment, I was frankly surprised to hear from her on the phone.

"I have an incredible job for you to make up for my bad behavior in the past," she said.

"And what is this great job?" I asked her hesitantly.

"I can't tell you yet but it involves scoring a major TV series," she said.

"I'm very interested, Debbie," I replied, taking a chance, but feeling secure at least that she wouldn't put herself up for *this* job.

In a few weeks, she called me, all out of breath. I was in New York playing a gig, and she had found me at my hotel.

"You gotta be at NBC at 9 a.m. tomorrow morning to watch a screening of this show," she blurted out excitedly. "If you like it, we can move to step two. It's called *Crime Story*, and it's being produced by Michael Mann, who did *Miami Vice*."

"I'll be there, Deb. Don't worry," I assured her.

Of course my gig was the night before, and I got to the screening at 8:59 the

(Left to right) Kooper, Howard Hesseman, Debbie Gold, and Michael Mann discussing the hidden meanings of Franz Kafka backstage in Hollywood at the Roxy, 1987. (Photo: Gary Nichamin/BOOM! Graphics.)

next morning. A secretary showed me to a room, plopped a tape into a VCR, cut the lights, and left me on my own, thankfully. The tape began, and in about fifteen minutes, I was fast asleep. This was caused by my getting to bed at about 5 a.m. after playing two sets the night before, as opposed to there being anything wrong with the program material itself as it unspooled in front of my closed eyes. I quite enjoyed what I saw as I woke up fitfully every few minutes to the sound of gunfire and watched a few minutes more before dozing off again. It was a two-hour pilot episode, so I think I saw half of it. But I knew I could score the show. I really thought I could bring this kind of genre to life with my music.

I flew back to L.A. and had a meeting with Michael Mann. He seemed like a really nice guy, and we talked music, mostly Chicago (where he was from) blues, for about forty-five minutes. Then he turned to me and said, "I want you to score episodes 1 and 2. Can you do a four-day turnaround on each episode?" I was so excited, I blurted out: "Of course I can! Thanks a million. I won't let you down!"

I walked out of his office and my brain was screaming. This was fantastic! I got in the car, got on the freeway, and immediately drove off the exit ramp of the entrance I had just gotten onto it from! This convulsed me. Boy, was I happy. One question kept burning in my mind the whole time though:

What in the hell was a four-day turnaround?[1]

---

[1]A four-day turnaround consists of delivering the finished music for an episode four days after initially viewing the episode.

1986-1990

CRIME STORY,

MICHAEL MANN,

JOHN WATERS,

B. B. KING,

CONVENTION HOPPING,

**AND FINALLY
LEAVING LOS ANGELES**

Having only scored one film and zero television shows, I decided to enlist the help of trusty Charlie Calello again. Charlie was already conversant with composing music on computers. At that time, a computer was the "enemy" to me, but I knew that a computer was exactly what this project needed—and if not for my work on the *Crime Story* series, Lord knows what I'd be doing today. So Charlie came in, and we split everything fifty-fifty. All the money and all the work. For the first episode, we spent two thousand dollars out of our own pockets because:

    A. We got carried away and
    B. We wanted to impress Michael Mann and
    C. We only had a four-day turnaround and
    D. We didn't have a computer yet!

It must have worked because, after we finished episode 2, Michael gave us episodes 5 and 6 to do. Now what of episodes 3 and 4, you say? Well, that's an interesting question.

When the series first was conceived, Todd Rundgren was hired on a contingency to do all the music. Todd did the two-hour pilot I saw half of, but Michael and Todd did not get along very well. Now Todd and I have always been friends and this presented a true test of our friendship. During this time period, we had lunch and I told him I hoped this whole situation wouldn't affect our friendship. He concurred and deferred to his problems with Michael. To fulfill his initial contract, Todd scored episodes 3 and 4, and then went back to work being the genius that he is, releasing the brilliant *Acapella* album. We are still friends today and no harm was done.

Debbie Gold was to receive a commission on every show we scored, as well she should have. I told her to call the Robert Light Agency, with whom I still had three months to go on my contract, and split her commision with them. Although they had gotten me no work in the nine months I'd been with them, and Debbie got me this veritable jewel alone, I was still under contract to them and they had to be dealt with. Things were working out brilliantly in general when the other shoe dropped rather abruptly. Robert Light decided, after first agreeing to split the commissions, that he wanted it all, and he sued Debbie and me. In a fair and just world, in my opinion, he should have walked away like a gentleman after not being able to secure one percent of work for me up to this point. As a matter of fact, he should have been *embarrassed* about it. But there rarely is a fair and just world in Hollywood Reality. And so off we went to court. Charlie went into a corner with Robert Light himself and negotiated successfully to pay him nine thousand dollars to go away. So this company that had gotten me no work got a nine thousand commission for doing nada. If that wasn't bad enough, Linda Livingston had the nerve to tell people—whom Debbie and I knew—at this time that she and her agency had initially secured the *Crime Story* job for me. Linda is currently the head of the film and television division of BMI. I don't really hear from her, as you can well imagine.

Michael Mann reminded me of Bob Dylan: They were both masters of intimidation, but both were sweethearts underneath it all. I decided to play a hunch and act toward Michael the same way I did toward Bob—as an equal who did not feel intimidated by him. It was risky, but it worked. It didn't hurt that we were born on the same day, either—Michael's exactly one year older than I am. When he would come in and bully me, I'd give him good-natured shit right back, and he enjoyed the banter. The work was deathly serious, though, and I learned many life lessons in short order.

To score a weekly TV series effectively, you must first adopt a "method." You have to zen out the most time- and cost-effective way of working that doesn't compromise your creativity. This can take anywhere from two weeks to two years, but it is the key to great work. Because Charlie and I had worked together seamlessly on many other occasions, we didn't trifle with any ego aspect of it. We simply divided up the work and got on with it.

On Mondays, the post-production team would meet in the morning to view the episode we would be completing that week. Foley people, dialogue loopers, sound effects guys, film editors, and yours truly (about eight of us) would sit around a movieola and watch the episode. When anything jumped out as needing fixing, the appropriate team would temporarily stop the film and make a note of it. If a scene wasn't playing well, and it was determined that music would help, that would constitute one of the usual twenty cues for that week. Cues are another name for the pieces of music that play behind scenes in a film. Pensive moments, action stuff, love scenes, places where music can help, all were identified and catalogued. At the end of the session, which usually took five hours for a one-hour episode, I would have a list of all the music cues for that episode.

By the time Charlie arrived at our little studio in the late afternoon, I had divided up the cues so that whoever was better at a certain mood would write that particular cue. Sometimes, I'd have a lot to do, sometimes not much, but I always chose the best man for each cue.

Charlie would work days—9 a.m. to 6 p.m.—and I'd come in at 6 p.m. to make sure he was doing okay and to start my shift. I'd usually work from 6 p.m. to 3 a.m. As each episode was completed, we took a large portion of our pay and put it aside to lease/purchase equipment we needed. Finally, three-quarters into the season, we had built our own recording studio, the Slammer, on the premises of Amigo Studios, a recording complex in North Hollywood. Now we would only pay a small amount of rent each month and *no* studio time. If we went to a second season, we knew, our profits would soar. It was a calculated risk we took, but we believed in the show and we believed in ourselves. And finally, the show believed in us: Lo, there came a second season . . . *and it was good.*

I used to say at the time: We were overworked and overpaid! After the spotting session on Monday, Charlie and I would write all the cues between Tuesday and Friday. On Saturday we would record and on Sunday I'd mix. Sunday night our music editor would show up at the mix, and take the recording tape to be transferred to film. He would then represent us at the final mixing sessions for each episode. (Let me add parenthetically that the music editor was an important part of the team. We went through four or five editors until we found Frank Fitzpatrick. Frank did brilliant work and saved our asses on more than one occasion.) Then Monday would roll around and the next spotting session would begin. It was an eight-day-a-week job, but we loved what we were doing. The show was made up of the kind of black humor that I really appreciated. When I would get advance tapes of an episode, it would be like getting a new Beatles album or something like that. I'd rush home and put it on and enjoy the hell out of it.

When I first started, there was a guy who selected the source music (records) played during the show. Now the era of the show was the early sixties, and that is my area of expertise in this world. I called Michael Mann and begged him to let me pick the source music for the show. It wasn't a greed thing—it was a knowledge thing. Well, he acquiesced and soon NBC television was playing Jimmy Reed, Muddy Waters, and Howlin' Wolf records in primetime. It was a blues lover's coup! I knew I was making *someone* happy out there, because the source cues generated a lot of mail all on their own.

The person who picks records on a show is called the music supervisor. Often he is selected before someone is chosen to score the film to participate in that decision as well. I didn't like the credit "Music Supervisor." I went into Michael Mann's office one day and said: "If you saw me walkin' down the street, Michael, would you say 'There's the music supervisor?' No, right? Then can I change my credit at the end of the show?"

When he found out I wanted "Guy That Picks the Music for the Show," he was amused enough to assent. And so, at the end of every show from about episode 8 on, that credit ran at the end of the show. An amusing "first" for primetime TV.

There was a huge A-bomb detonation in Nevada that ended the first year of the series and was kind of a cliffhanger. I made Michael a tape of ten records I thought were suitable for that sequence and let him choose the one he liked best. He picked the one that I would have chosen myself: "Bad Boy" by Clarence Palmer and the Jive Bombers. We cut it into the sequence and watched it in a screening room together.

"It's PERFECT!! I really love it," Michael screamed, as he watched the song play over the bomb blast and the final credits.

About a week later, on a Wednesday night, they were mixing the last reel of the season's last show. This is where they combine all the dialogue, looping, sound effects, music, and audio, balancing it all on two tracks of stereo for the final version. They were working about five blocks from my apartment in Hollywood, so I took the dog for a walk and ambled over to say my goodbyes for the summer to everyone. When I walked in, Paul Huntsman and Kiki Morris, heads of post-production, rushed over to me yelling: "Oh, we are so glad you're here! You have got to stop him—he's in the cutting room changing the last song! We're *never* gonna get out of here tonight!"

These were a nervous bunch of people, let me tell ya. Plus, Mann was pulling "Bad Boy" out, our mutual choice, and a good one. I walked into the cutting room,

Kooper and Charles Calello at work once again. The Slammer, North Hollywood, 1987. Note the dichotomy of shirts and wristwatches. (Photo: Al Kooper Collection.)

∽

dog-on-leash. Michael was in there with Dick Wolf, one of the producers of *Miami Vice* (who later went on to create the series *Law and Order* on his own). When I walked in, Michael looked up from the editing bay, caught like a child with his hand in the cookie jar.

"Boy, I can't leave you alone for five minutes without you fucking up the whole show, can I?" I said, laughing with the usual aplomb I reserved for "The Master of Intimidation."

"Al! I . . . uh . . . just wanted to make sure we were doing the right thing . . . ," he answered, actually red-faced at seeing me appear before him unscheduled in the studio.

"Well, then, how about you, me, and Dick going back out there and watching the last five minutes of the show with "Bad Boy" cut back in and seeing how it plays?" I suggested.

Michael assented, and we did just that. As the lights came up, Michael turned to me, smiled, and said: "Okay. Okay. You're right, it's great. You win. That's a wrap, gang!"

And that is exactly how the first season ended.

For one of the first times in my life, I wanted to take a vacation. With a weekly TV series, there is *no* traveling all year, and I missed it. My friend Shep Gordon, who managed Alice Cooper, Luther Vandross, and Teddy Pendergrass, had a beautiful house on the beach in Maui. I asked him if it was available for a week in July, and before you could say "Aloha," my new gal Vivien and I were eating papayas and lying on the sand. We had a great time, other than burning our skin real badly. *Amateurs.* We came home and I geared up for the onslaught otherwise known as the second season.

This year, we *had* our "method." We would alternate shows. I would score the odd numbered ones (how apropos!) and Charlie the even ones. If any guy wanted help from the other guy, he could rightfully request it. I would still come in for the recording and mixing even when it wasn't my week. I played guitar on many of Charlie's cues, and I usually mixed the entire show anyway.

We owned the studio now, so our costs were greatly reduced. All the gear had been paid off the first season, and we'd gotten a slight raise for the second season. *Things were excellent.* The bad part was that NBC kept moving the show around and our core audience never knew when it was on anymore. That, coupled with a lot of pre-empts in a row, made our ratings not as good as they should have been. It was possible the end was in sight, and I psyched myself up for that eventuality as the season progressed.

The show itself was a landmark on TV. Without it, there would have certainly been no *Twin Peaks* or *Northern Exposure*. And many composers borrowed heavily from some of the ideas that Charlie and I came up with every week. There was even a bootleg MIDI sample making the rounds called *"Crime Story* Horns." However, all good things must come to an end, and the close of *Crime Story*'s second season was indeed the end of the series. So Charlie's and my "good thing" also came to a halt. Debbie Gold, who was representing us now, was requested to get us more work, but alas she was too busy. She was doing music supervision for a commercial film and one of Michael's mini-series at the same time.

The momentum of Charlie's and my scoring careers began to stall. Debbie's career was doin' fine, though. Does this sound familiar?

Al and Dennis Farina share a laugh on the set of Crime Story *before they find out the series has been canceled. Las Vegas, 1987.* (Photo: Leslie Leaney.)

∽

One job came through, however. This was producing some prerecorded material for John Waters' next film, *Cry Baby*. This was to be his first musical, and all the musical numbers had to be finished *before* filming began for lip-syncing purposes. Johnny Depp was the star and he actually could sing, but Waters insisted on a stand-in voice for him. James Intveldt was chosen to ghost Depp's vocals. James was a local favorite rock-a-billy singer and bass player in the Los Angeles area. Rachel Sweet was chosen to do the singing for Amy Locane, who played the female lead. Rachel had made some records for Stiff, the English cult label. She was a joy to work with (not that James wasn't).

There was one epic number I was worried about called "Please Mr. Jailer." The original record from the fifties was by Wynonna Carr. I changed a lot of the words to fit Waters' storyline, and the changes were quickly approved. We cut the track as a duet with James and Rachel and two sets of background singers, white and black, male and female. When we handed it in, they came back and wanted structural changes based on the choreography of the scene. Out came the trusty razor blade, and a plethora of edits were made to satisfy the choreographer's demands.

Now I had been hired by the music supervisors of the film. After a short time, they called and told me *never* to call John Waters and to communicate only with *them*. I saw this as trouble. I was forbidden to talk to the person I was trying to please; the man who had the whole vision for the film. How could I *really* know what he wanted? Sure enough, after more tracks were sent in, the last two were rejected by Waters and my employment was terminated. I certainly saw this coming as a result of the diverted communication.

Now it's common practice in the recording studio business not to release master tapes to a client until the bill is paid. Universal had not sent us one check (all of our recording for *Cry Baby* was done at our studio, the Slammer) for over a month's worth of studio time. At this point, of course, Universal needed these tapes to shoot film to, and we needed the money to pay the studio expenses, i.e., rent, maintenance, engineers, tape costs, etc. But Universal simply refused to pay the bills.

At one point, a lawyer Debbie Gold had engaged to represent us in this venture called me and said: "You had better release those tapes to Universal or no one's *ever* going to hire you in this town again."

I held the phone away from ear and looked at it incredulously. Then I lost my cool. "Do you work for *us*?" I asked the attorney. "Are you trying to recover the monies that are owed to *us*? Or are you threatening us because Universal got to you? I don't feel very much support here. Not to mention that uncreative cliché you ended your sentence with. . . ."

I was furious and fired her the next day. Then Universal's lawyer called, and *she* was quite nice. She wanted to know *my* side of the story, and she was very calm. She stepped into the middle and negotiated a deal where we got half of what Universal owed us. I *still* didn't like it, but I went along with the deal to end all the negativity. Big company like that holding up the little guy for money they actually owed—*not cool at all*.

A good friend of mine, Dave Alvin, replaced me on *Cry Baby*, and all of a sudden I was in Todd Rundgren's position from *Crime Story*. Dave's way of handling the situation was to not call me until he finished the gig. Well, we're still friends today. And after the fuss was all over, I hired that Universal lawyer to represent *me*!

Cry Baby was a box-office dud (bad karma), but it's on cable every once in awhile, and I smile when I hear the work they used that I *did* do in the film.

Meanwhile, it was 1988 and I moved into a lovely rented home on the Valley side of the Hollywood Hills, and married Vivien, in front of the waterfall in the garden of that house. Would the third time be the charm?

Moving right along, I got a call to produce two tracks for the next B. B. King album and was very excited. During the eighties, it was fashionable to hire five different producers and have them produce two tracks each. I guess the record companies figured the odds for a hit were better that way. To me, it usually resulted in uneven sound, and a shambles of an album. The ironic part was that B. B. recorded for MCA Records, owned by Universal; so I guess I *would* work in this town again!

B. B. and I had been friends since 1967, when I played on his *Alive and Well* album. Now *that* was an evening I'll never forget! Bill Szymczyk was producing B. B. then and called me two months ahead to book me for four nights of sessions. I was so excited, I was literally counting the days on my calendar until the session. The big night finally arrived, and I got there, and it was kinda . . . well . . . disorganized. So I jumped in, as I was wont to do in those days, to try and help the session along. As I was suggesting some arrangement changes and groove things, I said to drummer Herb Lovelle, "What if you just play it with a fatback groove right at the top?"

Well, he looked at me with the most disdain an African-American can muster to look at a Caucasian with and repeated back to me: "*Fatback?*"

The air, as they say, could have been cut with a knife (that is, if a knife *could*, in fact, cut through frozen air). I immediately got the worst migraine headache I had ever had in my life and just clammed up. Somehow I got through the session, but the chemistry between Herb and me was so bad that I couldn't wait to get outta there. I called Szymczyk the next day and told him to replace me on the rest of the sessions in an effort to end the bad vibes and have regretted it ever since. On the very next session they cut "The Thrill Is Gone" and lucky Paul Harris got to play keyboards on it. Well, although I have certainly tried, *you can't play on everything*.

For these new B. B. sessions that I was producing, I had selected two songs that other people had recorded but that seemed like B. B. should have done in the first place: Joe Simon's "Drowning in the Sea of Love," and Benny Lattimore's

---

[1]The technology had escalated in such a way that a musician could set up a bank of synthesizers and assign each one a different instrument sound, then program into a sequencer what each synth would play and have the whole synthesized band play back at the same time in perfect synchronization. This could all be done on a computer, and that is how our work on *Crime Story* was performed each week. This new technology changed the face and sound of music when introduced in 1985.

"Let's Straighten It Out." I met with B. B. to select keys for the songs, and then retired back to the Slammer to cut tracks while he went on the road. I used the MIDI system[1] to cut the tracks (no musicians to argue with this time!).

I put a reference guitar track on to show B. B. where to play, and I hired a singer to do a reference vocal to show B. B. where to sing. I sent him a cassette with the guitar and vocal on it so he could learn where his parts went. I cut the tracks on thirty-two-track digital format because we had the machine available to us for a few months.

B. B. came in to sing one night, and because of his grueling road schedule he had not had time to work with the tape I had sent him. So we had to start from scratch, and he had to learn the songs right there in the studio. On "Drowning in the Sea of Love," he was unsure where each line began in the arrangement. I physically went out into the studio and stood next to him while he sang, and tapped him on the arm one beat before each of his vocal entrances. His musicianship and a copy of the lyrics in front of him took care of the rest. We made it into a fun evening and had a good time. Hopefully, there was no pressure on him.

I did four different takes of him singing, then let him take a dinner break while I put the final vocals together from the four tracks that he had sung. This is called "comping" vocals in studio language. After you've recorded a few tracks of vocals, you go in and listen line by line to each performance; picking the best performance of each line from the different tracks, dissecting words and syllables from different vocals if necessary, and recording the composite of the different tracks that work onto an open master track. Painstaking, but worth the two hours it takes to construct a master vocal.

So B. B. came back from dinner, and I played him the combined finished vocal (which, incidentally, was wonderful). "How did you do that?" he exclaimed, amazed. "I don't even *know* this song yet!"

I guess he had never comped a vocal before, but he appreciated the expediency involved. We did the next song the same way and called it a night. The next evening he returned, and we added his guitar to both tracks. He sounded great. We were very relaxed and laughing, and I must confess I clandestinely recorded some candid moments between us for posterity. In my entire forty years in the music business, I have not met one person nicer than B. B. King. It's always a pleasure to work with him, and it's an honor to be his friend today.

Unfortunately, there was a bad ending to this story from the eighties.

Weeks after I had handed in the mixes, the studio called and said MCA had requisitioned the thirty-two-track master tapes. I knew that this meant they were going to remix my mixes. I called then-president of MCA Irving Azoff, and explained to

B. B. King and Kooper walk the runway for Tommy Hilfiger, Los Angeles, 1988. King, ever the consumate professional, pretends to enjoy Kooper's couture and guitar playing.
(Photo: Leslie Leaney.)

☙

him that there were things on the tape that neither B. B. nor I would want used, and it would probably save time if I could attend the remix and show whoever was mixing just what those things were.

"Stop whining!" said Azoff, and I said, "Fine," and hung up.

When the album *King of the Blues* was released, my worst fears were confirmed. In "Drowning in the Sea of Love," there is no snare drum in the verses, and half of the guitar solos are *me* playing from the reference tracks I put on as guides for B. B.!

I was extremely embarrassed, to say the least, so I called B. B. to explain. He took my call right away. "I know why you're calling, Al," he interrupted, "and, most of all, I know it's not your fault. So let's not even talk about it. How are *you*, my friend?"

That was all I needed to hear. I just put the CD back in its case, and never listened to it again. I also never did any work for MCA again. Azoff was soon replaced by Al Teller, Killer of Kooper Albums.

This was the beginning of the end. Too many times people who had *no* business doing so came in with the musical equivalent of spray cans and "painted" graffiti all over my work. I was growing older and no longer wanted to be treated like that. I began to understand that I had to retire from my business life as it was, or I would end up hanging myself like those two poor guys in Badfinger. If B. B. hadn't been the multilayered, sugar-coated, human being that he was (and is), he might have resented me for something that was not even *remotely* my fault. Not to mention the embarrassment of having other listeners think that what they heard on that album was the result of *my* decisions. And since there is only one B. B. King in the business, I couldn't allow the record companies to constantly put me in situations like that.

I decided it was time to "get out gracefully." But first:

Every January, the National Association of Music Merchandisers (NAMM) holds its winter convention in Anaheim, California. Since the mid-seventies, I had attended it to see what new products were being introduced, and to see old friends. This event was always an oasis for musicians from all over the world, a gathering place where we could all get together and visit with each other, no matter what the rest of the year held in store for us. It was also an opportunity to set up relationships with individual companies and beta-test their equipment in exchange for free goods. In addition, the Consumer Electronics Show (CES) would hold *its* convention in Las Vegas, usually the week before the NAMM show. This was where all the stereo equipment, modern gadgets, and video games were displayed for the coming year. and was a blast to attend. In later years, sandwiched between those two shows was the MacWorld Expo in San Francisco (Macintosh computer stuff), and I would make a trifecta out of it and attend all three shows in a two-week period.

The wildest was always the CES show in Las Vegas. Some old friends of mine ran a video business in Los Angeles, and they would take over the top floor of one of the older hotels every year to "entertain" clients. They were nice enough to always comp me a room in their plethora of penthouse suites, and I would go along and watch the show. Not necessarily the CES show, either. My friends would arrive with a bevy of beauties from L.A., who were there specifically to please the clients. Drugs would be dispensed like company pens, and the alcohol ran like tap water. It was almost as good as the old Record Plant, but the bill was much steeper! Let me tell ya, though, these people knew how to party. Concurrently, the adult video companies (porno in plain terms) displayed their newest tapes at the show (in their own area, of course, which just happened to be in the basement of the hotel where we occupied the penthouse suites), and various of these companies brought their biggest film stars to sign posters and pictures, and please the clients. So when these supernovas collided . . . *Yikes!* You have never seen so much debauchery in one hotel at one time. It was a wonder I made it to the other two conventions each year. Finally, I stopped going to the CES show, so that I could live to tell the rest of this story—and here it is:

Back in Los Angeles, as the eighties drew to a close, I was reaching the end of my rope. I hadn't made a record since 1982 as an artist, I was increasingly leery of doing business with the major record companies because of past experiences, and I was watching the city ferment all around me and become increasingly more dangerous. I never really fit into Los Angeles. Ultimately, it's a keep-up-with-the-Joneses-kinda-town, with too much emphasis on physical beauty and no emphasis on inner beauty, especially in the film and record industries. I did not choose to wear designer clothing, did not belong to the Friars club, did not live in the 90210 zip code, and did not drive a Beamer or a Jeep. I did not love the earthquakes or smog and felt a growing sense of dread over the racial unrest. I lived there because the weather was nice and it was good for business. Period. Now that the business was beginning to smell like the garbage, there was no reason to participate in it. *So I stopped.*

I actively stepped back from hustling for work. My plan, from the jump, had been to get out gracefully. If I could help it, I didn't want to play oldies shows, I didn't want to kiss someone's ass who knew far less than me, and I didn't want to be walking around in flannel shirts and speedos at age fifty-five. However, dropping out of the business but staying in town was not enough. I would still run into these bastards in the market, at concerts, in restaurants, and I never wanted to see them again.

One day, I was grocery shopping at Ralph's Market in Studio City when I ran into Steve Cropper. Steve, an original member of Booker T. & the MGs, one of the architects of the Memphis Stax-Volt sound, and one of the best guitarists/writers in the history of soul music, was someone I was always *glad* to see. I asked him how he was doing, and he said: "Oh, Al, I am just trying desperately to sell my house here. I moved to Nashville, and it is fantastic. You should move down there—you'd love it!"

This seemed like the word of the Lord as channeled through Steve Cropper. Maybe *this* was the answer to the L.A. problem. I had spent a great deal of time in Nashville in the early seventies, but hadn't really been there since then. So I replied: "That sounds like a great idea, Steve. I'm gonna check it out right away."

I got home and called my friend Sam Bush, a Nashville resident who had extended me an open invitation awhile back to stay at his new home there. I asked if I could stay for a week, as I was interested in moving there and wanted to "check it out." I believe his exact words were: "Come on down, Alvis!"

I rented a video camera so I could show my new bride what the future might hold in store for us as Souls of the South. I went there solo and had an appointment-filled week. I spent one day with a real estate broker, and it was extremely eye-opening. This was 1989 Nashville, and the prices for great homes were unusually inexpensive. Certainly not in the inflated Los Angeles league. I ran into other people I knew who had settled there and whom I was actually glad to see. But the thing that really got me was no matter how far I walked or drove in any direction, I did not bump into *one* person from Geffen Records. *This was fabulous!*

I flew home to show Vivien the video I'd made, and was ready to pack up and move. Amazingly, she hated what she saw. Even without being an amateur Sven Nykvist, I admit my depiction of the town looked grey and dreary. But hell, it was in the middle of November! Still, the town looked more Bergman than DeMille, and she didn't like it.

"Hey—we'll go house-hunting for a few days, then you'll see it first-hand and be as charmed as I was," I said hopefully.

"I better be," she warned.

And, of course, she loved it. We found a house on the first day we looked, and we made our plans. The house was available May 1, 1990, and all the paperwork could be concluded easily in the time period beforehand. I was jazzed. I was finally getting out of Los Angeles. Charlie and I split up the studio fifty-fifty. He got the console, the tape machine, and the giant TV. I got all the MIDI gear, synthesizers, processors, and the computer. All that stuff had been built into these two huge metal road cases on wheels, each of which literally weighed a ton. When you added my possessions at home (which included ten thousand LPs, twenty-five hundred CDs, and four thousand singles), the movers were dealing with literally ten tons of stuff! That intimidated even me, especially when I got the movers' cost estimate. I have always been such a pack rat, but in my later years I've been glad I've been the "keeper of the memorabilia" because that stuff has come in handy for books and archival album releases.

Anyway, we began to pack. In this time period, someone broke into our L.A. house, but was interrupted by the maid and thwarted from taking anything. This freaked me out, because I still had Jimi Hendrix's guitar—which was beginning to escalate in price—in the house. Glad to be getting outta here, I kept thinking.

I had begun working with Bob Forrest, leader of the L.A. band Thelonious Monster. We were writing together and doing pre-production for what was gonna be a Bob Forrest solo album or T. Monster's second album. Bob had a heroin problem and was in and out of rehab in the year we worked together. He was a wild talent; a good poet and singer, but a crazed personality. I asked one of my cured Narcotics

Anonymous friends to sponsor him, and I hope the friend forgives me one day for that "favor." It came time to move, and Bob and I were half done with our project. We decided we would finish it in Nashville. When the movers came to finally lead me out of California, the only tears in my eyes were from the smog and the moving bill—and, finally, still no tan.

1990-1995

We arrived in Nashville in the spring, which is one of the two best seasons there are (the other being the fall, natch). The blossoms were out, everything was blooming; it felt like flower power all over again. I guess that's why I never noticed that every ten steps there was another way to break into our house. Besides, I was in this blossom-peace-love-out-of-California groove and I thought Nashvillians would never rob anybody's house.

After living there about a month, Vivien returned to California on some family business for a week. Bob Forrest was in town finishing his tracks with me. I had located a studio called Sound Emporium two blocks from my house that approximated Record Plant's Studio B, and I was ecstatic. One night, I went to one of the musician hang-out bars, hooked up with some imbibing friends, and closed the place about 3:30 a.m. It was the first time I'd done that since I lived there, and as I drove up the driveway to my house, I noticed a window was broken in the kitchen area. Probably some baseball kids, I remember muttering. I got my keys out and . . . the door was ajar! I put two and two together real quick and *ran* to the Hendrix guitar. *Still there—whew!* The only things I noticed missing were some glass jars of change that we kept in the kitchen. I surmised that the burglars had just broken in when I drove up and had high-tailed it out of the house taking off through the back yard. I was spooked, though. That's when it hit me how really vulnerable the house was and that an alarm system was mandatory.

I refused to leave the house until the alarm system was installed and working. I slept on the couch where I could see the back-door-scene-of-the-crime. When Vivien came back, she noticed that all her jewelry was missing, so the burglars might have been inside a little longer than I thought. It took me two or three months to trust the alarm system, but finally, I loosened up. Then someone went in the back shed and stole the power mower and the weeder.

That did it. I called my friend Albert Molinaro, who owns Guitars R Us , a vintage instrument store in L.A.

"Albert," I said, "will you broker the sale of my Hendrix guitar for me? I gotta get it out of my house ASAP!"

I know what you're saying: Why didn't I just put it in storage? Well, because a guitar like that, in my possession, would not have made its owner happy in storage, that's why. Either I played it and felt safe owning it, or I sold it. It's all Mitch Mitchell's fault. He sold his Hendrix guitar for $250,000, and people will murder you for that amount of money. I felt my Hendrix guitar was a magnet drawing bad stuff to my new home. I had owned it for over twenty years, gotten tremendous use out of it, and now it had outlived its usefulness. I knew that in just a few short years it would fetch a cool million, at least, but I was not in a position to wait that long now.

Albert made some calls, and a speculator in Japan bought it for six figures soon thereafter. I used the money to redecorate and furnish the house. Who would have thought that a block of wood with some wires on it could command such a price? It's now referred to as the "Al Kooper-Hendrix guitar." A few years ago the new owners put it up for auction at Sotheby's. It did not fetch the unrealistic minimum they had predetermined and went back on the shelf. As of this writing, it strangely has returned to Albert Molinaro, who was asked to broker it for a second time. What a long strange trip that guitar has had. Many people think I still own it. But you know I don't. So please stop breaking into my house if you're reading this. Which reminds me of the classic story of that guitar:

When we were recording Skynyrd's first album, I brought the guitar to the studio, in case the sound of it might be suitable for any track we were doing. One of the Skynyrd boys picked it up and starting jamming with it unplugged.

A rare shot of me in public playing the guitar Jimi Hendrix gave me. Accessorizing by the use of strap, wristband, and belt, I discreetly attempted to draw attention away from the guitar. (Photo: Gary Nichamin/BOOM! Graphics.)

"Hey, Al—this guitar plays nice," he said admiringly. From across the room, Ronnie Van Zant looked up and said: "That guitar used to belong to Jimi Hendrix. He gave it to Al. . . ." The guitar player immediately let it fall out of his hands onto the couch. "*OOOO . . . I just got some nigger on me!*" he screamed irreverently. Without missing a beat, Ronnie answered him: "You better pick that guitar up and see if you can get some *more* of that nigger on ya."

And no, I'll never tell who the irreverent one was.

After I did what I could with Bob Forrest, China Records of England hired me to produce Green on Red. They were a band from L.A. that had made a few albums which were critically well received, especially in Europe. About three years before, an A&R man from PolyGram had tried to put us together. He set up a meeting for them at my house in Hollywood, and they came over with another producer, Jim Dickinson from Memphis. It kinda pissed me off. I chose to make the best of it, however, so I had them go out and get a twelve-pack, and I got Jim to autograph a copy of his solo album from the seventies that was in my collection. We sat around and told old soldier stories all night. The next morning I called the A&R guy up and chewed him out. They had already picked their producer; so why bother me?

But now Green on Red was ready for me. We made an interesting album called *Scapegoats* that only came out in Europe (one of those). The deal was set up by my old PolyGram boss Jerry Jaffe, and I was happy to be involved with him again. No hard feelings. But . . . no hard sales, either.

A call came from David Spero, Joe Walsh's manager, about being a sideman on Joe's summer tour for 1991. Joe had a new album out with a hit single. *The Ordinary Average Guy Tour* was mostly opening for The Doobie Brothers in sheds (outdoor amphitheaters that staged summer shows for between fifteen and twenty thousand people). I actually hadn't done the touring sideguy thing in ten years since Dylan's tour in 1981. I was kind of curious as to whether a forty-seven-year-old couch potato could physically stand up to that sort of abuse. Since Vivien would be left mostly alone for three months if I went on the tour, I left it up to her to make that final decision. She gave it her blessing, so I took the job. Rehearsals took place in L.A. during the NBA basketball playoffs, and being a Bulls fan, I was horrified to miss the actual final game the first year Jordan and company took it all. I did get to see the last five minutes at the rehearsal studio and went berserk when they won.

The relationship between Joe and me went back to the mid-sixties. By the time The James Gang (Joe's first band) was successful, I was working in A&R at Columbia. We met and really hit it off. I gave him some advice and kinda took him

Discussing the hidden meaning of Kierkegaard's Journals *with Joe Walsh.*
(Photo: Al Kooper Collection.)

☙

under my wing. Extremely talented, he didn't stay where he was long. Pete Townshend "adopted" him next, and his career really took off.

Joe had assembled a buncha pirates for this sojourn: I played keyboards and rhythm guitar, Joe's old friend Joe Vitale played drums, flute and keyboards, Chad Cromwell, a hot, new young drummer, also living in Nashville, played drumkit number two, and Joe's running buddy, Rick "the bass player" Rosas, lived up to his nickname. I was playing much more guitar than I thought I would, but was not complaining. The set-list was new album stuff, Eagles stuff, and Joe's greatest hits. It was a tight one-hour set, and we usually slayed 'em every night.

About two weeks into the tour, we had a night off in Pittsburgh (one of those places that sounds like what it is . . . like Flushing, New York). I called home, as I usually did, to check in. After about five minutes of chit-chat, Vivien said: "I can't be married to you anymore." I thought she was joking, but as she continued talking, my heart sank into the pit of my stomach. I couldn't believe she was actually leaving me *while I was out on the road*! There was another guy involved (there usually is), and evidently, this had been building up for awhile. No wonder she gave this tour her blessing! Later I would write a song about it called "Women Paint Signs (That Men Cannot Read)." But at that moment, I was devastated. Fortunately, the band was off that night, 'cause I was a mess, children! For about a week, I was not a hundred percent, but everyone on the tour was really understanding. In retrospect, I'm glad it happened that way because I was a million miles away from it and had the gig to take it off my mind for an hour every night. Who knows what I might have done if I'd been back home? Could I have afforded Johnnie Cochran?

Two weeks later, I was home on a week's break and began to put the pieces back together. Vivien had moved out by then, taking what she pleased. And so began the period of adjustment. Can a rock guy be successfully married? I had three divorces in my life so as to think not. Marriage? I can only think I'm getting better at it. The fourth one's da bomb!

I got a great call that week from Jim Yukich, a director friend, who hired me as musical director for *Ray Charles 50th Anniversary* TV special. This was to take place in Pasadena right after the Walsh tour ended. Once again, I hired Charlie Calello to watch my back. Ray Charles was my idol. I modeled my career after his, and his influence on me can be found everywhere in my work. But I knew that he could be difficult to work with. Stories had always gone around about stuff like that. So I was mentally prepared for anything.

The show's stage designer had worked out a configuration for the layout of Ray's band onstage. The first morning, everyone was setting the stage and putting the mics in place for his sprawling eighteen-piece band. At 1 p.m. Ray arrived and said in no uncertain terms that he would not perform unless his band was set up *the way he was used to* every night. The stage had to be ripped down and reset, microphones and all. This delayed our day by two and a half hours. Rehearsal began at 3:30 p.m. instead of 1:00. I had hired additional musicians, and I knew they were booked only until 6 p.m. Things got bogged down, performers got backed up, and at 6 p.m. my hired guns left—for other, previously booked sessions, I imagine. When Ray heard that the additional musicians "walked out on him," he insisted that they be *fired*. He could not be reasoned with. This left us without a guitar player. I grabbed a guitar out of the trunk of my car, plugged it in, and started sight-reading charts. Never a dull moment!

Now we had quite a star-studded line-up; Stevie Wonder, James Ingram, Michael Bolton, Gladys Knight, Michael McDonald, Randy Travis, and Tevin Campbell had all come to pay tribute to the Genius. We had written an arrangement of "Hallelujah I Love Her So" for Stevie Wonder to sing—one of Ray's compositions that Stevie had recorded at the dawn of his career. After he had run through our arrangement once with the band, Stevie took Charlie and me aside, played a hip-hop arrangement on piano that he had come up with, and politely asked if a new arrangement could be struck. We recorded Stevie singing and playing the piano, and we wrote a new arrangement overnight. But the highlight of the show was Stevie and Ray performing together *for the first time ever*, doing Stevie's "Living For the City." I sat in the band playing guitar as they ran it down, having the time of my life.

I remember when they were getting the guest line-up together, I called Steve Winwood, another Nashville resident, and asked if he would like to participate. "I could never sing with, open for, or follow Ray Charles. I'd be much too intimidated," he confessed.

That prospect, however, did not deter Michael Bolton, who had the unenviable task of singing "Georgia on My Mind" with Ray. Bolton had recorded a version that was on the charts at the time. We had to write the arrangement with key transitions, as each of them sang the song in different keys. The run-through went fine. Next up was Randy Travis. He was doing "Your Cheating Heart" by himself, and for fun we wrote a lot of jazz voicings in the horn parts to try and mess with the then much heralded country star. I gained a lot of respect for Travis that afternoon. The horn parts didn't faze him in the least, and he sang the devil out of that Hank Williams classic.

The rest of the rehearsal went fine. The next day we ran over Ray's tunes alone. I stood about ten feet from him as he did the most amazing version of "Just For A Thrill." The man could still easily mass-mesmerize anytime he got ready to, and at that moment he most assuredly was ready! Then there followed a discussion between Ray and the producers about the conclusion of the show:

PRODUCERS: Okay, Ray. . . . So then you say, "I've enjoyed the first fifty years. Are you all ready for the next fifty?" The audience will say,

"Uh huh!" and then you do the song and the credits roll.

RAY: What song do I do?

PRODUCERS: The Uh Huh Song [from Ray's Pepsi commercial]. . . .

RAY: Well you better get you some tape, 'cause I'm not gonna do that song. I get *paid* to do that song. Pepsi pays me to go all over the world and do that song. Why in the fuck would I just want to do that song for nuthin'?

PRODUCERS: Okay—now let's just calm this down. . . .

RAY: Look, this is not a song that I'm naturally inclined to do. . . .

PRODUCERS: Well, we did discuss it with you at the last meeting. . . .

RAY: I don't know nuthin' about no meeting. . . . I'm just not gonna play that song. If you want to play a tape of it, that's fine with me. Now what's next?

Somehow, on Friday night, we taped the show. There were a few glitches. James Ingram's teleprompter malfunctioned during his version of "I Can't Stop Loving You," and he was really depending on it for the lyrics. He improvised quite well. I didn't play on Michael Bolton's tune, as he was worried about walking out at the right moment in the middle of Ray doing "Georgia." I stood in the wings with him to give him his cue instead. As the song began, I started laughing to myself. "What's so funny?" Bolton asked. "I was just thinking how funny it would be if I sent you out at the wrong time," I answered, giggling. "That's not funny, Al," he said as his eyebrows came a little closer together. I got him out at the right time anyway. I had a wonderful time playing guitar behind all these people, especially Gladys Knight and Ray and Stevie. That's what I remember most about that event.

Years later, I played organ in the house band at a charity show at the Grand Ole Opry in Nashville. Michael Bolton was on the bill again, and our band was set to accompany him on Otis Redding's "Dock of the Bay." But, first, he came onstage with just his pianist backing him up and sang an *aria* from an opera for this stunned country music audience.

"What were you thinking?" I asked later.

Bolton answered: "Well, it's the Grand Ole Opry. . . . I thought maybe they'd enjoy some *real* opera singing. . . ." Yeah. Like these people listen to the 3 Tenors when they head to the bar for a Cold One.

Perhaps . . . but bad guess, Mikey!

The next "work" I got was perhaps the strangest of all. Kathi Goldmark, a media escort (it's not what you think—she squires authors around to TV and radio interviews and book signings when they're in San Francisco) came up with the idea of putting a band together made up of famous authors who owned instruments or had fantasies about singing/playing in a rock group. I was asked to be musical director of this aggregation. It was to be called The Rock Bottom Remainders and consisted of Stephen King—rhythm guitar and vocals; Dave Barry—lead guitar and vocals; Amy Tan—background, lead vocals, and whips; Barbara Kingsolver—keyboards, vocals, and one of the most disarming smiles on the planet; Robert Fulghum—mandocello, wisdom, and vocals; Ridley Pearson—bass and vocals; Tad Bartimus—background and lead vocals; Kathi Goldmark—background and lead vocals (it was *her* ball, remember?); plus two *real* musicians we hired to make it all coalesce, Josh Kelly on drums; and Jerry Petersen on saxophones. It also included a Critics Chorus that consisted of: Dave Marsh, Joel Selvin, Matt Groening, Greil Marcus, and Roy Blount, Jr.

The plan was to play for the American Booksellers Association (ABA) convention in Anaheim on Memorial Day Weekend 1992. And so, three days before the show, we put this big lump of humanity in a room, and my job was to sculpt it into something recognizable as a musical group. We were quite heinous, but we had spirit and a great sense of humor. We put together a show that was entertaining (if you owned earplugs; if you didn't, we threw them out to the audience between songs) and funny. Unbeknownst to all of us, we were in the infancy of our career as a group, and unfortunately we made the mistake of having an amateurish video shot of our escapade that is occasionally still available in the random sadistic record store. If you should come across this dubious piece of merchandise, resist the impulse to see famous, intellectual, grown men and women making fools of themselves. Later on, we elevated the gig to an art form, but only I was there to tape *that*!

After the show had been over for weeks, we began to fax each other about resurrecting the behemoth and doing this again. Steve King wanted the whole nine yards: a tour, a tour bus, bad food, groupies, etc. To this end, he proposed that we pre-sell a book that we would all co-author about said upcoming tour, and fund the tour with the advance from the book. It was extremely expensive to get the fifteen members of this band together and keep them together for three weeks—in the six-figure range actually. But somehow, with King's clout, his fantasy came true. This time, at the first rehearsal, these troupers were good! They had done their homework with the scent of greasepaint lurking in their synapses, and our quality went up a hundred fifty percent.

This was more like summer camp than anything else to these stars. Their livelihoods were usually earned solo, in quiet, undisturbed rooms myopically staring down typewriters, word processors, or computers. Now they were thrown together with more of their own ilk, to commiserate and question each other, liberated from

Remainders Tour. New York City, 1992. Stephen King (not related to B. B.), Dave Barry, and I mug for the camera secure in our collective heterosexuality. (Photo: Al Kooper Collection.)

☯

the quiet writing rooms, and thrust onto a tour bus that took them to blue collar beer joints all along the Eastern seaboard. They were ecstatic! (The poll result onboard the bus for the question an author most *hates* to hear or answer was "Where do you get your ideas?") Robert Fulghum and Matt Groening could not be there for the whole tour because of commitments in their real lives, but they showed up at the last performance. We played Rhode Island, Boston, Cambridge, Northampton, New York, Washington, DC, Philadelphia, Atlanta, Nashville, and Miami. All monies actually earned went to Volunteers for Literacy, as did the proceeds from sales of our signed tee shirts, which we sold at our concerts.

There were many highlights on this tour: Amy Tan singing "These Boots Were Made for Walking" in full dominatrix gear replete with whip; Stephen King singing

"Teen Angel," with everyone in the band wearing haloes and Dave Marsh in drag as the dead girlfriend in the song; Dave Barry singing and playing an anthemic version of Van Morrison's "Gloria"; the Critics Chorus dropping their pants mid-tune to reveal brightly-colored boxer shorts. There was much, much more, all of it chronicled in a book you can try and locate at masochistic bookstores everywhere. It's called *Mid-Life Confidential*, and it's packed with photos by Tabitha King (some of which, I must say, are extremely unflattering—and I mean that in the best possible way) and some of the funniest writing you will ever read. I promise. No disappointments, no refunds.

We played some more, and then the usual band in-fighting took the fun out of it all. I made a few wonderful, hilarious life-long friends (and enemies) as a result of this caper. Why, Stephen King wrote the liner notes to my next album and dedicated his book *Insomnia* to me (how apropos). But for more than just one "gloria"-ous moment, it was Our Shining Hour. I shot a tedious home video of the whole tour. I'm threatening to edit it someday—and who knows what might happen then???

In 1993, Sony Records decided to honor Bob Dylan with a thirtieth anniversary concert at Madison Square Garden. In 1963, John Hammond, Sr., had signed the lad who was soon known in the hallways of Columbia Records as "Hammond's Folly." Now these same name-callers were ready to admit defeat, but not to the face of the by then-expired Hammond. Just to turn the screw, his talented son, John Hammond, Jr., was invited to perform (not, however, during the three-hour-plus PPV part of the show!).

This was a goonbash with an amazing backstage cast. I brought a camcorder and got some great footage of the rehearsals and the backstage antics. Neil Young called it "Bobfest." I called it "Night of a Thousand Bobs." The hallways backstage yielded some impressive guests and visitors: Richie Havens, Tom Petty, Don Was, Lou Reed, Lenny Kravitz, Wynonna, Chrissie Hynde, George Harrison, and yours truly, all co-existed with grace and decorum in an effort to honor their friend and inspiration, in the face of Sony's blatant hucksterism. I was scheduled to reprise my organ part on "Like A Rolling Stone" behind John Mellencamp and his band. This turned out to be the opening song of the concert that was beamed to millions of households. During rehearsal and prior to performance, Mellencamp spoke not a word to me. I was truly surprised when he introduced me to the crowd between songs. All in all, it was a great hang and I have a lovely backstage home video of the event.

So between Joe Walsh, Ray Charles, and Stephen King, my first two years in Nashville actually were spent mostly on the road. When I returned there, someone called me about a charity softball game that was taking place at Greer Stadium, Nashville's minor league ballpark. At first I almost hung up, because even playing softball would have probably put my unexercised body into cardiac arrest. But what they really wanted was for me to play the organ at the game. *What a great idea!* Now *there* was something that was not on my résumé yet! I jumped at the chance and had a wonderful time watching George Jones pitch as I wailed out "Green Onions!"

In between getting divorced and rebuilding my life once again, someone actually hired me to play on a country record. A man with the unlikely name of Garth Fundis called to have me play on the debut album of an artist he was producing. Now I knew Garth from Sound Emporium, the studio two blocks away, and I was glad when he called. I love studio work because of the challenge. You walk in, you have no idea what you're gonna hear, and you have to create something on-the-spot that will enhance it. Garth had a ballad that needed organ, and in just a few moments of work after I walked into the studio for Garth's latest production, I had played on another classic record—the first Trisha Yearwood album. The track was called "Fools Like Me" and you know I could relate to *that*! Later on during my Nashville stay, I played on Trisha's movie track "Devil in Disguise" from *Honeymoon in Vegas*, and on her contribution to the Eagles' *Common Thread*, "New Kid in Town."

In this same time period, an A&R guy from Virgin Records called about my producing one of their artists, Danny Tate. He sent Danny down to Nashville for a week, and we hung out, cut one track together, and got along pretty well. Then the guy from Virgin called back and offered me the *least amount of money I had ever been offered in my entire career* to produce "a few" tracks for Tate's album. I told him that his offer was far below what anyone had ever paid me, and he rewarded me with the cliché "Well, what have you done lately?"

I grimaced and replied, "Turned *you* down, for one thing!" and hung the phone up on him. This validated my moving to Nashville and ceasing to produce records. I knew then I had made the right choice and that I was, indeed, getting out *almost* gracefully. "What have you done lately," indeed. My first year in the music business eclipsed *that* guy's entire career résumé. Who needed this??

The other negative/positive experience took place in Los Angeles. Stephen King invited me as his guest to the Rock and Roll Hall of Fame Dinner. Now this was something I would not normally attend at $1,000 a plate. On top of that, the money goes back to the RRHF and doesn't feed, save, or teach anybody anything, in my opinion. I selected my good friend Bonnie Bedelia, the actress, as my date. (She had just finished appearing in one of Stephen's movies, *Needful Things*. I thought it would suit the motif, and Bonnie loved music as well.) Stephen's table consisted of all horror-film people—John Carpenter, Tobe Hooper, etc. I was the only rocker at the table.

Now, even with the lovely Bonnie at my side, I was totally snubbed by everyone in the current music community (with the exception of Shep Gordon and the house band). So, rightfully, this should be one of those tell-all, skeletons-in-the-closet books, because I really have *nothing* to lose here. But plenty of people are waiting in line to put *those* puppies out, and you'll rarely see a book like *this*, so I'll just control myself. That dinner was my second and final affirmation of having done the right thing. Plus, while they were giving out these awards to families of dead people (i.e., Frankie Lymon and The Teenagers), these bastards were out in the lobby smoking cigars and schmoozing. I don't need that, believe me. I support MusicCares, a division of NARAS that doesn't need a museum and actually tries to help people while they're still alive. At what point do you get a message when practically everyone you're inducting from a genre that's less than fifty years old is deceased?

While in Los Angeles in early January getting ready to attend the winter NAMM show of 1994, a truly life-changing event took place. I was staying at the home of my lawyer Mike Goldsmith and his wife Karon in Beverlywood, California, between Beverly Hills and Santa Monica. I got in late one night, and fell asleep in my clothes in their guestroom. I awakened to the familiar grunts of an earthquake. I started groaning as I had cut my yearly L.A. stay to five days and now, on one of those five days, I had to endure an earthquake.

As it continued, it became apparent this was not just another earthquake. The house was rockin' back and forth and stuff was falling and sliding everywhere. The quake continued on for forty-five seconds. The screams by Mike's wife from the next room added to the cacophony. Usually, during the other six quakes I had lived through, I would calmly walk to a doorway and brace myself under it. This time, it was impossible to navigate off the bed because of the intensity of the quake. I hung on for dear life. Mercifully, it finally shuddered to a halt. The power was out and my watch said 4 a.m.-ish. Because I had fallen asleep in my clothes, I was the only one with shoes on who could then brave the broken glass. I hesitantly walked into the hall, begging for a flashlight. Mike brought me one, and my hand was shaking so hard it was useless. I gave it back to him and *his* hand was shaking as well. *None of the three of us could hold the flashlight steady.* We listened to a Walkman radio and found out nothing. So we just sat there and tried to calm down and wait for dawn to survey the damage.

As the sun rose, people hesitantly inched out of their homes to see what was what. Mike's chimney was down, there were cracks in all his walls, and his record room, containing thousands of rare LPs, had imploded. All the shelves had pulled out of the walls, crashing inward. I had been given the choice of sleeping in that room, and if I had accepted I would surely have perished. Great news story: *"Rock producer Al Kooper was killed today when ten thousand LPs crashed down on him, crushing him instantly."* Death by vinyl! The ultimate record collector's death.

The refrigerator had slid a full ten feet into the middle of the glass-encrusted floor of the kitchen. It was a mess. By 9 a.m. I had ascertained that the airport had escaped unscathed, and I went into forward motion to fly out of Gomorrah before tomorra. By noon I was in the air, winging southward to the comparative safety of Nashville. As I stood waiting at bagagge claim in Country Music City, I saw on the TV monitors for the first time that day the widespread damage and fires in L.A. Two minutes from where I had been staying, the freeway had split in half. The full impact finally hit me and I was in shock. I was lucky to be alive! I went home and it took me hours to calm down and sleep. I decided right then and there that I had spent enough time in California, and that I would *not* be returning there again in this life. And I haven't.

Jeff Nissim owns a record club and label based out of Ocean, New Jersey. His company, MusicMasters, has mostly put out jazz and classical releases and collected a few Grammys doing so. In 1990, he released a blues-rock album by Killer Joe, a collection of New Jersey-bred musos including Max Weinberg, Jimmy Vivino, and Joe DeLia. The record didn't do well, but Jeff had whetted his appetite. He asked Jimmy Vivino about me: Would I be interested in making a new album? At the time, Max Weinberg was headquartering out of MusicMasters and so Jeff asked Max to call me. Jeff and Max came to see me at my home in Nashville.

> **JEFF:** We'd like you to make an instrumental album for our label.
> **AL:** Does it have to be jazz?
> **JEFF:** It can be whatever you want it to be, so long as its cost doesn't exceed $40,000.
> **AL:** Come over here and shake my hand, 'cause we have a deal.

It was that simple. Max didn't say a word.

There was a project in the back of my head I had always wanted to pursue, and Nissim was now giving me a chance to make that project a reality. It was a tip of the pork-pie to all the instrumental albums I had grown up with, which were now extinct. Artists like Duane Eddy, Booker T. and The MG's, The Ventures, Bill Black's

Combo, The Meters, and so many others who made my teen years so joyous. No one made records like this anymore, and I wanted to pay homage to my roots and at the same time maybe turn some younger listeners on to a whole era of music they missed. Toward this end, I built a core band of Jimmy Vivino, Anton Fig, Harvey Brooks, and the Uptown Horns. On some other tracks I used a Nashville band consisting of Kenny Greenberg on guitar, Jim Fielder on bass, John Gardner on drums, and Paul Franklin on pedal steel. I tried to touch elements from the fifties through the eighties. Stephen King wrote the liner notes, and a curious cover was concocted of sixteen photos depicting the artist (i.e., me) from age nine to forty-nine. I called it *Rekooperation*, because it was my first album in twelve years. It came out to universally great reviews, but sold universally not so great.

I always had misgivings about signing with a small label because of history. Anyone in the past who had been with a major label, and subsequently aligned themselves with a small label, was never able to return again to a major label. At this point in my life, however, such a thing was *desirous*. One had to give up tour support, ad campaigns, videos (still haven't made one), and all other cash-funded trappings to be with a small label. In return, you could bring your vision to fruition untouched, and that was worth it to me at that point in my life. I may perish without ever having made a video. Then a hundred years from now, people won't be able to see me prancing around with scantily-clad women, lip-synching to some song I was forced to cavort around to in somebody else's vision. I can suffer that hardship.

I should point out, however, that with the help of Cheech Marin (of Cheech and Chong fame) I did appear in two videos in the guise of a rabbi! Cheech was making a video for his lampoon of Springsteen's *Born in the USA*, called *Born in East L.A.* (later to become a feature film). He cast me as a rabbi with two speaking lines. For those who recognized me in it, it must have been hysterical. Shortly after its release, my friend, video-director Jim Yukitch, called to ask if I wanted to be in a Jeff Beck video he was directing called *Ambitious*. The plot line involved various people coming down to audition as the lead singer for Beck's group. I suggested I reprise the rabbi and have Cheech in it with me. It was hilarious if you ever got to see it.

Jim Yukitch, who also got me the Ray Charles gig, was directing a Phil Collins special and also asked me to appear in that. In one segment, Phil was doing one of his new songs à la Dylan '65, and they wanted me to appear in the shot playing organ; kind of an inside joke. I tried to dress like 1965 for it (not too difficult a task for my wardrobe at that time), and it worked out pretty well. If you don't count the myriad interviews and talk show appearances, that's pretty much my entire videography. Okay, ENOUGH ALREADY!!! Now back to our story. . . .

Rekooperation was released on my fiftieth birthday, February 5, 1994. To coin-

Cheech Marin directs me in a difficult role for his Born in East L.A. *video, 1985.*
(Photo: Al Kooper Collection.)

೧೨

cide with all this, MusicMasters threw me a fiftieth Birthday Bash at the Bottom Line in New York. They invited the two bands I had been in to reunite and join the Rekooperators, my current band, in a life-retrospective performance beginning with *The Blues Project*, continuing with *Child Is Father to the Man* (BS&T), and closing with *Rekooperation*. Right up to the day before the concerts, MusicMasters was negotiating with a video company. Finally, they came to an agreement, and releases had to be circulated among the musicians at the various rehearsals that day. We were going to record and videotape all the performances for future release. Most people signed the releases as soon as they were handed to them. Steve Katz, however, from the Blues Project and BS&T, took exception to being handed something like that a day before the actual show. He refused to sign it until his brother/lawyer Dennis had checked it out thoroughly. He also successfully urged other members of the bands to join him in his boycott and to take advantage of the negotiations his brother was performing gratis for Steve.

With the investment that MusicMasters was making in this event, this was definitely a boulder in their passageway. The shows went on in the face of this controversy, but bad feelings abounded. I got the flu the night before the first show and had to play the entire three-day event sick as a dog. The last night Roy Blumenfeld, the Project's drummer, got the flu too. In spite of all this in-fighting, there were some wonderful moments captured on audio and video. Danny Kalb's incredible version of "Two Trains Running," a high-powered trumpet duet between Randy Brecker and Lew Soloff during "My Days Are Numbered," and a great spontaneous rendition of Pat McLaughlin's "Don't Tell Me" were just some of the high points. Guest appearances by Stephen King, Dave Barry, Peter Riegert, John Sebastian, and Johnnie Johnson rounded out the shows each night.

After the smoke cleared, Steve's brother, Dennis, renegotiated the paper with MusicMasters, and those that had taken Steve's offer signed off on it. Twenty-four musicians had now signed the contract and still no Steve Katz signature. Finally, he asked for twice as much money as each of the other twenty-four musicians had agreed to be paid and a gratis shopping spree of the MusicMasters classical catalog.

He was turned down cold.

It then became my responsibility, since Steve would not sign the contract everyone else signed, to clear out his tracks on the album and replace them. This was extremely costly and time-consuming and, in some cases, seemed impossible because of leakage. Even when his tracks were erased, occasionally you could hear his parts or his unintentional screams of feedback being captured by other microphones. Somehow, though, it all got done. For awhile it looked like "Two Trains Running" was unusable because of said leakage, but harp player Mike Henderson from Nashville came in one afternoon and painstakingly worked with me covering all the leakage in that song with some masterful harp-playing.

Jimmy Vivino replaced most of Steve's guitar parts, as he had been playing those songs with me for over ten years anyway and was totally conversant with them. Jerry Douglas played some amazing lap-steel on "I Can't Keep from Cryin'," and the over-all quality level of the music went up a notch or two. We got a better CD. However, because Steve appeared in two out of the three bands, *we lost the video*. I'm doomed never to have a video, I guess.

Naturally, this closed the door on any future relationship with Steve. The other members of The Blues Project could not really defend his behavior on any level. We were never really great friends, and I think he saw this as a chance to really fuck with me (which he did *not*—it was actually MusicMasters that bore the brunt of his behavior and had the most to lose) and he played it out to its illogical conclusion. Love ya, Steve.

The album came out on Valentines Day, 1995. It's a two-CD set titled *Soul of a*

The Mighty Rekooperators, 1994. (Left to right) Harvey Brooks (recently retired to Scottsdale, Arizona, and currently replaced by Mike Merritt), Al, Jimmy Vivino, and Anton Fig. (Photo: Steve Eichner—Al Kooper Collection.)

Man, accompanied by a forty-page booklet and with intensive liner notes written by *Goldmine* ex-editor Jeff Tamarkin. In theme it is the musical equivalent of this book—its soundtrack, in effect. So if you've enjoyed the reading so far, I'm pretty sure you'll enjoy the listening. With God's help, the album will still be available in stores as you read this.

In the summer of 1995, Jeff Rosen, who runs Bob Dylan's office, called me out of the blue. Bob was scheduled to play in London the next week at *The Prince's Trust Concert* in Hyde Park, and he had requested that I join the band for that show. The show's line-up included Alanis Morrisette, Bob, The Who performing *Quadrophenia*, and Eric Clapton closing out the festivities. I had studiously avoided "crossing the pond" to England ever since I had lived in London in 1979. I had to make a quick decision because of the time frame, and I opted to attend. I figured I knew everyone on the show except Morrisette, and it would be nice to see them all again, including Bob.

The plan was to warm up with two theater shows in Liverpool and then play the big London gig. I soon found myself winging eastward to meet up with the troops, and got to Liverpool the day before the first show there. I walked around Liverpool (first-timer) and took in all the Beatles tourist crap. The next day, we soundchecked in the afternoon, and I played the show pretty much with that soundcheck as my only rehearsal. Well, at the next day's soundcheck I was asked to change the parts I had played the night before. I was basically recreating the riffs I played on the original records because I thought that's why Bob had hired me and because that's what I would naturally play anyway. But Tony Garnier, the bassist and leader of the band, admonished me: "Those parts are being played by other instruments in the band now, Al. Find something else to play."

Now I have to say, I found that request insulting and unprofessional. If Keith Richards sat in with *my* band and we played "Jumpin' Jack Flash," I wouldn't say: "Hey Keith, lay out at the top. I got it covered on the organ!" Ludicrous, actually. But seeing that Bob rarely attended soundchecks, I couldn't just look him in the eye and say: "This is what you flew me here for?" So, with the benefit of the wisdom of my years, I followed orders and complied with Tony's bizarre request. This took most of the fun out of playing the gigs for me, but I knew how to behave and it seemed I had no choice. At the soundcheck for the Hyde Park gig, Bob's old friend, Rolling Stone Ron Wood, joined us on guitar for the whole set. It was nice to see Ron again, but with two guitars jamming away in there already, he was basically in the same playing position I was.

Day of show in London arrived, and we rode in vans to the venue. It was so people-dense around the park that we had to enter through the handicapped area; an ironic but fitting omen when one has to perform in front of two hundred fifty thousand people. I am not one who is disarmed by crowd size. Hey, I'll play to a hundred people or one million people and not bat an eyelash. But believe me, I'd prefer a hundred. Big shows like that rarely make it possible to connect with the audience, and the feeling onstage is abnormally surreal. This is not to say you can't pull off a great performance every now and then in that situation, but chances are, you won't.

Bob stuck with the odds that day. He walked onstage with a scowl on his face, and it remained there the entire show. Ron Wood, trying desperately to have a good time, kept smiling at Bob, who just returned his glance with the perennial scowl. HBO taped this event and, with due respect to whoever mixed it, the balance was way off. This did not help one's appreciation of the show when it was reduced in size to fit the home TV screen format. But I enjoyed the look on my face the rare times I could see it. I look like I was thinking, "BEAM ME UP, SCOTTY!!! ON THE DOUBLE!!!" as I tried valiantly to invent new parts while the pedal steel played all *my* licks.

They showed this program on TV on New Year's Eve that year, and I didn't know it was scheduled to be on. I was sitting curled up on the couch, channel surfing with some new Nashville female acquaintance, when my face appeared on the screen. "Look!!!!" she squealed. "You're on TV!!! Turn it up louder!!!" I must have appeared to be the most blasé guy she had ever met, as I aggressively convinced her we should watch something/anything else. That was my last date with her (her choice) as I recall.

Coincidentally, it seemed that my self-imposed "retirement" was rapidly coming to a conclusion. I had basically—except for a few and far between gigs—just dropped off the face of the earth for seven years. I had never taken any kind of sabbatical before this, and it was thoroughly enjoyed by me in Country Music City. But restlessness was rearing its head again. What could I do, *now*?

1996-1998

**THE GREENING OF
NASHVILLE,**

DOCTOR AL,

BOSTON,

BERKLEE,

THE NEW OLD BOOK, AND

THAT'S ALL HE WROTE

As the years went passing by in Nashville, the town began to erupt and meta-morphize into something that was more akin to California than Tennessee.

Originally, when I moved there in 1990, I admired the cunning stunt the city fathers had pulled off: They took all the tourist attractions and put them in a giant amusement park/hotel/concert hall complex called Opryland. Geographically, it was totally out of downtown Nashville, over by the airport. When tourists came to town, most of them convened out there, and the locals could move along with their everyday lives without fear of being overrun. The downtown area still reeked of the forties and fifties, and was a wonderful trip down memory lane to anyone raised in that era. I always found it very comforting and retro-nurturing.

Then in the early nineties, some geniuses thought it would be great to gentrify the downtown. Bad idea. All of a sudden: POOF! There was a Hard Rock Cafe. BAM! A Planet Hollywood. BOOM! A Hooters and a Wildhorse Saloon. The streets crawled with people who craved buying commemorative tee shirts in shitty souvenir shops disguised as restaurants. KAPOOWIE!! A twenty-thousand-seat arena went up right in the heart of downtown, with no added mass transit to accommodate it. Traffic became ugly. Gone was the original ambience. You can struggle down Second Avenue today and not even be able to tell *what* city you're in. Clubs began to open that charged exorbitant cover charges and booked big name acts. The people I had moved away from L.A. to avoid began to move to Nashville in droves. I knew it was over for me, but *where to go*???

Over the course of the years covered in this book, I had lived in New York, Atlanta, Los Angeles, London, Austin, and Nashville. My tenure in Nashville had been seven years of self-imposed vacation-like retirement. I knew I did not wish to return to the music biz per se. But I really felt like getting back to work. *So what to do?*

Beverly Keel, a close and scrumptious (I don't think that word is in the dictionary; use your imagination) friend of mine and a native Nashvillian, had given up a full-time job as a journalist at the now-defunct local paper, *The Nashville Banner,* to work in publicity for PolyGram Records. In no time at all, she was miserable and longed to be back at the paper, where her job had unfortunately been snapped up immediately. She decided to join the Music Business program at Middle Tennessee State University and teach publicity and artist management. I monitored a few of her classes and spoke at a few. She was really happy in her new job, and a light bulb went off in my head: "Why not dispense all this information I'd learned over the past forty years to people who could really use it *now*?"

I wanted to be at a school where the learning curve was high and the classes small, and the students would "get" what I was teaching. The first place that came to mind was the Berklee College of Music. This institution is located in Boston, a city I hadn't lived in yet. That was a perk. There were, however, a few minor problems:

> **A.** No one had asked me to teach at Berklee.
> **B.** I did not possess a teaching degree.

Pshaw! I could deal with those obstacles. I called an old friend of mine who was now a department head at Berklee. Here's how the conversation went:

> **ME:** Hi! It's Al Kooper. Remember me? How ya been?
> **HIM:** Al. It's nice to hear from you. What can I do for you?
> **ME:** Well, actually, I've reached that time in my life when I was thinking about teaching at Berklee. . . .
> **HIM:** Ohhhh. . . . [Incredibly loooooooooooong pause] Do you have any

. . . uhh . . . teaching degrees, Al?

ME: Uhhhh. . . . [Incredibly looooooooooonger pause] No, actually I don't. But Freddie Lipsius, who was with me in Blood, Sweat & Tears, has been teaching there for many years, and he never had a teaching degree.

HIM: Yeah, it used to be like that, Al. But nowadays, they're more critical about your qualifications.

ME: [Beginning to get *very* depressed] Well, it was nice to talk to you again. Say hi to the wife and kids for me.

HIM: Okay. Bye, Al.

Maybe this wasn't the way in. Perhaps he thought I wanted a full workload and a high salary, etc. All I *really* wanted was maybe two classes a week to get my feet wet and the money was of no consequence whatsoever. Then, if all went well, maybe two years down the line, I would consider joining the faculty full time. Undaunted, I called the President of the school, Gary Burton. Gary and I had come up together in the Greenwich Village music scene. He is a highly respected jazz vibraphonist, and we might have even played on the same bill back in the sixties. He was much more encouraging, and when he found out I was only interested in part-time work initially, he virtually guaranteed me a position. Soon I had a letter from Berklee offering me employment.

Shortly thereafter, Five Towns College, a music school located on Long Island and not related to Berklee, called out of the blue to inform me I had been selected to receive an Honorary Doctorate of Music from their school and speak at their commencement exercises. I accepted gladly and was now Doctor Kooper. I took this as an omen that everything was falling into place.

I remember the first day of teacher orientation at Berklee. I was nervous. I was in over my head as usual, and I humbly sat down to learn a thing or two. By the end of the day, I had been offered many wonderful teaching tips, and was made aware of all the help and assistance that was available to me should I seek it. The next week I faced my first class, and two hours later I was virtually unscathed. Hell, I had learned a lot in the last forty years, and I genuinely wanted to pass this knowledge on. When the students were willing to share in my knowledge and began to ask great questions, I was reassured. To my advanced record production class, I brought twenty-four-track master tapes from my home library. We played them in the studio/classroom and dissected them to find the heart and soul of a record production. The class was fascinated. I was ecstatic. My songwriting class had never heard of Laura Nyro. I sat and watched the expressions on their faces as I played

A Doctor of Bluesology accepts his degree. Lawn Guy Land, 1997.
(Photo: Barbara Torre).

them their first taste of "Poverty Train" and "Eli's Coming." This was energizing.

As the semester moved on, I began to look at certain classes like a chess game. In two hours I had to take their Queen. They knew it when they walked in and sat down, but I had to do it surreptitiously, and when they were checkmated, I needed smiles. I had to get them from point A to point B and make it an enjoyable journey as well. It's a stimulating exercise. As each semester ended, I hated to let my classes go. I had developed a genuine affection for them and I never felt like I was finished. The last question on the first midterm exam I authored was: "I did well on this exam—True/False." I warned the students as I handed out the tests, "You can get that last question wrong, so be careful!" I look forward to each semester now, glad to be giving something back and getting something back myself.

I decided to edit, revise, and update my book from 1977, *Backstage Passes*. Twenty years had passed, and a lot of new, interestiing events had transpired that were worth writing about. Bob Nirkind, senior editor at Billboard Books, had been a big fan of the original book. When he saw the first draft of the new version, he snapped it up for publication and I then had a serious deadline to add to my regular workload.

It took me four months to find a house in Boston. Initially I looked in Cambridge, but settled on Somerville, a dense blue-collar town right next to Cambridge. That's usually the drill. People all come to Boston wanting to live in Cambridge. When they quickly find out that they're about $400,000 short to be buying a home there, they quickly pick someplace adjacent like Somerville and quietly settle down to reality. There is currently a renaissance going on in Somerville. *The Utne Reader* called it one of the top up and coming communities in the country, something like ". . . the Paris of the Nineties." Those of us that live here don't really dispute that. We just know the author of that statement meant Paris, Texas.

It is here in Somerville that I now sit pounding out the final draft of this opus de funk. I have already taught an advanced record production class and an advanced songwriting class at Berklee. In my second semester now, I am teaching the history of record production, and the history of American popular song writing. I can safely say my vacation and retirement are over. What I actually did was take an early retirement at an age I could enjoy it. Seven years later, I was ready to return to work. Most people end their retirements in the boneyard. That will not happen here—like my heroes, Muddy Waters, B. B. King, and Ray Charles, I will play the blues until my hands can't move anymore. The most wonderful thing is that while I'm very busy, I am not a card-carrying, full-time music business lifer. Now I can take the time to pursue things that are music-related, but far removed from the record business—teaching, free-lance writing, dee-jaying, graphics work, etc. Things I always wanted to do but never had the time for in my past lives.

I feel blessed to have an almost normal life now, with some terrific memories that I hope you have enjoyed sharing with me. I wouldn't trade the ups and downs of the last forty years for anything. Seeing the transformation of my students over the course of a semester is as rewarding as any gold record on the wall. On the other hand, the house would really smell if I started putting the students up on the wall.

The band I'm in now, The Rekooperators, is probably the best band I've ever been a member of. To a man, the musicianship is certainly the highest of any of them. With Jimmy Vivino on guitar, Mike Merritt on bass, and Anton Fig on drums, I feel I am invincible when I sit down to play accompanied by a cast like that. Except for myself, they are all employed as musicians on late-night television shows: Jimmy and Mike with Conan O'Brien, and Anton with David Letterman. This makes touring problematical. When we do go out and play (on weekends), we do it because we love to play, not because it's financially rewarding, because it ain't. So we are out there performing because we genuinely enjoy playing music together. I think the audience can sense this difference and share that same joy with us. It remains one of the best things in my life now.

Over the last fifteen years, I've probably written fifty really good songs. I feel like I'm still growing and maturing as a writer. However, I can't face the indignity of the music business to try and do anything with them. I'd be proud to put them out for sale and show my continuing growth as a songwriter, but even without that recognition I'll just keep writing and playing my songs. Maybe my son will have the fortitude to deal with getting them all released when I'm gone. I'm having too much fun with my other projects to return to the negativity of my past life. I just wish I had looked after my royalties more carefully so I that I didn't have to chase all these bastards around for my rightful due *now* (and I could be living in *Cambridge!*). I'd like to be done with all the legal rigamarole, get what's coming to me, and move on without looking back.

I realize I still have much life to live. I've tried to document the life I have already lived up to now because it was exciting, different, and humorous. From now on, it should be humorous and rewarding, but not much different than anybody else's humorous and rewarding life. So I feel safe ending the book here, even though this life could drag on for God knows how long.

Thanks for traveling this bizarre voyage with me. I hope to see you sometime at a concert. Come up and say hi, and if you bring this book with you, I promise to sign it (that is, if you ask me to!). And remember, I'm a professional—*don't try any of this at home*!!!!

1998–2007

TRIALS,

TRIBULATIONS,

AND A SOULFUL AGGREGATION

When I first started teaching and I hadn't been in town very long, a guy called me up and said, "Hi, I'm Bob Doezema, I teach at Berklee, and we put a band together for a fund-raising event every year and play. Our regular keyboard player can't make it this year, and I wanted to invite you. I figured you're new in town and you probably haven't had the chance to play much."

I said, "Boy, you got *that* right!"

Bob continued, "We're just playing blues, so you don't have to rehearse! We'd *love* for you to come down and play with us."

So I said, "I'll be there."

It was simple; it was fun; and it was comparatively menial in my schedule and a wonderful diversion. I participated again a year later. The events are called "galas" at Berklee. And at the second gala I got them to rehearse once, so that I could sing a couple of my songs. By the third one, I made them *really* rehearse, and we had added horns. So after the third one, I said, "This is pretty good. Do you guys want to go play out in front of a paying audience somewhere?" And they said, "Yeah, we'd love to do that!" I went through two other drummers to get the correct one, and one other bass player. There are six of us total now, and early on I named us The Funky Faculty. We've been together about eight years, and the lineup is Bob Doezema, guitar; Jesse Williams, bass; Jeff Stout, trumpet and flugelhorn; Daryl Lowery, reeds and flute; and Larry Finn on drums. I play mostly organ and piano with a minor on guitar and mandolin.

I needed a band like this because my concurrent band, The Rekooperators, had been taken out of my grasp by guitarist Jimmy Vivino. Now normally this is a negative thing, like losing BS&T to Bobby Colomby. But Jimmy was one of my "discoveries," and I had supported him as a player and as a person for decades. He just happened to grow into making The Rekoops *his* backing band instead of mine. I was actually proud of him and his ascent to leader.

And having the pressure of being the front man reduced to fifty percent made the gigs a lot more comfortable for me. I eventually came to think of myself as a sideman in The Rekooperators and I had zero problems with that. It is a classic jam band, and all the members love it because it's a blowing-off-steam vehicle. Except for myself, Jimmy, Mike Merritt, and Anton Fig, all play on late-night TV shows, and when they have the time to blast off, The Rekooperators is their first choice. However, when Jimmy took over, I lost a band to play Al Kooper music exclusively. And so God delivered The Funky Faculty, and that's what we did and still do. We've been all over Europe, playing Italy, Norway, Denmark, the Czech Republic, and three tours in Japan. It's my biggest joy now. At sixty-four, I really love playing live gigs more than anything else. It's my favorite thing to do.

Arthur C. Clarke's prophetic year, 2001, was a *very* bad year for me: my mom died; my dog died; 9/11. But let's discuss the even worse parts of that year for me.

I noticed that something was a little weird with my sight, but I didn't know what it was until I actually shut one eye and went, *Whoa!* My vision was *much* worse than usual. So I went to the ophthalmologist, and he rushed me over to the head of neurology at Mass General in Boston. She was an older British woman, and she said, "What you have is very rare. What happened is you had a stroke in your eye that, for whatever time period, prevented the flow of blood to your optic nerve and then damaged your sight in that short amount of time, permanently. It's irreparable, but it won't get worse. We don't know much about it, but I have something I'd like to try with you." Her "treatment" involved two really dangerous drugs, and I had to sign forms absolving them of guilt if anything serious happened to me—Al, the guinea pig. I had to go to the hospital every day and have my blood checked. The other medication she put me on was steroidal, and since I'm diabetic, it jacked my blood sugar *way* up, which was also not good. This went on for three weeks, and I remember it was around Christmastime, because it wasn't so jolly. As a joke, I used to say, "I'm the Jewish Ray Charles—half-off." Nine months later, the same thing happened to the other eye. And then, of course, I lost that Ray Charles line. It was such a good line, too.

And the British specialist woman was back in Britain doing something. So they sent me to another guy, and he said, "I see how you were treated for the first eye." He said, "I just wanna tell you: I'm not gonna go that way." And I just said, "Thank you so much!" 'Cause that was so rough and scary the first time. So that was a relief. And he was very nice, and let me see what the damage was through new tests he gave me They prescribed three different pairs of glasses for me. The everyday pair are trifocals. Then I have another pair that's just for sitting at the computer. It's sort of measured for how far I am from the screen. And those are really my lifesavers, because I spend most of my time there. And then there's reading glasses. Not too much use for *them* anymore. . . . It takes so much effort to actually read smaller type that my actual endurance time is, at the most, forty-five minutes—and then it's a for-sure nap. So reading a book has been neutralized forever. Good thing I was such an avid reader before 2001. But ultimately, I feel I was blessed that this affliction was aimed at my eyes instead of my hands or my ears. Hell, most times I'm playing, my eyes are closed anyway! Adjustment to everyday life was not that difficult. With thirty-five percent of my sight, I feel able to easily get through most situations, and I capitalize on touch to get me through dealing with musical instruments and various TV remote controls.

Six months after the second eye diagnosis, I had to have an MRI to see how things were going. When they got the results, my regular doctor called me and said, "The eyes checked out great, *but* . . . they found a *brain tumor.*" And I went, *This is unbelievable! First the one eye, and they say the odds of having it in both eyes are eighty-five percent against and so then both eyes, and now, a brain tumor!* And she said, "That's the bad news." I said, "What's the good news?" She said, "I know the greatest doctor for that, and with your permission I'd like to call him and see if I can get you in there." And I said, "You need my permission for that?" I said, "Go!" Living in Boston provides a great medical community. Her referral, who is world famous—people come from all over the world to have him work on them—was Dr. Peter Black. So I went and saw him. He had great office-side manner and made me very comfortable, helped me understand what the problem was. He said, "I'd like to wait a few months and see what goes on with this."

So I said, "Okay." Three months later he went in and looked again, did the MRI. And he said, "Maybe another three months; I don't see anything happening, so I don't feel like I want to go in and operate." And I'm thinking, *I don't feel that way. . . . I want you to go in and get this thing out, because I'm not getting any younger, and it's not getting any smaller.* I figured, as you get older the odds increase against you. So at the third exam, I was gonna verbalize this, but he said, "Well, it's starting to grow a little bit, I think I'd like to go get it." And I thought, *Thank God!* and I said, "When do you want to do this?" and he said, "How about in two weeks?" and I said, "Fabulous." I've always been of a mind that I can do *anything* if I have a week to prepare for it. With diabetes there's always the threat that you're gonna lose your feet. So I have an advance, and I'm thinking, *Maybe someday you'll lose your feet, so just be ready for that.* As you can see, I have a positive outlook. The day of the tumor operation, we had to be there about 6 a.m. And I really was thinking, *Okay, let's go.* It wasn't like, *Oh, my God, I may not come out of this*, or *Oh, I'm so scared*, or anything like that. I was fine.

I do not have a fear of death. I've had such a wonderful, amazing life, I'm not gonna miss anything. I've already lived the life I wanted to live. Anything else is a bonus.

Well, this was a big one for me . . . I had miraculously never broken a bone, and the only other time I was under the knife was for a kidney stone. I basically felt lucky. I had the best doctor and the best attitude. I remember they anesthetized me and said, "Count backwards." The last thing I remembered was *ninety-eight* . . . and then I woke up, and Dr. Black was there, and my wife Susan was there. He said to me, "Everything went fine. You're okay. I only shaved a quarter of your hair along the left side where I operated. The operation took eight and a half hours, got a bit bloody at the end, but all is well." I had a bandage on at the time, and felt okay; I was taking everything in. Let's say they operated on a Monday. So it was Monday night when I came out of it. Tuesday was a tough day; I didn't like being in the hospital and I hated the bed. The doctor visited and said, "You're doing very well, so I'd like to get you home Wednesday afternoon." *Brilliant.* But I thought they must really need hospital space to check somebody out after brain surgery in two days!

And I was just so glad to be able to get home. I went up to the bedroom, which is on the second floor of our house. I lay down, and they had a visiting nurse who would come in and put a machine on my legs just to stimulate them because of the inactivity. She would come in every four or five days and do that. It was a six-week recovery. I was on a lot of painkillers, which worried me, because in the past, as you've previously read, I had an addiction to painkillers, and now I was taking the same thing I was addicted to, and the same amount I'd been taking at the height of my addiction.

The doctor said to me at the three-week point, "I'm going to stop the pills Thursday. I'm just telling you, and then you can take these other pills, which don't deal with the same area, but they're painkillers." So I said, "Okay," and I stopped on Wednesday, because I really wanted to know what was going to happen . . . and it was a very smooth changeover. There was still pain, but there wasn't that withdrawal thing, because before I was treating *mental* pain, and this time I was treating physical pain. And there's a big difference . . . speaking as far from a doctor as one can be, although I am a Doctor of Music.

So it was a totally smooth transition, and that meant a lot to me. Well, those six weeks, I was mostly bedridden. Susan had to pulverize every bit of food I ate, because I couldn't open my jaw very far because of the operation being just above my ear. I don't know why this was, but I couldn't chew properly, so then that was part of the *fun* . . . asking for steak shakes! So I think the first three months plus, I was also waiting for the hair to grow. I wasn't gonna go out there with a left-headed mullet. Tumorettes syndrome? Now, for those people who are reading this and are married or have a significant other, if you're the one being operated on and recovering in this six-week period, your task is *much* easier than the other person's. My wife, God bless her, made it through that. It was *much* tougher on her than it was on me. And it was tough on me! But taking care of an immobile, complaining mate for a month and a half is not suggested for happy marriages.

So the hair grew back pretty fast, which was good. But the six weeks were brutal for both husband and wife.

As I've said before, I was concerned about the vision loss, but I felt that I could overcome whatever the drawbacks were gonna be. Even when the second eye went, I said, "I know I can deal with this," in terms of playing. The biggest loss there was the reading, but fortunately, I'd read a lot of books before. Unfortunately, since the brain tumor, I can't remember *which* books! I noticed a certain memory loss right away; it was comparatively small. I expected it anyway. But it wasn't as bad as I thought it'd be. And now, it's gradually getting a little worse, but I suspect that's the age factor.

So I don't think either of those problems hurt my performing abilities. The eyesight thing just changed them a little bit.

Diabetes is something they haven't cured yet, and I'm not the best diabetic patient who ever walked the earth, so that's something that I'm *constantly* fighting. And that's an everyday battle. Everything that I like to eat, I'm not allowed to eat anymore.

Carbohydrates are the joy of life. So it's very tough. I can still have carbohydrates, but in very small amounts.

I could be a better patient if I were another person. But I'm sixty-four years old; I've sort of grown into who I am. And I do what this person can do, and that's all I can do. At the end of the live show, I thank the audience for coming, and I say that I will sign anything they've brought. "I just have to go in the dressing room for twenty minutes . . . and shoot up." And everybody laughs. The really funny part is I used to say that *before* I got diabetes. And now I say, "The bad part is . . . it's insulin." And they laugh again, this time a little more knowingly, because the average age of a person who comes to see me live is . . . deceased. But I think my life changed around sixty. Up to that point, I laughed at the birthdays. "I don't look so bad. I feel good. I'm still doing what I like to do." At sixty, the physicalness of my age started to matter more. But as soon as I could, I was out playing again. I had to put a rider in my booking contracts that they had to get this exact musical equipment rented for me, because I was playing by touch, and there couldn't be any substitutes. So that was the main difference. I had taught myself in that time period—before I went out and played again—to operate everything by touching. For instance, I can work the entertainment center remote control better than my wife can, because I don't need the lights on to see it. I *definitely* don't think of myself as blind, or really, not even close. I think I see as well as you do. I really do. I'm in my world, and in *my* world I see fine. And that's the best way to be with it.

I was very upset when they took my driver's license away. There are only two cities I need to drive in, Nashville and Los Angeles, so it doesn't matter. But now it causes me problems because I can't get around easily in those cities. It's great not to drive in Boston, though, let me tell you. It's a gift.

So there were very few good things that happened in 2001; maybe two. One was the release of a two-CD set called *Rare and Well Done.*

Sony came to me—they own most of my album catalogue—and they said, "We want to put out a two-album look at your career, and we'd like you to be involved." And I said, "I would really *love* to be involved." My contact guy at Sony has always been Bruce Dickinson. Bruce conveys what I want to the suits and saves me from dealing with them so I can get the creative parts of reissues done. In this two-CD set we took one CD and made it a sort of "greatest hits." But we went in and remastered the tracks we chose, which had never been done before. In other words, we upgraded the sound of each track using comparatively modern technology rather than what was available when the tracks were originally recorded and mastered. For the second CD, I decided to unearth as many unreleased tracks, alternate takes, and rarities as I could find. Once I decided that, I was able to come up with the title of the album. The *Well Done* was obviously the first CD of my most popular tracks over the years, and the *Rare* was stuff that I didn't think many people had heard before. I had a single out in 1965 that's very rare, called "New York's My Home," and we included that after Bruce tracked down the master. And then the demo of "Somethin' Goin' On," a track from the *Child Is Father to the Man* album, which was lying in a box of demos in my basement. I was aiming that at fans of that album, and the basement was a great source of material for the *Rare* CD. I was, for the first time, trying to think, *Would I like this if I were a fan?* and I'd never done that before. I think that's the only time I really approached the content of an album that way.

Jaan Uhelszki, my friend who wrote the liner notes for the album, suggested that she go and get comments from various peers, about a particular song or about me in general. And she said, "I'd like to get a list from you of people you think would be interesting, and then *I* would like to pick some people." And I said, "Well, don't tell me the people that you're gonna pick." And, you know, the result of that was better than *any* award that I could get from *any*body. I didn't know that was gonna be the case, but . . . people I really admire, like the band XTC, to have the two guys that are the key guys in the band say really nice things about me—I was totally surprised! And Billy Gibbons from ZZ Top, who I worship. It just was the best thing for me about that album—to have the blessings of my peers is so much more important than any statuette. And I lead a hermetically sealed life in the confines of my Somerville home, so I would've had no way of knowing any of this. So that's a great thing that Jaan did. And also, it made my awardless life really enjoyable. I don't care—the way things are *politically*, I really have no desire, and don't *need* to be in the Rock and Roll Hall of Fame, because it's not *really* that; it's the Rock and Roll Hall of *Sales*. I think that the music speaks for itself. I don't have a blank area in the breakfront, you know, to display awards or anything like that.

I'm an insomniac, so I only sleep two to four hours a night, as a rule. I was examined at UCLA and the University of Texas for this condition, and they said that when I go to sleep, I go into the deepest sleep there is immediately——it takes other people three and four hours to get to it—and that two to four hours may be sufficient for me, and not to worry about it. Which was great news. The other thing is, I sleep on the living room couch, because by the time I get upstairs, I'm awake.

I go, "I could sleep right now." *But if I go up those stairs, I'll be awake.* So I just go right for the couch, and no rituals. *I'm just going to sleep right now, and I know I'll be up in two hours*. If I sleep properly in *my* schedule, then getting up in the morning is sometime between 4:30 and 6:30 a.m.

The wonderful thing about insomnia is I have *so* much time to work that other people don't have. And I get so much work *done* in that time. And the studio is a timeless place. I'll go down at midnight, and then I'll see it's 6 a.m. or I'll see the light coming in the window, and I'll go, *Jeez, I think I should stop now!* but it's *great* like that. So that's what my days and nights are primarily like.

Around 1975–76 I stopped making solo albums because they stopped selling. I was aware of that, so I concentrated on producing records for other musicians rather than attempting to do something people were basically rejecting. Financially, I hit a low point in the early '80s and supported myself by playing local clubs in the L.A. area and taking an A&R job at PolyGram Records. In '94 I released an instrumental album just for fun and followed with a strong live album in '95.

When I got an iPod for the first time, I made a playlist, "Unreleased Al." And then I had a home for all my closeted solo stuff, and I took the different formats and got everything into the playlist. And then I stepped back and looked, and there was, like, 140 songs in there. And I'm going, *Jeez. Maybe it's time now, I think I can make an album.* Prior to this, in 1995, the songs were yelling at me, saying, "Get us out of the basement!" and there were some very good ones there. So I went out and traipsed around and tried to get a record deal, and I couldn't really get one because I was over fifty. I went back to the songs and said, "I'm so sorry, I tried, but I'm afraid this is what your life is gonna be—trapped in a basement!" And in 1995 I laughed it off and went on with my solo-albumless life.

Then in 2004 I met some guy—you know, I would always keep a current bunch of the songs on the iPod—so I played him some of the songs and he said, "That's very good," and "I have a friend who has a label, do you mind if I play this for him?" I stammered back, "So long as it's just that guy, yeah, okay, sure." Then he came back to me and said, "They want to put this out." I said, "Well, I need to re-record it. They're sort of demos, most of them." He said, "Let me put you two on the phone," and it turned out to be Steve Vai, the metal shred guitarist. I didn't really know him; we're in completely different fields. And I'd seen pictures of him—you know, the long hair, the hand on the crotch, and like that—and I'm going, *I don't know what this phone conversation is gonna to be like.* And I remember specifically that I had the current picture of him in front of me, and I got on the phone with him, and it was not the guy in the picture *at all.* It was so far afield I was amazed. And he was knowledgeable, he was *very* nice, and those are two very important things to me. And he really enjoyed the music, which was a shocker to me completely, and he wanted to put the record out.

So he said, "Would you like to make an album?" I said, "Oh, absolutely." Then we worked the details out, because I needed a budget to re-record the demos, and that's how it came to be. And that was thirty years after I had released my last solo album. Like I said, I tried at fifty and didn't succeed. So here I was at sixty-one by the time the deal and the record was done. In '95 I was just shut down everywhere, nobody would see me. I thought I might *never* make a solo album in my lifetime . . . it was sobering, but I could live with it. Ten years later, suddenly I was enabled again after thirty years.

I originally was going to call this album *I Am Where I Want to Be*. That was the working title. And then, when I finished it and it was in sequence and I played it back, there were some very dark things in there, some dark subject matter and dark songs, and I said, *This is not where I want to be!* laughing to myself. *I can't call this album that!* So I had to come up with another title, and it was *Black Coffee*. I thought, *This is a sobering look at life*. In retrospect, it was the perfect title for what that album became. It got the *best* reviews of any album I had ever done, which was interesting, as far as reviews are concerned. And I don't think I increased my sales much, but they didn't go down either. And then I won Comeback Album of the Year in the Memphis Blues Awards. Awards aren't much to me, but *that* meant something.

Well, the reviews plus the award were good for my head. I don't really make a record for anybody but myself. I try to do the best I can artistically, and if I prove that to myself, then I've reached my artistic goal; then I've made a successful record. Then I pray that the fans know of its existence, buy it, and enjoy it. I always hope that they'll get it, because I love my fans. I have great fans. Plus, it was miles ahead of the records I had done before. Then I wanted to do another one because I was very lucky. One of the things that's very important to understand about *Black Coffee* is, I had something that most artists don't have, which is 140 songs to choose from. Now what that means is if you take the *best*—I took nine original songs for the last album—you take the best *nine* of those 140 tracks . . . WOW. What are you gonna have there? It's going to be better than what you normally have the choice of, which is what you wrote between the last album and this album. And I still have that . . . there are new ones written since the last album. So I still have about 140 to choose from. Plus, on *Black Coffee*, I wrote a song with one of my heroes, Dan Penn. He wrote "Do Right Woman," "I'm Your Puppet," "Cry Like a Baby," "Dark End of the Street," some really great songs. We became friends when I lived in Nashville. I remember the first night we tried to write together—we did not succeed, but boy, did we laugh! We had a great time, and then eventually we did successfully write together. I love Dan, he's a great guy, he's very special. He's very talented. A very *under*rated singer—an amazing singer, but known as a songwriter and a producer. I wish that his voice was as recognized as everything else about him.

So one of the songs Dan and I wrote together was on the album, called "Going Going Gone," which was about getting older, which we both knew a bit about. And because I put *Black Coffee* out, I was then able to realize a lifelong dream and write two songs with Gerry Goffin, who was, *is*, one of the major lyricists of all time. It came about because I got a note from this woman I dated very briefly in the '70s. You know, one of those e-mails out of the blue: "Hi, how are you? I don't know if you remember me . . ." and I thought, *I remember you*. And it continued, "Just want to see how you're doing. I'm living in L.A. I'm married to Gerry Goffin." And I went, *Boing! I have an intro to Gerry Goffin!* so I wrote back . . . *Of course I remember you!* "How nice to hear from you!"

And it was, because ambitious me got to ask him if he'd be interested in writing together. I quickly mailed him *Black Coffee* and he loved it, and that's all it really took. We worked over the phone and the Internet, because of geography, and we wrote two songs, and I got to meet him the next time I played L.A. He's manic-depressive, and I think he deals with it quite well. I'll tell you one thing, he's not suffering as a lyricist; he's as great as he ever was. He may speak a little haltingly. I was very nervous about meeting him, and then I met him, and he was so sweet. We had a ton of things in common, knew the same people.

I truly understand him. He was so wonderful, and we spent a little more time, and now, he's really become a good friend. We talk to each other on the phone quite a bit, and I think we'll be able to write some more songs. But I adore him now, and I didn't even know him before I got that e-mail.

The follow-up to *Black Coffee*, which is *White Chocolate*, contains the two new Goffin-Kooper songs. I like the album title a lot, because it really says what's on the record. I spent more time on it than on any record I'd done before. What happened was, I called Steve Vai's record company, Favorite Nations, and said, "I have to start this record now, and I know we haven't finalized our deal for the second album. But I have to start now because 2008 is my fiftieth anniversary in the music business, and I want to get a certain amount of product available in 2008 to celebrate that, and this is certainly one of them. And I'm hoping for a certain amount of synergy so that people will know about these things." So they said, "Okay," and I said, "And we'll work the deal out." So we started making the record, and I invested about twenty grand to keep it going. And then they called back and said, "We'll do the same deal as last time, but we can't give you any front money."

Which is another way of saying, "No deal."

Because that's really *all* the record companies do, in many respects, is pay for you to make another record—and because I work in an old style, I can't really do an entire record in my home studio. I have to go to a real studio at some point. So I was really in a jam, and twenty grand in debt as well. While I waited to solve this problem, I kept working on the record at home, which didn't cost anything except time. And then I said, "The only way I can do this is to find someone to invest in this record, and I don't even *know* anybody like that." To make a long story very short, I found someone who would do that. I needed probably at least three times the amount of money that I had already invested—because that's what *Black Coffee* cost—and I got someone to do that. I can't even put into words how much this saved my life and meant to me. It's one of the biggest things anyone's ever done for me. (I have preserved his anonymity to keep the sharks from his generous door.) And I really feel that this record surpasses the quality of *Black Coffee*. It wasn't my initial approach, but I started paying more attention to detail than I ever had before. And I met a gentleman a few years ago, when I had to change from tape as a storage medium to hard drives, which had become the new storage—I had to change my system at home to deal with this . . . going digital. So I studied, for about nine months, all the products that were available, and I went and had a demo at this company called Mark of the Unicorn, which is near my house in Boston. And the guy gave me a demo, and it was great. The most popular system is ProTools, but it's very expensive, and I wasn't being supported by anyone. Mark of the Unicorn would do the same thing that ProTools would do, and cost me one quarter what ProTools cost . . . so it was no contest.

Plus I was sort of angry at ProTools, because they became the industry standard, but they didn't really pass their success on to the consumer; they actually *raised* their price. So this guy who did the demo for me and caused me to go with Mark of the Unicorn—I'm going to call them MOTU so I don't have to keep saying that—their product is called Digital Performer. And when I started scoring TV shows in 1986 I found that I had to work on the computer, and I had no computer experience, so that's when I learned how to use the computer, when I did *Crime Story* for Michael Mann. And the program that I picked then was Performer, again MOTU, albeit in their infancy. So to go to Digital Performer, I didn't have to adjust my learning curve too much; I was very facile on Performer by this time.

This MOTU gentleman, Dave Roberts, who has worked there for many years, comes over to the house in his spare time and helps me with anything that's over my head in the product, and that's a big help. And he really came in and helped me *tremendously* on *Black Coffee*, but not as *ultra*tremendously as he did on *White*

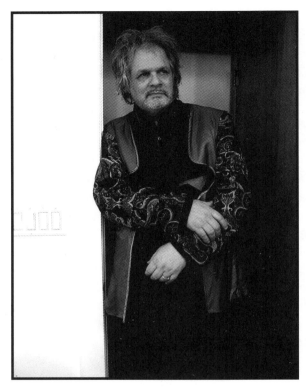

The current Mr. K–2007. (Photo: Susan Monosson.)

෨෨

Chocolate. Because I wanted to go into detail on that album and I didn't know how to do it, and he taught me how. Digital Performer is capable of doing much more than I take out of it. And I started taking a little more on this album, and it changed the record, I think, in an interesting way. It's a little *better*, for lack of a better word. It's not as rough. I don't know if that's a bad thing; I don't think so. It's passed my test. I think I still have the funk of The Funky Faculty; I don't think I've lost that. In fact, it's probably the most musically ambitious album I have ever attempted. There are two tracks with the rhythm section of the younger band Ollabelle and the Memphis track with Steve Cropper, Anton Fig, and Duck Dunn for good measure. At the time of this writing, I am starting the mixing process, which will take three weeks. When the album is completely finished, I will decide how it will be marketed and by whom. This is a revolutionary and precarious time for the music biz, and I must very carefully take my next step. Time will tell, my friends, stay tuned. . . .

For writing, like reviews and essays and things like this, I always try to speak in the same voice as the one I'm using now. Again, I'm only trying to satisfy myself. So I found a good voice for writing, and it satisfies me. And I love to write, too. I'll do a review once in a while for the music editor at the *Boston Herald.* He calls me from time to time and asks me to write pieces for them, which I do very happily, because he allows me to write about new talent. If I can help those people, I'm just delighted to do that. But I love to write, and there's a great quote, a *wonderful* quote, that Tom Waits said: "The bad thing about history is, that the people who were *there* are not talking, and the people that *weren't* there, you can't shut them up." So I *love* to write about the things that I was there for, because I feel like I'm a knight on a horse with an antirevisionist sword in my hand. There are so many interesting things that I was in the room for in my life that I've seen reported falsely, that it makes me worry about all of history. That's why I love that quote.

Yeah. One thing that really annoys me is reading untrue reporting of things that I was very close to. *The* thing that bothers me the most about music history is calling the pop music of the early '60s the "Brill Building Sound." This drives me *nuts*, because ninety percent of that music was not created in the Brill Building, which *peaked* in the '40s, and by the end of the '50s, everybody had bailed out. Not even bailed out: nobody was going to the Brill Building, except the people who were already there that had survived that time period. So people who wanted to start new businesses in the late '50s, they went to 1650 Broadway because it had a more modern look, it had been renovated. And 1619 had the frosted glass-on-brown wood doors with gold decals on them, so you could have just been going to a dentist's office instead of to a record company or a music publisher or something like that. 1650 had black steel doors with, still, the gold decals, but there was something about those black doors that was more modern.

I've never gone to a dentist's office that had a steel black door, sorry. So people went to 1650 Broadway, and it became *the* building. Carole King and Gerry Goffin, Barry Mann and Cynthia Weil, Dionne Warwick, B. J. Thomas, Bobby Lewis, all these people . . . Chuck Jackson . . . Sedaka, Feldman, Goldstein and Gottehrer, who wrote "My Boyfriend's Back" and "I Want Candy," and me. We were all in 1650 Broadway, and it was not called *any* "Building," it was just 1650 Broadway. So calling that the Brill Building Sound is completely unfactual. In all fairness, in the Brill Building were Leiber and Stoller—one of the greatest writing teams in the foundation of rock 'n' roll—and Hal David and Burt Bacharach. So that's at least a good twenty percent of the music of that time between those two teams, but all the rest was at 1650, and that's what it should have been called. So that bothers me, a lot.

I know that when I die, nobody else will be yelling about that Brill Building Sound, and I also know that it's too late and I can't change it. But I like to contradict it. Because it's *true*, it's the truth.

In 2005, a strange change began in my life. I started getting awards. It all started with the Memphis Blues Award for *Black Coffee*: Comeback Album of the Year. Prior to this I had been involved in albums that went rewardless, such as *Odessey and Oracle*, *Child Is Father to the Man*, *Super Session*, *Second Helping*, etc. So

I sort of grew up in the music industry just doing the best I could, and certainly not expecting any undue recognition for it. Hell, today, there are many people who have no idea of my Lynyrd Skynyrd involvement. So what? I know it, and really, that is all that matters. In 2006, Numark Industries gave me a Milestones Award, which is basically a lifetime achievement award. In 2007, I was inducted into the Rock Walk of Fame in Los Angeles, and received the Les Paul Award in New York, both lifetime achievement nods. This change makes me feel honored and quite old at the same time. When people ask me how it is being in my sixties, I usually reply:

"I enjoyed the *first* sixties much more!"

I have lived my fifty years in the industry with the same mantra: "If you don't expect anything, you're never disappointed." I will never change that. It kept me sane and dedicated all my life, and there's no need to change anything now.

Thank you all for joining me on this journey of musical lunacy, and I hope you had a wild, insightful, hilarious ride.

Al Kooper
January 2008

(Photo: Jeff Tamarkin.)

Selected Discography

(With special thanks to *Goldmine* magazine, Bonni Miller, and especially Jeff Tamarkin)

SINGLES AS AN ARTIST

With Leo De Lyon and the Musclemen

1960   "Sick Manny's Gym"/ "Plunkin'"
        Musicor 1001

As Al Kooper

1963   "Parchman Farm"/"You're The Lovin' End"
        Mercury (U.K.)

1965   "New York's My Home"/"My Voice, My
        Piano And My Foot"
        Aurora 164

1967   "Changes"/"Pack Up Your Sorrows"
        Verve-Folkways 5026

1969   "You Never Know Who Your Friends Are"/
        "Soft Landing On The Moon"

        Columbia 4-44748

1970   "Brand New Day"/"Love Theme From *The
        Landlord*"
        Columbia 4-45179

1970   "God Shed His Grace on Thee"/"She Gets
        Me Where I Live"
        Columbia 4-45148

1970   "I Got A Woman"/"Easy Does It"
        Columbia 4-45243

1971   "Dearest Darling"/Medley: "Oo Wee Baby I
        Love You"/"Love Is A Man's Best Friend"
        Columbia AE7-1034

1971   "John The Baptist"/"Back On My Feet"
        Columbia 4-45412

1972   "Jolie"/"Be Real"

Selected Discography

Columbia 4-45735

1972 "The Monkey Time"/"Bended Knees"
Columbia 4-45566

1972 "Sam Stone"/"Be Real"
Columbia 4-45691

1976 "This Diamond Ring"/"Hollywood Vampire"
United Artists XW879

1982 "Two Sides (To Every Situation)" (with
Valerie Carter)/"Snowblind"
Columbia 03312

With The Blues Project

1965 "Back Door Man"/"Violets Of Dawn"
Verve-Folkways 5004

1966 "Catch The Wind"/"I Want To Be Your
Driver"
Verve-Folkways 5013

1966 "Goin' Down Louisiana"/"Where There's
Smoke, There's Fire"
Verve-Folkways 5019

1966 "I Can't Keep From Crying Sometimes"/
"The Way My Baby Walks"
Verve-Folkways 5032

1967 "No Time Like The Right Time"/"Steve's
Song"
Verve-Folkways 5040

With Blood, Sweat & Tears

1968 "I Can't Quit Her"/"House In The Country"
Columbia 4-44559

With Mike Bloomfield and Steve Stills

1968 "Season Of The Witch"/"Albert's Shuffle"
Columbia 4-44657

1969 "The Weight"/"Man's Temptation"
Columbia 4-44678

ALBUMS AS AN ARTIST
As Al Kooper

1968 *I Stand Alone*
Columbia CS 9718 (released on CD in

Japan in 1992)

1969 *You Never Know Who Your Friends Are*
Columbia CS-9855 (released on CD in
Japan in 1992)

1970 *Easy Does It*
Columbia G 30031 (released on CD in
Japan in 1992)

1970 *The Landlord* (soundtrack)
United Artists UAS 5209

1971 *New York City (You're A Woman)*
Columbia C 30506 (released on CD in
Japan in 1992)

1972 *Naked Song*
Columbia BL 31723 (released on CD in
Japan in 1992)

1972 *A Possible Projection Of The Future/
Childhood's End*
Columbia KC-31189 (released on CD in
Japan in 1992)

1974 *Al's Big Deal—Unclaimed Freight: An Al
Kooper Anthology*
Columbia PG 33169 (released on CD in
the U.S. in 1990)

1976 *Act Like Nothing's Wrong*
United Artists UA-LA702-G (released on
CD in the U.S. in 1995)

1982 *Championship Wrestling*
Columbia FC 38137 (released on CD in
Japan in 1992)

1992 *Joy Of Flying*
Sony (Japan) XDCS-93089 J (compilation,
Japan only; promotional item—very rare)

1994 *Rekooperation*
MusicMasters 01612-65107-2

1995 *Soul Of A Man*
MusicMasters 01612-65113-2

With The Blues Project

1965 *Live At The Cafe Au Go Go*
Verve-Folkways FV 9024 (M)/FVS 9024 (S)

1966 *Live At The Cafe Au Go Go*

Selected Discography

Verve-Folkways FT(M)/FTS 3000(8) (a reissue of Verve/Folkways 9024; released on CD in the U.S., Germany, and Japan)

1966 *Projections*
Verve-Forecast FT(M)/FTS-3008(S) (released on CD in the U.S. and Germany)

1967 *Live At Town Hall*
Verve-Forecast FTS-3025

1970 *Best Of The Blues Project*
Verve-Forecast FTS-3077

1973 *Reunion In Central Park*
MCA/Sounds of the South MCA2-8003

1989 *The Best Of The Blues Project* (CD; includes five bonus tracks, including one unreleased live cut)
Rhino R170165

1997 *Anthology*
PolyGram 31452 9758-2

With Blood, Sweat & Tears

1968 *Child Is Father To The Man*
Columbia CS-9619 (released on CD in the U.S., Germany, and Japan)

1972 *Greatest Hits*
Columbia KC-31170 (released on CD in the U.S., Germany, U.K., Canada, and Japan)

1973 *Greatest Hits* (Quad)
Columbia CQ-31170

1981 *Child Is Father To The Man* (half-speed master)
Columbia HC-49619

1996 *Child Is Father To The Man* (gold edition CD; contains a bonus of six early demos)
Columbia CK 64214

(*Note:* Other BS&T anthologies contain Kooper-era material.)

With Mike Bloomfield and Steve Stills

1968 *Super Session*
Columbia CS 9701 (released on CD in the U.S., Germany, U.K., Canada, and Japan)

1974 *Super Session* (gold label)
Columbia PCQ-9701

1996 *SuperSession* (gold master; contains previously unreleased track: "Blues for Nothing")
Columbia CK 64611

2003 *Super Session* (CD) (best-sounding remastering with two bonus tracks)
SONY Legacy CK63400

With Mike Bloomfield

1969 *The Live Adventures Of Mike Bloomfield & Al Kooper*
Columbia KGP6/CS 9742

1997 *The Live Adventures Of Mike Bloomfield & Al Kooper*
Columbia, CD, (U.S.) C2K-64670

2003 *Fillmore East: The Lost Concert Tapes 12/13/68*
SONY Legacy CK85278

With Shuggie Otis

1969 *Kooper Session*
Columbia CS-9951 (released on CD in Japan in 1992)

With Jimmy Vivino and the Rekooperators

1997 *Do What, Now?*
MusicMasters 01612-65157-2

On Various Artists' Compilations

1966 *What's Shakin'* (track: "I Can't Keep from Crying Sometimes")
Elektra EKL-4002 (MVEKS-74002 (released on CD in the U.S.: Elektra 9 61343-2)

1988 Green Linnet: *Christmas Guitars* (CD) (track: "Winter Wonderland")
GLCD-1103

1995 *For The Love Of Harry* (Harry Nilsson

tribute) (track: "Salmon Falls")
MusicMasters 01612-65127-2

1997   *Badfinger Tribute* (CD) (track: "Maybe Tomorrow")
Copper CPR2181

2001   *He's A Rebel: The Gene Pitney Story Retold* (track: "One Day")
To M'Lou Music PIG7

AS A SONGWRITER

(Songs recorded by artists other than Kooper)

1959   Anastasia: "That's My Kind Of Love"
Laurie 3066

1963   Freddie Cannon: "The Old Rag Man"
Warner Bros. 5666

1963   Lorraine Ellison: "I'm Over You"
Warner Bros. 5879

1963   Tommy Sands: "A Young Man's Fancy"
ABC-Paramount 10466

1963   Keely Smith: "Goin' Thru The Motions"
Reprise R20-149

1963   Johnny Thunder: "The Chain"
Diamond SD-5001 (LP)

1964   Sammy Ambrose: "This Diamond Ring"
Musicor 1061A

1964   Pat Boone: "Rainy Days Were Made For Lonely People"
Dot 45-16754

1964   The Essex: "When Something's Hard To Get"
Roulette 4564

1964   Eddie Hodges: "The Old Rag Man"
Aurora 161

1964   Eddie Hodges: "The Water Is Over My Head"
Aurora 156

1964   Lulu: *Tell Me Like It Is* (now on CD)
Carnaby 552030

1964   Gene Pitney: "Hawaii"
Musicor MU-1040

1964   Gene Pitney: "The Last Two People On Earth"
Musicor MU-3019 (LP)

1964   The Surfer Girls: "One Boy Tells Another"
Columbia 4-43001

1965   Ernie Andrews: "Where Were You When I Needed You"
Capitol 5448

1965   Eight Feet: "Bobby's Come A Long Way"
Columbia 4-43505

1965   Gary Lewis & the Playboys: "This Diamond Ring"
Liberty 5576

1965   Gene Pitney: "Don't Take Candy From A Stranger"
Musicor MU-3056 (LP)

1965   Gene Pitney: "I Must Be Seeing Things"
Musicor MU-1070

1965   Gene Pitney: *She's Still There* (LP)
Musicor MU-3056

1965   Eddie Rambeau: *I Fell In Love So Easily* (LP)
Dyno-Voice 9001

1965   Bruce Scott: "You Can't Lose Something You Never Had"
MGM K13455

1965   Alan Lorber: *Flute Thing* (LP)
Verve V6-8711

1966   Modern Folk Quintet: "Night Time Girl"
Dunhill 45-D4025

1966   Rockin' Berries: "The Water Is Over My Head"
Reprise 0442

1966   Bobby Vee: "Fly Away"
Liberty

1968   Arbors: "I Can't Quit Her"
Date 2-1645

1968   Don Meehan Project: "House In The Country"
Columbia 4-44791

1968   Ten Years After: *I Can't Keep From Cryin'* (LP)

Selected Discography

	Deram-DES 18009
1970	*The Landlord* (soundtrack) (features several Kooper compositions, including the Staples Singers performing "Brand New Day" and Lorraine Ellison performing "Doin' Me Dirty") United Artists UAS 5209
1971	Rufus: "Brand New Day" Epic 5-10691
1971	T. D. Valentine (Tommy Mottola): "Love Trap" Epic 5-10523
1972	Frankie & Johnny: "LifeLine," "Don't Tell Ma," "Lonesome Song" Warner Bros. 2675
1972	Donny Hathaway: "I Love You More Than You'll Ever Know" Atco 6903
1972	Latimore: "Jolie," "Be Real" Glades 6502
1973	Dawn: "Jolie" Bell 1112
1973	Lynyrd Skynyrd: "Mississippi Kid" Sounds of the South MCAD 1685
1973	Betty Wright: "Let Me Go Down" Alston SD7026
1974	Carmen McRae: "I Love You More Than You'll Ever Know" Atlantic 45-2691
1975	Long John Baldry: "Brand New Day" Casablanca 7012
1975	Lynyrd Skynyrd: "Cheatin' Woman" Sounds of the South MCAD 31003
1976	Cold Blood: *I Love You More Than You'll Ever Know* (LP) ABC917
1977	Roger McGuinn: "Please Not One More Time" Columbia
1977	Leo Sayer: *Lost Control* (LP) Warner Bros. 3200

1977	Libby Titus: "Fool That I Am" Columbia 34152
1993	Thelonious Monster: "Body & Soul" Capitol 0227-2
1993	Guitar Shorty: "I Love You More Than You'll Ever Know" Black Top BT-1094
1994	Beastie Boys: "Flute Loop" Capitol 72438-28599-2 5
1996	Tony Terry: "I Love You More Than You'll Ever Know" Virgin 39861
1997	Kevin Mahogany: "I Love You More Than You'll Ever Know" (CD) Warner Bros. 9 46226-2
2001	Jay-Z: "Soon You'll Understand" Roc-A-Fella 31454 82032 (CD)
2002	Joe Bonamassa: "Nuthin I Wouldn't Do (For A Woman Like You)" Okeh BK61088 (CD)
2004	The Alchemist: "Hold You Down" ALC/Koch KOC-9548 (CD)
2007	Marc Broussard: "I Love You More Than You'll Ever Know" Vanguard 79826-2 (CD)

(*Note:* The above selections omit songs Kooper wrote and recorded himself either on solo albums, with The Blues Project, or with Blood, Sweat & Tears.)

AS A PRODUCER

(Selected titles—albums only)

1967	Don Ellis: *Autumn* Columbia 9721
1968	Al Kooper: *I Stand Alone* Columbia CS 9718
1968	Al Kooper/Mike Bloomfield/Steve Stills: *Super Session* Columbia CS 9701
1968	Linda Tillery: *Sweet Linda Divine* Columbia CS 9771

Selected Discography

1969   Mike Bloomfield/Al Kooper: *The Live Adventures Of Mike Bloomfield & Al Kooper*
Columbia KGP6/CS 9742

1969   Al Kooper: *You Never Know Who Your Friends Are*
Columbia CS-9855

1969   Al Kooper and Shuggie Otis: *Kooper Session*
Columbia CS 9951

1970   Bob Dylan: *New Morning*
Columbia KC-30290

1970   Al Kooper: *Easy Does It*
Columbia G 30031

1970   Various artists: *The Landlord* (soundtrack)
United Artists UAS 5209

1971   Appaloosa: *Appaloosa*
Columbia 9819

1971   Michael Gately: *Gately's Cafe*
Janus JLS 3039

1971   Al Kooper: *New York City (You're A Woman)*
Columbia C 30506

1972   Frankie & Johnny: *The Sweetheart Sampler*
Warner Bros. 2675

1972   Al Kooper: *A Possible Projection Of The Future/Childhood's End*
Columbia KC-31189

1973   Blues Project: *Reunion In Central Park*
MCA/Sounds of the South MCA2-8003

1973   Elijah: *Fanfares*
Sounds of the South 377

1973   Al Kooper: *Naked Songs*
Columbia BL 31723

1973   Lynyrd Skynyrd: *Pronounced Leh-Nerd Skin-erd*
Sounds of the South 363

1973   Mose Jones: *Get Right*
Sounds of the South 329

1974   Lynyrd Skynyrd: *Second Helping*
Sounds of the South 413

1975   Al Kooper: *Al's Big Deal—Unclaimed Freight*
Columbia PG 33169

1975   Lynyrd Skynyrd: *Nuthin' Fancy*
Sounds of the South 2137

1975   The Tubes: *The Tubes*
A&M SP-4534

1976   Al Kooper: *Act Like Nothing's Wrong*
United Artists UA-LA-702-G

1976   Nils Lofgren: *Authorized Bootleg*
A&M SP-8362

1976   Nils Lofgren: *Cry Tough*
A&M SP-4573

1976   Peter John Morse: *On The Shoreline*
MCA 2299

1977   Christopher Morris Band: *Christopher Morris Band*
MCA 2282

1977   Libby Titus: Unreleased album CBS

1978   Marshall Chapman; *Jaded Virgin*
Epic 35341

1978   Rick Nelson: *Back To Vienna* (unreleased)
Epic
(*Note:* Four tracks appear on Epic/Legacy EK 48290-2, *Stay Young: The Epic Recordings.*)

1978   Lenny. White: *Adventures Of Astral Pirates*
Elektra 6E 121

1979   Four on the Floor: *Four On The Floor*
Casablanca NBLP 7180

1979   Freddy Henry: *Get It Out In The Open*
Clouds 8809

1980   Eddie & the Hot Rods: *Fish And Chips*
EMI

1980   Joe Ely: *Texas Tornado* (CD)
MCA MCAD 10816

1980   David Essex: *BeBop The Future*
Mercury 6359 064 (U.K.)

1980   Johnny Van Zant: *No More Dirty Deals*
Polydor PD 1-6289

1981   Johnny Koonce: *Got My Eye On You*

A&M SP6 4936

1982   Johnny Van Zant: *Last Of The Wild Ones*
Polydor PD1-6355

1983   Phil Judd: *The Swinger*
MCA 36007

1984   Q-Tips: *Live At Last Rewind*
RELP 1001 (U.K.)

1984   St. Regis: *Parts* (unreleased album)
PolyGram

1989   B. B. King: *The King Of The Blues*
MCA 42183

1990   Various artists: *Cry Baby* (soundtrack; 3 tracks)
MCA MCAD-8038

1991   Green on Red: *Scapegoats*
China WOLCD-1001 (U.K.)

1991   Thelonious Monster: *Beautiful Mess* (1 track)
Capitol 80227 2

1992   Al Kooper: *Joy Of Flying* (compilation)
Sony XDCS-93089J (Japan only)

1994   Al Kooper: *Rekooperation*
Music Masters 01612-65113

1994   Al Kooper: Soul *Of A Man*
MusicMasters 01612-65107-2

1995   Various artists: *For The Love Of Harry* (Harry Nilsson tribute album)
MusicMasters 01612-65127-2

1997   Jimmy Vivino & the Rekooperators: *Do What, Now?*
MusicMasters 0162-65157-2

AS A SIDEMAN

(*Note:* Italics indicate an album, quotation marks indicate a single song.)

1962   Gene Pitney: *The Many Sounds Of Gene Pitney*
Musicor MM-2001

1965   Judy Collins: "I'll Keep It With Mine"
Elektra 45601

1965   Bob Dylan: *Highway 61 Revisited*

Columbia CL-2389

1966   Joan Baez: "Pack Up Your Sorrows"
Vanguard 35040

1966   Bob Dylan: *Blonde On Blonde*
Columbia C2S-41

1966   Jim and Jean; *Changes*
Verve-Folkways 5005

1966   Phil Ochs: "I Ain't Marchin' Anymore"
Elektra

1966   Tom Rush: *Take A Little Walk With Me*
Elektra EKS 7308

1966   Simon and Garfunkel; *Parsley, Sage, Rosemary And Thyme*
Columbia CS-9363

1967   Eric Andersen: '*Bout Changes And Things Take 2*
Vanguard VSD-79236

1967   Peter, Paul and Mary: *Album 1700*
Warner Bros. W-1700

1967   The Who: *The Who Sell Out*
CA DL-74950

1968   Jimi Hendrix Experience: *Electric Ladyland*
Reprise 2RS-6307

1968   Moby Grape: *Wow/Grape Jam*
Columbia CS-9613/MGS-1

1968   Eric Andersen: *More Hits From Tin Can Alley*
Vanguard VSD 79271

1968   Paul Butterfield Blues Band: *In My Own Dream*
Elektra 74025

1968   Paupers: *Ellis Island*
Verve 3051

1968   Taj Mahal: *Natch'l Blues*
Columbia 9698

1969   B. B. King: *Live And Well*
Bluesway BLS-6031

1969   Rolling Stones: *Let It Bleed*
London NPS-4
(*Note:* Kooper also played on alternate, unreleased takes of "Brown Sugar" and

Selected Discography

1970   "Memo from Turner" in this time period.)

1970   Bob Dylan: *New Morning*
Columbia KC-30290

1970   Bob Dylan: *Self-Portrait*
Columbia C2X-30050

1971   Appaloosa: *Appaloosa*
Columbia 9819

1972   Rita Coolidge: *Lady's Not For Sale*
A&M SP-4370

1972   Frankie & Johnny: *Sweetheart Sampler*
Warner Bros. 2675

1973   Bob Dylan: *Dylan*
Columbia PC-32747

1973   Lynyrd Skynyrd: *Pronounced Leh-nerd
Skin-nerd*
Sounds of the South 363

1973   Betty Wright: *I Am Woman*
Alston SD7206

1974   Brewer and Shipley: *Brewer And Shipley*
Capitol ST 11261

1974   Latimore: *Latimore*
Glades 6502

1974   Lynyrd Skynyrd: *Second Helping*
Sounds of the South 413

1974   Roger McGuinn: *Peace On You*
Columbia 32956

1975   Lynyrd Skynyrd: *Nuthin' Fancy*
Sounds of the South 2137

1976   Jeffrey Comanor: *A Rumor In His Own
Time*
Epic 34080

1976   Randy Edelman: *Farewell Fairbanks*
20th Century 494

1976   Nils Lofgren: *Authorized Bootleg*
A&M SP 8362

1976   Nils Lofgren: *Cry Tough*
A&M SP 4509

1976   Bill Wyman: *A Stone Alone*
Rolling Stones COC 79103

1977   Terence Boylan: *Terence Boylan*
Elektra 7 E 1091

1977   Alice Cooper: *Lace And Whiskey*
Warner Bros. 3027

1978   Marshall Chapman: *Jaded Virgin*
Epic 35341

1978   Nitty Gritty Dirt Band: *American Dream*
United Artists LA 854

1979   Leo Sayer: *Here*
Warner Bros. 3200

1980   Eddie & The Hot Rods: *Fish And Chips*
EMI America 3344

1980   George Harrison: *Somewhere In England*
Dark Horse 49725

1980   Johnny Van Zant: *No More Dirty Deals*
Polydor PD1-6289

1983   Bob Dylan: *Infidels*
Columbia 38819

1985   Bob Dylan; *Biograph*
Columbia C5S-38830

1985   Bob Dylan: *Empire Burlesque*
Columbia 40110

1988   Was (Not Was): *What Up, Dog*
Chrysalis 41664

1990   Bob Dylan: *Under The Red Sky*
Columbia 46794

1990   Shaking Family: *Dreaming In Detail*
Elektra 60900-2

1991   Dion: *Bronx Blues* (1962-1965) (CD)
Columbia CGK 46972

1991   Webb Wilder: *Doo Dad*
Zoo/Praxis 72445-11010-2

1991   Trisha Yearwood: *Trisha Yearwood*
MCA MCAD10297

1992   Various artists: *Honeymoon In Vegas*
(soundtrack) (Kooper appears on Trisha
Yearwood's "You're The Devil In Disguise")
Epic 52845

1993   Bob Dylan: *The 30th Anniversary Concert
Celebration*
Columbia C2K 53230

1993   Shaver: *Tramp On Your Street*
Zoo/Praxis 72445-11063

Selected Discography

1993   Various artists: *Common Thread: The Songs of the Eagles* (Kooper appears on Trisha Yearwood's "New Kid In Town")
Giant 24531

1995   Tom Petty: *PLAYBACK* (boxed set)
MCA MCAD6-1137

1996   Tracy Nelson: *Move On*
Rounder CD-3143

1996   Sam Bush: *Glamour & Grits*
Sugar Hill SHCD3849

1997   Dion: *The Road I'm On: A Retrospective* (CD)
Columbia C2K 64889

1997   Honeydogs: *Seen A Ghost*
Mercury/Debris 314 534 9592

1998   Phoebe Snow: *I Can't Complain*
House of Blues 51416 1352

Soundtrack Work

(Not comercially released.)

1986/87 *Crime Story* (TV series)
New World Television (2 Seasons)
Produced by Michael Mann

1990   *Cry-Baby* (film)
Imagine Films
Directed by John Waters

1990   *Drug Wars: The Camarena Story* (TV miniseries)
Artisan Entertainment
Produced by Michael Mann

1991   *Ray Charles: 50 Years In Music, Uh-Huh!* (cable TV special)
Image Entertainment
Music direction by Al Kooper

1994   *Against Their Will: Women In Prison* (TV movie)
Monarch Entertainment
Directed by Karen Arthur

2000   *By Courier* (film short)
Two Tequila Productions
Directed by Peter Riegert

2004   *King Of The Corner* (film)
Elevation Filmworks
Directed by Peter Riegert

Index

Index

Index

320

Index

Index

Index

Index

Index

Index

Index